Seeking the Identity of Jesus

Seeking the Identity of Jesus

A PILGRIMAGE

Edited by

Beverly Roberts Gaventa & Richard B. Hays

William B. Eerdmans Publishing Company
Grand Rapids, Michigan / Cambridge, U.K.

Published 2008 by
Wm. B. Eerdmans Publishing Co.
2140 Oak Industrial Drive N.E., Grand Rapids, Michigan 49505 /
P.O. Box 163, Cambridge CB3 9PU U.K.

Printed in the United States of America

14 13 12 11 10 09 08 7 6 5 4 3 2 1

Library of Congress Cataloging-in-Publication Data

Seeking the identity of Jesus: a pilgrimage / edited by
Beverly Roberts Gaventa & Richard B. Hays.
p. cm.
Includes bibliographical references.
ISBN 978-0-8028-2471-4 (pbk.: alk. paper)
1. Jesus Christ — Biography — History and criticism.
2. Jesus Christ — Historicity. I. Gaventa, Beverly Roberts.
II. Hays, Richard B.

BT303.S44 2008
232 — dc22

2008031701

www.eerdmans.com

Contents

Permissions

The authors, editors, and publisher are grateful for permission to reprint material from the following sources:

"Christ Is Alive," by Brian Wren. Copyright © 1969, 1995 Hope Publishing Co., Carol Stream, IL 60188. All rights reserved. Used by permission.

Markus Bockmuehl, "Seeing the Son of David," in *Seeing the Word: Refocusing New Testament Study* (Grand Rapids: Baker Academic/Baker Publishing Group, 2006).

Dale C. Allison Jr., *Studies in Matthew: Interpretation Past and Present* (Grand Rapids: Baker Academic/Baker Publishing Group, 2005).

Boris Pasternak, "Hamlet," from *Selected Poems: Boris Pasternak,* trans. Jon Stallworthy and Peter France (London: Allen Lane, 1983), p. 125. Copyright © Peter France, 1983. Reproduced by permission of Penguin Books Ltd.

Unless otherwise indicated, Scripture translations are those of the authors.

Acknowledgments

The present volume had its origins in a collaborative research initiative — "The Identity of Jesus Project" — sponsored by the Center of Theological Inquiry (CTI) in Princeton, New Jersey. It is a sequel to *The Art of Reading Scripture* (Grand Rapids: Eerdmans, 2003), a collection of essays that grew out of an earlier research initiative at CTI, "The Scripture Project." That project touched only briefly on the question of Jesus' identity. It was Wallace Alston, the Center's director, who conceived the vision for a second study group focused explicitly on this topic. He and Robert Jenson, at that time the Center's senior research scholar, enlisted the editors of this volume and provided strong encouragement and organizational support for the launching of this new undertaking. On behalf of all the contributors to this volume, we would like to thank both of them for their patient persistence in moving things along, as well as their gracious hospitality to our little community of scholars, who met at the Center twice a year over a period of three years.

Before the completion of the project, Wallace retired from his position as director. His successor, William F. Storrar, graciously continued to welcome the group to CTI and to support our work; we owe him our thanks. Thanks are due also to Kathi Morley, Marion Gibson, and Heather Kaemingk, the staff members at CTI who arranged the complicated logistics of gathering, housing, and feeding this far-flung group of scholars.

The editors would especially like to express our deep sense of gratitude to Carol Shoun, faculty editorial associate at Duke Divinity School. She has done the intensive work of copyediting these essays and shepherding the book toward completion. Her impeccable sense of style, her extraordinary organizational skills, and her good-humored tolerance of the quirks of our group have made the finishing of this book a joy rather than a burden. Her contributions to this volume, as well as to *The Art of Reading Scripture,* have been indispensable.

We would also like to record our thanks to David Moffitt, a doctoral student in New Testament at Duke, who undertook the task of proofreading the Greek and Hebrew words and phrases in the manuscript and standardizing the fonts, and to Anne Weston, faculty editorial assistant, who provided timely research support. We appreciate the work of Brittany Wilson, a doctoral candidate at Princeton Theological Seminary, who assisted with the final proofreading, and Sean Larsen, a doctoral student in theology at Duke, who prepared the indexes. Sam Eerdmans and Michael Thomson of Wm. B. Eerdmans Publishing Company have kindly encouraged this book project and waited patiently over the past four years for it to come to fruition.

Finally, the editors would like to acknowledge that it has been a great privilege to work together with all the members of this research group. In contrast to the competitive spirit that so often attends academic gatherings, we experienced within the Identity of Jesus Project a profound and joyful spirit of cooperation among friends. The end of our meetings was bittersweet: we were glad to have completed our work, but saddened that our times of laughter and mind-stretching common labor had to come to an end. It is our hope that readers will encounter within this book some measure of the enrichment we received from one another.

BEVERLY ROBERTS GAVENTA & RICHARD B. HAYS
Princeton Theological Seminary and Duke Divinity School
August 16, 2007

Contributors

Dale C. Allison Jr.
Errett M. Grable Professor of New Testament Exegesis
and Early Christianity
Pittsburgh Theological Seminary

Gary A. Anderson
Professor of Old Testament
University of Notre Dame

Markus Bockmuehl
Professor of Biblical and Early Christian Studies
University of Oxford

Sarah Coakley
Norris-Hulse Professor of Divinity
University of Cambridge

Brian E. Daley, SJ
Catherine F. Huisking Professor of Theology
University of Notre Dame

Beverly Roberts Gaventa
Helen H. P. Manson Professor of New Testament Literature and Exegesis
Princeton Theological Seminary

A. Katherine Grieb
Associate Professor of New Testament
Virginia Theological Seminary

Richard B. Hays
George Washington Ivey Professor of New Testament
Duke Divinity School

Robert W. Jenson
Senior Scholar for Research (ret.)
Center of Theological Inquiry, Princeton, N.J.

Joel Marcus
Professor of New Testament and Christian Origins
Duke Divinity School

Walter Moberly
Professor of Theology and Biblical Interpretation
Durham University

William C. Placher
Professor of Philosophy and Religion, LaFollette Distinguished Professor in the Humanities
Wabash College

Katherine Sonderegger
Professor of Theology
Virginia Theological Seminary

David C. Steinmetz
Amos Ragan Kearns Professor of the History of Christianity
Duke Divinity School

Marianne Meye Thompson
George Eldon Ladd Professor of New Testament
Fuller Theological Seminary

Francis Watson
Chair of Biblical Interpretation
Durham University

Abbreviations

AASF-DHL	Annales Academiae scientiarum fennicae: Dissertationes humanarum litterarum
AB	Anchor Bible
ABRL	Anchor Bible Reference Library
ANF	*Ante-Nicene Fathers*
ANTC	Abingdon New Testament Commentaries
BNTC	Black's New Testament Commentaries
BThSt	Biblisch-theologische Studien
BZNW	Beihefte zur Zeitschrift für die neutestamentliche Wissenschaft
CCSG	Corpus Christianorum: Series graeca
FRLANT	Forschungen zur Religion und Literatur des Alten und Neuen Testaments
GBS	Guides to Biblical Scholarship
GNO	Gregorii Nysseni Opera
HSem	Horae semiticae
IRT	Issues in Religion and Theology
JB	Jerusalem Bible
JSHJSup	Journal for the Study of the Historical Jesus: Supplement Series
JSNTSup	Journal for the Study of the New Testament: Supplement Series
JSOTSup	Journal for the Study of the Old Testament: Supplement Series
JSPSup	Journal for the Study of the Pseudepigrapha: Supplement Series
LCC	Library of Christian Classics
LCL	Loeb Classical Library
LNTS	Library of New Testament Studies
LXX	Septuagint
NHS	Nag Hammadi Studies
NICNT	New International Commentary on the New Testament

NIV	New International Version
NJPS	*Tanakh: The Holy Scriptures: The New JPS Translation according to the Traditional Hebrew Text*
NPNF[1]	*Nicene and Post-Nicene Fathers*, Series 1
NPNF[2]	*Nicene and Post-Nicene Fathers*, Series 2
NRSV	New Revised Standard Version
OBT	Overtures to Biblical Theology
OTL	Old Testament Library
PG	Patrologia graeca [= Patrologiae cursus completus: Series graeca]
RSV	Revised Standard Version
SBT	Studies in Biblical Theology
SMRT	Studies in Medieval and Reformation Thought
SNTI	Studies in New Testament Interpretation
SNTSMS	Society for New Testament Studies Monograph Series
TU	Texte und Untersuchungen
WMANT	Wissenschaftliche Monographien zum Alten und Neuen Testament

Seeking the Identity of Jesus

Beverly Roberts Gaventa and Richard B. Hays

Seeking Jesus: Conflicting Images

"We wish to see Jesus."

These words are uttered in the Gospel of John by an anonymous group of seekers, identified only as "some Greeks" (John 12:20-21).[1] Similar words are spoken today by uncounted numbers of people. The vast majority of these people are committed Christians who hunger for a clearer sense of who Jesus Christ is and what he means for their lives. But many others seek Jesus as well, including the historically curious, the spiritually hungry, and the openly skeptical.

And those who seek will surely find — or at least find *something.* The contemporary marketplace offers an astonishing, even bewildering, variety of interpretations of the identity of Jesus. The problem for seekers of Jesus is to sort out what is genuine from what is spurious.

In many ecclesial circles, Catholic and Protestant alike, Jesus has been seen as a quietistic "personal Savior" who offers individuals forgiveness of sins, a close relationship with a loving God, and assurance of heaven.[2] In some versions of popular evangelicalism, there is also a vivid expectation that this same Jesus will come, in the near future, on the clouds of heaven,

1. Scripture quotations not otherwise identified are from the NRSV.

2. An analogous, but more nuanced, portrayal of Jesus is found in Joseph Ratzinger, Pope Benedict XVI, *Jesus of Nazareth: From the Baptism in the Jordan to the Transfiguration* (New York: Doubleday, 2007). This book focuses on Jesus' personally intimate union with God the Father and his mission to invite all humanity to share in a close, loving relationship with God.

to judge the world, punish the wicked, and reward the righteous. Even so, this Jesus keeps generally aloof from real-world affairs in the present; his mission is a purely "religious" one: to offer hope for the afterlife.

In the last quarter of the twentieth century and the early years of the twenty-first, however, the Jesus of popular evangelicalism has become more deeply enmeshed in conservative politics and nationalism. This Jesus often seems to come attired in red, white, and blue as the inspiration and authorizer of the American empire. To be sure, he still offers salvation to those individuals who confess faith in his name, but he also serves as the spokesman for a platform of "family values," capitalist economics, and a strong national defense policy. At the same time, we have witnessed an odd mutation of this figure in the preaching of a "prosperity gospel," which invokes him chiefly as the provider of financial abundance and personal fulfillment. This Jesus — in contrast to the hard-edged culture warrior of the religious right — is a sweet and generous benefactor who desires to give material blessings to all who call on him.

Partly in reaction against such aberrant portrayals of Jesus, one also finds in the religious marketplace other, strikingly different representations of the figure who stands at the center of Christian faith. During the 1990s, a group calling itself the Jesus Seminar attracted much media attention by claiming to offer a new, more factually reliable account of the historical Jesus. They gathered a team of scholars to study and eventually vote on the authenticity of sayings attributed to Jesus, producing a new, color-coded edition of the Gospels that would identify the "real" sayings of Jesus and distinguish them from churchly accretions. Their finding? Fewer than 20 percent of the sayings attributed to Jesus in the canonical Gospels are authentic. Though many of their presuppositions and working methods have been widely employed since the nineteenth century, the Jesus Seminar presented their cut-and-paste reduction of the Gospels as a new historical breakthrough that offered a more secure factual basis for our understanding of Jesus. This portrait was of a strikingly non-Jewish Jesus, a laconic wandering sage who loved witty aphorisms but had no particular interest in Israel's heritage or destiny, and no interest in leading a new religious movement. Most emphatically, the Jesus Seminar's Jesus had no aspirations to be regarded as divine.

In other circles, there has been an effort to rehabilitate the extra-canonical Gnostic gospels as illuminating sources of insight into the identity of Jesus. These texts originated in a second-century religious and philosophical environment that regarded the material world as evil and the God of the Old Testament as an inferior, malicious power. In recent years, however, they have sometimes been read selectively to underwrite a form of individualistic, therapeutic spirituality. The Jesus of this neo-Gnostic revival is a mysterious guru who calls his followers to inner spiritual illumination and disengagement from the world. This representation of Jesus received its greatest publicity boost in 2006, with the publication of the newly discovered *Gospel of Judas.*

Recent years have also brought us the startling popularity of the pulp novel *The Da Vinci Code,* which depicts a Jesus who was married to Mary Magdalene and produced children with her. According to Dan Brown's potboiler, the "real" story of this purely human Jesus was violently suppressed by the emperor Constantine in the fourth century in favor of a fictional divine savior and a Christianity that denigrates sexuality and denies leadership to women. Despite — or perhaps because of — its flagrant distortion of historical information, and because of its suspicion of any notion of church authority, this book has somehow struck a nerve in popular culture and offered a Jesus that many would like to believe in.

No survey of recent popular portrayals of Jesus would be complete without mentioning the Jesus of Mel Gibson's film *The Passion of the Christ.* Gibson presents Jesus as neither teacher nor healer but as the passive victim of seemingly arbitrary and unending physical torture, which is somehow redemptive.

And, of course, Jesus has also long been seen as a prophetic figure who stood against the religious and political authorities of his day, offering an example of nonviolent resistance. Many forms of liberation theology find in Jesus the inspiration for their preferential option for the poor, and movements advocating peace and justice for the downtrodden often look to Jesus as their inspiration and champion.

In view of this profusion of conflicting images of Jesus in the church, in the academy, and in popular culture, it is no wonder that the identity of Jesus might appear more elusive than ever. It was this confusing state of affairs that led some of us to conceive the idea of a research project on the identity of Jesus, under the sponsorship of the Center of Theological Inquiry (CTI) in Princeton, New Jersey.

The Identity of Jesus Project

During the years 1998-2002, the Center of Theological Inquiry had sponsored a collaborative, interdisciplinary scholarly venture called "The Scripture Project," which culminated in the publication of a book entitled *The Art of Reading Scripture,* edited by Ellen Davis and Richard Hays. This collection of essays sought "to explore, to exemplify, and to nurture habits of reading Scripture theologically" in a culture in which the church had lost touch with many of the skills and practices necessary for the careful and life-giving reading of the Bible.[3] In light of the Scripture Project's findings and the enthusiastic reception of *The Art of Reading Scripture,* Wallace Alston and Robert Jenson, the Center's director and senior research scholar, proposed another project as a sequel to the first, this time focusing specifically on the interpretation of the figure of Jesus. They asked Beverly Gaventa of Princeton Theological Seminary and Richard Hays of Duke Divinity School to serve as co-chairs for what was christened "The Identity of Jesus Project."

Once again, an interdisciplinary team was assembled, comprising several of the scholars who had participated in the Scripture Project, along with a number of others whose expertise would be especially crucial for addressing the complicated problems surrounding the quest for the identity of Jesus. (Names of the participants can be found in the list of contributors on pp. xi-xii.) This group met twice annually in Princeton for three years, from 2003 to 2006. Our meetings included worship, the presentation and critique of papers prepared for group discussion, and the study of biblical texts, as we, like the Greeks in John 12, inquired after Jesus. Although about half the members of the Project are scholars whose primary expertise is in the field of New Testament and early Christianity, it was an important part of the project design to include theologians, church historians, and scholars specializing in the study of the Old Testament. As the collection of essays offered here attests, the contributions of these diverse disciplinary perspectives were vital to producing a rounded account of our endlessly fascinating subject.

While all the members of the project are confessing Christians, no one should read this collection of essays expecting to find a single party line or

3. Ellen F. Davis and Richard B. Hays, eds., *The Art of Reading Scripture* (Grand Rapids: Eerdmans, 2003), p. xv.

narrowly conceived consensus position. The identity of Jesus is too complex to permit simple description; furthermore, our participants represent not only different academic specializations but also different religious and cultural backgrounds — Catholic and Protestant, American and British, high church and low church, male and female. Our discussions were spirited, candid, humorous, moving, and illuminating. Sometimes we found cherished ideas challenged by other members of the group; other times we encountered new insights into Jesus that we had never before considered. At the end of the three years, all of us had the sense of a converging collective vision of the identity of Jesus, even though the precise articulation of that vision remained difficult. Just as significantly, we had a sense that we had experienced the fulfillment of Jesus' promise that "where two or three are gathered in my name, I am there among them" (Matt 18:20).

The essays included in the present volume are the fruit of those three years of conversation. Each essay was discussed thoroughly by the group, revised in light of that discussion, and brought back for further conversation before being edited for inclusion here. Thus, while the views expressed in the essays remain those of the individual authors, each of us has profited richly from the generous critical wisdom of our colleagues, in ways too complex to credit neatly in footnotes.

Many scholarly presentations of Jesus operate on assumptions that resemble those of an archaeological expedition. The "real" Jesus is thought to lie buried beneath historical artifacts — texts and traditions. The work of the Jesus Seminar is but an extreme example of attempting to "get down to" the actual Jesus of history by separating him from the church's Gospels and the church's creeds. By contrast, the Identity of Jesus Project came to believe that Jesus is best understood not by separating him from canon and creed but by investigating the ways in which the church's canon and creed provide distinctive clarification of his identity. The church's ancient ecumenical creeds are not artificial impositions on Scripture but interpretative summaries of the biblical narratives. Therefore, they offer us an overarching sense of the meaning of the whole Bible, and of Jesus' place within that story.

What you will find in this book has less in common with an archaeological expedition than with a pilgrimage. Pilgrims begin their treks from differing locations and require varying equipment, but they all hope to converge at a common destination. And as they travel, they are reliably guided by the reports of those who have preceded them on the journey. In the same sense, our authors work with a variety of "reports" offered by the biblical canon, church tradition, and contemporary experience. While we affirm the importance of historical investigation and the location of Jesus' identity in first-century Palestine, we also affirm that Jesus is not reducible to what can be learned from historical research alone.[4] What, then, are the sources we can turn to for knowledge of Jesus, and how should they be employed?

Sources for Knowledge of Jesus

The Testimony of the Biblical Witnesses

The primary source for our knowledge of Jesus is the collection of early Christian writings that came to be called the New Testament. These writings, virtually all of which were composed during the second half of the first century C.E. (i.e., within seventy years after the death of Jesus), are the earliest testimony we have about him, and they preserve the memories and traditions that circulated within the earliest communities of his followers.[5]

The most ancient writings in the New Testament are the letters of the Apostle Paul. Initially a devout Pharisee who was a fierce foe of the first followers of Jesus, he experienced a dramatic reversal through an encounter with the risen Lord, and he found himself called to preach the good news about him to the Gentiles (Gal 1:11-24). He subsequently founded a network of congregations around the Mediterranean, particularly in Asia Minor and Greece. Some of his letters to these communities were preserved and collected; they give us our earliest glimpse of the emergent Christian movement.[6] While offering only a bare sketch of historical infor-

4. For a reflection on the word "identity" and the work that it does, see the essay in this volume by Robert Jenson.

5. For a clear presentation of the modern scholarly consensus about the authorship and dating of the various New Testament writings, see Raymond E. Brown, *An Introduction to the New Testament,* ABRL (New York: Doubleday, 1997).

6. Scholarly consensus acknowledges seven of these letters as authentic letters written by Paul himself (Romans, 1-2 Corinthians, Galatians, Philippians, 1 Thessalonians, and Philemon). Six more letters that claim Pauline authorship (Ephesians, Colossians, 2 Thessalonians, 1-2 Timothy, and Titus) were eventually included in the Pauline collection, but many scholars believe that some or all of these are actually the work of second-generation followers or associates of Paul.

mation about Jesus, the material they do contain is of great importance because of its early date.[7]

The heart of the New Testament's witness to the identity of Jesus is to be found in the four Gospels — Matthew, Mark, Luke, and John. All four of these texts, which preserve extensive traditions about Jesus' teaching and activity, were written in their present form during roughly the last thirty years of the first century. Precise dates are difficult to determine, but the firm consensus among modern New Testament scholars holds that Mark is the earliest, and that it was composed shortly before or after 70 C.E.[8] Both Matthew and Luke used Mark's Gospel as a major source for their narratives, while adding substantial amounts of material from other sources. (Luke explicitly claims to have read several other accounts about Jesus and to have investigated the testimony of eyewitnesses [Luke 1:1-4].) The best guess is that these two Gospels were composed somewhere around 80-90 C.E. Because major portions of Mark, Matthew, and Luke follow a similar narrative line, they can easily be laid out in parallel columns for comparison; thus, they are often called the Synoptic Gospels, indicating that they can be "seen together." The Gospel of John, despite a few points of overlap with Mark and Luke, is a distinctive and seemingly independent composition,[9] offering a richly meditative rendering of Jesus' identity and mission. It is the most difficult of the four to date precisely, but it was probably composed no later than the last decade of the first century.[10]

Several observations about the character of this fourfold Gospel tradition are significant. First, all of these Gospels take the form of narratives.[11] They are not merely collections of sayings or theological treatises about Jesus; instead, they tell a story about him. And despite the significant differences among them, in every case that story focuses climactically on his crucifixion and resurrection.

7. For a discussion of what these letters say about the identity of Jesus, see the essay by Richard Hays.

8. On the problem of dating Mark, see Joel Marcus, *Mark 1–8*, AB 27 (New York: Doubleday, 2000), pp. 37-39.

9. See D. Moody Smith, *John among the Gospels*, 2nd ed. (Columbia: University of South Carolina Press, 2001).

10. For individual essays on the portrayal of Jesus' identity in each of these four canonical Gospels, see the essays by Dale Allison, Joel Marcus, Beverly Gaventa, and Marianne Meye Thompson.

11. See the essay by William Placher.

Second, all four narratives render information about Jesus as a historical figure situated in first-century Palestine under Roman rule. They are not timeless myths or fictions spun purely for the purpose of spiritual edification; rather, they make referential historical claims.

Third, they are not merely historical reports. All four Gospels are works of *proclamation,* seeking to present and interpret traditions about Jesus in such a way that readers (or hearers) of the story will be moved to acknowledge him as Son of God, whose death and resurrection are the definitive events through which the God of Israel is redeeming the world. Thus, these narratives are theological portraits of Jesus.[12]

Fourth, over time the church has insisted that all four distinct Gospel accounts are essential to a rounded picture of the identity of Jesus. We should neither conflate them into a single harmonized account (as Tatian did in his *Diatessaron*) nor pick a single Gospel as authoritative against the other three (as Marcion did); rather, we should receive all four together as complementary testimonies about the complex figure of Jesus the Christ.[13] If this is so, it follows that no single historical reconstruction of Jesus of Nazareth can supplant the fourfold testimony of the Gospels as a more adequate account of his identity. Historical investigation may shed light from new angles on Jesus and his significance — for example, by recovering more nuanced information about the Judaism of his day — but it can never replace the interpretations given to posterity by the four canonical Gospels.

The other documents in the New Testament each, in their distinctive ways, bear additional witness to the identity of Jesus. The Acts of the Apostles — an account of the expansion of the earliest Christian mission from Jerusalem into the wider Mediterranean world — was composed by the author of the Gospel of Luke as a second volume to accompany and extend his story of Jesus. It provides a fascinating window into the ways in which the significance of Jesus' life, death, and resurrection was interpreted and

12. For careful reflection about how we might acknowledge and weigh both the historical and the theological elements of the Gospels, see the essay by Francis Watson.

13. For an illuminating account of the very early date and theological importance of the church's adoption of the fourfold Gospel canon, see Graham Stanton, *Jesus and Gospel* (Cambridge: Cambridge University Press, 2004), pp. 63-91. This chapter, originally Stanton's Presidential Address to the 1996 Society for New Testament Studies General Meeting in Strasbourg, France, was first published as "The Fourfold Gospel," *New Testament Studies* 43 (1997): 317-46.

proclaimed by first-century communities, particularly as the message about Jesus took root in Gentile soil.

The miscellaneous documents sometimes categorized as the Catholic Epistles (James, 1 and 2 Peter, 1, 2, and 3 John, and Jude) offer moral exhortation to early Christian communities facing adversity and opposition. Particularly in 1 Peter, there is a strong appeal to see Jesus as an example to be emulated through patient endurance of suffering (1 Pet 2:18-25). The three short Johannine Epistles illuminate the ways in which the distinctive testimony of John's Gospel was received and contested within particular communities at the end of the first century or the beginning of the second.[14] Of special note is the insistence of 1 John on the confession that "Jesus Christ has come in the flesh" (1 John 4:2). This letter indicates that already by the end of the first century there were emergent groups of Jesus-followers who denied his fleshly humanity and viewed him exclusively as an otherworldly divine figure. The author of 1 John emphatically labels such people "false prophets," animated not by the Spirit of God but by "the spirit of the antichrist" (4:1, 3).

The two remaining texts in the New Testament stand apart from the others, both in their literary genres and in their distinctive portrayals of Jesus. The Letter to the Hebrews is not really a letter but rather an extended sermon, written in a complex and sophisticated rhetorical style, that powerfully portrays Jesus both as the obedient, suffering Son of God and as the eternal high priest who leads the way for his brothers and sisters into the heavenly sanctuary.[15] And the last book of the canon, the Revelation to John, is a fantastically imaginative apocalyptic vision that symbolically portrays the ultimate triumph of Jesus — "the lamb who was slaughtered" — over the powers of the present age.

All these texts provide crucial angles of vision on the identity of Jesus. While we could not include individual essays on every one, we hope that the volume's representative sample will amply illustrate the rich diversity and complexity of the New Testament witness to Jesus.

Still another layer of complexity comes to light when we take into account the church's historic confession that the Scriptures of Israel also constitute crucial testimony about Jesus. The Old Testament witness was

14. On these epistles, see Raymond E. Brown, *The Community of the Beloved Disciple* (New York: Paulist, 1979).

15. See the essay by A. Katherine Grieb.

understood as offering prophetic prefiguration of one who was to come, one in whom the character and purposes of the one God of Israel would be at last fully revealed and accomplished. The present volume contains only two essays considering the ways in which the identity of Jesus might be understood in light of Israel's Scripture;[16] these essays must stand as pointers to a broader area of inquiry beyond the modest scope of this book. For example, the disclosure of the identity of Jesus in the Psalms — read retrospectively in light of the story of Jesus — is a topic that demands much further study and discussion.[17]

What Is the Role of Extracanonical Writings?

As the foregoing discussion indicates, the Identity of Jesus Project has taken the canonical Scriptures of the Old and New Testaments as the primary ancient textual evidence for seeking the identity of Jesus. In view of many other recent publications, however, some readers may wonder whether other ancient writings *not* included in the Christian canon might have equal or better claim to offering truthful testimony about Jesus.[18] It is therefore necessary to say something briefly about these extracanonical texts.

First, there is the question of the sources that may have been used by the Gospel writers. Particularly prominent in recent critical discussion has been the hypothetical source called Q (short for German *Quelle,* "source"). This source has been posited by New Testament scholars to account for the sayings material that is common to the Gospels of Matthew and Luke but absent from the Gospel of Mark. It is important to emphasize that there is no extant manuscript of Q and there are no references in any ancient texts to such a document.[19] Q is purely a hypothesis, a speculative creation of

16. See the essays by Gary Anderson and Walter Moberly.

17. For some preliminary reflections on this question, see Richard B. Hays, "Christ Prays the Psalms: Israel's Psalter as Matrix of Early Christology," in *The Conversion of the Imagination: Paul as Interpreter of Israel's Scripture* (Grand Rapids: Eerdmans, 2005), pp. 101-18.

18. See, for example, Bart D. Ehrman, *Lost Scriptures: Books That Did Not Make It into the New Testament* (New York: Oxford University Press, 2003); Ehrman, *Lost Christianities: The Battles for Scripture and the Faiths We Never Knew* (New York: Oxford University Press, 2003).

19. The so-called *Critical Edition of Q* (ed. James M. Robinson, Paul Hoffmann, and

modern scholarship. While the hypothesis has enjoyed widespread acceptance in the New Testament guild, there are other credible explanations for the close parallels between Matthew and Luke, including the possibility that Luke used Matthew as a source.[20] Among the members of the Identity of Jesus Project, there are varying opinions on this question. One member of the group has written two books about Q,[21] while others remain deeply skeptical. In any case, acceptance of the Q hypothesis would add very little to the database for seeking the identity of Jesus, since this speculative source necessarily contains nothing that is not already present in Matthew and Luke. If in fact Q did exist and consisted of nothing other than a collection of sayings, it would bear witness to an early form of Jesus-tradition that lacked the story of Jesus' passion, death, and resurrection. But there is no way to confirm or disconfirm such a theory. Thus, for the purposes of our project, Q — along with other hypothetical pre-Gospel sources — played no more than a passing role in discussions of the portrayal of Jesus in the Synoptic tradition.

Of course, beyond Matthew, Mark, Luke, and John, there are other ancient "gospels" that offer various representations of Jesus. Perhaps the most important of these is the *Gospel of Thomas.* The text of this gospel, written in Coptic, was unearthed in a group of manuscripts found at Nag Hammadi, Egypt, in 1945. Unlike the canonical Gospels, it does not tell the story of Jesus; it is simply a collection of 114 sayings, introduced by a single sentence: "These are the secret sayings which the living Jesus spoke and which Didymus Judas Thomas wrote down."[22] A number of sayings in *Thomas* roughly parallel sayings found in the Synoptic Gospels, but there are also numerous sayings that are distinctive. Consider this example:

John S. Kloppenborg [Minneapolis/Leuven: Fortress/Peeters, 2000]) is nothing other than a careful attempt to work out the hypothesis through collation of the parallel texts from Matthew and Luke. Normally, a "critical edition" would work from ancient manuscripts. In this case, there are no such manuscripts.

20. For a strong challenge to the Q hypothesis, see Mark Goodacre, *The Case against Q* (Harrisburg, Pa.: Trinity Press International, 2002).

21. Dale C. Allison Jr., *The Jesus Tradition in Q* (Harrisburg, Pa.: Trinity Press International, 1997); *The Intertextual Jesus: Scripture in Q* (Harrisburg, Pa.: Trinity Press International, 2000).

22. *Gospel of Thomas* quotations translated by Thomas O. Lambdin, in *Nag Hammadi Codex II,2-7,* ed. Bentley Layton, vol. 1, NHS 20 (Leiden: Brill, 1989).

> Jesus said, "If they say to you, 'Where did you come from?', say to them, 'We came from the light, the place where the light came into being on its own accord. . . .' If they say to you, 'Is it you?', say, 'We are its children, and we are the elect of the living father.' If they ask you, 'What is the sign of your father in you?', say to them, 'It is movement and repose.'" (*Gos. Thom.* 50)

As this quotation suggests, the theological perspective of the *Gospel of Thomas* is closely connected to Gnosticism, a religious and philosophical movement that gave rise to hybrid gnosticized versions of Christianity in the second century. According to Gnostic thought, escape from the evil material world is possible only through the secret *gnōsis* (knowledge) that is available to an elite chosen few who have a spark of light, that is, of otherworldly divine essence, within themselves.

Some scholars have argued that the *Gospel of Thomas* should be dated in the first century, perhaps even earlier than the canonical Gospels — or at the very least that it contains independent traditions about the teaching of Jesus that are older than the Synoptics. This claim is often combined with the hypothesis that *Thomas* represents a very early form of Christianity that was focused not on Jesus' death and resurrection but rather on the teaching of a contemplative wisdom.[23] Such assertions, however, seem highly questionable when subjected to historical scrutiny. There is no evidence for the existence of the *Gospel of Thomas* in the first century. Its Gnostic theological tendencies, along with its systematic stripping away of Jewish elements and references to Israel's Scripture, mark it as a second-century composition derived from a cultural context distant from first-century Palestine. The parallels between *Thomas* and the Synoptic Jesus sayings can be shown to demonstrate *Thomas*'s dependence on the Synoptic tradition.[24] It is of course possible that the *Gospel of Thomas* also pre-

23. For the proposed early dating of the *Gospel of Thomas,* see Stephen J. Patterson, *The Gospel of Thomas and Jesus* (Sonoma, Calif.: Polebridge, 1993); April D. DeConick, *Recovering the Original Gospel of Thomas: A History of the Gospel and Its Growth,* LNTS (London: T&T Clark, 2005). For arguments favoring a later date, see Risto Uro, *Thomas: Seeking the Historical Context of the Gospel of Thomas,* JSPSup (London: T&T Clark, 2003); Larry W. Hurtado, *Lord Jesus Christ: Devotion to Jesus in Earliest Christianity* (Grand Rapids: Eerdmans, 2003), pp. 452-79; Nicholas Perrin, *Thomas, the Other Gospel* (London: SPCK, 2007).

24. Christopher Tuckett, "Thomas and the Synoptics," *Novum Testamentum* 30 (1988): 132-57; Klyne R. Snodgrass, "The Gospel of Thomas: A Secondary Gospel," *Second Century* 7 (1989/90): 19-38.

serves some sayings or traditions, apart from those transmitted in the canonical Gospels, that actually do go back to Jesus. Such claims must be assessed on a case-by-case basis. But the overall portrayal of Jesus in *Thomas* tells us far more about the admittedly interesting phenomenon of second-century Gnosticism than about Jesus of Nazareth.[25]

If that is so in the case of the *Gospel of Thomas,* it is true a fortiori of other ancient gospels that have attracted much recent media attention. The most celebrated recent example is the *Gospel of Judas,* newly discovered and translated, and promoted with great media fanfare by a *National Geographic* television special in 2006. This text is a fourth-century manuscript of a writing that was probably composed in the late second century. It presents Judas as a hero because, by betraying Jesus, he enables Jesus to escape confinement in his body and in this present evil material world. Jesus himself scornfully laughs at his disciples for their preoccupation with prayer and sacraments and offers recondite speculations about the realm of the "72 luminaries" and "360 firmaments." Even more clearly than the *Gospel of Thomas,* the *Gospel of Judas* overtly manifests second-century Gnostic views far removed from earlier, historically authentic traditions about Jesus.[26] Similarly, another of the Nag Hammadi Coptic texts, the *Gospel of Philip* — which received widespread attention because it is cited in *The Da Vinci Code* — comes from precisely the same later Gnostic milieu.

These texts tell us virtually nothing about the Jesus who lived and walked in Capernaum and Jerusalem in the first decades of the first century. Instead, they manifest a studied avoidance of Jesus' Jewish heritage and of the central ancient proclamation about his death and resurrection as saving events. Their newfound popularity in America in our time may

25. Recently, some scholars have questioned whether "Gnosticism" is an adequate category for interpreting the diverse ancient religious phenomena often included under that description. It is also sometimes suggested that the term reinforces anachronistic distinctions between orthodoxy and heresy. See, e.g., Michael Allen Williams, *Rethinking "Gnosticism": An Argument for Dismantling a Dubious Category* (Princeton: Princeton University Press, 1996); Karen L. King, *What Is Gnosticism?* (Cambridge, Mass.: Harvard University Press, 2003). The present brief introduction does not permit us to enter this debate. Our continued use of the term "Gnosticism," reflecting long-standing scholarly practice, is informed by Bentley Layton's magisterial work *The Gnostic Scriptures* (Garden City, N.Y.: Doubleday, 1987). For Layton's helpful historical framing of the Gnostic texts, see especially pp. xv-xxvii, 5-22, and (on the *Gospel of Thomas*) 376-79.

26. For a fuller discussion, see N. T. Wright, *Judas and the Gospel of Jesus* (Grand Rapids: Baker, 2006).

well derive from popular suspicion of the church and popular longing for a sort of "spirituality" that can be detached from tradition, from history, or from accountability to anything other than one's own inner spiritual stirrings. Insofar as these second-century writings belong to the history of interpretation of Jesus, they must be seriously examined for what they might tell us about Jesus' character and identity. But by the same token, they must be critically evaluated in light of the most ancient traditions of testimony to him.

It is precisely the need for critical evaluation of claims about Jesus that led over time to the formation of the New Testament canon. It is of course impossible to set forward here a full account of the historical developments that produced what we know today as the New Testament.[27] But in light of the misinformation promulgated in recent years by *The Da Vinci Code* and other best-selling books, a few clarifications are in order.

The list of twenty-seven books that make up the New Testament was first set forward, so far as we know, by Athanasius, the bishop of Alexandria, in 367 C.E., and this same list was finally given conciliar ratification at the Council of Carthage in 397 C.E. But the core of the canon had been firmly established in the churches long before that time, as early as the time of Irenaeus in the late second century. That core consisted of the fourfold Gospel (Matthew, Mark, Luke, and John), the Acts of the Apostles, the collection of thirteen Pauline letters, and the letters 1 Peter and 1 John. These writings were widely accepted as authoritative in churches both East and West, so that "in the decades just before and after AD 200, church writers in Greek and in Latin widely accepted a collection of twenty works as a NT alongside the Jewish OT."[28]

The Epistles of James, 2 Peter, 2-3 John, and Jude were sometimes included in early lists of authoritative writings, sometimes not. Likewise, the Letter to the Hebrews and the book of Revelation — particularly the latter — were controversial and not universally accepted in the churches until the fourth century. A few other early Christian writings were sometimes

27. For clear scholarly accounts of the formation of the New Testament canon, see Harry Y. Gamble, *The New Testament Canon: Its Making and Meaning*, GBS (Philadelphia: Fortress, 1985); Bruce M. Metzger, *The Canon of the New Testament: Its Origin, Development, and Significance* (Oxford: Clarendon, 1987). For brief summaries, see Brown, *Introduction to the New Testament*, pp. 3-15; Luke Timothy Johnson, *The Writings of the New Testament*, 2nd rev. ed. (Minneapolis: Fortress, 2002), pp. 595-619.

28. Brown, *Introduction to the New Testament*, p. 15.

treated as authoritative, read in churches, and included in canon lists in the early centuries. These writings included the *Epistle of Barnabas*, the *Shepherd of Hermas*, and the *Apocalypse of Peter*. It should be noted that nowhere in our ancient sources do we have any indication that texts such as the *Gospel of Thomas* or the *Gospel of Judas* ever enjoyed widespread acceptance in Christian churches; they seem to have been produced and read only in and for small, secretive, esoteric groups.

As this brief sketch indicates, it is simply not the case that the Council of Nicaea (325 C.E.) or the emperor Constantine forcibly imposed the New Testament canon we know today and suppressed numerous other gospels. Constantine had no role whatever in the process of canon formation, and the heart of the canon was firmly established more than a hundred years before he was born. While ecclesiastical councils eventually did ratify a formal canon list, the basic discernments about canonicity had been worked out in the life of the church long before any official action to confirm those decisions.

The criteria that seem to have been employed in this organic process were simple: (1) apostolicity — that is, some historical connection to the earliest circle of apostolic witnesses; (2) accordance with the rule of faith — that is, general consistency with teachings that the community recognized as faithful to the basic story of the gospel; and (3) acceptance and use in the churches, particularly the major metropolitan centers such as Antioch, Alexandria, and Rome. As the last point indicates, political factors did play a role in this process, as in any human deliberative process. But the notion that there was some nefarious conspiracy by elite ecclesiastical bureaucrats to stamp out widely popular gospels or to suppress the truth of the humanity of Jesus could not be further from the truth. Indeed, it is precisely the later Gnostic gospels that effectually deny the humanity of Jesus; one of the major reasons for the early church's steadfast insistence on the fourfold Gospel canon was its desire to *affirm* the humanity of Jesus and the goodness of the created material world.

The Testimony of the Church

As the foregoing remarks on canonization suggest, the role of the church as *a tradition-bearing community* is crucial to serious inquiry about the identity of Jesus. Nils Dahl, the great New Testament scholar who taught for many years at Yale Divinity School, suggested that the best way to understand Jesus' identity was — in the words of one of his book titles — to seek *Jesus in the Memory of the Early Church.*[29] Jesus is best understood in light of the recollections of the community of his followers, the community that originally preserved and interpreted traditions about him. Dahl's incisive comment on historical reconstructions that treat these traditions with suspicion is worth quoting in full:

> In no case can any distinct separation be achieved between the genuine words of Jesus and constructions of the community. We do not escape the fact that we know Jesus only as the disciples remembered him. Whoever thinks that the disciples completely misunderstood their Master or even consciously falsified his picture may give fantasy free reign.[30]

The church in its early years understood this point very well and consequently placed great emphasis on the faithful transmission of traditions about Jesus through the chain of witnesses proceeding from the apostles to subsequent generations of teachers and leaders. Irenaeus, the bishop of Lyons, writing near the end of the second century, made a passionate case that the truthfulness of the church's testimony, in contrast to the esoteric, speculative fabrications of the heretics he opposed, was secured precisely by continuity of tradition, the continuity of the church's memory. He declared that the gospel was "handed down to us in the Scriptures, to be the ground and pillar of our faith,"[31] and that the teaching of the apostles was passed from one generation to the next through the public testimony of an unbroken line of bishops:

> In this order, and by this succession, the ecclesiastical tradition from the apostles, and the preaching of the truth, have come down to us. And this is most abundant proof that there is one and the same vivifying faith, which has been preserved in the Church from the apostles until now, and handed down in truth.[32]

29. Nils A. Dahl, *Jesus in the Memory of the Early Church* (Minneapolis: Augsburg, 1976).

30. Nils A. Dahl, "The Problem of the Historical Jesus" (1953), in *Jesus the Christ* (Minneapolis: Fortress, 1991), p. 94.

31. Irenaeus, *Against Heresies* 3.1.1, ed. A. Roberts and J. Donaldson, *ANF* 1:414.

32. *Against Heresies* 3.3.3 (*ANF* 1:416).

One way in which the tradition was carried forward, in addition to the textual materials of the emergent New Testament canon, was through the church's practices of worship, prayer, and sacraments. The identity of Jesus was constantly re-presented in the community every time believers prayed the prayer he had taught his disciples, every time the community proclaimed his death through the practice of the Eucharist. These communal practices not only guaranteed continuity in the church's testimony to Jesus but also continued over time to produce fresh encounters with him. In its worship, the community both remembered Jesus and found itself instructed and empowered to extend his mission in the world, and thereby to realize his identity more fully. If, as Luke writes in Acts 1:1, the Gospel informs us of the things that "Jesus *began* to do and to teach" (NIV), it is in the ongoing narrative of the church's life that we discover what Jesus subsequently *continued* to do and to teach.[33]

Of course, such a claim imposes upon those who would affirm it a stringent demand to distinguish between faithful and unfaithful developments, between those aspects of the church's witness that truthfully present the identity of Jesus to the world and those that betray it.[34]

What Is the Role of Contemporary Experience?

Finally, the necessity of discernment applies not only to the testimony of texts and traditions from the past but also to testimony about the presence and character of Jesus in the present time. The opening paragraphs of this introduction gave a few examples of claims about how Jesus may be experienced in our time. As we suggested there, some such claims must be judged to be distortions or delusions. But if in fact Jesus was raised from the dead, he is alive: it follows that he continues to speak and to act, to express his redemptive love for the world. In the words of a hymn by Brian Wren:

> Christ is alive! No longer bound
> to distant years in Palestine,

33. On this approach to understanding Jesus in terms of the unfolding history of his impact in the church, see especially Markus Bockmuehl, *Seeing the Word: Refocusing New Testament Study* (Grand Rapids: Baker Academic, 2006), pp. 161-88.

34. These matters are engaged in the essays by Brian Daley, David Steinmetz, Katherine Sonderegger, and Sarah Coakley.

but saving, healing, here and now,
and touching every place and time.[35]

It is therefore a basic element of the grammar of Christian faith that, in the wonderful image of Gerard Manley Hopkins, "Christ plays in ten thousand places."[36]

But how do we recognize those places? And how do we know that the Jesus we encounter there is for real? It is part of the burden of this book to argue that all such experiential claims must be tested for consistency with the testimony of Scripture and the church's tradition. So, for example, the Jesus who is enlisted to support war or *apartheid*, or the Jesus who promises wealth and ease to his followers, cannot be the same person we know from the New Testament and the Eucharist. Such representations are flatly inconsistent with all that has been disclosed about his identity in the past. On the other hand, both Scripture and tradition bear consistent witness that Jesus is truly to be found among the poor and those who suffer, in solidarity with them. This aspect of Jesus' identity surfaces in several of the essays in this book. One point on which participants in the Identity of Jesus Project agreed is that precisely by listening carefully to the church's tradition, we may find ourselves led unexpectedly into learning the disciplines of prayer and attention that will enable us to experience the presence of Jesus.

Converging Visions of Jesus

Readers of this book will find that certain themes recur throughout the essays. Taken together, these themes articulate something like a common understanding that emerged from our work together. Some of them have to do with the methods appropriate to interpreting the evidence about Jesus, and others have to do with the picture of Jesus' identity that results from such interpretative work. It is not easy to keep these matters cleanly separated, because any account of Jesus is closely bound up with the hermeneutical methods and epistemological presumptions at work in our en-

35. Taken from "Christ Is Alive," by Brian Wren. Copyright © 1969, 1995 Hope Publishing Co., Carol Stream, IL 60188. All rights reserved. Used by permission.

36. Gerard Manley Hopkins (1844-1889), "As kingfishers catch fire, dragonflies draw flame . . . ," in *The Poems of Gerard Manley Hopkins*, ed. W. H. Gardner and N. H. MacKenzie, 4th ed. (Oxford: Oxford University Press, 1967), p. 90.

counter with him. In any case, the affirmations that follow do not constitute a formal declaration by the members of the group. They are, rather, an attempt by the editors to characterize the substantial areas of broad consensus in our deliberations.

Jesus of Nazareth was a Jew. Any attempt to describe Jesus' identity must recognize that he was a historical figure who was very much a part of the Judaism of his day. The essay by Markus Bockmuehl, "God's Life as a Jew," gives special emphasis to this point, but all of the essays presuppose it, and many of them thematize it explicitly. Jesus' teaching and activity make sense only within the context of Israel's history and Israel's Scripture. For that reason, his identity is forever bound up with God's people Israel. It is highly significant that his first followers acclaimed him as the Christ: the Messiah of Israel promised by the Scriptures. Therefore, all attempts to set Jesus against Jewish law and tradition must be critically scrutinized, and all attempts to portray him as a non-Jewish figure must be emphatically rejected.

The identity of Jesus is reliably attested and known in the Scriptures of the Old and New Testaments. The four canonical Gospels (Matthew, Mark, Luke, and John) are the earliest extant accounts of the story of Jesus. These writings have been received as true and authoritative by the Christian church from the first centuries of Christianity. Their authoritative role was not artificially imposed by fiat of emperor or council at some late date; rather, they emerged from the life and worship of Christian communities in the first two centuries of the Christian era as the definitive and reliable portrayals of Jesus. For this reason, these Gospels have unique importance for Christians seeking the identity of Jesus.

Further, *the entirety of the canonical witness is indispensable to a faithful rendering of the figure of Jesus.* We cannot see Jesus clearly by reading only one Gospel to the exclusion of the others, for their differing portrayals are complementary and essential to the wholeness of our understanding of this multifaceted figure. Similarly, we cannot understand him rightly apart from the other writings in the New Testament (the Acts of the Apostles, the letters of Paul and other early Christian leaders, and the book of Revelation), which grapple with the meaning of the story of Jesus and interpret his significance for the ongoing life of the community. Finally, the Gospel stories themselves are unintelligible apart from the larger and older body of Scriptures that provide the historical, literary, and theological context for understanding Jesus. The New Testament writers repeatedly insist that the significance of Jesus' life, death, and resurrection is to be interpreted "in accordance with the Scriptures," by which they mean Israel's sacred writings: the Law, the Prophets, and the Psalms (see, e.g., Luke 24:44; 1 Cor 15:3-5).

One corollary of the preceding two points is that *in order to understand the identity of Jesus rightly, the church must constantly engage in the practice of deep, sustained reading of these texts.* If Jesus is to be known rightly through the testimony of the apostolic witnesses, one primary means of access to him will be through disciplined, faithful engagement with the texts through which that testimony is mediated. This sort of attentive reading of Scripture can and must serve as a constant critical check on our tendency to make Jesus in our own image and thereby turn him into an idol to serve our purposes.

It follows also that *to come to grips with the identity of Jesus, we must know him as he is presented to us through the medium of narrative.* The New Testament discloses the identity of Jesus chiefly through telling his story, not through abstract dogmatic propositions or anthologies of his sayings. This attention to narrative is one of the factors that has encouraged us to include in this book separate essays on most of the major New Testament witnesses: rather than rendering a homogenized account of the New Testament's testimony, we want to pay careful attention to the distinctive ways the story of Jesus is told by Matthew, Mark, Luke, John, Paul, and Hebrews. Even the letters of Paul and the Letter to the Hebrews — probably the most "theological" documents in the New Testament — are rightly understood as reflective commentary on the story of Jesus as it comes into contact with the life of the communities of his followers.

The trajectory begun within the New Testament of interpreting Jesus' identity in and for the church has continued through Christian history. For that reason, the creeds of the church and the interpretative testimony of the church's tradition must be taken seriously into account. The identity of Jesus is disclosed partly through his impact on many generations of Christians who have served and worshiped him, as well as through the reflections of the church's great theologians who have thought deeply about who he is. One of the pervasive illusions of modernity is that we can dispense with tradition and replace it with more scientific modes of knowing. But in the case of Jesus, his identity is inseparable from the accounts offered by the great cloud of witnesses who have known him before us.

Jesus is not dead; he lives. God vindicated Jesus Christ by raising him from the dead. Therefore, he is alive.[37] The implications of this claim are enormous. First, it requires us to rethink what is possible and how God in fact acts in history. Second, it means that Jesus can be known not only as a figure of the historical past but also as the living Lord of the church, and of the world. One of the challenges of understanding the identity of Jesus, then, is to discern the ways in which Jesus is present and active in the world today. Third, if indeed Jesus' resurrection has foreshadowed God's ultimate new creation of all things, this means that our vision of the identity of Jesus remains filtered "through a glass darkly," awaiting the full final disclosure that will be accessible only eschatologically. But the resurrection has given us the decisive clue to understanding and trusting the life-giving power of Jesus.

Because Jesus remains a living presence, he can be encountered in the community of his people, the body of Christ. This encounter takes place in many ways: in preaching, in the sacraments, and in the community's life together in service. Such claims are mysterious, but they are strongly grounded in both the testimony of Scripture and the experience of the church across time. One way in which Jesus may be particularly encountered as present is in the experience of the poor and those who suffer, as suggested by Matthew 25:31-46.

One motif that repeatedly surfaced in our group's deliberations was the recognition that *Jesus is a disturbing, destabilizing figure.* In his own historical time he was a controversial figure who generated a social movement that the guardians of order considered a threat to the status quo. For this reason, he was executed as a dangerous revolutionary. And it has remained true across time that Jesus' teachings and presence have a way of unsettling things, challenging privilege, calling people to radical and costly service. Wherever Jesus is invoked as the guarantor of an established order, we may rightly suspect that some sort of identity fraud is being perpetrated.[38] The Jesus we know through Scripture and the creeds does not leave us at ease; rather, he calls his followers to deny themselves and take up the cross. He teaches us that we are sinners and that we are called to actions of costly discipleship that bear witness to God's coming kingdom of justice in an unjust world.

37. For discussions of the identity of Jesus that take seriously the claim that Jesus is alive, see Leander E. Keck, *Who Is Jesus? History in Perfect Tense* (Columbia: University of South Carolina Press, 2000); Luke Timothy Johnson, *Living Jesus: Learning the Heart of the Gospel* (San Francisco: HarperSanFrancisco, 1999).

38. This point is strongly emphasized by Wayne A. Meeks, *Christ Is the Question* (Louisville: Westminster John Knox, 2006).

Finally, *the identity of Jesus is something that must be learned through long-term discipline.* This is already suggested by the shape of the Gospel narratives, in which Jesus calls disciples who follow him around for years without fully grasping who he is. Only after their extended exposure to him and after the shattering revelatory events of cross and resurrection do they even begin to grasp his identity. Likewise, we should not suppose that the identity of Jesus is something we can learn by reading one book, discovering one new ancient text, or polling one panel of experts — including the experts whose essays are collected here. Learning the identity of Jesus is a costly, lifelong process in which we grow, under the tutelage of Scripture and the church's disciplined practices of worship and service, toward a deeper comprehension of the Jesus we know now inadequately. As Paul describes this life of discipleship: "I want to know Christ and the power of his resurrection and the sharing of his sufferings by becoming like him in his death" (Phil 3:10). This is not a pilgrimage to be undertaken lightly or with impatience. One of the problems with many popular books and television programs about Jesus is that they neglect this costly call to discipleship as a prerequisite to knowing his identity. We come to know him rightly insofar as we are conformed to the pattern of his life. And, as Paul well knew, that will cost us not less than everything.

Unresolved Issues

Partly for that reason, it would be an act of great presumption for our collaborative group of scholars to suppose that we could answer all questions or give an adequate account of Jesus by producing this collection of essays. All we can do is to offer some pointers to insights that we have found helpful. We hope that these insights will provide a useful guide for other pilgrims who follow us in seeking the identity of Jesus.

At the same time, honesty compels us to report that despite our converging visions of Jesus, several important issues were unresolved in our common deliberations. Careful readers will discern several unresolved methodological tensions among the various essays. We have made no attempt to disguise these tensions: they are a sign of the group's vigorous engagement with perennially challenging problems. Differences of opinion — or at least significant differences of emphasis — remain among the participants. Three of these unresolved issues are particularly salient, and these should be identified at the outset.

First, what is the relationship of historical reconstruction of the figure of Jesus to "canonical" interpretation and the church's rule of faith? All members of the group agreed in principle that historical criticism of the Bible can contribute important insights about the identity of Jesus not only by setting him in his proper historical context but also by clarifying the transmission and development of the early church's traditions about him.[39] And all of us agreed in principle that the wholeness of the New Testament canon is essential to a rounded picture of Jesus, and that the church's rule of faith, as expressed in the ancient ecumenical creeds, provides a truthful and reliable guide to the interpretation of the canonical witnesses. The difficulty is to know how these two agreed-upon principles are to be linked *in practice* in giving an account of the identity of Jesus. Do the findings of historical criticism serve as a constraint and corrective to the church's confessional traditions? Or is it the other way around? Or is some more complex dialectical hermeneutical process required to bring these different ways of knowing Jesus into a mutually fruitful relation to one another? Readers will readily see how different authors in this collection of essays have given different weightings to these different approaches to interpretation.

Second, how do we deal with the unity and diversity within Scripture itself? The Bible is a collection of documents composed and edited by many different people over a very long period of time. Even the New Testament is made up of diverse writings composed by several different authors over a period of at least fifty years. Do all these writings somehow say "the same thing" about Jesus? Or does our account of Jesus' identity have to acknowledge the irreducible particularity of and differences among the various witnesses? Within this overarching question of unity and diversity we may identify several issues that surface throughout the volume:

- What is the relationship of Israel's Scripture to the New Testament, and in what way, if at all, can the Old Testament be read as disclosing the identity of Jesus?
- How do we deal with the fact of four different Gospels in the New Testament? Should they be somehow harmonized into a single account,

39. This is not to say that the common methods and conclusions of historical criticism are beyond critique and reformation. See on this question particularly Dale Allison's essay "The Historians' Jesus and the Church." Readers should note well that Allison is calling not for the rejection of historical inquiry about Jesus but for its refinement.

or should they be treated as distinct witnesses? The design of the volume favors the latter approach, but the question of a unified fourfold witness is never far from sight.

- What about the diversity of literary genres in the canon? Do the various New Testament epistles, the historical narrative of Acts, the hortatory sermon of the "Epistle" to the Hebrews, and the visionary book of Revelation stand alongside the Gospels as equally important testimony to the identity of Jesus? If so, how do these very different literary forms contribute to the overall picture?

We regret that the design of our project did not include a study of Revelation, but all the other literary genres in the New Testament are represented by the essays in this volume. Readers will find that the authors of the essays grapple in various ways with the relation of the individual writings to the larger shape of the canonical witness to Jesus.

Finally, apart from interpretation of the biblical texts, how much weight should we place on the experience of Jesus by the faithful, who regularly claim to encounter him in prayer, in sacramental worship, in the gathering of the community, in spirit-inspired prophetic utterances, or in the faces of the world's poor and suffering people? What criteria are to be used in assessing these accounts of Jesus as a living presence? Do they give us reliable information about the identity of Jesus? Or are they merely sentimental fantasies that hang the name of Jesus on diverse spiritual experiences only loosely connected with him? Of course, all such experiential claims need to be tested for congruity with the biblical testimony about Jesus' character and teaching. But because Jesus was raised from the dead, he is in fact alive and able to be mysteriously present in the world. Readers of this book will find that some of the essayists (for example, Sarah Coakley) place far more emphasis on the living encounter with Jesus than do others. It would be fair to say, however, that all of us in the Identity of Jesus Project acknowledge that if we are going to join the Greeks of John 12:21 in wishing to see the Jesus of whom the New Testament speaks, we must also open ourselves to the possibility of encountering him today.

These questions remain unresolved in this book, but they do sketch out some of the rocky terrain that must be traversed in the pilgrimage. In the essays that follow, we offer a collection of reports from along the way, and we invite others to join us in seeking the identity of Jesus.

Sources and Methods

How the Gospels Mean

William C. Placher

Suppose I start to tell you a story: "A dog walked into a bar, sat down, and ordered a gin and tonic. . . ." If you rush out eagerly and dead serious to tell others that I have found a dog who not only talks but orders mixed drinks, you are not faithfully reporting me. You have misunderstood me — I meant to be telling a joke. Conversely, if I see a car crash and rush into the room yelling, "Call an ambulance; there's been an accident," you have misunderstood me if you say, "Not bad," and assume that I was trying out a dramatic sketch.

Before we can even ask about the truth or falsity of stories people tell, we need to understand what they mean, and that involves, among other things, understanding what *kind* of stories they are — that is, "how" they mean. The beginnings and endings of stories often help particularly in this regard. Most contemporary Americans would recognize my dog story as an intended joke from the first few words. Similarly, when John Bunyan ends part 1 of *Pilgrim's Progress* with "So I awoke, and behold it was a dream,"[1] we understand differently what has gone before.

So how *do* the Gospels mean? I propose that the four canonical Gospels (the ones in the New Testament) are *history-like witnesses to truths both historical and transcendent.* What follows attempts to explain the meaning of that cumbersome phrase, drawing primarily from the Gospels' beginnings and endings to do so. It seems helpful to begin by contrasting the Gospels with some things they are not: they are not works of fiction, not (in at least one sense of the word) myth, and not the usual form of modern history.

1. John Bunyan, *The Pilgrim's Progress* (London: Penguin, 1965), p. 148.

What the Gospels Are Not

Not Fiction

Works of fiction — novels, for example — operate in their own secondary world, usually designed to seem plausible in the events they narrate, perhaps connected to our world by the insights they offer into human character, but not consistently recounting events that have happened in the same real world in which we live. Historical novels may use some characters and events from our world, but at some point they deliberately veer off in a "fictional" direction — that's the point of the exercise. The Gospels are different. They refer to characters on the grand stage of history well known to many of their first readers: Herod, Pontius Pilate, Quirinius the governor of Syria. And so might historical novels. Something more, however, happens in the Gospels. Particularly in their endings, they reach out to include their readers in their world.[2] John is the clearest case. At the end of John 20 (some think the original end of the Gospel), the narrator steps out of the narrative frame and declares that "these [things] are written so that you may come to believe that Jesus is the Messiah, the Son of God, and that through believing you may have life in his name" (John 20:31).[3] Readers become figures in the world of the story, invited to belief.

Even more dramatically, the end of John 21 announces that the beloved disciple "is the disciple who is testifying to these things and has written them, and we know that his testimony is true" (21:24) — presenting here not only an author who testifies to the truth of the narrative but, with "we," a community that knows that his testimony is true. The great Johannine scholar Raymond Brown notes how, until this point, the world of the Gospel has been self-contained, as if its readers were in a darkened auditorium watching a play. "But now, as the curtain is about to fall on the stage drama, the lights in the theater are suddenly turned on. Jesus shifts his attention from the disciples on the stage to the audience that has become visible and makes clear that his ultimate concern is for them — those who have come to believe in him through the word of his disciples."[4]

2. The authors of the Gospels, to be sure, would have pictured their typical "readers" as an audience listening to the text read aloud rather than solitary figures with books in hand.

3. Scripture quotations are from the NRSV.

4. Raymond E. Brown, *The Gospel according to John* (Garden City, N.Y.: Doubleday, 1970), p. 1049.

Mark's narrative strategy is almost exactly the opposite of John's, and yet he invites a similar relation between readers and text. Where the Fourth Gospel steps out of the frame of the narrated world to address its readers, Mark's enigmatic ending leaves its readers enclosed in the world of the story, and with no apparent way out. Mary Magdalene, Mary the mother of James, and Salome have found the tomb empty of Jesus' body and encountered a mysterious young man. "So they went out and fled from the tomb, for terror and amazement had seized them; and they said nothing to anyone, for they were afraid." The only witnesses remain in fearful silence, with even an awkward and abrupt grammatical ending to add to the sheer strangeness of the final sentence.[5] As Robert Fowler puts it, "The story *in* Mark's Gospel seems to preclude the telling *of* Mark's Gospel."[6] Except that here, somehow, is this text. We are addressed from a community of faith, although no such community appears within the story itself. "The key to understanding the ending of Mark," Fowler concludes, "is not to understand the women or men in the story, but to understand what is happening in the women or men reading the story."[7] We as readers become part of the story we are reading, and thereby the world of the story and our world merge.

Something similar happens at the end of Luke and of Matthew. Consider, for instance, just how odd is Luke's introduction of the good news of Jesus' resurrection. On the first day of the week, a group of women goes to Jesus' tomb, only to find the stone rolled away and the tomb empty. The women are perplexed (Luke 24:4). Then two men in dazzling clothes appear to them, and they are terrified (24:5). In the end, they tell the news to the apostles, to whom the words "seemed . . . an idle tale, and they did not believe them" (24:11). Peter goes to the tomb himself, and he is amazed, astonished. The whole first section of resurrection accounts has passed by without a single unambiguously positive verb to describe a response. Even later, when Jesus appears to the eleven, the only description of their reaction is that "they were startled and terrified, and thought that they were seeing a ghost" (24:37).

5. The last word of the Greek text (in the oldest manuscripts) is a conjunction, γάρ *(gar),* or "for" — an odd way to end a sentence, much less a book.

6. Robert M. Fowler, "Reading Matthew Reading Mark," in *SBL Seminar Papers, 1986,* ed. Kent Harold Richards (Atlanta: Scholars Press, 1986), p. 14.

7. Robert M. Fowler, "Reader-Response Criticism: Figuring Mark's Reader," in *Mark and Method: New Approaches in Biblical Studies,* ed. Janice Capel Anderson and Stephen D. Moore (Minneapolis: Fortress, 1992), p. 80.

Likewise, at the very end of Matthew, as the eleven disciples come to the mountaintop for their final commissioning, "they saw him, they worshiped him; but some doubted" (Matt 28:17). References to doubt appear in a number of later resurrection traditions, but there, as in the story of doubting Thomas, they have an apologetic function. Doubts provide the occasion for decisive evidence.[8] Here, however, no such demonstration follows, and the only role of the doubt seems to be to leave the response within the narrated world ambiguous and thus thrust readers into the story as people called to make a decision, inviting us to think of the world of the story as the world in which we live.

The literary critic Erich Auerbach rightly insisted on the "tyrannical" character of these texts. Reading the *Iliad* or the *Odyssey,* Auerbach noted, we can escape to Homer's imagined world for a time, and even learn lessons about the meaning of heroism or the call of home. But "the Scripture stories do not, like Homer's, court our favor, they do not flatter us that they may please us and enchant us — they seek to subject us."[9] These stories claim to offer a framework — a beginning, an end, a center — for all of history, and they propose that our lives and all other events have meaning only to the extent that they fit into that framework. These stories purport to *define* reality.

Their tyrannical character, particularly when combined with their content, ought to make them deeply disturbing. Most of us, most of the time, understand our world in terms of getting and spending, comfort and security. These stories declare that those who would find their lives must lose them; they call on their readers to pick up their own crosses and follow in the path of the Crucified One. If they are thereby not merely describing one eccentric corner of the world or offering us one option we might choose among others but defining the world in which we live, then we have a chance to find peace only on the other side of suffering, and we are called to reject the comfortable values that dominate our society.

Now of course this is the *claim* they make. It may be false. Their au-

8. See Luke 24; John 20:25; Mark 16:11-14 (in the longer secondary ending of Mark, probably added sometime in the second century); *Epistula Apostolorum* 1-10.

9. Erich Auerbach, *Mimesis: The Representation of Reality in Western Literature,* trans. Willard R. Trask (Princeton: Princeton University Press, 1968), p. 15. See, almost identically, Bonhoeffer's account of the "complete reversal" that takes place when Christians read Scripture. Dietrich Bonhoeffer, *Life Together,* trans. John W. Doberstein (New York: Harper & Row, 1954), p. 54.

thors may have been misled, confused, or lying. But novels cannot, *in this sense,* be "false." They are not even making the sort of claim that raises such issues of truth and falsity.[10] Since the Gospels do raise such questions, they are not fiction.

Not Myth

Nor are the Gospels, in one sense of a word with many senses, myth. I use "myth" here to mean a story about events occurring in a primordial time that is also, in Mircea Eliade's words, "a sort of eternal mythical present that is periodically reintegrated by means of rites."[11] The Babylonian creation myth, *Enuma Elish,* for instance, tells how Marduk, the deity of Babylon, defeated the earth monster Tiamat and made the physical world out of her dead body. The story was recited each New Year's Day in a ritual that established order (an order that included the king's rule) for the coming year.

One could say of such a myth what Auerbach says of Scripture: it claims to define the framework for reality, a framework within which our own lives need to be lived. But in other ways such myths are different from the Gospel stories. The Babylonian myth does not take place "while Quirinius was governor of Syria." It would not make sense to ask how many years have elapsed between Marduk's victory and this New Year; mythical time is not like that. It is related to our time, not by chronological distance, but by its eternal availability for ritual repetition.[12]

The Gospels, by contrast, narrate datable events. Here their beginnings effectively make the point. Matthew begins with a genealogy, locating Jesus in a line of well-known characters in Israel's history. Indeed, the fourteen generations each from Abraham to David, David to the deportation to Babylon, and the deportation to Jesus (Matt 1:17), however symbolic their significance, could hardly, in their specificity, be more unlike the "once upon a time, long ago" characteristic of myth's temporal loca-

10. There are other senses in which novels may be false — if their authors, for instance, deliberately manipulate characters down paths foreign to their identities in order to make an ideological point.

11. Mircea Eliade, *The Sacred and the Profane,* trans. Willard R. Trask (New York: Harper & Row, 1961), p. 70.

12. See Paul Ricoeur, "Myth and History," *The Encyclopedia of Religion,* ed. Mircea Eliade, 16 vols. (New York: Macmillan, 1987), 10:273.

tion. As soon as the story narrates Jesus' birth — indeed, in the very next phrase — it mentions Herod, a political figure known to the story's first readers, whether Roman, Greek, or Hebrew, as their near contemporary.

Luke adopts the beginning characteristic of a Greek historian, acknowledging previous writers and making reference to eyewitnesses before announcing his intention, as someone who has "investigat[ed] everything carefully from the very first, to write an orderly account for you . . ." (Luke 1:3). In terms of the conventions of Greek writing, he could not make it clearer that what follows is not myth. Mark's characteristic abruptness, by contrast, makes his genre initially less clear. He simply starts telling his story. Still, he does include a quotation from Isaiah, anticipating the events he narrates and thereby locating them clearly *after* the historical figure Isaiah. Moreover, the very ordinariness of his scenes and characters draws us away from the world of myth. These are not Hesiod's gods or Homer's heroes but fisherfolk from a small village, in a time and place familiar to the story's first readers.

John's Gospel offers the most complicated case. How would one define the genre of its prologue? That "beginning" when the Word was with God might well be a kind of mythical time. But even in the prologue, the story quickly shifts to a different kind of time: "There was a man sent from God, whose name was John" (John 1:6) — not, we soon learn, long ago and far away, but fairly recently and in known territory. And the Word made flesh occupied the same time and place as this John. Here too the story emerges as one not far from its first readers' own time and place.

Not the History of a Modern Historian

So are the Gospels history? That depends, of course, on what we mean by history. Reading Shelby Foote's magisterial account of the Civil War,[13] I trust that when he says that the road was muddy, he has established by evidence that the road *was* muddy. If he reports that first the general died and then the line of troops broke and fled, I believe that that is the order in which the events occurred. (I actually do trust these things, even though Foote's three very long volumes contain not a single footnote. Foote had

13. Shelby Foote, *The Civil War: A Narrative,* 3 vols. (New York: Random House, 1958-74).

his critics, and he knew the rules of the game of modern history writing; he would not have risked bluffing.) By contrast, as John Calvin noted long ago, "We know that the Evangelists were not very exact as to the order of dates, or even in detailing minutely every thing that Christ did or said."[14] Details are inconsistent; chronology varies from one Gospel to another; events are reported (such as Jesus' prayers in the garden of Gethsemane) that it seems unlikely anyone could have known. Either the Gospel writers were not writing history with the same goals as most modern historians, or they did a bad job of it.

But ancient historians *in general* had different methods than their modern equivalents. Thucydides, in many ways the most "modern" of them, assures us near the beginning of his *History of the Peloponnesian War:* "Either I was present myself at the events which I have described or else I heard of them from eye-witnesses whose reports I have checked with as much thoroughness as possible."[15] So far so good. But his history includes many speeches given on key occasions, and in this case, he admits: "I have found it difficult to remember the precise words used in the speeches which I listened to myself and my various informants have experienced the same difficulty; so my method has been, while keeping as closely as possible to the general sense of the words that were actually used, to make the speakers say what, in my opinion, was called for by each situation."[16] He is following conventions different from those accepted by historians today; he differs from other ancient historians only in the clarity with which he explains himself.

The Gospels likewise provide "history" in the minimal sense of stories about an actual human being who lived at a particular time and place not all that far distant from the time of their authors. Their authors rearranged details — Calvin took it for granted that the Sermon on the Mount combined sayings originally delivered at different times.[17] Confident that they

14. John Calvin, *Commentary on a Harmony of the Evangelists,* trans. William Pringle, vol. 1; *Calvin's Commentaries,* vol. 16 (Grand Rapids: Baker, 1989), p. 216.

15. Thucydides, *History of the Peloponnesian War* 1.22, trans. Rex Warner (London: Penguin, 1972), p. 48.

16. *History of the Peloponnesian War* 1.22 (Warner, p. 47). I am not sure how to reconcile "keeping as closely as possible to the general sense of the words that were actually used" and making the speakers say "what, in my opinion, was called for."

17. "Pious and modest readers ought to be satisfied with having a brief summary of the doctrine of Christ placed before their eyes, collected out of his many and various discourses." Calvin, *Commentary on a Harmony of the Evangelists,* p. 259.

understood who Jesus was, they put down stories that seemed to them to capture his identity without worrying overmuch about the accuracy of the particular stories. Likely, they made up some such stories themselves. They would have been dramatically different from other historical writers of their time had they done differently.

We would therefore misread the stories if we evaluated their truth in terms of the percentage of things they report that Jesus actually said or did (assuming that some method permitted us to do this reliably). That would not be faithful to the character of these narratives. Rather, we should think about them as David Kelsey says Karl Barth did: "as a source of anecdotes about what Jesus said or did which one would tell to show 'what he was like.' The anecdotes that fall together into a given group are interchangeable. Barth is not interested in them for themselves but for the *patterns* that recur in a number of them. The incidents the anecdotes recite serve to *illustrate* Jesus' personhood, not to constitute it."[18] The stories concern who Jesus was — someone who healed others, someone who hung out with outsiders, someone who argued with Pharisees about the law, and so on — rather than the chronology of his ministry or the accuracy of every saying or deed they report.

This is one of the places the Jesus Seminar's method goes wrong. The Seminar votes on the historical reliability of individual sayings and stories, and its members then create their portraits of Jesus out of whatever particulars have been defined as reliable. If we cannot be sure of the historicity of any particular exorcism, for instance, then by this method we have no basis for concluding that Jesus performed exorcisms. As Dale Allison explains so well in his essay on the historical Jesus for this volume, however, such an approach to evidence contradicts ways we reasonably argue all the time.[19] I can remember quite clearly that my grandfather was a curmudgeon even if

18. David H. Kelsey, *The Uses of Scripture in Recent Theology* (Philadelphia: Fortress, 1975), p. 43.

19. Cf. also Hans Frei: "In the instance of Jesus, it may well be that certain of his sayings or specific, isolated episodes recounted from his brief ministry, which are quite enigmatic in character and tell little about him, such as his condemning a fig tree because it would not yield fruit out of season (Mark 11:12-14), are much more nearly reliable historical reports than those in which his over-all personal intention is more clearly depicted." Frei, *The Identity of Jesus Christ: The Hermeneutical Bases of Dogmatic Theology* (Philadelphia: Fortress, 1975), p. 141. I am in this whole essay following the conclusions, albeit inadequately, of my teacher Hans Frei.

I cannot reliably recall any particular curmudgeonly thing he said or did. Similarly, one would expect Jesus' followers' memories about the sort of person he was to be clearer than their ability to recite particular things he said. Yet the Jesus Seminar insists that lacking any trustworthy particulars, we cannot possibly have a trustworthy generality.

An emphasis on general characteristics does not dodge the question of truth. A character portrait of Adolf Hitler that made him out to be a nice guy would be false — even if every report within it of kindness to dogs and small children were true. So too the Gospels, if they did not convey the person Jesus was, would be false. Many of their episodes we can take to be illustrative anecdotes; nevertheless, some stories narrate an event so central to the picture of Jesus they present that, in Hans Frei's words, it "allows and even forces us to ask the question, 'Did this actually take place?'"[20] He could have healed one person rather than another, spoken one parable rather than another, and still have been the same person. But not, for instance, if he had lived to a ripe old age rather than dying on a cross.

Where do we get these rules for deciding what matters and what doesn't? We have to get them first and foremost from the stories themselves. There are, to be sure, endless borderline cases, but that does not mean that we cannot identify some matters as clearly on one side or another of a line. How could we read any of the Gospels and think that the crucifixion is simply an illustrative anecdote showing Jesus' compassion? How could we notice how John dates the crucifixion differently from the other three Gospels and think that chronological accuracy is central to the truth of the matter? And so on — to be sure, soon to harder cases. Is Mark 6:45-52 an attempt to show how Jesus was always mysterious to his disciples, even when in their midst, or is it telling us that one of Jesus' characteristics was that he could walk on water? I myself would favor the first interpretation, but I concede that the argument would have to be complex.

The fourfold character of the Gospels reminds us that the church has not characteristically taken them as history in the modern sense. Each story is different; there are inconsistencies. While Christian scholars have often engaged in various forms of harmonizing, the church down the centuries has consistently resisted combining them into a single narrative; perhaps we should pause in surprise at this fact more than we do. What

20. Frei, *Identity of Jesus Christ*, p. 140. This seems to me so clear that I am always puzzled at the number of Frei's readers who ignore it.

would have been more natural, it might seem, than conflating disparate accounts into a single, consistent story? But Christians have apparently realized that doing so would distort the kind of material the Gospels represent.[21] Indeed, each Gospel has its own narrative logic. The way it begins and ends, its ordering of incidents, the manner in which its picture of Jesus emerges — these and other factors are part of the way in which the particular Gospel renders Jesus' identity, and they would be lost if we conflated all the Gospels into a single narrative.

What the Gospels Are

Witnesses

The Gospels, then, to return to my thesis, are *history-like witnesses to truths both historical and transcendent.* They are, first of all, *witnesses.* Their authors give testimony to events that have transformed their lives. Paul Ricoeur's analysis of testimony draws out at least three relevant features. First, witnesses relate what they have seen or heard.[22] "You are witnesses of these things," the risen Christ tells disciples in Luke 24:48 — meaning that they should now narrate to others what they have themselves encountered. Second, "witnesses" evokes the setting of the courtroom, where, in Ricoeur's words, "the solemnity of testimony is eventually enhanced and sanctified by a special ritual of swearing or of promising which qualifies as testimony the declaration of the witness."[23] Thus, for instance, in Acts 5:32 Peter and the apostles "are witnesses" before the Sanhedrin of things related to Jesus. Witnessing is not idle storytelling. In a trial, something important is at stake. As a witness, one commits oneself to the truth of that to which one witnesses. And third, witnessing involves risk on the witnesses' part. As Aristotle says, witnesses "share the risk of punishment if their evidence is pronounced false."[24] Indeed, witnessing on behalf of an unpopu-

21. And thus the church did not choose to receive as canonical Tatian's second-century Gospel conflation, the *Diatessaron.*

22. Paul Ricoeur, "The Hermeneutics of Testimony," in *Essays on Biblical Interpretation,* ed. Lewis S. Mudge (Philadelphia: Fortress, 1980), p. 123.

23. Ricoeur, "Hermeneutics of Testimony," p. 124.

24. Aristotle, *Rhetoric* 1.15, 1376a, lines 12-13, ed. Richard McKeon, *The Basic Works of Aristotle* (New York: Random House, 1941), p. 1376. Even more strongly, from Deuteronomy:

lar person or cause risks punishment even when speaking the truth. So in the early church, "witnesses" (μάρτυρες, *martyres*), or "martyrs," came to mean those who died for their faith.

History-like Witnesses

The Gospels are, more specifically, *history-like* witnesses. They do not primarily witness to scientific truths or poetic insights or myths but to events in time and place near to that of their authors and first readers. As already noted, they are not the kind of narrative most historians today would write — far more casual, for instance, about details and chronology, far more willing to include their understanding of the events' ultimate meaning in the telling of their stories. Nevertheless, they are *witnesses.* Once we understand the points of the story, we can be confident of the authors' commitment to their truth. This is the person Jesus was: the *sort* of person he was as anecdotally illustrated by characteristic sayings and actions, and the *particular* person he was as manifested in the events of his life that most defined his identity. This is the event that happened in Jesus: the way things have changed in the world because of him, the difference that makes to the Gospels' authors, the difference it can make to the Gospels' readers. On such matters, their authors commit themselves.

History-like Witnesses to Truths Both Historical and Transcendent

The Gospels witness to *truths both historical and transcendent.* Some of what they witness to involves plain events describable without reference to miracle or mystery. There was a man named John, who baptized Jesus. Jesus ate with tax collectors, taught in parables, helped those who were sick and outcast, and died on a cross. The words in these claims have their most literal and everyday meaning. Other cases are different. Jesus declares, in

---

"If the witness is a false witness, having testified falsely against another, then you shall do to the false witness just as the false witness had meant to do to the other. So you shall purge the evil from your midst. The rest shall hear and be afraid, and a crime such as this shall never again be committed among you. Show no pity: life for life, eye for eye, tooth for tooth, hand for hand, foot for foot" (Deut 19:18b-21).

Mark's Gospel: "Then they will see 'the Son of Man coming in clouds' with great power and glory. Then he will send out the angels, and gather his elect from the four winds, from the ends of the earth to the ends of heaven" (Mark 13:26-27). In John, Jesus describes himself as "the light of the world" (John 8:12) and says: "The Father judges no one but has given all judgment to the Son" (John 5:22). The Gospel writers clearly mean to witness to the truth of these sayings. I use "transcendent" as a convenient if vague way of saying that such claims reach beyond ordinary history, toward either an eschatological future or a realm different from that of events in this world.

The Gospels, to be sure, often make the relation of historical and transcendent claims complicated. It is a historical event that a Jewish woman named Mary or Miriam had a baby or that a particular Jewish teacher was crucified outside Jerusalem by the Roman authorities. But the Gospels claim that these are *also* transcendent events: the incarnation of God's Son and his redemptive death for the salvation of the world.

The complexity reaches its peak in the accounts of Jesus' resurrection. Some women went to Jesus' tomb and found it empty; the disciples had not stolen the body. On the one hand, such claims are true or false in a quite ordinary sense. On the other hand, when the Gospels move from the narratives of Jesus' trial and death to the events after his resurrection, they shift from relatively parallel and clear accounts to a jumble of very different stories — different in location, in character, in how they seem to picture how Jesus "appeared." As Rowan Williams puts it, "The stories themselves are about difficulty, unexpected outcomes, silences, errors, about what is not readily accessible or readily understood. . . . In short, it is not a straightforward matter to say what the gospels understand by the resurrection of Jesus; but this seems to have something to do with the fact that the Christian communities of the last quarter of the first Christian century didn't find it all that straightforward either."[25] Nor should this be surprising. If these witnesses are truthful, then Jesus' resurrection was not an ordinary historical event but one that transformed the whole of history. Even temporal issues get complex. On the one hand, if Jesus was raised from the dead, that must have happened between the time he died and the time his disciples began to preach that they had seen him alive, and this is a datable and specific period. On the other hand, if Karl Barth is right to talk about Jesus' resurrection as an "eternal" event contemporary with every believer,

25. Rowan Williams, *On Christian Theology* (Oxford: Blackwell, 2000), p. 187.

then it can no longer simply be assigned a particular temporal location,[26] and how we talk about it has to get more complicated.

Indeed, whenever we deal with transcendent events — whether they transcend history in the direction of the eschatological future or the eternal — such complexities arise. We are using words to point toward realities we cannot understand. Thomas Aquinas offered a particularly helpful way of conceiving this. In such cases, he said, our words refer truly to the "thing signified" but not to the "mode of signification."[27] To use the kind of example that Aquinas had in mind, if it is true that God is wise, then, confronted with God, I would see that, yes, "wise" is an appropriate term to apply to God (the "thing signified"), but the *way* "wise" applies to God (the "mode of signification") is beyond anything I could have imagined. Analogously, one who fully understood what it meant to say that Jesus was raised from the dead would recognize the appropriateness of the language of "raised" and "now lives" but find the *way* in which it is true unexpected and astonishing, though incorporating the already specified "historical" elements of this event.

Conclusion

So how do the Gospels mean? They are history-like witnesses to truths both historical and transcendent. Neither fiction nor myth nor history in the modern sense, they narrate events that convey who Jesus was and is — some as illustrative anecdotes, some as claims about specific events that define his identity. Their narration involves historical elements, where they use words in quite ordinary senses, and transcendent elements, where they use words in extraordinary senses, the manner of whose truth we cannot now imagine. If we believe them, such should be the complex object of our belief.

26. Karl Barth, *Church Dogmatics* 4/1, trans. G. W. Bromiley (Edinburgh: T&T Clark, 1956), pp. 291, 318.

27. Thomas Aquinas, *Summa Theologica* I.13.3, trans. Fathers of the English Dominican Province (1948; reprint, Westminster, Md.: Christian Classics, 1981), p. 62; *Summa Contra Gentiles* 1.30.2, trans. Anton C. Pegis (Notre Dame: University of Notre Dame Press, 1975), p. 140. See Victor Preller, *Divine Science and the Science of God* (Princeton: Princeton University Press, 1967), p. 173; George A. Lindbeck, *The Nature of Doctrine* (Philadelphia: Westminster, 1984), pp. 66-67.

Why *should* we believe them? That question admits of two kinds of answers, one negative and the other positive, each requiring at least another essay to expound. But brief comments can point in the directions those answers might take.

First, if we do not believe the Gospels' truth in the sense here described — do not believe that they grasped Jesus' fundamental identity — then we cannot know who Jesus was.[28] Evidence from outside the Gospels can provide historical context, and the work of critical historians on the Gospels themselves can establish some sayings and deeds as more probable than others according to the criteria of such a method. But many questions remain, and the fundamental character of a person's life is often one of the hardest judgments for historians to make on the basis of limited evidence. In the end, if the Gospels get Jesus wrong, then we must either pick our own favorite interpretation of him and impose it on the evidence — the examples of this are legion — or else admit that he is one of those very many historical figures about whom we know some facts without understanding them very well.

Such negative conclusions, however, do not themselves imply reasons for belief. Maybe we cannot know much about Jesus. To claim that we can, we need positive arguments. Augustine famously declared: "I should not believe the gospel except as moved by the authority of the Catholic Church."[29] This is a remark, no doubt, bound to make many Protestants nervous, but considered just at an empirical level, it is a simple statement of fact. The church formed and preserved the canon of Scripture, and most Christians have encountered the Bible first and most commonly in the life of the church. If we ask, "Why do *these* texts have authority?" (and not, say, the noncanonical gospels), on a human level the answer is simply that they are the texts given such authority by a community of faith and worship that treats them as Scripture.

Such function within a community is what it means to call something "Scripture." As David Kelsey has argued, "to call a set of writings 'scripture' is to say that they ought to be used in certain normative and rulish ways in the common life of the church."[30] Thus, to ask, "Why do you accept the au-

28. Nils Alstrup Dahl, *Jesus the Christ* (Minneapolis: Fortress, 1991), p. 94; Dale Allison, "The Historians' Jesus and the Church," p. 88 in this volume.

29. Augustine, *Against the Epistle of Manichaeus* 5.6, trans. Richard Stothert, *NPNF*[1] 4:131.

30. Kelsey, *Uses of Scripture in Recent Theology,* p. 164.

thority of these texts?" is finally just another way of asking, "Why do you belong to the church?" and that in turn is another way of asking, "Why are you a Christian?" And the reasons for becoming a Christian are, as Kelsey puts it, "complex, unsystematic, and idiosyncratic."[31] Each Christian comes to faith through a different combination of the haunting power of the biblical stories, the moral inspiration of the lives of other Christians, the way life seems to make sense when guided by Christian values, and who knows what other factors. But if one does become a Christian, accepting Scripture's authority comes as part of the package. Scripture can, to be sure, function as "authority" in many different ways, but it is hard to think of how one could simultaneously take the Gospels as authoritative in any sense faithful to their own meanings and believe that they give us a fundamentally mistaken picture of Jesus' identity.

Christians have generally, at a different level, understood their coming to faith as "the work of the Holy Spirit." "They who strive to build up firm faith in the Scripture through disputation are doing things backwards," Calvin insisted. "The same Spirit . . . who has spoken through the mouths of the prophets must penetrate into our hearts to persuade us that they faithfully proclaimed what had been divinely commanded."[32] So the New Testament itself invites us to think. As Francis Watson puts it, "[T]he coming of the Spirit of truth is — from a Johannine perspective — the precondition for grasping and being grasped by the truth incarnated in the Gospel story. . . . We do not find out the truth, from our own resources; rather, the truth finds us."[33] The work of the Spirit is already part of the Gospel stories, and even more of what we learn of the early church in Acts and the Epistles — and the Spirit functions, among other things, to bring people to faith in the truth of witnesses to Christ. "No one can say 'Jesus is Lord' except by the Holy Spirit" (1 Cor 12:3).

So with Christians today. We find ourselves understanding the world, and living in the world as part of a Christian community, in a way that would make no sense if the witness of the Gospels were false. Understanding and living in the world in this way, we find ourselves persuaded of the complex truths they propose, and of a way of seeing the world that has

31. Kelsey, *Uses of Scripture in Recent Theology,* p. 164.

32. John Calvin, *Institutes of the Christian Religion* 1.7.4, trans. F. L. Battles, LCC 20:79.

33. Francis Watson, "*Veritas Christi:* How to Get from the Jesus of History to the Christ of Faith without Losing One's Way," p. 113 in this volume.

those truths at its center. They may be inaccurate in all sorts of ways, but we are convinced that they fundamentally tell us who Jesus was and is. That conviction emerges both from the persuasive power the stories themselves have on us and from the power we find in a way of seeing and living in the world that presupposes these stories are true.[34]

34. If such an argument seems philosophically implausible, see Willard Van Orman Quine, "Two Dogmas of Empiricism," in *From a Logical Point of View,* 2nd ed. (New York: Harper & Row, 1963), pp. 41-42; John Rawls, *A Theory of Justice,* rev. ed. (Cambridge, Mass.: Harvard University Press, 1999), p. 18.

Identity, Jesus, and Exegesis

Robert W. Jenson

I

Faith and theology ask, "Who is Jesus?" because the primal proclamation of the gospel, "Jesus is risen," is a simple subject-predicate proposition, with the personal name "Jesus" as the subject. That the gospel is indeed gospel therefore depends on who Jesus is; the proposition "Stalin is risen" would not be good news for many. "The unconditional friend of publicans and sinners is risen" is good news to anyone willing to try those shoes on; "the chief keeper of the gulag is risen" would be good news to very few.

Thus, those who encounter the gospel and try to understand it must know who Jesus is. If they do not already know, they must ask, and the church must respond. We will find that our hypothesized inquirer's demand turns out to involve several different but related requests for identification.

In what follows, we will briefly consider the general notion of identity. We will go on to sketch its role in the theological tradition; the survey will along the way encounter places where the tradition impacts the question before this group. We will then turn more directly to some of the different but related senses of "Who is Jesus?"

II

The notion of identity is hard to specify directly, which is not necessarily a deficiency. Proceeding in the oblique fashion often appropriate to fundamental notions, we may begin by noting that we successfully, and often interchangeably, make use of proper names[1] and what Bertrand Russell isolated as "uniquely identifying descriptions." We successfully say things like "Mary Jones [proper name] is happy," attributing happiness to one person and not necessarily to any other, that is, *identifying* her as the one of whom we wish to say this. And we successfully say, "The current president of the United States [identifying description] is a Republican," attributing being a Republican to one person and, so far as this sentence goes, to none other. What these sentences must first succeed in doing, in order to do what they set out to do, is to specify an identity, which it seems they indeed manage to do. This may be all we need to know about the notion of identity as such.

It does seem, however, that the temporality of the things that might have or be such an identity requires a further observation. Identities must surely be diachronic: an entity's identity is what allows it to be identified by the same proper name or identifying description on different occasions without equivocation. If I cannot meaningfully say, "Mary Jones is now happy but may not be tomorrow" — whether this is true or false — it does not seem that "Mary Jones" succeeds in its mission of identification. My identity is my identity *with* myself across time; and here we are getting into more problematic and metaphysical waters, for it is possible to lose faith in one's own diachronic self-identity, as did the protagonist of Sartre's *Nausée.*

Thus, "self" and "identity" are closely related notions and indeed are often used interchangeably. To lose myself or to lose my identity would be the same disaster. This leads to a further point: the most natural use of "identity" is not in discourse about pots and pans or galaxies but in discourse about persons. Doubtless this is because the diachronic self-identity of persons can become problematic, as that of cookware or galaxies does not.[2] Whether it can actually be lost is another question, to which I suspect the answer is no. Having an identity is something *persons* do — or want or hope to do, or even not to do.

Let us say that an identity, in recent usage, is what can be repeatedly specified by a proper name or an identifying description,[3] particularly

1. In the commonsensical sense, not in that of logical positivism.

2. Though when we get to quantum behavior, things are not so clear.

3. Or perhaps by other of the devices linguistic analysts call "indexicals."

with respect to what, again in more recent usage, may be called a person. There is doubtless more that could be said, but I think this is enough to be going on with.

III

In the theological tradition, much of the semantic field now covered by "identity" was covered by *hypostasis,* and its various — invariably unsuccessful — translations.[4] The word was adapted, during the trinitarian and christological labors of the fourth and fifth centuries, from antecedent philosophical use. There it had been used more or less interchangeably with *ousia* — which we sometimes translate "nature" and sometimes "substance"[5] — for "real something." For the purposes of their trinitarian proposals, the fourth-century "Cappadocian" fathers made an ontologically innovative distinction between *hypostasis* and *ousia.* They appropriated the former for one aspect of being a real something: that a real something is *distinguishable* from others that otherwise are the same, and just so is *countable.* The *hypostasis* of something is the distinguishable and so countable *x* that has/is some *ousia* — for example, "Peter" picks out an *x* that has/is the *ousia* "human," just as do "Paul" and "Andrew" and others. Thus, a fundamental piece of Cappadocian trinitarian analysis:[6] Father, Son, and Spirit are three *hypostaseis* who have/are one *ousia,* deity.[7] Of course, the Greek thinkers had known about persons being countable somethings that share humanity but would have regarded stipulating Father, Son, or Spirit — or indeed Peter, Paul, or Andrew — *by* such relations as an ontological put-down. In their view, it was *what* I am that is worthy of note, not *that* I am it or that *I* am it.

Thus, the creed of Nicaea-Constantinople affirms of the Son — who is Jesus — that he is *homoousios* (note the *ousi* between prefix and suffix)

4. By and large, scholars have given up and now simply take the transliteration as a loanword.

5. Thereon hangs a tale of endless conceptual confusion.

6. Which won out at Constantinople and became the linguistic vehicle of the ecumenical dogma.

7. This of course raises the question why Father, Son, and Spirit are not three gods, as Peter, Paul, and Andrew are three humans. The question was brilliantly answered, but pursuing that would be afield from our purpose.

with God the Father; we struggle to translate, and have most recently come up with "of one being." It was the Cappadocian analysis that the Father and the Son are nonetheless two, as being distinguishable *hypostaseis*, that enabled the affirmation.[8]

That the Son is *homoousios tō patri*, "of one being with the Father," is said without qualification of the Son of God and of the subject of the following creedal narrative; and so it is said simultaneously of one of the three who are God *and* of the second-Temple male Jew Jesus of Nazareth. This of course provoked a question about the relation between this one person's being God and his being a human. The Council of Chalcedon in 451 once again recruited the term *hypostasis*,[9] now from its trinitarian use. There is in Jesus the Son, they said, but one *hypostasis* of two *ousiai:* there is but one identifiable and countable *x* to be whatever is to be said of the Son because he is God and whatever is to be said of the Son because he is human. The lively concern behind this rather lifeless formulation was the insistence by Cyril, the great fifth-century bishop of Alexandria, that there is but one protagonist of all that the Gospels narrate of the Christ, whether what he is said to do or suffer is a divine thing to do or suffer or a human thing to do or suffer.[10] God the Son was born of Mary[11] and hung on the cross;[12] and Jesus of Nazareth saves sinners and rules the universe from the Father's right hand.

Thus, it is ecumenical dogma,[13] now in more modern terms: you can-

8. At Constantinople. At Nicaea, folk had little idea what they were saying when they said the Son was *homoousios tō patri;* they just knew that Arius had once said he wasn't.

9. By way of a compromise formula of Cyril of Alexandria.

10. To see what Cyril and, less decisively, the council opposed, one might read Theodore of Mopsuestia's commentary on John, which laboriously labels each deed or experience of the protagonist according to whether he does it as God or as man. Or, most unfortunately, one might consider Pope Leo the Great's *Tome*, affixed to Chalcedon by his legates' insistence, which in effect says that in Christ deity and humanity each does its thing. To be sure, since Leo was a great pope and the council did accept the *Tome*, we must in other contexts interpret his language *in bonam partem.*

11. Thus, affirmation of Mary as *Theotokos*, the Mother of God, became and has remained a chief test of orthodoxy and indeed of theological acuteness. *Sancta Maria, mater Dei . . .*

12. It later became dogma that *unus ex trinitate passus est pro nobis*, "one of the Trinity has suffered for us."

13. I am aware that "dogma" has acquired a variety of adventitious associations, most of them likely to put readers off. But there is no satisfactory other word to denote that small body of teaching that the church has formally determined is essential to the gospel. And it is

not accurately pick out Jesus of Nazareth without in fact simultaneously picking out the second person of the Trinity, and you cannot accurately pick out the second person of the Trinity without in fact simultaneously picking out Jesus of Nazareth. It seems to me that this is already a rather important result for our project. Unless we are willing to reject the historic teaching of the church at its very heart, we must obey the rule: when we ask about the identity of Jesus, historical and systematic questions cannot be separated.

IV

We can come to the same result by another route, which leads more directly back into the question of Jesus' identification. The character of the predicate ". . . is risen" imposes a sort of conceptual backflip, for ". . . is risen" is not only a concept predicated of Jesus' story; it is itself part of the story.[14]

Indeed, that Jesus is specifically *risen* is the precise point of identity (that word again!) between the various common names and concepts or titles that may be predicated of Jesus, and the particularity of this person. "Lord" or "Messiah" or "divine" or ". . . redeems" or ". . . saves" can — even if in some or all cases falsely — be predicated of anyone, for they are not themselves biographical items. But ". . . is risen" *at once* ascribes a universal significance to the one of whom it is predicated and is an item of that one's particular story. Thus, in the case of "Jesus is risen," the person determines the universal significance, and the universality is that of the individual person — which is, of course, the great offense of the gospel. "Is risen" is of a logical sort not contemplated by the Greek thinkers; it predicates universal significance of a particular person and is itself an identifying item of his biography.

---

a very small body of teaching indeed; it is certainly *not* the mass of what churches have mostly taught or "theologians" opined.

14. The principal error of Rudolf Bultmann's students was to deny this — the case of Bultmann himself is complicated by his denial that any story at all needs to be told. Neither Ebeling nor Fuchs denied that Jesus is risen. What they taught was that "Jesus is risen" is our necessary true *response to* the Gospel narrative, not *part of* the narrative itself. In this, they intended to carry on the tradition of Wilhelm Herrmann. They were in my judgment wrong, but if they are to be charged with error, the error must be properly located.

When, then, we ask — and now, we should note, we find ourselves following the pattern of the Gospels — "Who is this one who was born of Mary and taught Torah as if he were the author and cast out the demons and . . . and was crucified *and rose?*" we are asking a question that is at once historical and dogmatic. That Jesus is, for example, "of one being with the Father" — or that he is not — is part of a possible answer. Note that this answer responds to a question about "the one who was born of Mary" and so on, so that *if* it is true, no narrative of "the historical Jesus" can be correct that conflicts with it.

And then there is another flip — the last such, I think. It is itself an item in the Gospels that the Crucified and the Risen are the same one person, that ". . . is risen" is not predicated of Jesus of Nazareth in any tricky sense; a chief locus is the story of "doubting Thomas." Also according to dogma, the two must be straightforwardly the same one embodied person; consider, for example, the confession required of Berengar,[15] that the body that was broken on the cross and the body broken on the eucharistic table are the same body.[16] Therefore, no item even of the narrative by which we make that first identification, of who it is that is supposed to be risen, can be — historically! — true if it conflicts with dogma. (Of course, this rule holds only if he is indeed risen and if the church's dogma rightly construes that.) Precisely for the sake of historical truth, we are bound to construe also the pre-resurrection story of Jesus by the christological and trinitarian dogmas.

V

A first sense of the question, "Who is Jesus?" is often referred to as a search for "the historical Jesus." The question in this case is, "Who is it of whom '. . . is risen' is predicated?" Already this question is theologically decisive.

15. An eleventh-century advocate of an extreme Augustinian view of the sacrament, who recanted by signing a confession beginning, with splendid rhythm, *Ego Berengarius. . . .*

16. They are, to be sure, that body in different ways. According to Paul, the risen body is a *sōma pneumatikon,* whereas the body that died is a *sōma psychikon.* In Paul's view, however, this does not mitigate either the bodiliness of the Risen One or the identity of his body as dead and risen (1 Cor 15:43-44). As to what "body" means in "Jesus' dead organic body and risen spiritual body are the same body," discussing that would take us far beyond the bounds of this volume. Here we must rest with the proposition itself.

For disputes about "the historical Jesus" cannot, in cases where the identifying descriptions proposed are not mutually compatible, be disputes within the same religion. For example, what members of the "Jesus Seminar" say they believe in, and what those who think of Jesus as the final prophet of the kingdom and the final interpreter of the Torah believe in, are two different gospels. No one can simultaneously cling, for life and death, to "Jesus, the ultimate beach guru, is risen"[17] and, with the Gospels themselves, to "Jesus, the final prophet of Israel's kingdom, is risen."[18]

"The historical Jesus" is not, however, a reliably univocal term.[19] In scholarly jargon, it often refers to the figure reconstructed by historical-critical research. But in normal usage, "the historical Jesus" will less counterintuitively be taken to name someone who occupied time and space together with, for example, Tiberius Caesar and the reader of these pages, and who must be supposed to have done and suffered many things not now recoverable by research.

It does not detract from the necessity of historical-critical research — to which we will come — to note that simple identification of the historical Jesus with any critically obtainable reconstruction will not do for Christian theology. For such an identification depends on a radically idealist notion of "historical" — unless the historical-critical investigation in question is in the mind of God, or is one that humans could continue forever. In the following I will therefore mean by "the historical Jesus" what really happened with the person of that name, however we find (or do not find) out about it. For the class of historians' reconstructions I will use "the historians' Jesus."

Nor is identification of the historical Jesus with the historians' Jesus philosophically necessary. The Jesus who occupied time and space with us surely did much that is not recoverable by historians. Moreover, we are

17. This formulation of course gives the seminar too much credit; most of its members do not apparently suppose that anyone is risen.

18. Nor will a Fregean account of reference allow this, as was once suggested in our consultation. "The morning star" and "the evening star" can indeed refer to the same thing, even though they are different descriptions. But many sets of descriptions predicated of the same thing make contraries, that is, a set of propositions of which at least one must be false. "The ultimate beach guru" and "the final prophet of the kingdom," given any historically plausible account of "guru" and "prophet of the kingdom," make such a set.

19. For a longer account, see Robert W. Jenson, *Systematic Theology,* 2 vols. (New York: Oxford University Press, 1997-99), 1:171-78.

with equal surety entitled to suppose that some of this may be beyond historians' grasp not only in fact but in principle.[20] That any event that actually happened in time and space must be able to appear in a proposition of the form "On the available evidence, it is very likely/unlikely that *x* occurred" is a metaphysical doctrine that carries no certainty on its face. It is a doctrine deeply embedded in modernity's habits of thought, but no more necessary for all of that.

The phrase "however we find . . . out about" the historical Jesus points to a decisive circumstance for the project of this book. For we now have to note that believers' grasp of *this* historical Jesus has never depended only on the evidence to which "historical critical" scholarship has confined its efforts — the New Testament, a sparse offering of other very early mentions, and a more or less arbitrary selection of other "gospels."

Besides the New Testament, there are two bodies of testimony to which believers have in fact turned for information about Jesus. There is the messianic witness of the Old Testament; and it does not matter to the present point how we understand that witness to have been made. And there is the spiritual tradition of the church. Thus, two phrases from Isaiah, evoking a "man of sorrows, acquainted with grief," and the church's iconography these phrases shaped, have doubtless more determined what believers know as the Jesus who came from Nazareth and had a mission in Israel than have any five pages of the Gospels. To be sure, it is a founding dogma of modern exegesis that believers' reliance on such sources is a naive mistake; but whether this dogma is true is the very question at issue.

Believers' ordinary procedure is of course as preposterous as modernity thinks it is — *unless* it is indeed true that God is the specifically triune God; that Jesus, just as the historical Jesus, is the second identity of this God; and that this God is the Creator, so that what is true for him is all the facts there are. I have just listed two dogmas straight and given Cyril's construal of another. Our troubles with the historical Jesus — and historical Paul and historical whomever — were inaugurated by thinkers who exploited modernity's historical consciousness specifically and intentionally to escape "the yoke of dogma." But what if the church's dogma were a necessary hermeneutical principle of historical reading, because it describes the true ontology of historical being?

20. If Jesus did "miracles," perhaps these belong in this epistemological category. The resurrection itself is of course the key and central matter.

Because the church Fathers worshiped the specifically triune God, they understood the word of the Old Testament as the Word who is eternally with God and is God, and who has as the very same Word appeared among us "in these latter days"; they heard the testimony of the Old Testament as the voice of Christ and indeed *could* not hear these texts otherwise. And it is of course a commonplace of churchly awareness that the gospel-word in the church is Christ speaking. Now then, whose testimony to the historical truth about Jesus might the scholarly reader more want than that of the very person — remember, there is just one identity here — whose biography she or he is pursuing?

The question must of course arise, Are there then no limits to what believers may rightly say they know about the historical Jesus? It is here that we should in my judgment see a role for "historical-critical" research. There is undoubtedly much more to the historical Jesus — as the term is here used — than such research can recover; and I have proposed that other parts of Scripture and the church's tradition can discover some of this to faith. But we should not claim to know anything about the historical Jesus that plainly conflicts with what we at any time take to be historical-critically established.[21] To be sure, "the assured results of critical research" are notoriously not all that assured; today's certainty may be the victim of tomorrow's new research paradigm. And indeed, what occasions reexamination of an accepted bit of historical-critical reconstruction may be precisely its clash with what believers think we know from, say, Isaiah. Together with the general probabilism of historical-critical knowledge, all of this means that we must carry our working picture of Jesus with a certain tentativeness — which is a theological good thing.

VI

So what indeed if the church's dogma were a necessary hermeneutical principle? What if we did take seriously those backflips that the resurrection performs on "Who is Jesus?" It will, I think, be much the best if we finally abandon sheer abstraction and display the consequences by doing an actual piece of exegesis. I choose the scene of Gethsemane because the mu-

21. We must remember that such negatives as "Jesus did not do miracles" or "Jesus was not raised in the body" are *not* results of research and could never be.

tual impact of dogma and text is in this case not far to seek, and because the questions the mutuality raises are formidable and important.

The story by itself immediately provokes a question of dogmatic proportions: Could Jesus in Gethsemane have chickened out? Could he have said, "Father, you want this coming confrontation but I do not," and fled to Galilee? And a reader with even the most minimal theological concern cannot help asking also, If he had, what then?

Neither simple answer to the first question seems satisfactory. If we come to the text from a usual churchly catechesis, we are likely to say that since Jesus is God he could not have given in to fear; but this answer ruins the Gethsemane story, turning the prayer and anguish into pretense.[22] If, on the other hand, we are unbothered by the claim for his divinity, or suppose that we can bracket it out methodologically,[23] we are free to say that the story clearly supposes he could have fled, choosing his wants over the Father's. But this reading also turns out to ruin the story. For the Gethsemane scene has its drama only as part of the larger Gospel narrative; and this narrative, particularly in its presumably earliest canonical version by Mark, is shaped by the sense that Jesus' life is governed by a certain divine necessity, and that this necessity is not external to his personhood.

Indeed, it would appear that the only answer that preserves the narrative integrity both of the pericope itself and of the story of which it is one incident is that he could have fled and that this too, if it had occurred, would have belonged to the divine necessity that determined his life. That is, crudely, that he is God and could also in that capacity have ceased to be godly. But where does that leave us theologically?

There was some discussion among participants in this project whether attention to dogma might limit the range of readings available for a particular text, and whether this would be a good or a bad thing. In the present case, dogma clearly does exclude some readings: precisely the two readings initially considered. If we follow church dogma, we cannot say that Jesus could obviously have decided for what he himself wanted, thus reading the story simply as a dramatic turning point in a human life; for dogma insists on his inseparable deity. And we cannot say that he could not have decided

22. A path that all too many preachers and teachers have taken, great thinkers among them.

23. I do not think we can do that, but of course the exegetical establishment has for centuries thought we could.

for his wants rather than God's; for dogma insists on his humanity — and since even if Jesus did not in fact sin, as the tradition has maintained, the whole point of noting that he did not sin is that he was genuinely tempted.[24]

Thus, the readings excluded by concern for the Gospels' narrative integrity and those excluded by dogma coincide. Perhaps this observation can teach us something both about the *way* in which dogma should guide exegesis and about the root of dogma itself.

The Gethsemane pericope narrates one side of a conversation. A conversation between whom? Since the conversation is in prayer, and since Jesus is a Jew, the one partner must clearly be the God of Israel, whom Jesus here as elsewhere addresses as his "Father." But who is the other partner in the conversation, the speaker of the side that we hear? Who says, "Remove this cup from me; yet, not what I want, but what you want"?[25] The obvious — indeed tautologous — answer is the man Jesus of Nazareth, shortly to be in deadly conflict unless this Father relents. But if we follow standard christological teaching, that answer poses a problem — or rather a whole nest of them.

Who prays here? According to church teaching defined by the Council of Chalcedon (451), the protagonist of all scenes in the Gospels' narrative is a single person, who is truly God — the Son — and truly man — the individual Jesus of Nazareth, the Christ of Israel.[26] If we say it was simply the man Jesus of Nazareth who prayed, and observe that he did so in such fashion as to distinguish what he wanted from what the Father wanted, where does that leave the Son? Outside the conversation? Or, supposing that the Son agrees with the Father, are we to suppose a diversity of wants between God the Son and the man Jesus, internal to the one person? Is this supposition intelligible at all? It should be noted that we cannot rescue it by invoking psychological phenomena such as "being of two minds," since God the Son does not inhabit Jesus as a factor of his psychological structure[27] — in-

24. Hebrews 2:18; 4:15.

25. Mark 14:36 NRSV. The crudity of this translation, over against earlier English versions, rises almost to confessional significance. But it is the translation in use, and it answers to my needs in this essay.

26. Council of Chalcedon, *Definitio fidei, Decrees of the Ecumenical Councils,* ed. Norman P. Tanner (Washington: Georgetown University Press, 1990), 1:86.14–87.2.

27. The great attempt to solve christological puzzles on that line was made by Athanasius's overzealous disciple Apollinaris and was quickly found wanting.

deed, the Son does not "inhabit" Jesus at all; he simply *is* Jesus, as Jesus then simply *is* the Son.

Should we therefore instead say that it is God the Son who says to the Father — by himself or jointly with Jesus — "Not my wants, but yours"? But is a divergence of wants between the Father and the Son, who with the Spirit are supposed to be but one God, thinkable? Jürgen Moltmann has made it an axiom of his theology that it is. His chief proof text is the so-called cry of dereliction on the cross, which he understands as marking an actual abandonment of God the Son by God the Father, a rupture of the concord between them. For my own part, I can only say that I am always tempted by such dramatic excess but cannot persuade myself that it is here justified by Scripture as a whole.

We have been noting ways in which dogma can constrain our reading of a text, in the case of the present text in considerable part by making it a puzzlement. Yet at the beginning of this essay we noted how the same or related puzzlements emerge from the narrative structure of the text itself, suggesting that our use of the dogma as a hermeneutical principle is not an imposition from outside. And now we may begin to perceive how the text can, vice versa, exert pressure on dogmatic thinking: is there indeed any way out of the questions the text poses but the frightening one earlier mentioned, that at Gethsemane — or over against the temptation to summon the angels and come down from the cross or at a hundred other points of the Gospel narrative — the triunity and so, by the dogma of Trinity, the godhead of God was somehow at risk? We will come back to that.

The Gethsemane pericope narrates, besides a conversation, the making of a decision: that Jesus would do what the Father wanted rather than what he wanted. Who made this decision? The man Jesus of Nazareth? God the Son? Both? If we say just Jesus, and if we presume the concord of God the Son's will with that of the Father, this posits two possibly differing wills in one person of Jesus the Son. Does that make sense — psychology again not being to the point? If we say God the Son, as somehow other than the man Jesus, either this means that Jesus has no will, or it results in the same antinomy.

This last quandary was the issue in the most decisive of the christological controversies that racked the ancient Eastern church in the aftermath of the Council of Chalcedon's decisions: the monothelite/dyothelite, the "one-willite/two-willite" controversy of the later seventh century.[28] Chalcedon had laid it down: Christ is a single integral person, who does and suffers all that the Gospels narrate about their protagonist; and given what the Gospels in fact narrate about him, this person must be God and man at once — in the formulaic language of the decree, he must have/be "two natures," deity and humanity. So far so good, and this is the dogma we have been invoking. But the more abstract part of the council's text is patient of, and even sometimes seems to invite, a construal of the Gospels' story that in effect says that in Christ's life and work deity and humanity each does its own thing, that is, that Christ is not a single dramatic protagonist after all.[29]

Whole regions of the Eastern church, followers of Cyril of Alexandria who had been put on edge by recent history, read the decree with suspicious eyes, decided that this is what Chalcedon would indeed turn out to mean in theological practice, and rejected it. As the dispute widened into schism, these became known as "monophysites," "one-naturites," for their insistence that the incarnation once given, the distinction of two natures is a distinction of concepts only and not of actual entities. Theologians of the imperial church set out to find formulas that would entice the monophysites back,[30] and succeeded only in triggering a series of further controversies. The last of these provoked one of the last great intellects of the ancient world, Maximus the Confessor, to strenuous thought.

The imperial theologians proposed: we must indeed think of two natures in Christ, but the legitimate monophysite concern may be accommodated by saying that there is only one *will* in Christ — they proposed "monothelitism," "one-willism." One can see why they thought this proposal had to carry even those loyal to Chalcedon: what, after all, would a person with two wills be?[31] Appealed to for his judgment, Maximus turned to Scripture, and therein to long meditation on the Gethsemane pericope. To his great credit as an exegete of the plain sense, Maximus refused to back off from the simple observation that clearly there are *two* wills in play

28. By this time, the Western church was not up to much theologically. It should be noted that the controversies and settlements after Chalcedon are customarily dismissed in Western seminary education as nit-picking. Looking into them, one discovers the contrary: only with them do the christological questions really become interesting.

29. To this, the reference easiest for me to make is Jenson, *Systematic Theology,* 1:127-33.

30. They wanted to do this for two reasons: sincere concern for the unity of the church and concern for the unity of the empire, toward the end, in the face of Islam's military advance.

31. Again, psychological abnormalities are not relevant.

in the Gethsemane story, and that on the side of the one who prays, it will not do to say either that this is just a man praying to God or that the struggle is pretense.

Within the terms of the imperial proposal, the two wills could not simply be the wills of Jesus and his Father. For the imperial proposal assigned having will to "nature" rather than — for a possibility that might occur to moderns — to "person":[32] it is "natural" to "humanity" to have will. Moreover, if will were not assigned to nature, positing one will would give nothing to the one-naturites. To the consternation of the imperial theologians, Maximus perceived that if the terms of their own proposal are maintained[33] and the plain sense of the text honored, a "dyothelite" position results. One of the wills displayed in the story must be the one that belongs to the Son's human nature. And since the Son's other nature is the divine nature and since divine will is assigned to divine nature and not to divine personhood, the divine decision displayed in the story must belong to this other one of the Son's "two natures." Which gives two wills in Christ, one for each nature, one divine and one human.[34] But however are we now to construe the story? Surely blatant mythology is just around the corner?

Maximus's attention to the story compelled him to maintain that in Gethsemane the man Jesus made a hard human decision in fully human fashion. What then of the divine decision? To lay out Maximus's solution in his own language and follow his dialectics would take more space than could be justified within the purpose of this essay; what follows is my rewriting of Maximus's suppositions and argument.

Human nature and divine nature are ontologically asymmetrical.[35] Human nature is individuated, so that according to Jesus' human nature he is one individual of the human race, who thus makes his own decisions. But the divine nature is not individuated in *this* fashion; the Son

32. The dominant term in the East was, indeed, not "person" but "hypostasis"; and a hypostasis does not have qualities other than those of the nature of which it is a hypostasis.

33. Martin Luther arrived at a position remarkably similar to that of Maximus, with far fewer dialectics that follow, by implicitly denying the terms in which the old debate was conducted.

34. This sabotaged the imperial politics, over against monothelites, but now over against Islam as well, for which treason Maximus was tortured — apparently unintentionally — to death.

35. This is standard thinking in the tradition.

has the divine nature only by and in the mutual relations of Father, Son, and Spirit — as likewise the Father and the Spirit each have the divine nature only in these mutual relations. Therefore, precisely because will belongs to nature, the divine decision made at Gethsemane must be thought of as made not by any one divine person but only in the mutuality of the Three.

Then Maximus makes his most daring move: since Jesus and the Son are but one person, it is the very decision made by the man Jesus that constitutes the Son's concrete role in the triune decision. Perhaps we may put it so: the man Jesus' human decision is the content of the triune decision — as, perhaps, the Father is its absoluteness and the Spirit its freedom. If we let Maximus — or anyway what I take from Maximus — guide our vision, we will see in Gethsemane a man making a hard decision, and we will see this very event as an event in the triune life, as nothing less than the triune deciding that this man will in fact be faithful, that is, that there will be an atonement.[36]

Could Jesus have fled? No, because his life, like all else, is governed by the triune will, here by the triune decision that he will be faithful. Yes, because his human decision is itself the Son's presence in that triune decision.

I would have thought this result an exegetically very good thing. The hard dogmatic thinking just sketched did not, as generations of critical scholars have supposed it must, lead away from the text but rather to discovery of the text's own power, in its plain reading.

Part of that power is the pressure that, vice versa, a text can exert on the understanding of existing dogma and perhaps on an eventual necessity of new definition — or, since in the situation of a divided church, formulation of dogma becomes problematic, perhaps we should rather say on dogmatic thought.

It does not seem possible to take the Gethsemane pericope — or the temptation in the wilderness or the passersby's challenge to Jesus on the cross or the Akedah or Joshua's question to Israel at the Jordan or . . . — seriously without thinking a thought forbidden by the weight of theological tradition: that at such junctures in God's scriptural history, the godhead of God is somehow at stake. Trying to specify that "somehow" would be alto-

36. It should be recorded that I know two eminent authorities on Maximus, one of them a member of this consultation. One of them thinks my use of Maximus goes too far; the other supports it.

gether too audacious an attempt to penetrate God's mystery.[37] But the "somehow" alone is sufficient challenge to our metaphysical prejudices.

God is undoubtedly beyond any threat we or any creature might pose to his omniscience and omnipotence — or to any of the *omni*-s that enjoy at least quasi-dogmatic status. But without positing any actual rift in the divine unity, we can ask whether the triune life may not encompass something that if it occurred among *us* would surely be at least the *threat* of rupture. Jesus could not have fled Gethsemane — but his own free human decision belongs to the triune decision that he could not. It seems, therefore, that in some not-further-to-be-penetrated sense, God's unity, which is inseparable from his godhead, might not have been sustained.

What if Jesus had fallen? A metaphysical style more dramatic than most can approve would perhaps say: then precisely *nihil*, then the world would have been precisely what postmodernity takes it to be. Even more à la Heidegger: Being held its breath between "Remove this cup from me" and "yet, not what I want. . . ." But enough of such extravagances.

Because there is the plain sense of the Gethsemane text and others like it, we must ask, not indeed *whether* God is "impassible," to use the word that sums up the *omni*-s, but *how that works* in the case of the specific biblical, triune God.[38] It would lead far beyond the confines of this essay to go any more deeply into that.

VII

There is much current discontent, among both exegetical and systematic theologians, with the hegemony of "historical-critical" exegesis. A variety of other modes of reading are therefore proposed: rhetorical, reader-response, literary, and so on. It is not, however, at all clear that either supplementing or replacing historical-critical reading with some other sort of reading will in fact reach the true cause of the discontent — or indeed satisfy our responsibility to truth.

It will be seen from the above that restoring the ancient mutual dependence of dogmatic thinking and exegesis is another matter altogether; their

37. Though one may perhaps remark that with God necessity and absolute contingency are the same thing.

38. Thus, God surely knows everything, which does not itself say how he knows it.

relation cannot be contained within modernity's ontological assumptions and so requires us to rework them drastically. Just so, in my judgment, the interdependence goes directly to the deep cause of our discomfort. To be sure, such a metaphysical fruit-basket-upset is uncomfortable to live through.

God's Life as a Jew: Remembering the Son of God as Son of David

Markus Bockmuehl

"Jesus the Jew" — a platitudinous commonplace?[1] What difference could it possibly make for serious reflection about him? Whether we think it matters or not, any historically and theologically honest search for the identity of Jesus soon stumbles on the precariousness of several seemingly self-evident assertions one might wish to make about that identity. In this essay I wish to explore Jesus' Jewishness and the significance it might have for an understanding of him that is not only "creedally credible" but also, indeed ipso facto, true to what that same creed asserts about the historical past.

Some Prickly Preliminaries

We face an inevitable measure of methodological throat clearing if our conversation about Jesus' Israelite identity is to be meaningful. Four particular issues arise immediately.

Identity?

The fashionable term "identity" may seem transparent to popular culture in the late- or postmodern West. Philosophical and theological clarity on

1. This essay is a revised and significantly abbreviated version of Markus Bockmuehl, "Seeing the Son of David," in *Seeing the Word: Refocusing New Testament Study* (Grand Rapids: Baker Academic/Baker Publishing Group, 2006). Permission granted. Scripture quotations are from the NRSV.

this matter, however, is rather more elusive: we may agree that it involves intentional agency in the light of historical antecedents and social consequences,[2] but is that enough? Our need for a definition seems underscored by the vagueness of common usage, where someone's "identity" can comprise a bewildering range of qualities derived from the expression of habits and preferences of culture or lifestyle — vegetarian socialite, day-trading eco-warrior, "queer" theorist, feminist earth mother, Stetson-topped "neoconservative," Wahhabi Web designer. People choose such terms to identify themselves or others as "who they are," both to themselves and to those diversely "identified" others.

What is intriguing is the extent to which such seemingly subsidiary and often volitional or impermanent qualities have in large areas of society fused with an almost metaphysical ontology of "identity." Contemporaries who take this "essentialist" view of identity will set out to "find themselves"; they may base moral or lifestyle preferences and habits ranging from the trivial to the life changing on the earnest conviction that "this is who (or how) I am," "that's just (not) me," or even "that's how God made me." Leaving aside the problem of whether such an essentialist anthropology can ever be compatible with a theological view of creation, vocation, and redemption, the examples cited suggest that popular notions of "identity" may not be self-evidently useful in establishing the meaning of that word for a theological inquiry concerned with Jesus.

Dictionary definitions of "identity" highlight distinguishing characteristics that express individuality or identification. More eloquently, and perhaps more appositely for our question, Paul Ricoeur has written about *narrative* identity as a function of permanence over time, established by self-constancy (being true to one's word) and by perseverance of character (the acquired habits and identifications that constitute "the 'what' of the 'who'").[3] This clarification may suffice for present purposes.

2. Amélie Oksenberg Rorty, introduction to *The Identities of Persons,* ed. Amélie Oksenberg Rorty (Berkeley: University of California Press, 1976), p. 15.

3. Paul Ricoeur, *Oneself as Another* (Chicago: University of Chicago Press, 1992), pp. 113-39, esp. 118-23. Cf. Sarah Coakley's comments on identity in her essay "The Identity of the Risen Jesus: Finding Jesus Christ in the Poor," in the present volume.

Jesus' Identity?

Such definitions immediately become slippery in the attempt to speak christianly of Jesus, whose "self-constancy" and "perseverance of character" attest his permanence both in time *and beyond time.* In Jesus of Nazareth, we hear, God's own identity came to full expression — and that in bloody historical concreteness, *sōmatikōs.*

Nor is this all. In other cases we might claim to find God powerfully revealed in a saintly life, festive worship, or meditation on Scripture — or, for that matter, in a Tuscan hillscape or a Boccherini cello concerto. But in none of these cases could we say that the saint herself *is* God, or that sunset vespers at Sant'Antimo reveal *all* that can be known of God.

Precisely that reverse assertion, however, is what the New Testament uniquely affirms of Jesus. His self-constancy and perseverance of character, in other words, are consistently construed in relational terms as between the Son and the Father. God was "in Christ" (2 Cor 5:19), but also, Jesus is the identity of God. What you see is what you get; indeed, what you see here is all you could possibly get. Not every writer states this in explicitly maximal terms, but for the Fourth Evangelist and others it is crystal clear. To see Jesus is to see the Father of Jesus (John 14:9), Abraham's and Isaiah's thrice-Holy Lord made flesh (John 8:56-58; 12:41), the unique Son who alone bears the ineffable Name (Phil 2:9; Eph 1:21; John 17:11-12), "the Messiah who is over all, God blessed forever" (Rom 9:5), who sits on the heavenly throne, at God's right hand (e.g., Mark 14:62; Rom 8:34; Eph 1:20-23; Heb 12:2; Rev 7:17), and to whom is due the worship of all creation (e.g., Phil 2:10-11; Heb 1:6; Rev 5:12-14; 22:3). In keeping with that conviction, several of the authors go so far as to claim that *only* here can God be seen: *no one* comes to the Father except through Jesus (e.g., John 14:6; Acts 4:12).

The New Testament tends to state such convictions constructively and even somewhat delicately, more as an article of *eschatological* confession and confidence in the Lord's Chosen One than as a disciplinary instrument, here and now, for the eternal elimination of the unconfessing many. Nevertheless, the Christian church went on before long to conclude that this placed Jesus and the church fundamentally at loggerheads with all those outside it, and Judaism for its part returned the compliment. Thus, at some time during the complex and often unhappy history of their relationship and self-definition between Bar Kokhba and Justinian (mid-second through mid-sixth centuries C.E.), the overwhelming majority of

Jews and Christians came to agree, tragically, that one could not both follow Jesus and practice Judaism.[4] On the Christian side, this conclusion has always found a degree of succor in quasi-Marcionite readings of Paul; but it remains tragic all the same, in that it soon generated a Jesus who had for both Jews and Christians ceased to be recognizable as the Messiah of Israel.

Jesus' Jewish Identity? A Historic Oxymoron

And that brings us to our third opening conundrum. As the ancients concluded, to assert the Jewishness of Jesus is in the end a dangerous nonsense; it substitutes semantic games for a truthful account of either Judaism or Christianity. Though Jewish and possibly even observant in appearance, Jesus had in fact put an end to Jewish life based on the Torah by revealing the new dispensation that would henceforth displace it. Thus, the first Gentile bishop of Antioch, born less than a generation after Jesus' death, bluntly affirms that "it is monstrous to talk of Jesus Christ and to practice Judaism."[5] One could argue that opposition to "Gnostic" and Marcionite views partly attenuated this position in later second-century writers such as Justin, Irenaeus, or Tertullian, although their polemics never quite extended to a positive appreciation of Jesus qua Jew. By the fourth century, however, the leading Christian authors articulate what was by then a truism: Jesus had come quite simply to replace Judaism with Christianity, teaching that law observance was henceforth lawbreaking.[6] Twenty-first-century readers should need no reminder that the wedge thus driven between Jesus and Judaism by Jews and Christians alike has, from antiquity to the period of living memory, wrought consequences of incalculable horror.

4. Daniel Boyarin, *Border Lines: The Partition of Judaeo-Christianity* (Philadelphia: University of Pennsylvania Press, 2004), maps the tenuous complexity of this history with acute perception; cf. also, e.g., Judith Lieu, *Christian Identity in the Jewish and Graeco-Roman World* (Oxford: Oxford University Press, 2004); Seth Schwartz, *Imperialism and Jewish Society, 200 B.C.E. to 640 C.E.* (Princeton: Princeton University Press, 2001).

5. Ignatius, *To the Magnesians* 10.3, trans. Kirsopp Lake, *The Apostolic Fathers,* vol. 1, LCL (London: Heinemann, 1912), p. 207; cf. 8.1-2 (though he concedes that the Christianity of the circumcised may be a lesser evil than the Judaism of the uncircumcised [*To the Philadelphians* 6.1-2], and he emphatically claims Jesus "our God" as Son of David, born of Mary according to the divine economy of salvation [*To the Ephesians* 18.2]).

6. E.g., Eusebius, *Demonstration of the Gospel* 1.6.39; similar arguments about Torah observance as "lawbreaking" are present in other patristic authors.

All of this leaves us in an awkward position when trying to address the Jewishness of the person and aims of Jesus. Historically, the supposed Judaism of Jesus was acknowledged almost universally, by both Jews and Christians, to be an oxymoron — an idea as plausible as an orthodox rabbi hosting the annual neighborhood hog roast.

This dichotomous heritage is by no means straightforwardly "anti-Semitic," although scholarly discussion in the last twenty-five years has sometimes chosen to caricature it in that fashion. To some extent, it is in fact deeply bound up with the early church's quest for self-definition — and thus, at least in that historically fraught sense, with "Christian identity." Be that as it may, as far as the person and identity of Jesus are concerned, opposition to Judaism, to Christianity, and perhaps above all to Jewish Christianity have all played a part in reinforcing that classic denial of a Jewish Jesus. What we may call the "genetic predisposition" to such denial has expressed itself particularly among interpreters of Paul — a revisionist and iconoclastic trait that, as Harnack thought, reached from Marcion (via Origen and Augustine?) to Luther and culminated in the "assured results" of nineteenth-century German scholarship.[7]

Some scholars have found a cognate trend in the recent, almost uniquely North American school of thought around a liberal-minded, egalitarian Jesus as a social reformer conversant with populist philosophical aphorisms rather than religious dogma or observance. Although the writers associated with the Jesus Seminar never explicitly deny Jesus' Jewishness (and generally take vociferous exception to the charge that they do), their Jesus does appear to be largely stripped of Jewish religious specifics. Such Jewish moral or eschatological themes as may have found their way, against the odds, into the "Q gospel" (the hypothetical collection of Jesus' sayings, or "logia," supposedly used as a literary source by Matthew and Luke) are invariably ascribed to the effect of a later Judaizing editorial veneer — a distortion of the gentle mystic's original intentions in the direction of an Israel-centered messianism preoccupied with an eschatological kingdom of God.

All in all, we are clearly caught on the horns of a dilemma: even allow-

7. Adolf von Harnack, *Marcion: Das Evangelium vom fremden Gott*, 2nd ed., TU 45 (Leipzig: Hinrichs, 1924). For Harnack's convictions about the need for hermeneutical "violence" and "iconoclasm," see his 1885 correspondence with Friedrich Loofs, quoted in Agnes von Zahn-Harnack, *Adolf von Harnack* (Berlin: Bott, 1936), pp. 102-3.

ing that Jesus' Jewishness is historically plausible, can a Christian point of view affirm the essential Jewish particularity of Jesus' identity without thereby denying a part of its own heritage? The answer to that question might conceivably require a degree of theological "gene therapy" — a task that has begun to be noted and addressed in recent discussions of church and Israel.[8]

"Jesus the Jew": The Historical Quest's Unstable Cliché

Historically, as we have seen, the idea of "Jesus the Jew" has been an oxymoron. Within the world of Jesus scholarship, however, it had by the end of the twentieth century become something of a platitude — so much so that few brows could now be wrinkled by books like Vermès's *Jesus the Jew* or Sanders's *Jesus and Judaism*, which in their day caused storms of excitement and debate.[9] Aside from an articulate, vociferous, and intellectually introspective minority of academic and church circles sympathetic to the North American Jesus Seminar, it has in fact become difficult to find serious Jesus scholarship prepared to deny that Jesus of Nazareth's message and ministry have their appropriate setting within the highly diverse framework of first-century Jewish belief and practice in the land of Israel — about which recent textual and archaeological discoveries have enabled us to know more than perhaps any other generation of Christians since the second century.

Whether or not one accepts the rather problematic identification of the current wave of scholarship as a "Third Quest" (after the nineteenth-century "lives" of Jesus work and the mid-twentieth-century form-critical hunt for authentic logia), it seems reasonable to suggest, as John Meier has

8. See, e.g., R. Kendall Soulen, *The God of Israel and Christian Theology* (Minneapolis: Fortress, 1996); Bruce D. Marshall, "Israel: Do Christians Worship the God of Israel?" in *Knowing the Triune God: The Work of the Spirit in the Practices of the Church*, ed. James J. Buckley and David S. Yeago (Grand Rapids: Eerdmans, 2001), pp. 231-64; Robert W. Jenson, "Toward a Christian Theology of Judaism," in *Jews and Christians: People of God*, ed. Carl E. Braaten and Robert W. Jenson (Grand Rapids: Eerdmans, 2003), pp. 1-13; also Mark S. Kinzer, *Postmissionary Messianic Judaism: Redefining Christian Engagement with the Jewish People* (Grand Rapids: Brazos, 2005).

9. Géza Vermès, *Jesus the Jew: A Historian's Reading of the Gospels*, 2nd ed. (London: SCM, 1983); E. P. Sanders, *Jesus and Judaism* (London: SCM, 1985).

done, that the recovery of Jesus' thoroughly Jewish religious context is perhaps the single most important result of the recent flood of research.[10]

The present consensus on the Jewish Jesus, however, remains fragile and under constant challenge: even those who share it cannot agree on what it means or entails — in part because "Judaism" itself found complex and diverse expressions in first-century Palestine. The different interpretative options invariably carry significant ideological freight and legitimate strikingly diverse ulterior motives or "subtexts."[11] New Testament scholars, even if they talk the talk of a Jewish Jesus, do not always walk the walk — tending rather to generalize context-specific texts for ideological ends or, more commonly, to continue in blithe disregard of all particularities. Challenges arise not only from historical skeptics and the protagonists of the Jesus Seminar but also from the proverbial force of old scholarly habits.

Whether for conventional or confessional reasons, many continue to favor the notion of Jesus' opposition to Jewish faith and praxis — not perhaps to "Judaism" *tout court* but certainly to the teaching of any and all Jewish individuals and groups actually known to us. This applies especially in the case of law, where a majority still assume that at least in a handful of programmatic words and actions Jesus deliberately "broke" or "annulled" the Torah and thereby did place himself consciously over against "Judaism."[12] Quite how one should envisage this kind of comprehensive dissent from all possible Jewish options is often opaque, especially if one bears in mind a religious context as complex as pre-70 Galilee and Judea. What is clear is that conservatives are often just as keen on this theme of Jesus' superiority or separation from contemporary religious Judaism as ostensibly more liberal interpreters. Making Jesus more of a Jew seems still to entail making him less of a Christian — or at any rate less palatable as a figure of Western Protestantism.

10. John P. Meier, "The Present State of the 'Third Quest' for the Historical Jesus: Loss and Gain," *Biblica* 80 (1999): 486.

11. A point rightly stressed by William Arnal, "The Cipher 'Judaism' in Contemporary Historical Jesus Scholarship," in *Apocalypticism, Anti-Semitism, and the Historical Jesus: Subtexts in Criticism,* ed. John S. Kloppenborg and John W. Marshall, JSNTSup 275, JSHJSup 1 (London: T&T Clark, 2005), pp. 24-54.

12. Classic examples of such misreading, represented even in major Third Quest scholars such as E. P. Sanders, include the Matthean antitheses (Matt 5:21-48) and, above all, the instruction to "let the dead bury their dead" in Matt 8:22 par. Luke 9:60, on which see my remarks in Markus Bockmuehl, *Jewish Law in Gentile Churches: Halakhah and the Beginning of Christian Public Ethics* (Edinburgh: T&T Clark, 2000), pp. 23-48.

Quite what this might mean either for history or for faith is a question on which we remain very far from a consensus. The remainder of this essay will attempt to offer a thumbnail sketch of Jesus of Nazareth's Judaism and conclude by asking what difference this might make for a Christian theological understanding of his identity.

Eschatology and Identity: The Case of Jesus "Called the Christ"

We will begin with a reconstruction. As such, it can at best be of only ephemeral value to theology; as such, too, it has weaknesses, many of which mirror my own and those of my environment of work and worship. Nevertheless, as John Dominic Crossan declaimed in a famous half-truth to conclude his own very differently construed argument, "If you cannot believe in something produced by reconstruction, you may have nothing left to believe in."[13] The point may be put in more theological terms: as long as salvation matters to history (and vice versa), then to seek to understand them both becomes a sacred obligation.[14]

Regardless of whether any particular historical reconstruction stands or falls, one point remains indispensable to any viable Christian interpretation of the identity of Jesus. Against obscurantist dogma of both the skeptical and the fideistic kind, even the most theological of New Testament authors insist that the entire Christian enterprise depends on the basic trustworthiness of Gospel testimony. Contra certain "postliberal" views sometimes (rightly or wrongly) associated with Hans Frei, for the early Christian church the identity of Jesus is *not* accessible simply in "stories" about him that may or may not have a bearing on history.[15] It is the *referential truth* of that apostolic testimony that undergirds the very possibility of faith (John 19:35; 21:25); indeed, "if Christ has not been raised, your faith is futile and you are still in your sins" (1 Cor 15:17). And what is "doubting"

13. John Dominic Crossan, *The Historical Jesus: The Life of a Mediterranean Jewish Peasant* (San Francisco: HarperSanFrancisco, 1991), p. 426.

14. Cf. on this relationship the pensive remarks of Martin Hengel, a doyen of New Testament historians, "'Salvation History': The Truth of Scripture and Modern Theology," in *Reading Texts, Seeking Wisdom: Scripture and Theology*, ed. David F. Ford and Graham Stanton (London: SCM, 2003), pp. 229-44.

15. Hans W. Frei, *The Identity of Jesus Christ: The Hermeneutical Bases of Dogmatic Theology* (Philadelphia: Fortress, 1975).

(*apistos,* "faithless") about the Fourth Gospel's Thomas is not his desire for facts but his emphatic refusal to trust the apostolic testimony: unless he personally sees and touches the evidence, he "*will not* believe" (John 20:25, 27, 29). Unless at some basic level we are prepared to receive, trust, and inhabit a given communal embodiment of memory and witness, we can know nothing at all. The solipsism of *cogito ergo sum,* "I think, therefore I am," is logically compelling only in the madhouse.

Jesus' birth in Bethlehem of Judea, with its Davidic connotations, remains contested as to its historicity; arguably, the debate about its function in understanding Jesus' identity is well worth having. All agree, however, that his main formation and early ministry were set in a wholly Galilean context during the reign of the emperor Tiberius (14-37 C.E.) and his puppet king Herod Antipas (4 B.C.E.–39 C.E.), son of Herod the Great (37-4 B.C.E.) At the same time, Jesus evidently had some followers in Judea, where his ministry concluded during a Passover pilgrimage to Jerusalem that began with a controversial demonstration in the Jewish temple and ended on a Roman cross.

Against repeated assertions to the contrary, recent literary and archaeological studies show early first-century Galilee to have been thoroughly Jewish in population, in worldview, and, to a surprising extent, in praxis.[16] Despite significant Phoenician and Hellenistic influence until the third century B.C.E., Galilee remained at most very superficially Hellenized in the aftermath of Maccabean expansion and resettlement. Periodic attempts to recast Jesus as a philosopher in the Greek Cynic vein are therefore intrinsically implausible, being further compromised by Jesus' apparent avoidance of the Hellenistic cities that surrounded Galilee (in Syria, on the coast, and in the Decapolis) and indeed by the absence of identifiable Cynics or their ideas within first-century Galilee. In terms of culture and above all of religion, it is at best misleading to characterize Galilee's peasants and artisans in terms of a generically "Mediterranean" social anthropology. (Cultural-studies approaches typically ignore the role of religion for the definition of identity, whether Jewish or otherwise.)[17]

16. See, e.g., Mark A. Chancey, *The Myth of a Gentile Galilee: The Population of Galilee and New Testament Studies,* SNTSMS 118 (Cambridge: Cambridge University Press, 2002); Seán Freyne, *Jesus, a Jewish Galilean: A New Reading of the Jesus-Story* (London: T&T Clark, 2004).

17. David Kaufmann, "What Are Jewish Cultural Studies?" *Council of Societies for the Study of Religion Bulletin* 34 (2005): 19-22, follows Jonathan Boyarin in suggesting that cul-

Jesus' development and praxis as a religious Jew find ample expression in the Gospel narratives: after his genealogy and infancy, we find his apprenticeship in the renewal movement of John the Baptist; his inaugural message about the imminent kingdom of Israel's God; his enactment of divine forgiveness and call to repentance; his exorcism of unclean spirits, including the Roman "Legion" personified; his calling of twelve disciples to evangelize and ultimately to judge the twelve tribes of Israel, together with his general avoidance of Gentiles; his classic teachings and miracles steeped in scriptural typologies of the Israelite prophetic tradition; and his disputes with contemporaries about how to be faithful to the shared norms of the Torah.

Others called him "rabbi," "teacher," "prophet," or "Messiah"; like the later rabbis, he in turn called his followers "disciples" *(mathētai, talmidim)* and made at least some of them his empowered "emissaries" *(apostoloi, sheluchim).* The Jesus of the Synoptic tradition endorsed tithing, sacrifice, and voluntary gifts to the temple; he even paid the controversial temple tax, however grudgingly. Jesus said grace before meals and wore tassels on his clothes. "His" prayer is quintessentially Jewish, and particularly close in form to the ancient Kaddish prayer of the synagogue.[18]

The very nature of his repeated disputes about matters such as vows, food and corpse impurity, divorce, the Sabbath, and the temple presupposes Jesus' affirmation of the Torah's authority. At issue are the hermeneutical priorities within Scripture, as well as between Scripture and subsequent innovation, some of which he rejected (e.g., in the area of secondary purity). Jesus consistently stood in dialogue, and remarkably often in agreement, with known moral and halakic positions within Pharisaic

---

tural studies' purely pragmatic anthropology always risks "erasing Jewish difference" (p. 21). Mutatis mutandis, cf., e.g., Markus Bockmuehl, review of *The New Testament World: Insights from Cultural Anthropology,* 3rd ed., by Bruce J. Malina, *Bryn Mawr Classical Review* (2002.04.19), http://ccat.sas.upenn.edu/bmcr/2002/2002-04-19.html.

18. Cf. Franz Mussner, *Tractate on the Jews: The Significance of Judaism for Christian Faith,* trans. Leonard Swidler (Philadelphia: Fortress, 1984): "It is the prayer of the *Jew* Jesus with which every Jew without inner reservation can pray. . . . The Our Father is the great 'bridge prayer' between the Jewish and the Christian communities" (p. 130). Cf. further Asher Finkel, "The Prayer of Jesus in Matthew," in *Standing before God: Studies on Prayer in Scriptures and in Tradition,* ed. Asher Finkel and Lawrence Frizzell (New York: Ktav, 1981), pp. 131-69; Joseph Heinemann, "The Background of Jesus' Prayer in the Jewish Liturgical Tradition," in *The Lord's Prayer and Jewish Liturgy,* ed. Jakob J. Petuchowski and Michael Brocke (London: Burns & Oates, 1978), pp. 81-89.

Judaism or at Qumran: he repeatedly espoused views that also featured, and sometimes prevailed, in subsequent rabbinic debate. In this connection, he occasionally restricted or forbade what the Torah permits, but he never permitted what it clearly forbids.[19]

His story climaxes in a Passover pilgrimage to Jerusalem complete with an enactment of a messianic entry into the city and passionate concern about the corruption of the temple, the place of God's dwelling, which to him meant the universal house of prayer. During a Passover (or Passover-like) meal on the eve of his crucifixion, he brought all these concerns to a sharp focus by taking what would have been understood as a Nazirite vow (which commits a lay Israelite to priestly holiness, usually for a finite period) in anticipation of the coming kingdom (Mark 14:25 par. Matt 26:29). Even his classically Roman execution listed as his crime the only version of his Jewish messianic claim that Roman executioners could understand: *Rex Iudaeorum,* "King of the Jews."

The preceding four paragraphs give a deliberately synthetic, cumulative reading. The constituent features need not in every case be unambiguously "authentic" or straightforwardly retrievable in order to secure the overall picture of a Jesus whose Jewishness of faith and praxis inalienably defines his identity as the "what" of the "who." Some cited assertions are peculiar to Matthew; some are wholly absent from John. The argument capitalizes on the Jewish cultural and religious way of life Jesus shared with

19. Mark 7:19 is often cited as definitive proof to the contrary. Several considerations make this highly unlikely. Notably, the context as even Mark himself presents it clearly shows Jesus talking not about pork or other nonkosher foods but about acquired impurity. "No food can defile" in 7:15 means "no food that the Torah permits can defile," as Menahem Kister, James G. Crossley, and others have rightly noted — a position also attested in other Jewish sources. Mark's Jesus objects to the view that permissible foods can defile if they come in contact with unwashed hands. Moreover, as Heikki Sariola and Gerhard Dautzenberg, among others, have shown, Mark has no consistent or systematic position on the law: if he meant 7:19 as a comprehensive statement about the abolition of food laws, nowhere in the Gospel does he seem to follow through on this — indeed, his Jesus is remarkably observant. See Kister, "Law, Morality, and Rhetoric in Some Sayings of Jesus," in *Studies in Ancient Midrash,* ed. James L. Kugel (Cambridge, Mass.: Harvard Center for Jewish Studies/Harvard University Press, 2001), pp. 145-54; Crossley, *The Date of Mark's Gospel: Insight from the Law in Earliest Christianity,* JSNTSup 266 (London: T&T Clark, 2004), pp. 183-205; Sariola, *Markus und das Gesetz: Eine redaktionskritische Untersuchung,* AASF-DHL 56 (Helsinki: Suomalainen Tiedeakatemia, 1990), pp. 248, 261, and passim; Dautzenberg, "Markus und das Gesetz: Überlegungen zur gleichnamigen Untersuchung von Heikki Sariola," *Biblische Zeitschrift* 42 (1998): 91-95.

the apostolic Palestinian communities that first passed on his tradition (settings that historical criticism often cannot reliably distinguish in practice). A vigorous historical case can indeed be made for virtually all of the cited traditions, including the interesting correlation, observed also at Qumran and among the Pharisees, of an integrated concern for both eschatological hope and Jewish praxis (or halakah). It is particularly significant that the preservation of such "obsolete" elements in the Gospels arguably runs against the grain of redaction: they have become politically incorrect for evangelists committed in every case to the gospel's post-Easter outreach to *Gentiles.*

What is striking in the Gospels is not so much their adaptation to the needs of post-70 C.E. Gentile communities but precisely the remarkable *lack* of such accommodation, whether linguistically, religiously, geographically, historically, legally, or theologically. At least as documents for the constitution of a Gentile mission and church, the Gospels remain extraordinarily anachronistic in their presentation of a Jesus who manifests a great deal more Jewish particularity than was often found congenial by later Christians.

In the remainder of this section, I wish to illustrate this point by singling out two aspects of Jesus' ministry likely to be of particular importance for his distinctive "identity," namely, his views of Israel and of himself. It seems appropriate to view the key issues here through the lens of two pivotal texts, one pertaining to Jesus' view of the destiny of the Twelve (Matt 19:28 par. Luke 22:30), and the other to his public self-presentation (Mark 12:1-9 par. Matt 21:33-41; Luke 20:9-16; cf. *Gos. Thom.* 65).

The Destiny of the Twelve — Matthew 19:28 par. Luke 22:30

All four Gospels affirm that Jesus singled out twelve men as an inner core of the larger group of disciples, although relatively less is made of this in John. Their appointment is generally regarded as authentic by all except those who, failing to find it in "Q1" (the supposed earliest layer within Q) or the presumably early *Gospel of Thomas,* ascribe it to the evangelists. Moreover, their symbolic association with the twelve tribes of Israel is not in serious doubt. Viewed on the canvas of its scriptural and Jewish setting, Jesus' eschatological institution of the Twelve conveys a theocentric and specifically *messianic* reconstitution of the entire biblical Israel under the leadership of tribal judges and their king.[20] The theme of twelve phylarchs, or tribal "princes," continued to be an important part of Jewish interpretation in the early Roman period. In the saying reported in Matthew 19:28 par. Luke 22:30, the judges rule over their tribes within the kingdom of the Son of Man, just as the synagogue's ancient *Amidah* prayer explicitly anticipates the restoration of the tribal judges and the Davidic king.

Matthew

19:27Then Peter said in reply, "Look,
we have left everything and followed
you. What then will we have?" 28Jesus
said to them, "Truly I tell you, at the
renewal of all things, when the Son of
Man is seated on the throne of his
glory, *you* who have followed me *will*
also sit on twelve thrones, judging the
twelve tribes of Israel."

Luke

22:28"You are those who have stood by
me in my trials; 29and I confer on
you, just as my Father has conferred
on me, a kingdom, 30so that you may
eat and drink at my table in my
kingdom, *and you will sit on thrones*
judging the twelve tribes of Israel."

Our central saying occurs in two very different settings during Jesus' last week in Jerusalem. Matthew includes it in a discussion of the costs and rewards of discipleship following Jesus' encounter with the rich young man (cf. Mark 10:17-31 par. Luke 18:18-30), while Luke makes it part of his unique discourse after the Last Supper on the subject of greatness in the kingdom (cf. Mark 10:42-45 par. Matt 20:25-28). Since it belongs to the remainder of a subtraction of Markan material from Matthew's agreement with Luke, it is typically included in the supposed sayings source Q. In fact, however, neither the classic Two-Source Hypothesis (literary dependence of the later Matthew and Luke on the earlier Mark and Q) nor any of its major rivals (literary dependence of Luke on Matthew or of Matthew on Luke) offers a satisfactory source-critical explanation of what is more likely a case of independent, quite possibly oral transmission of the same saying in different settings. Yet the virtual disappearance of the original Twelve in the narratives of the early church renders the persistence of Je-

20. Cf., e.g., William Horbury, *Messianism among Jews and Christians: Twelve Biblical and Historical Studies* (London: T&T Clark, 2003), pp. 157-88; W. D. Davies and E. P. Sanders, "Jesus: From the Jewish Point of View," in *The Cambridge History of Judaism*, vol. 3, *The Early Roman Period*, ed. William Horbury et al. (Cambridge: Cambridge University Press, 1999), pp. 635-36.

sus' promise to them all the more remarkable (and the promise itself more probably authentic, whatever its original setting). More interestingly for our purposes, this prediction graphically demonstrates the vital importance of the restoration of biblical Israel's twelve tribes for Jesus' message and expectation. The lost sheep of the kingdom of Israel is the one that Jesus would rule and whose tribes the Twelve would judge.

The Mission of the Son — Mark 12:1-9

Narratively, at least, our second passage seems uncomplicated. Jesus has been challenged by the religious authorities about his authorization to act as he did in the temple. His reply launches into an evidently programmatic parable, which characterizes his understanding of himself, his mission and identity, in terms of an Old Testament symbol for Israel and its leadership that was well known and understood by Jesus' contemporaries (Isaiah 5; cf., e.g., 4Q500). We will here concentrate on the Markan version of the parable, which most commentators regard as having shaped the two Synoptic parallels (Matt 21:33-41; Luke 20:9-16; cf. *Gos. Thom.* 65).

> 12:1 A man planted a vineyard, put a fence around it, dug a pit for the
> wine press, and built a watchtower; then he leased it to tenants and went
> to another country. 2 When the season came, he sent a slave to the ten-
> ants to collect from them his share of the produce of the vineyard. 3 But
> they seized him, and beat him, and sent him away empty-handed. 4 And
> again he sent another slave to them; this one they beat over the head and
> insulted. 5 Then he sent another, and that one they killed. And so it was
> with many others; some they beat, and others they killed. 6 He had still
> one other, a beloved son. Finally he sent him to them, saying, "They will
> respect my son." 7 But those tenants said to one another, "This is the heir;
> come, let us kill him, and the inheritance will be ours." 8 So they seized
> him, killed him, and threw him out of the vineyard. 9 What then will the
> owner of the vineyard do? He will come and destroy the tenants and
> give the vineyard to others.

Despite the tenants' reckless obstinacy, the divine protagonist's desire for his vineyard Jerusalem-Israel does not fail but is fully vindicated. When the Son is killed and thrown out of the vineyard, God brings his purpose for it to fruition in removing the tenants who have failed to honor the Father in the Son. The Son's self-giving death stirs the Father to action that is both redemptive (of the vineyard) and destructive (of those charged with its care).

In all three Synoptic versions, the parable is in different ways at once *antisupersessionist and supersessionist* in intent.[21] Christian interpreters even in recent years have often read this parable as if it ends with the owner's destruction of the *vineyard* and the transfer of his favor to a new and different one. It does not. Indeed, the parable is *deeply antisupersessionist in relation to Israel.* The whole object of the action of the Father and the Son is the protection and prospering of the vineyard of Israel in the purpose for which it was made. In all three Gospels the vineyard is saved — a point that echoes ancient Jewish interpretation but is nonetheless remarkable because in several Old Testament antecedents the opposite appears to be the case. Indeed, in this respect the conclusion of the parable differs strikingly from that of the vineyard parable in Isaiah (5:5-6). There is in the Gospels a radical "supersession" and even replacement, apparently without remnant — but it applies to the *tenants* in charge, Israel's religious and political guardians, the "shepherds" who destroy and trample down the vineyard, to cite another prophet's striking image (Jer 12:10). The vineyard itself is entrusted "to others" (Mark 12:9), who will care for it properly.[22]

Most poignantly for the identity of Jesus, *the mission of the Son is to give his life in the service of Israel's rescue from oppression,* for the restoration of her relationship with God. He stands in this respect in solidarity with other servants who have gone before; his sacrifice, however, is the one that prompts God's rescue of the vineyard. He also markedly differs from his predecessors in that the tenants recognize his true identity ("this is the heir"), murder him, and cast him out precisely for this: the aim is nothing short of disinheriting God. His is the defining mission; as the heir he represents all that the Father means to the vineyard. Recalling Abraham's gift

21. Definitional problems of "supersession" are usefully discussed in Marshall, "Israel," p. 232 and passim.

22. Matthew famously adds "to a people" (21:43). Contrary to a widespread misreading, however, even for Matthew those from whom the vineyard is taken are not "Israel" but its failed leaders (21:45), and the "people" to whom it is given is emphatically *not* "another" or a "different" *ethnos* but rather the restored nation, the twelve tribes whom the disciples will "judge" (i.e., govern) in the eschaton (19:28).

of that other "beloved son," Isaac, as understood in contemporary Jewish interpretation, here the Father — by not withholding even his only Son — gives everything he has in a plea for reconciliation with his own vineyard. Through the Son's self-giving sacrificial suffering, death, and expulsion, God takes action to save the vineyard from its unlawful oppressors.

Israel's Christ in History and Christian Memory

Our journey has led from definitional and methodological conundrums about the "identity" of Jesus to a reconstruction of his Israel-centered mission and message, with two illustrations of how this concern comes to concrete expression in his eschatology and self-understanding.

While these and other issues continue in inevitable suspense, it seems clear that the identity of Jesus remains incomprehensible apart from the evangelists' apostolic memory and testimony to the migrant prophet and Messiah from Nazareth "on a mission from God": he walked the biblical Holy Land in search of the lost sheep of the house of Israel, wept over Jerusalem and protested against her temple's corruption, and finally bound his own fate to that city and to the redemption of the twelve tribes of Israel.

To recover the text's implied reading on this point may sometimes mean to read against the grain of much patristic protestation to the contrary. What I have called theological "gene therapy" is emphatically not a matter of simply letting historical criticism trump Scripture or the creed. Nor is it a case of creating a new doctrinal mutant, a kind of "designer Christianity" in our own postmodern image, resplendent in the assurance of our own superior insight and innovation. On the contrary, it is quite simply a matter of returning to the text: holding the church accountable to its own most basic confession about a two-testament Scripture that bears witness to the Messiah of God's elect people. The New Testament documents, both early and late, recall that the Word became *Jewish* flesh and lived, died, and rose among us. Amidst a good deal of attention deficit and hyperactivity disorder among biblical scholars, this may indeed prove to be the abiding contribution of the recent wave of Jesus scholarship.

In the parable of the wicked tenants, Jesus understands his identity as unique Son of the Father to be inextricably linked to his mission for the deliverance and renewal of Israel. No theologically conscionable construal of Jesus' identity can finally bypass this vital and personified commitment to the salvation of Israel, centered on the city over which Jesus lamented and where he died. Jesus' apostle to the Gentiles saw his own mission as directly instrumental to that same end (Rom 9:5; 11:1-2, 26), a point obscured for centuries under the forgetful Gentile superiority complex that Paul himself explicitly condemned (11:18-24).

In our own time, it has taken the twentieth century's near destruction of the vineyard to awaken the church to the New Testament's implication that, as Pope John Paul II put it in his historic visit to Rome's great synagogue in 1986, the covenant remains unbroken. Judaism, he said on that occasion, is profoundly "intrinsic" to Christianity, just as Jews are uniquely the favored and elder brothers of Christians. That is to say, Gentile amnesia on this point is in fact a denial of Jesus and of Christianity as much as it is a denial of Judaism. It rides roughshod over the "text's intention" *(intentio operis)*, as Umberto Eco calls it. The history of Christian thought and praxis, as we saw at the beginning of this essay, suggests something of a genetic predisposition against a Jewish Jesus — and thus at various times against an incarnate Jesus, born of a Palestinian Jewish mother called Miriam, against one whose ministry was to seek the lost sheep of the house of Israel, against one who held that God's word in Scripture cannot be broken, against one who physically suffered and died under Pontius Pilate, against one who was raised on the third day.

That predisposition may indeed call for a measure of theological "gene therapy" if the church is to reappropriate the meaning and significance of the Word made — and raised! — Israelite flesh. The Fourth Evangelist grasps the meaning of that Word most provocatively when he finds in the historic soil of Palestine the Bethel of Jesus — and Jacob's ladder made tangible in the thirsting, weeping, bleeding Son of Man upon whom the angels descend and ascend as they gaze on the "place of God" on earth as it is in heaven (John 1:51; cf. Gen 28:12). Thus, Scripture itself, as shared word of life to Jews and Gentiles, precludes for its implied readers the very possibility of asking the outsider's *Judenfrage* ("Jewish question"). Instead, it compels those who convert to faith in Jesus to cease wondering "what to make of the Jews" — coming instead to recognize *themselves* as having their identity in relation to the Messiah and the chosen people.

I wish to close, however, on a note that has been largely implicit thus far. The abiding significance of this remembered Israelite identity of Jesus is vitally underscored by his *resurrection*. Far from being the brainchild of a

Pauline rush into a Hellenistic savior cult, the apocalyptic claim of "resurrection" is itself a deeply and irreversibly Jewish affirmation,[23] in both the pre- and post-Easter contexts of the New Testament.[24] No Roman soldier who might have guarded the tomb that first Easter Sunday morning could have described the events in terms of "resurrection"; that language was simply unavailable.[25] Only a Jew, indeed, only a religious, possibly Pharisaic Jew, could predict — or identify, or *remember* — someone's being "resurrected."

To be sure, the reality of a resurrection after three days inevitably strained and transformed the Jewish linguistic register too, as Rowan Williams rightly suggests.[26] But it remains significant that scholars who otherwise affirm the Jewish identity of Jesus are often content to sideline his resurrection as irrelevant. Even those who do take it seriously do not always make enough of one crucial fact: the one who is raised is none other than the crucified Messiah of Israel and "King of the Jews." For the early Christians, it was the resurrection that confirmed this identity; indeed, it is theologically vital for the New Testament witnesses that Jesus' identity did not change on Easter Sunday (Acts 2:36; 17:3; 26:23; cf. Luke 24:26; Rom 1:3-4; Phil 2:9-11; John 20:28-31). In the resurrection God made Jesus visibly "both Lord and Messiah" of Israel, the Son of David who is "Son of God with power" (Acts 2:36; Rom 1:3-4) — and, in one of the most radically Jewish and radically Nicene of all early christological affirmations, God bestowed on him "the name that is above every name" — the very name of YHWH (Phil 2:9; cf. Eph 1:20-21; Heb 1:3b-4; also John 17:11-12; Rev 1:4-8).[27] For the first Christians, in other words, it was "seeing the Word" in the resurrection that crucially corroborated the identity of Jesus the Jew as

23. See, e.g., Dan 12:2-3.

24. See N. T. Wright, *Christian Origins and the Question of God,* vol. 3, *The Resurrection of the Son of God* (Minneapolis: Fortress, 2003), pp. 129-206, esp. 200-206.

25. See Wright, *Resurrection of the Son of God,* pp. 32-84.

26. The resurrection stories "are in fact about laborious recognition . . . , the gradual convergence of experience and pre-existing language in a way that inexorably changes the register of the language." Rowan Williams, "Between the Cherubim: The Empty Tomb and the Empty Throne," in *Resurrection Reconsidered,* ed. Gavin D'Costa (Oxford: Oneworld, 1996), p. 91; cf. Markus Bockmuehl, "Resurrection," in *The Cambridge Companion to Jesus,* ed. Markus Bockmuehl (Cambridge: Cambridge University Press, 2001), p. 113.

27. Cf. Markus Bockmuehl, *A Commentary on the Epistle to the Philippians,* BNTC (London: A&C Black, 1997), pp. 141-48; and more broadly, C. A. Gieschen, "The Divine Name in Ante-Nicene Christology," *Vigiliae Christianae* 57 (2003): 115-58.

Messiah and Lord God of Israel.[28] In the witness of the apostles — including the apostle to the Gentiles — the New Testament's implied readers firmly appropriated this truth. Access to the identity of Jesus was for them, and perhaps still is for us, diversely but inalienably tethered to the apostles' memory of the one who walked, gave thanks, and broke bread with them that first Easter evening. "Remember Jesus Christ, raised from the dead, a descendant of David" (2 Tim 2:8).

28. Marshall, "Israel," pp. 245-47 and passim, illustrates the extent to which New Testament (especially Johannine) and patristic texts identify the God of Israel with the Logos and the Son, that is, the second person of the Trinity.

The Historians' Jesus and the Church

Dale C. Allison Jr.

Three Problems

For several decades now, so-called criteria of authenticity — chiefly, multiple attestation, dissimilarity, embarrassment, and coherence[1] — have been the tools of choice for most scholars seeking the historical Jesus. They have constituted the winnowing fork by which the experts have separated pre-Easter materials from the later ecclesiastical chaff. But these criteria have not led to any uniformity of result, or any more uniformity than would have been the case had we never heard of them. They have brought us the Jesus of the Jesus Seminar as well as the very different Jesus of John Meier.[2]

My explanation of this odd outcome is that the criteria themselves are seriously defective. They cannot do what is claimed for them. It is not, as I

1. The criterion of *multiple attestation* presupposes that a tradition (that is, a saying or story) attested in two or more independent sources has a better chance of being authentic than one attested singly; the criterion of *dissimilarity* seeks to isolate materials that are different from typical emphases in Jewish and early Christian sources and so unlikely to have been borrowed from or created by them; the criterion of *embarrassment* holds that a saying or story is likely original if there is evidence that it discomfited early Christians; and the criterion of *coherence* requires that a tradition not be judged authentic unless it coheres with other traditions already regarded as genuine.

2. Robert W. Funk, Roy W. Hoover, and the Jesus Seminar, *The Five Gospels: The Search for the Authentic Words of Jesus* (New York: Macmillan, 1993); Robert W. Funk and the Jesus Seminar, *The Acts of Jesus: The Search for the Authentic Deeds of Jesus* (San Francisco: HarperSanFrancisco, 1998); John P. Meier, *A Marginal Jew: Rethinking the Historical Jesus*, 3 vols. (New York: Doubleday, 1991-2001).

once supposed, that this or that criterion is problematic or needs to be fine-tuned but rather that the whole idea of applying criteria to individual items to recover the Jesus of history is a problematic endeavor.

1. Proof is often beyond us.

The gap between what happened and what we can show to have happened is much larger than we care to imagine. Aristotle seemingly preferred to speak of Pythagoreans in general instead of Pythagoras in particular because he found it too hard to extract the historical philosopher from the later material assigned to him; and why should anyone think that contributing allegedly apocryphal material to the Jesus tradition is a deed that we, two thousand years later, can regularly detect? Origen wrote that the attempt to "substantiate almost any story as historical fact, even if it is true, and to produce complete certainty about it, is one of the most difficult tasks and in some cases is impossible."[3] Maybe it would be closer to the truth to say that such certainty is in *most* cases impossible.

In Mark 9:43-48, Jesus warns against sins of the hand, foot, and eye: "If your hand causes you to stumble, cut it off; it is better for you to enter life maimed than to have two hands and to go to hell, to the unquenchable fire. . . ." This saying does not satisfy the criterion of multiple attestation, because there is no independent parallel in the Synoptics or John or elsewhere in first-century Christian sources. There is, however, an amazingly close Jewish text in the Babylonian Talmud,[4] so the criterion of dissimilarity can hardly be invoked. One also cannot obviously invoke the criterion of embarrassment to uphold Jesus' authorship of the complex, so all we seem to be left with is coherence. Some would argue that this criterion is fulfilled, because Jesus was morally earnest, liked hyperbole, called for un-

3. Origen, *Against Celsus* 1.42, trans. Henry Chadwick (Cambridge: Cambridge University Press, 1965), p. 39.

4. *b. Nid.* 13b: "Have we here learned a law as in the case where R. Huna [really] cut off someone's hand? Or is it merely an execration? Come and hear what was taught: R. Tarfon said, 'If his hand touched the membrum let his hand be cut off upon his belly.' 'But,' they said to him, 'would not his belly be split?' He said, 'It is preferable that his belly shall be split rather than that he should go down into the pit of destruction.'" In both Mark and *b. Nid.* 13b, the hand that sins should be cut off. In both, this act of mutilation is preferable to going to "the pit of destruction" or "Gehenna." And in both the thought is expressed in the "better . . . than" form.

compromising self-sacrifice, and invoked eschatological judgment as a motive for right behavior. Others, however, would respond that coherence by itself is a pretty weak indicator, which is true enough; and if, in addition, they are antecedently inclined to suspect that all the other references to eschatological fire in the Jesus tradition are secondary — a fairly common view today — then they will have the same suspicion here.

None of what has been said gives us good reason to attribute Mark 9:43-48 to someone other than Jesus, and my own strong intuition has always been that the verses go back to him. But if I am candid, I am not really sure what arguments or criteria I might muster to persuade others who are inclined to a different opinion or even no opinion at all. I can say that the language is vivid and shocking. My mind's eye beholds a bloody stump and an empty eye socket when it encounters these words, from which it follows that if Jesus did say something like Mark 9:43-48, it would stick in the memory. But this begs the question: Did he really speak something like it?

I have reluctantly come to the conclusion that the situation with regard to Mark 9:43-48 is representative of much of the academic effort to recover Jesus. The usual sorts of arguments that critics deploy, and that unfortunately I myself have repeatedly deployed, for saying yea or nay to a pre-Easter origin are not very weighty. Only a few Synoptic traditions are obviously secondary because they clearly contain purely post-Easter convictions (e.g., Jesus' assurance to John, "Let it be so now; for it is proper for us in this way to fulfill all righteousness," Matt 3:15); and only a few are almost certainly historical because church invention is wildly implausible (e.g., the accusation that Jesus was a glutton and drunkard, Matt 11:19 par. Luke 7:34). The origin of the rest of the material, which means almost all of the material, is open to interminable debate, and precisely because our arguments and criteria are just too weak to resolve much of anything. Despite all the ingenious efforts, has anyone really unveiled good public arguments for concluding that Jesus uttered or did not utter the golden rule (Matt 7:12 par. Luke 6:31), the parable of the rich man and Lazarus (Luke 16:19-31), the command not to let the left hand know what the right hand is doing (Matt 6:3), or the parable of the wicked tenants (Mark 12:1-12)? And who has established that a herd of pigs did or did not run over a cliff when Jesus was nearby? Is it not time to quit pretending that such things can be done?

My candid guess is that some of us look upon some arguments with favor because we like the result. The desired end blinds us to the inadequate means. Maybe some of us are also deceived about our own abilities because we have a Sherlock Holmes complex, naively believing that there must always be clues, and that if we seek them we will find them and so be able to demonstrate this or that. QED. But Sherlock Holmes is a fictional character. In real life, and that means in history, questions often go unanswered.

2. The line between fiction and nonfiction can be indistinct.

Sorting the tradition with the standard criteria presupposes that there is a clear distinction between authentic or historical items and those that are not authentic or historical. Almost everything, however, is instead a mixed product, that is, a joint product of Jesus and the church. Matthew 4:1-11 and Luke 4:1-13 tell us that Jesus went into the desert and that the devil tempted him there. Like Origen long ago, many modern scholars have judged this story to be unhistorical. I think that they are right: the dramatic temptation story is a haggadic fiction produced through reflection upon Scripture. Yet whoever first told the tale did so in the knowledge that Jesus (i) was a miracle worker, (ii) refused to give self-authenticating signs, (iii) thought himself victorious over demonic forces, (iv) could quote the Bible, (v) had faith in God, and (vi) associated his ministry with God's Spirit. So the temptation narrative, which recounts events that probably never happened, nonetheless rightly catches Jesus in several respects. It accordingly illustrates the obvious fact that fiction need not be pure fiction, that fiction can indeed preserve the past, so that the line between the two can be indistinct.

Although the assumption that a complex originated either with Jesus or with the early church is facile, the disjunction is the raison d'être for the standard criteria, which attempt to sort fiction from nonfiction, as though all the later expansions and commentary lead us away from the historical Jesus. This is just false.

3. Our criteria often point in different directions.

What do we make of the fact that our criteria are regularly at variance with one another? Some have attributed the words of Jesus at the Last Supper to the church for three reasons: (i) they belong to Christian liturgy and so do not satisfy the criterion of dissimilarity; (ii) they do not fit a Palestinian environment, for no Palestinian Jew would have spoken, even metaphorically, of others eating his body or drinking his blood;[5] and (iii) they interpret Jesus' death as an atonement, which not only gives Jesus clear foreknowledge of his fate but also places upon that fate a meaning otherwise barely attested in the Jesus tradition; in other words, they do not satisfy the criterion of coherence. Yet these arguments are seemingly balanced by three others: (i) the words of institution are attested in Paul, in Mark, and in an independent tradition in Luke, so we have early and multiple attestation; (ii) it was Jesus' habit to say shocking and outrageous things for the sake of effect, and one may interpret the words about eating his body and drinking his blood in that light; and (iii) the eschatological content of Mark 14:25 ("I will never again drink of the fruit of the vine until that day when I drink it new in the kingdom of God") harmonizes with Jesus' expectation of martyrdom within the context of his imminent eschatological expectation; in other words, they do satisfy the criterion of coherence. All of which is to say: the criterion of multiple attestation points one way (for), the criterion of dissimilarity the opposite way (against), and the criterion of coherence points both ways at once (for and against). There are of course additional arguments in the literature as well as refinements of those just given, but it goes without saying that they too do not exclusively throw their collective weight behind one alternative.

How should we respond to such conflict, or to like cases in which the criteria do not speak with united voice? One could perchance urge that we should simply do the math. If, for instance, three criteria favor authenticity and one other goes against it, the majority wins. Such an unimaginative approach would not, however, speak to the issue of an apparent tie. One might, alternatively, urge that one criterion carries more weight than another. Maybe multiple attestation is more important than dissimilarity, or coherence than embarrassment.

But all of that would be to miss the obvious, which is this: if our criteria point in different directions for the very same unit, then they are not very good gauges. What more proof does one need? If Jesus said A and yet some criteria imply otherwise, or if he did not say A and yet some criteria insinuate that he did, then our measuring instruments are crude and unreliable. Why then rely upon them anymore?

5. Many critics hold that whatever does not readily fit a Palestinian or Jewish environment must be secondary.

An Alternative

Fishing for Jesus in the sea of tradition using the criteria of authenticity wrongly privileges the part over the whole. When we look back upon our encounters with others, we see that our most reliable memories are often not precise but general. I may, for instance, not remember exactly what you said to me last year, but I may recall approximately what you said, or retain what we call a general impression. It is like vaguely recollecting the approximate shape, size, and contents of a room one was in many years ago — a room that has, in the mind's eye, lost all color and detail. After our short-term memories have become long-term memories, they suffer progressive abbreviation. I am not sure that I remember a single sentence that either of my beloved grandparents on my father's side ever said to me. I nonetheless know and cherish the sorts of the things that they said to me.

All of this matters for study of the Jesus tradition because it goes against common human experience to suppose that early Christians, let us say, accurately remembered many of Jesus' words but somehow came away with false general impressions of him. If those who passed on the Jesus tradition got the big picture or the larger patterns wrong, then they also got the details — that is, the sentences — wrong. It is precarious to urge, as has the Jesus Seminar, for example, that we can find the truth about Jesus on the basis of a handful of parables and a few dozen sayings deemed to be authentic if those parables and sayings are interpreted contrary to the general impressions often conveyed by the early tradition in its entirety. If Jesus was, for example, a "secular sage," devoid of eschatological interests, then the Synoptic tradition, which everywhere depicts a religious man with an eschatological vision, is so misleading that we cannot use it for investigating the pre-Easter period, and so we cannot know that Jesus was a secular sage. Here skepticism cancels itself.

What, however, is the alternative to skepticism? The early traditions about Jesus are not an unsortable mess. On the contrary, certain themes, motifs, and rhetorical strategies are consistently attested over a wide range of material; and surely it is in these themes and motifs and rhetorical strategies, if it is anywhere, that we are most likely to have some accurate memories. Indeed, several of these themes and motifs and strategies are sufficiently well attested that we have a choice to make. Either they tend to preserve pre-Easter memories or they do not. In the former case, we have some possibility of getting somewhere. But in the latter case, our questing for Jesus is probably pointless and we should consider surrendering to ignorance. If the tradition is seriously misleading in its broad features, then we can hardly make much of its details.

To illustrate, let me briefly review the evidence that Jesus and his disciples saw his ministry as implementing the defeat of satanic forces.[6] This conviction is reflected in sundry sources and in various genres — parables, prophetic declarations, stories of exorcism, etc. Here is a sample:

- The temptation narrative, in which Jesus bests the devil (Mark 1:12-13; Matt 4:1-11 par. Luke 4:1-13)
- Stories of successful exorcism (Mark 1:21-28; 5:1-20; 7:24-30; 9:14-27; Matt 12:22-23 par. Luke 11:14; Matt 9:32-34; cf. the passing notices of successful exorcisms in Mark 1:32, 34, 39; 3:22; Matt 8:16; Luke 13:32)
- Jesus' authorization of disciples to cast out demons (Mark 3:15; 6:7; cf. 6:13; Matt 7:22; Luke 10:19-20)
- The saying about Satan being divided (Mark 3:23-27; Matt 12:25-27 par. Luke 11:17-19)
- The parable of binding the strong man (Mark 3:27; Matt 12:29 par. Luke 11:21-22; *Gos. Thom.* 35)
- The story of someone other than a disciple casting out demons in Jesus' name (Mark 9:38-41)
- The declaration that Jesus casts out demons by the finger/Spirit of God (Matt 12:28 par. Luke 11:20)
- The report of Jesus' vision of Satan falling like lightning from heaven (Luke 10:18)
- The announcement that the ruler of the world has been driven out (John 12:31; 16:11; cf. 14:30)

One infers from all of this material not only that Jesus was an exorcist but also that he and others saw his ministry in its entirety as a victorious combat with Satan. This holds, whatever one makes of the individual units, at least some of which may be difficult to think of as historical. What counts is not the isolated units but the pattern they weave, or the larger images they form. Indeed, even if one were, against good sense, to reckon all

6. For what follows I am indebted to C. H. Dodd, *History and the Gospel* (New York: Scribner, 1938), pp. 92-110. Dodd's observations about method seem to me more important and useful than many more recent discussions.

the stories and sayings just listed to be creations of the community, one might still reasonably retain a certain faith in the whole of them taken together and suppose that the recurring motif tells us something significant about Jesus' ministry.

One can draw an analogy here with medical experiments. Taken by itself, even a perfectly devised double-blind, randomized trial counts for little. What matters is replication. And in areas where issues are particularly controverted, what finally matters is meta-analysis, the evaluation of large collections of results from numerous individual studies, including those with possible design flaws. It is the tendency of the whole that counts, not any one experiment or piece of evidence. It should be the same with questing for Jesus. It makes the most sense to begin not by looking at individual units microscopically but by gathering what may be called macro samples of material. We might even find that collectives display features or a gestalt not discernible in their individual components.

We cannot, for example, generalize about Jesus' relationship to the Pharisees from one controversy story, but from a collection of such, some generalizations might be drawn. Similarly, consider the proposition that Jesus had a pre-Easter follower named Peter. Let us say that, after examination of all the relevant materials, someone decided that every single story or saying in which Peter appears was a creation of the community and without pre-Easter foundation. What would follow? While the evidence would be consistent with denying to Peter a pre-Easter role or even doubting his historicity, such a conclusion would hardly be necessary. One might think it prudent to take Peter's frequent appearance in various complexes from various sources as best explained by the supposition that, despite all the legends, Jesus did have a follower named Peter.

The motif of victory over Satan and the presence of Peter throughout the early sources, canonical and extracanonical, are only two of a large number of recurring themes and motifs. To cite a few more of importance:

- The kingdom of God is coming and is even now present.
- God is the loving Father.
- Jesus works miracles on behalf of the sick and the infirm.
- The poor and the faithful will receive eschatological reward.
- Those who oppose Jesus and his cause will undergo eschatological judgment.
- The saints must expect suffering and persecution.

- The intention of the heart matters profoundly.
- Wealth is dangerous.
- Certain religious authorities have distorted their religious heritage.

It is not naive or precritical to urge that we should probably regard all of these items as rooted in the teaching and ministry of Jesus. Either the tradition instructs us that he spoke often about God as Father and showed special regard for unfortunates, or the tradition is so corrupt that it is not a useful source for Jesus and the quest for him is hopeless. I admit that this conclusion is contained in my premise, which is that memory, if anywhere, must be in the larger patterns; but then nothing but this premise allows research to proceed.

Scholars often conduct business as though what I am saying is true. They do not eliminate from the teaching of Jesus the logia about the kingdom of God or expunge the exorcisms from the pre-Easter period, despite these items' failure to pass the criterion of double dissimilarity. They continue to assign them to Jesus, I suspect, simply because they are so frequently attested across most of the tradition. This is not a matter of multiple attestation — a particular saying or event being attested at least more than once in more than one source — but rather of what one might call recurrent attestation, wherein a theme or motif is repeatedly attested throughout the tradition. Surely this is why we are confident that Jesus was an exorcist and spoke about the eschatological utopia as "the kingdom of God." By the same token, this is why we do not regard the baptismal command in Matthew 28:19 as authentic. Nowhere else does Jesus speak of ritual baptism or sound like a proto-trinitarian. The truth is that one could, if so inclined, urge that Matthew 28:19 satisfies the criterion of double dissimilarity: Jewish sources certainly nowhere speak of baptism in the name of the Father, the Son, and the Holy Spirit, and (aside from Matthew) the earliest Christian sources also here fail us, knowing rather of baptism in the name of Jesus. Yet this would be a specious argument for the pre-Easter origin of Matthew 28:19.

The main point to take away from this discussion is that if we have memory in the tradition, then the first and most likely place to look for it is not in individual sayings that our traditional criteria might seemingly endorse but rather in themes and motifs, as well as in rhetorical strategies such as the use of parables and hyperbole, that recur across the sources. This judgment of course does not imply that individual sayings and particular events do not predate Easter; many of them surely do, because Jesus was a memorable character. I am rather just conceding our own inability to authenticate so many of the smaller bits out of which the whole is made. I am unsure how often we can mount much of a demonstration that this or that saying goes back to Jesus even if it does, or that he did this or that thing even if he did. Often the best we can do with any degree of confidence is to try to answer such questions as, Did Jesus say this type of thing? or Did he do this type of thing?

One upshot of my approach is that, at the end of the day, there is no substitute for our primary sources, by which I mean the Synoptic Gospels — from my point of view John is here a secondary source[7] — although the rest of the New Testament and extracanonical sources should not be ignored. Our reconstructions of the historical Jesus must always be derivative; that is, they can never be anything other than variations of and commentaries upon Synoptic themes and events. To stray too far from Matthew, Mark, and Luke is to run the risk of succumbing to fantasy. If the Synoptics fail us too much, then we must fail entirely. This is not a theological judgment but a historical judgment. If our best sources have the wrong memories, where can we go to get the right ones?

Self-Conception

Where does all of this leave us with regard to Jesus' self-conception? Who did he say or think that he was? Did he imagine himself to be, as he purportedly imagined John the Baptist to be, not just a prophet but more than a prophet? Did he think himself greater than "the greatest among those born of women"? It is customary, when asking such questions, to enter the well-worn debates about certain christological titles. Did Jesus refer to "the Son of Man," and if so, what could he have meant, and whom did he have in mind? And did he imagine himself to be Israel's Messiah, the fulfillment of the promises to David and so destined to reign in Jerusalem? Or did he apply the term "Son (of God)" to himself in a way he did not apply it to others?

7. On the use of John as a source for historical information, cf. Marianne Meye Thompson, "Word of God, Messiah of Israel, Savior of the World: Learning the Identity of Jesus from the Gospel of John," in this volume.

Theological prejudice may hinder a thoroughly honest evaluation of these questions. It seems likely enough that many orthodox or more conservative Christians may be anxious to give the historical Jesus as high a Christology as possible, so that his continuity with the later creeds is as great as possible. Alternatively, more liberal Christians may equally desire just the opposite result. Many have worried that if Jesus thought of himself as the Messiah or as destined to return on the clouds of heaven as "the Son of Man," then he probably had "serious psychological difficulties."[8] Similarly, if one wishes to promote ecumenism among the world's religious, then a Jesus who saw himself as pivotal for the salvation of the world may be less congenial than one with a less exclusive, more universal character, let us say that of a spirit-inspired prophet who promulgated general religious wisdom.

However we sort out our own prejudices on this matter, and whatever theological work we want the historical Jesus to do for us, the textual evidence is, I submit, fairly clear on one particular. Our earliest Christian document is probably 1 Thessalonians, and in this we read that Jesus, "through" (διά, *dia*) whom the resurrection will occur (4:14), will return from heaven and rescue the saints from the coming wrath (1:10; cf. 4:13-18). Jesus is the center of Paul's eschatological scenario.

The eschatological expectations of 1 Thessalonians are part of a larger pattern that shows up not just in Acts and the Epistles but is also fully at home in the Jesus tradition itself. The Synoptic Gospels are united in presenting Jesus not just as God's final envoy but as the locus of the whole eschatological scenario, and especially as the central figure of the last judgment, as someone akin to Melchizedek in 11QMelchizedek, or the Elect One in the Parables of *1 Enoch*. Here are some of the pertinent traditions:

- Jesus the Son of Man will return on the clouds of heaven, sending angels to gather the elect from throughout the world (Mark 13:26-27; cf. 14:62; Matt 10:23; allusions to Daniel 7's depiction of the last judgment are clear).
- The sons of Zebedee asked to sit at the right and left hand of Jesus and

8. John Knox, *The Death of Christ: The Cross in New Testament History and Faith* (Nashville: Abingdon, 1958), p. 58; cf. 67 and 70-71. Marcus Borg, in *The Meaning of Jesus: Two Visions*, by Marcus J. Borg and N. T. Wright (San Francisco: HarperSanFrancisco, 1999), pp. 146-47, approvingly cites Knox and adds this: "I don't think people like Jesus have an exalted perception of themselves."

so presupposed his eschatological enthronement (Mark 10:35-40; cf. 14:62).

- Jesus selected a group of twelve disciples, whose number must represent the tribes of Israel (cf. Matt 19:28); and as he was not among their number but instead their leader, his leadership of renewed Israel is implied (Mark 3:13-19).
- Peter thought that Jesus must be "the Messiah" (Mark 8:29; cf. 14:61-62).
- The fate of at least some individuals at the final assize will depend upon whether they have acknowledged or denied Jesus (Mark 8:38; Matt 10:32-33 par. Luke 12:8-9).
- When Jesus went up to Jerusalem, crowds hailed him with the words, "Hosanna! Blessed is the one who comes in the name of the Lord! Blessed is the coming kingdom of our ancestor David!" (Mark 11:9-10).
- Jesus prophesied that he would destroy and rebuild the temple (Mark 14:58; cf. John 2:19).
- When the chief priest asked Jesus whether he was "the Messiah," he replied by applying Daniel 7:13 and Psalm 110:1 to himself (Mark 14:61-62).
- The Roman governor, Pilate, asked Jesus whether he took himself to be "the King of the Jews," and Jesus did not say no (Mark 15:2).
- Jesus called himself "Lord" and warned that not to do what he commanded will bring personal destruction (Matt 7:21-27 par. Luke 6:46-49).
- Jesus, in response to a query from John the Baptist, equated himself with the latter's "coming one" (Matt 11:2-6 par. Luke 7:18-23; the answer draws upon prophetic texts in Isaiah and lays implicit claim to fulfill them).
- Cities that have rejected Jesus — not John the Baptist or someone else — will suffer for it at the eschatological judgment (Matt 10:15; 11:21-24 par. Luke 10:12-15).
- People who "receive" the disciples really "receive" Jesus, and to "receive" Jesus is to receive the one who sent him, God (Matt 10:40 par. Luke 10:16).
- Jesus interpreted his success in casting out demons "by the finger of God" — an allusion to Exodus 8:19 that makes him Mosaic — to mean that God's kingdom had arrived; he thereby made himself out to be

the chief means or manifestation of its arrival (Matt 12:28 par. Luke 11:20).

- Jesus' followers will "judge" — which means either "rule" or "pass judgment upon" — restored Israel, and he cannot be less than they are; indeed, he must be more (Matt 19:28 par. Luke 22:28-30).
- Jesus read from the beginning of Isaiah 61 and proclaimed that its prophecies are fulfilled in his ministry; he thus claimed to be the anointed prophet of Isaiah's eschatological vision (Luke 4:16-21).

As with my earlier argument that Jesus saw his ministry as the downfall of Satan and his demons, so here too: I am not contending (or denying) that Jesus formulated any of the sayings just cited or that any event or circumstance referred to must be deemed historical. I am rather displaying a pattern. Jesus' starring role in the eschatological drama is all over the tradition, in words attributed to him and in words assigned to others, in stories as well as in sayings. Mark firmly attests to it. So also does the so-called Q source (the material common to Matthew and Luke but not in Mark).[9] So too traditions unique to Matthew and Luke. And it would be easy enough to add material from John, the *Gospel of Thomas,* Acts, Paul, and elsewhere.

What, then, should we think? We have three options. First, we may trust the sources and decide that Jesus believed himself to be the eschatological redeemer of Israel. Second, not knowing what to make of the sources, we may shrug our shoulders and confess ignorance: we just do not know what Jesus thought about himself. Third, we may distrust and even contradict the sources and assert that Jesus did not think himself to be Israel's deliverer.

Of these three positions, only the first two make much sense. The third, although common enough in the modern literature, entails that although our primary sources are consistently wrong about how Jesus understood himself, we can nonetheless get it right. We can still espy all the post-Easter contributions, subtract them, read between the lines, and discover what he was really up to. But if the sources — all of them — mislead on the matter of Jesus' exalted self-conception, if they have everything upside down, how much confidence can we have in using them to ferret out

9. And even in supposed Q1 material, that is, in what John Kloppenborg conjectured was an early stage of Q. See Kloppenborg, *The Formation of Q: Trajectories in Ancient Wisdom Collections* (Philadelphia: Fortress, 1987).

what he really did have to say? As before, if the larger pattern is a false memory, one wonders how we can still disinter the truth beneath the obfuscating sources. How can we ever feel much at ease with a Jesus who is so different from the individual on the surface of our texts?

There is a related problem. If a witness on the stand avows, "A said B," and then we learn that the witness was lying, we have not discovered anything about A. False testimony establishes nothing. We certainly do not have reason enough to conclude that A could not have said B. Some historians of Jesus, however, have seemingly proceeded otherwise. They have excised from the original tradition every single item that assumes or asserts his central eschatological role, and then they have announced that he did not think of himself as Israel's king or redeemer. But, even granting their surgical prowess, unless they also can refer us to material in which Jesus clearly rejects an eschatological role for himself — something they have not done because it cannot be done — the only proper conclusion is agnosticism, not denial.

Here, however, agnosticism is not obligatory. Pre-Pauline tradition already bestowed upon Jesus the title "Messiah" (Χριστός, *Christos*);[10] and despite all the diversity in Jewish eschatological expectation, this term implied his status as the divinely approved leader of Israel. Where, then, did this idea come from? Surely few can doubt that Jesus was crucified, and the Gospels report that Roman authorities executed him precisely with the charge that he pretended to be "King of the Jews" (Mark 15:26).[11] This is credible on the view that Jesus and his followers believed him to be Israel's eschatological leader. Positing such a pre-Easter conviction also accounts at one stroke for the constellation of materials catalogued above, as well as for the apparent fact that the Romans contented themselves with crucifying Jesus, not his followers.

If there is a better story to tell, I do not know it. Every piece of evidence we have indicates that from the beginning, Jesus, whatever appellation he did or did not bestow upon himself, was the leader, and everyone else a follower. He was the teacher while everyone else usually listened; he was the main actor while everyone else for the most part observed. There is

10. Werner Kramer, *Christ, Lord, Son of God*, SBT 50 (London: SCM, 1966), pp. 19-64.

11. On the historical plausibility of this, see Nils Alstrup Dahl, *The Crucified Messiah and Other Essays* (Minneapolis: Augsburg, 1974), pp. 23-24. Dahl's entire essay remains valuable, even though he underestimates, in my judgment, the scope and significance of what he calls Jesus' "messianic consciousness."

no tradition in which Jesus is not front and center.[12] Moreover, the primitive proclamation "God raised Jesus from the dead," however one accounts for it, was no reason to crown him Israel's king or to see him as a ruling lord — unless he was antecedently hoped to be such.[13] The *Testament of Job* tells the tale of the disappearance of the bodies of Job's dead children and their glorification in heaven without turning them into messianic figures (*T. Job* 39–40), and the two witnesses in Revelation 11 rise from the dead and ascend without gaining further attention. The early interpretations of the Easter events *presupposed* Jesus' pivotal eschatological role; they were not its source. The first believers did not preach — as they might have if Jesus had not already been the focus of messianic hopes — that God has raised somebody from the dead, so the end must be near. They rather proclaimed that God has raised *Jesus* from the dead, installing him as both Lord and Christ (cf. Acts 2:32-36).

Social Identity and the Church

Some modern writers leave the distinct impression that we find the historical Jesus by ascertaining, to the best of our ability, what he said and what he did. In other words, we uncover his identity by uncovering his self-understanding. This, however, is a peculiar procedure. Personal identity is never merely an individual matter, as though we are what we think. Surely, identity is always a social product, the upshot of multiple perceptions.

If I may change the subject for an illustration, Who is William Jefferson Clinton? One could, I suppose, read the ex-President's speeches and his autobiography and be content with that. But Bill Clinton has spent his life interacting with other human beings, so his assessment of himself is only one assessment among many; he has a public identity. Who would deny that we would gain a fuller understanding of him by learning what, let us say, his wife and daughter have to say about him? They could surely tell us things about him that he himself does not perceive. We would also profit greatly by talking to some of Clinton's longtime friends, as well as to

12. Mark 6:14-29 par., the story of the Baptist's martyrdom, whatever its genesis, only seems to be an exception: in its canonical contexts, it reveals the fate of a true prophet and so foreshadows Jesus' end.

13. Johannes Weiss clearly saw this long ago; see Weiss, "Das Problem der Entstehung des Christentums," *Archiv für Religionswissenschaft* 16 (1913): 468-71.

former and current staffers. The more friends, acquaintances, and even enemies we hear from, the more we know about Bill Clinton. Indeed, given his status as a public figure, it would make sense to interview people who have never even met the man to find out what they think of him. In short, Clinton's identity is not housed within his skin but is instead an interpersonal phenomenon. How he has affected others and what they have seen in him belong to his person as much as do his intentions and thoughts about himself. Furthermore, one guesses that, in some ways, we may best understand him only after the passage of considerable time, when he and those who know him are dead, and when the long-term consequences of his actions and policies have become evident. His reception history, if I may so put it, belongs to his identity.

It is not otherwise with Jesus, however otherwise dissimilar he may be from Bill Clinton. His identity cannot be reduced to what he said or to what he thought of himself, much less to what good historians might determine that he said and thought. Confining ourselves to the "authentic" words and deeds of Jesus is a bit like confining ourselves to Clinton's autobiography. The external perceptions of others and Jesus' *Wirkungsgeschichte,* or "history of influence," count for much.

Jesus' identity cannot be sundered from a whole constellation of post-Easter circumstances: somebody attributed to him the remarkable Sermon on the Mount, and somebody else remembered his death by creating Mark's stark and moving passion narrative, and somebody else penned Luke's beautiful and humane Gospel, and somebody else produced the symbolically rich and mystically charged Gospel of John, and somebody else composed the paean to love in 1 Corinthians 13 and declared there to be no difference between Jew and Gentile. Jesus wrote none of this, but without him none of it would have been written; and if his character had been different, the character of these texts would be too.

The proclamation of Jesus' resurrection makes and extends my point for me. His vindication meant that he was not confined to the dead past, that he was instead alive and his influence ongoing. Paul believed this so much that he could speak of those under Jesus' continuing inspiration as "the body of Christ," which in some way identifies Christ with his church.[14] We may, if we choose, reject this astounding equation. But if we

14. For further discussion on the identification of Jesus in the life of the church, see Sarah Coakley, "The Identity of the Risen Jesus: Finding Jesus Christ in the Poor," in this volume.

accept it, does not the historical Jesus become the first half of an incomplete sentence? And does not the church, to the extent that it remains faithful to its Lord, then become, in both its historical and its contemporary manifestations, the continuation of that sentence and so an integral part of Jesus' identity?

Veritas Christi: How to Get from the Jesus of History to the Christ of Faith without Losing One's Way

Francis Watson

"You are the Christ," Peter replies to Jesus' question. The simplicity of the confessional statement corresponds to the divine simplicity of the truth it acknowledges. It represents the moment of disclosure in which the light of truth appears and is recognized as such.

Yet the moment of disclosure cannot be made into a permanent dwelling place. When Peter proposes that the experience of the transfiguration should be given permanent form by the construction of three tabernacles (one for Moses, one for Elijah, and one for Jesus), his proposal is not even rejected; it is simply ignored, and it is left to the evangelist to apologize for his foolishness (Mark 9:5-6). On the way down the mountain, a theological difficulty comes to light. Jesus' three disciples engage him in debate about how the figure of the suffering and rising Son of Man relates to Elijah, whose coming to restore all things they have learned of from the scribes (9:9-13). Theological debate is not silenced for long even by a voice from heaven.

For Christians, Jesus' true identity is established above all by the fourfold canonical Gospel.[1] It is within this sacred textual space that we discover who Jesus is and who we are in relation to him. Yet here too scribes have uncovered problems that we might otherwise have overlooked. For these more recent scribes, the way from the sacred text to a firmly grounded belief in the crucified and risen Son of Man is anything but straightforward. Rightly — that is, critically — understood, the texts are

1. On this see Hans W. Frei, *The Identity of Jesus Christ: The Hermeneutical Bases of Dogmatic Theology* (Philadelphia: Fortress, 1975).

now said to speak of someone else: "the Jesus of history," whom we are to differentiate from "the Christ of faith."[2] This scribal distinction cannot and should not be ignored. Once it has become lodged in a disciple's mind, the problem of the Gospel's apparent twofold referent has to be addressed.

How are we to understand this distinction between a Jesus of history and a Christ of faith? Is it perhaps the product of some theological or methodological error, diagnosis of which will reveal our problem as a pseudoproblem?[3] Or, if the problem turns out to be real, can the distinction somehow be transcended so that we can continue to confess "one Lord Jesus Christ" rather than two (or more)? These are the questions that I shall address in this paper, with two opposing skepticisms in view: on the one hand, skepticism about the viability and value of the historical Jesus project; on the other, skepticism about the fourfold canonical Gospel as a truthful rendering of the identity of Jesus. These two skepticisms share the assumption that historical and theological discourses on Jesus are simply incommensurable and that no communication between the two is possible or desirable. The purpose of this paper is to see if communication can be reestablished.

The Historical Jesus: A Qualified Endorsement

It was presumably the English translator of Albert Schweitzer's survey of life-of-Jesus research who coined the phrase "the quest of the historical Jesus."[4] No doubt his immediate concern was simply to find a marketable ti-

2. The terminology goes back to the title of D. F. Strauss's polemic against Schleiermacher's lectures on the life of Jesus, *Der Christus des Glaubens und der Jesus der Geschichte* (1865), ed. H.-J. Geischer (Gütersloh: G. Mohn, 1971).

3. See, e.g., Luke Timothy Johnson, *The Real Jesus: The Misguided Quest for the Historical Jesus and the Truth of the Traditional Gospels* (San Francisco: HarperCollins, 1997). In this trenchant critique of recent American historical Jesus scholarship, Johnson argues that this scholarship is not only defective in practice but also misguided in principle. The Jesus of the Gospels is "not simply a figure of the past but very much and above all a figure of the present. . . . Christians direct their faith not to the historical figure of Jesus but to the living Lord Jesus" (p. 142).

4. The translator was W. Montgomery. F. C. Burkitt already speaks of "the great Quest" in his preface to Schweitzer's work (*The Quest of the Historical Jesus: A Critical Study of Its Progress from Reimarus to Wrede* [ET, London: A&C Black, 1910], p. xviii). The German title was *Von Reimarus zu Wrede: Eine Geschichte der Leben-Jesu-Forschung* (Tübingen: J. C. B. Mohr, 1906).

tle for the English translation. Had the book gone out into the English-speaking world ponderously entitled *From Reimarus to Wrede: A History of Research into the Life of Jesus*, its success would hardly have been assured. Schweitzer himself no doubt intended this title, or its German equivalent, to ensure a hearing for the book within the German academy. In contrast, the romantic English title echoes the medieval legend of the quest of the Holy Grail, familiar to Schweitzer's potential English-speaking readership through Tennyson's popular Arthurian cycle, *Idylls of the King*, and perhaps also through Wagner's *Parsifal*. Like the Holy Grail, the historical Jesus is the infinitely valuable yet elusive object that promises nothing less than the redemption of humankind. Like Galahad, Percival, and Lancelot, New Testament scholars set forth on an arduous and perilous journey that is also a pilgrimage, fraught with significance for all. To this day, the imagery is almost irresistible.

Yet we live in unromantic, prosaic times. It will serve the interests of clarity if we conceive of modern historical Jesus research as a scholarly project operating within a shared paradigm — that is, a set of assumptions, priorities, and methodological tools that inform and direct the process of research. Other, related projects also operate within this paradigm. Alongside historical Jesus research, there are source criticism, form criticism, redaction criticism, and narrative criticism, approaches that investigate the Gospels' literary relationships, the history of tradition, and the individual Gospels in their final forms. Historical Jesus research is closely related to these other scholarly projects, which together constitute the modern, *wissenschaftlich* study of the Gospels. This is a tightly integrated nexus of concerns relating to Jesus himself, the traditions about Jesus, and the first literary embodiments of those traditions.

The working hypothesis underlying the entire scholarly paradigm is this: that the historical Jesus is other than the figure(s) we encounter in the fourfold canonical Gospel. In Martin Kähler's terminology, there is a "so-called historical Jesus" and there is a "historic, biblical Christ."[5] Practically speaking, we can study the historical Jesus or we can study the images of Jesus constructed by each of the four canonical evangelists — but

5. Martin Kähler, *Der sogenannte historische Jesus und der geschichtliche, biblische Christus* (Leipzig: A. Deichert, 1892); ET, *The So-Called Historical Jesus and the Historic, Biblical Christ*, trans. Carl E. Braaten (Philadelphia: Fortress, 1964). We note in passing that the German *sogenannte* need not have the dismissive connotations of the English "so-called."

we cannot do both simultaneously. The two forms of research are concerned with significantly different objects, whatever the area of overlap between them. In contrast, it is said, "precritical" study of the Gospels normally assumed that the Jesus of whom they tell is maximally identified with Jesus as he really was. If the Johannine Jesus turns water into wine and speaks of himself as the light of the world, then so too did Jesus himself: the text is a window onto the historical reality. Within "critical" scholarship, however, the text loses its transparency and becomes increasingly opaque. In the creative imagination of the early church, it is now claimed, Jesus becomes the object not only of historical reminiscence but also of dogmatic construction and legendary elaboration, and the Gospels attest this complex process. We must distinguish the historical Jesus from the early Christian images of him. Modern Gospels scholarship is based on this fundamental disjunction.

The disjunction is not just a scholarly construct, divorced from the experience of ordinary readers of the Gospels. It does not require any advanced scholarly training to find oneself asking whether a particular Gospel story really recounts an event in the life of Jesus. The involuntary inward question, "Did that actually happen?" is hardly an uncommon response to a Gospel story. The question may be a naive one, presupposing a watertight distinction between fact and fiction that is vulnerable to some rather obvious criticisms. Yet antipositivistic critique goes beyond its remit if it tries to outlaw *every* attempt to distinguish factual occurrence from legendary elaboration. Ordinary readers and trained scholars are not wrong to assume that some such distinctions may be ventured. There is nothing incoherent or implausible about commonplace scholarly judgments such as the following:

> On the one hand, Jesus clearly did address God as "Abba." On the other hand, he probably never uttered the words, "I am the bread of life." Jesus grew up in Nazareth, but in reality he was presumably not visited in infancy by magi guided to his Bethlehem residence by a star. Jesus was actually baptized by John, but no descending dove or heavenly voice would have been directly ascertainable on that occasion. Jesus gained a reputation as a healer and exorcist, but he did not really stride across the Sea of Galilee during a storm. Jesus and his disciples came to Jerusalem for the Passover, yet (*pace* Matthew) he did not really enter the city seated on two animals simultaneously. Jesus was indeed arrested, tried,

tortured, and crucified, but the darkness at noon, the rending of the temple veil, the splitting of the rocks, and the resurrection of the saints do not belong to the realm of empirical reality.

These judgments reflect not just rationalistic dogma but a sensitivity to the dynamics of the Gospels' textuality — their relation to each other, to antecedent texts and traditions, and to the world from which they derive. If such judgments are accepted, then in each case we have a de facto distinction between a "historical Jesus" (for want of a better expression) and legends or legendary motifs created by early Christian storytellers.[6]

Is this disjunction based simply on a mistake? It is argued in some quarters that the road that leads from Reimarus to Wrede and beyond is actually heading *away from* the reality of Jesus, since its direction has been determined in advance by dubious rationalistic presuppositions that do not stand up to philosophical scrutiny. On this account, to diagnose the presuppositions — above all, the "prejudice against the supernatural" so characteristic of the Enlightenment — is conclusively to refute the modern critical paradigm. When the inappropriate presuppositions have been removed, it is said, the historical Jesus can be reidentified with his images in the Gospels. In this way, the Gospels' transparency to historical reality is restored — instantly and with minimal effort. In spite of their differences of presentation, the four Gospels are once again united in telling the story of Jesus the way it was.

This line of reasoning claims to offer a way out of the dilemma posed by the modern critical paradigm. It asks us to see this as a false dilemma, created by the arbitrary presupposition that the Gospels' story of Jesus simply *cannot* be true at certain crucially important points (water just does not turn instantly into wine; people do not return physically from death). Yet, the argument runs, how do we know that what is normally the case also holds true in the unique case of Jesus? Christian faith itself strongly encourages us to think otherwise. Those held in thrall by the critical paradigm must undertake an act of epistemological repentance.[7]

Should we follow this line of reasoning, or something like it, so as to

6. The classic statement of the case for disjunctions of this kind is D. F. Strauss's *Life of Jesus Critically Examined* (1835-36; ET, Philadelphia: Fortress, 1972).

7. For a sophisticated version of this argument, see C. Stephen Evans, *The Historical Christ and the Jesus of Faith: The Incarnational Narrative as History* (Oxford: Clarendon, 1996), pp. 184-202, 331-55.

mitigate the disjunction between the historical Jesus and the fourfold Gospel image? There are three main reasons why we should not take this route — in spite of its apparent attractiveness from the standpoint of Christian faith. First, the critical paradigm possesses remarkable explanatory power in its analysis of the realities of the Gospel texts. While this claim cannot be demonstrated to everyone's satisfaction, it will be self-evident to anyone who has ever worked seriously with a Gospel synopsis. Second, it is not at all clear that to identify a Gospel story as a legend is to be guilty of an act of willful unbelief. As Origen already knew, recognition of a narrative's historical implausibility may actually help the interpreter draw out its underlying theological meaning.[8] Third, it is one thing to confess God's final, definitive saving action in Christ but quite another to claim that this divine saving action is such as to be empirically verifiable in principle or in practice. This claim tends to imply a certain apologetic strategy, which is (arguably!) out of keeping with the dynamics of the Christian gospel.

At some points, the distinction between a "historical Jesus" and the Jesus of the fourfold Gospel testimony is virtually inescapable. While the scope and the significance of this distinction still need to be clarified, the distinction itself is not the product of incoherent thinking or of willful unbelief. The New Testament scholarly consensus on this point is grounded in the realities of the texts and should not be lightly dismissed by those who aspire to follow the "historic, biblical Christ." The goal of the present argument is to show how the scholarly construct known as the "historical Jesus" can be *reintegrated* into the canonical image of the historic, biblical Christ. But it is necessary first to grasp and to acknowledge the rationale for the distinction.

If we accept that, at any point, a Gospel writer says *x* about Jesus but the historical reality was probably *not-x*, then we have begun to identify Gospel material whose relationship to empirical reality seems tenuous or oblique and to distinguish it from material where this relationship is probably more direct. The systematic investigation of this distinction is the starting point of the project known as the "quest of the historical Jesus."[9] The project pro-

8. See the brief discussion of Origen's position in my *Text, Church and World: Biblical Interpretation in Theological Perspective* (Edinburgh: T&T Clark, 1994), pp. 230-31.

9. For an alternative to this model, see N. T. Wright, *The New Testament and the People of God* (London: SPCK, 1992) and *Jesus and the Victory of God* (London: SPCK, 1996). Wright argues that the correct starting point is to reconstruct Jesus' Jewish context and to ask how far the Gospel presentation looks plausible within that context.

ceeds from a more or less radical attempt to sift out "secondary" material, whose origin is held to postdate Jesus' own lifetime. Secondary material is identified not only by invoking general criteria of credibility (which do not necessarily deserve the pejorative epithet "rationalistic") but above all by way of an intricate comparative analysis of the Gospels, normally based on the source-critical theory of Markan priority. The residue of primary, or "authentic," material then provides the basis for the attempt to reconstruct the main outlines of Jesus' life and ministry, typically organized under a series of headings relating either to specific events (the baptism by John, the incident in the temple) or, more commonly, to broad themes (the kingdom of God, the inclusion of the marginalized). Also relevant here is the mass of surviving literature from the Second Temple period, which, under critical interrogation, can yield crucial insight into the historical and religious milieu within which Jesus lived and acted.

It is notorious that scholarly work in the "historical Jesus" idiom has been beset by serious difficulties. The criteria for differentiating primary from secondary material have often proved hard to define and to apply, and this has resulted in major interpretative differences. For much of the twentieth century, Schweitzer's triumphant announcement that eschatology was the key to Jesus' activity seemed virtually beyond dispute. At the start of the twenty-first century, it is again an open question whether Jesus was even interested in eschatology; those who argue that he was are forced into the "conservative" role of defending an older consensus.[10] Another persistent problem is the distorting effect of the ideological motivations often perceptible in historical Jesus research. For many scholars, there must be a sharp dividing line between the real, authentic, historical Jesus and the later, spurious Christ images that shaped the course of Christian dogmatic development. This imperative stems not from considerations of historical plausibility but from a projection of contemporary concerns back into the first century. A Jesus who lends his prestigious support to our own antiecclesial leanings or political preferences is sure to attract wide public interest. From a purely historical point of view, the problems encountered in trying to distinguish primary from secondary material have a

10. See Dale C. Allison, *Jesus of Nazareth: Millenarian Prophet* (Minneapolis: Fortress, 1998): "Many of us have, since Johannes Weiss and Albert Schweitzer, been persuaded that Jesus was an eschatological prophet with an apocalyptic scenario. Our judgment is consistent with the Synoptics' testimony" (p. 34).

simple explanation: they reflect the considerable area of overlap between what mattered to Jesus and what mattered to the early communities of his followers over the next few decades. In the last resort, a historical Jesus who diverges from his earliest followers at most key points will be historically implausible. But such a figure may well seem highly attractive. If he underwrites our religious and political biases, we will want to believe in him. And if we want to believe in him, then most likely we *will* believe in him.

It is tempting to regard these deficiencies — lack of consensus, ideological distortion — as fatal to the entire historical Jesus project. Yet this temptation should be rather firmly resisted. All major historical figures continue to generate an interpretative disagreement that reflects conflicting ideological investments. Far from undermining the debate, the disagreement just *is* the debate. We can choose to join the debate or not, but we cannot sensibly argue that it should be wound up and that historical Jesus scholarship should find some better use for its time. If there are deficiencies that need to be addressed, then they can only be addressed from within the debate, not by holding piously aloof from it. If there is poor scholarly practice, slipshod argumentation, or dubious methodology, none of that gives any pretext for rejecting the project itself.

The question is whether this project can allow any room for the distinctive concerns of Christian faith, for which Jesus is the embodiment of a divine saving action addressed to the whole of humankind, and not just one historical figure among many. If, for Christians, it is this relation to God and God's agency that makes Jesus theologically significant, can this conviction be asserted in a historically responsible manner? One possibility is that the theologically significant Jesus should simply be identified with the historical Jesus — that is, with the modern scholarly reconstruction of a historically plausible figure from the "authentic" material in the Gospels and from the extant literary and archaeological material relating to Jesus' various religious, social, and political contexts.[11] Within such a reconstruction, a variety of potentially significant motifs is to be found: Jesus' sense of his own relation to God and of his mission, his overturning of conventional wisdom, his attitude toward the marginalized, his recourse to

11. For a popular presentation of an argument along these lines, see Marcus Borg, *Meeting Jesus Again for the First Time: The Historical Jesus and the Heart of Contemporary Faith* (San Francisco: HarperCollins, 1995).

parable, his announcement of the kingdom of God, his critique of Pharisees and Sadducees, the ethos he created among his followers — and so on. Theological significance is surely to be found in this material. The question is whether theological significance is to be found *exclusively* in these "authentic" strands of the Gospels and whether those strands of the Gospels deemed "inauthentic" can simply be set aside as of no further significance. The conventional distinction between "authentic" and "inauthentic" material has a certain value in distinguishing the material that can be used for historical Jesus research from that which cannot be so used; but it is quite another matter to elevate this distinction into a criterion for theological significance.

If the theologically significant Jesus were to be identified with the historical Jesus of modern scholarship, then the narrative framework of the Gospels would have to be set aside. In particular, the beginning and the end of the fourfold Gospel narrative would be deprived of significance; there would no longer be anything much to say at Christmas or at Easter. Historical research is unlikely to confirm an incarnation or a risen Lord.[12] And what of the Eucharist, in its relation to the Gospel narrative of institution? The members of the "Jesus Seminar" report that they "found nothing in this narrative that could be traced directly back to Jesus."[13] Of course, there might be room for debate about that. Yet if "authenticity" is the criterion of theological significance, the significance of the Eucharist itself will be open to question. Eucharist, Easter, and Christmas may be a matter of profound indifference to secularized scholars who maintain a wary distance from Christian faith and its social embodiments. For participants in Christian faith and community, however, such indifference is impossible. It is precisely at the beginning and end of the Gospel story of Jesus that its "vertical" dimension — its rendering of the relation between Jesus and his God — comes most fully to expression. To eradicate that beginning and ending is to deny God's own identity, constituted as it is for Christians by the single though complex divine act in which God gives, gives up, and raises God's Son.[14] Outside that context, a "historical Jesus" who projects

12. *Pace* N. T. Wright, for whom (it seems) all things are possible for historical research; see his *The Resurrection of the Son of God* (Minneapolis: Fortress, 2003), pp. 685-718.

13. Robert W. Funk, Roy W. Hoover, and the Jesus Seminar, *The Five Gospels: The Search for the Authentic Words of Jesus: New Translation and Commentary* (1993; reprint, New York: Scribner, 1996), p. 260.

14. On this point, see Robert W. Jenson, *Systematic Theology,* vol. 1, *The Triune God*

fatherhood into the unknowable realm beyond empirical experience can hardly be the object of unconditional commitment. The historical Jesus of modern scholarship is a figure of some significance, but he cannot be identified with the Christ of faith acknowledged by the church. So much the worse for the church's Christ? Christians are not obliged to think so.

On theological but also on historical grounds, we cannot be content with a historical Jesus who is complete in himself, detached from his own reception by his first followers in the decades following his death. Their reception of him is also his impact on them. In the discussion that follows, we shall try to analyze that reception in historically and theologically responsible ways.[15] The transition from "Jesus" to "Christ" need not be a move from fact to fantasy. It could be a journey from a partial truth to a comprehensive one.

The Dynamics of Reception

We may now venture the following thesis: *The theologically significant Jesus (the Christ of faith) is the Jesus whose reception by his first followers is definitively articulated in the fourfold Gospel narrative.*[16] The thesis seeks to bridge the chasm of presumed incommensurability between historical Jesus research and a theology that regards the fourfold Gospel narrative as a given. It is the concept of "reception" that can reconnect the two, pointing the way to the comprehensive truth that is the *veritas Christi,* the "truth of Christ." In what follows, readers will note that I am striving for succinctness, in order to map out as clearly as possible the main contours of a complex and contested terrain.

(New York: Oxford University Press, 1997), pp. 42-44, 59-60. For Jenson, God is identified *by* Jesus' resurrection but also identified *with* this event (p. 59).

15. The concept of "reception" here is dependent on Paul Tillich, who argues that "[t]he event on which Christianity is based has two sides: the fact which is called 'Jesus of Nazareth' and the reception of this fact by those who received him as the Christ." Tillich, *Systematic Theology,* vol. 2, *Existence and the Christ* (1957; London: SCM, 1978), p. 97. Further: "Without this reception the Christ would not have been the Christ, namely, the manifestation of the New Being in time and space" (p. 99). Thus, the New Testament itself "is an integral part of the event which it documents" (p. 117).

16. In place of "the fourfold Gospel narrative," the thesis might have referred to "the New Testament" or to "the Christian Bible." The more limited formulation reflects the decision to focus in this paper on the special problems posed by the Gospels.

The Ecclesial Context

The thesis assumes that there is such a thing as a "theologically significant Jesus" (a "Christ of faith"). This is a Jesus set in the context of a *theo-logy* (a discourse about God) that finds in Jesus the hermeneutical key to the divine relation to the world and the world's relation to the divine. This discourse about God has a specific social location. It is an ecclesial discourse, a language game in which some participate while others do not. It has its own characteristic term for such participation — "faith." The Jesus of faith comprehends the historical Jesus but is not to be reduced to him. As we have seen, a purely historical Jesus is far too limited a figure for the ultimate concern of faith. This ultimate concern represents a fundamental challenge to the assumption that final decisions about Jesus' identity can be reached on the neutral ground of historical research. Historical research may illuminate a range of significant issues, but it will not tell us whether Jesus' person and mission are truly from God, definitively embodying the divine saving action on the world's behalf. Within the Christian community, everything hangs on whether Jesus is confessed to be from God. The Christian community has its own compelling reasons to resist and reject any limiting of Jesus' reality to what is historically verifiable.

The Scriptural Matrix

The thesis acknowledges the historical process in which Jesus' living, acting, speaking, and dying were assimilated and reconfigured within the earliest Christian communities. In the post-Easter period, the remembered human figure was subjected to an interpretative process inspired primarily by scriptural texts that were now understood to point specifically to him. That this interpretative process is original to the Easter faith is explicitly acknowledged in the Emmaus road story, which is itself both a testimony to that process and a product of it. For the communities that first shaped the "Jesus tradition," Scripture was the interpretative matrix within which Jesus' full significance could be brought to light. That is why, again and again, early Christian legends prove to be *midrash,* stories arising out of a scriptural kernel. Even "authentic" recollections of Jesus' life and death had to be relocated within a particular construal of Scripture and of Jesus as Scripture's fulfillment. The first Christians recollected how Jesus had died, yet they spoke not of his death per se but rather of the fact that "Christ died for our sins according to the scriptures" (1 Cor 15:3). Naturally, Scripture was mediated to them by a Jewish, postbiblical interpretative tradition that was also open to influences from elsewhere. The first Christians did not reflect on Scripture in a social and cultural vacuum; Hellenism's profound impact on other Judaisms of the time also affected them. Yet in their own self-understanding, it was Scripture reread in the light of the resurrection that authorized their reconfiguring of Jesus' story.

Reception as Tradition

The term "reception" points to the dialectic of preservation and innovation within the process of tradition. At one point, an authentic saying of Jesus is handed down, in a form close to the *ipsissima verba,* his exact words; at another, a new legendary motif is created. Yet the preserved saying may now function within an entirely new context, assigned to it by an evangelist or some other early Christian storyteller. A Gospel synopsis discloses how even the most stable and best-attested elements in the tradition can move from one context to another with remarkable ease. If this is still the case with the canonical evangelists, it was surely also the case in the earlier period. Conversely, a later legend may articulate a conviction that is deeply embedded in the earlier tradition: the Emmaus road story is a case in point. In the process of reception, a fluid relationship between older and newer elements in the tradition comes to light. Indeed, the term "reception" enables us to overcome the division between "authentic" and "inauthentic" material — a distinction pragmatically useful in historical Jesus research but not to be absolutized if Paul is right to confess that there is "one Lord Jesus Christ" rather than many (cf. 1 Cor 8:6). The point is that *everything* in the fourfold Gospel's portrayals of Jesus comes to us through the mediation of the earliest Christian communities and represents their reception of him. At every point Jesus is filtered through early Christian tradition; at no point do we encounter him face to face. Let us imagine that in a Christian community in Jerusalem or Galilee in the early 30s C.E., one of the twelve recalls a saying that he heard from Jesus' lips a year or two earlier and introduces it into circulation so that it is added to the growing stock of Jesus material. The saying may preserve Jesus' *ipsissima verba,* but already it bears the marks of its later usage. The fact that it has been recalled and circulated at all implies that it is seen to possess enduring significance, illuminating some aspect or other of the community's ethos or worldview. In other words, the saying that is preserved is specially selected for preservation. The selection process occurs within the life of the early communities, for it is there that the criteria for the survival or otherwise of recollections about Jesus are established. We hear of Jesus only what the first Christians want us to hear. That is the grain of truth in the claim that the Gospels give us direct access only to the early Christian communities and not to Jesus himself. But it would be better to say that the Gospels give us direct access to Jesus *as he was received* within the early communities.

The Historical Foundation

If the theologically significant Jesus is the Jesus received by the early church, the "quest of the historical Jesus" has nevertheless performed an invaluable service. Above all, it has demonstrated that, at a certain level of generality, the Gospel story remains grounded in empirical historical reality. In all four Gospels, Jesus' story unfolds within a consistent set of geographical and historical coordinates. One thinks of locations such as Galilee and its lake, Nazareth and Capernaum, Judea and Jerusalem, and of figures or groups such as Caiaphas and Pilate, Antipas and Philip, Pharisees and Sadducees. Historical research has shown beyond doubt that coordinates such as these anchor the story of Jesus in empirical reality. For those familiar with this research, it is hard to take seriously the persistent though marginal claim that Jesus may never have existed. This empirical reality exercises a degree of control over the developing tradition about Jesus — although not an absolute control, for the tradition seeks to portray a Jesus who is more than merely an empirical figure of history. Yet Jesus is not *less than* an empirical figure of history. He is not a virtually fictional character in a narrative;[17] he is not a disembodied voice uttering context-

17. Hans Frei seems to me to stray too close to this position in his emphasis on "the story as story" and on "the storied Jesus," about whose being prior to his literary embodiment we are not to inquire (Frei, *Identity of Jesus Christ,* pp. 102, 114). Frei tends to assimilate the Gospels to the genre of the modern realistic novel, which is "the special vehicle for setting forth unsubstitutable identity in the interplay of character and action" (p. 82). It does not occur to Frei that a range of relations to the real can coexist within a single narrative

less aphorisms (as in the *Gospel of Thomas*). It is a merit of historical Jesus research that it makes it difficult to be a docetist. The Jesus received by the early church is a figure of flesh and blood who shares our own existence within time and space.

The Value of Legend

Equally valuable, in principle at least, is the quest's identification of major parts of the Gospel testimony as "nonhistorical" or "legendary." Here some qualifications are necessary. First, the simple, pragmatically useful distinction between "historical" and "nonhistorical," "fact" and "fiction," has often served to conceal the far more complex range of relations between Gospel text and empirical reality. There are fictive elements in history writing, and facts may be indirectly attested in legends.[18] Second, understanding of the Gospels has been severely damaged by the rationalistic assumption that to label a narrative as a "legend" is to discredit it. For early Christian storytellers, legend seems to have functioned as a way of communicating nonempirical theological truth, and there is no reason why it should not continue to do so. Third, the theological truth that legend attests is never anything other than the truth *about Jesus.* Unlike myth, legend does not risk sacrificing the concrete particular to some timeless universal. Early Christian legend seeks to articulate *God's act* in Jesus, but it knows of no divine saving action other than that which is embodied in Jesus.

Writing the Tradition

The term "reception" is virtually synonymous with "tradition." Yet not much is known about the development of the tradition, oral or written, prior to the composition of the canonical Gospels. We must assume that this tradition was developed initially within the "churches of God in Christ Jesus which are in Judea" (1 Thess 2:14), in which "the twelve" ap-

---

(also in a realistic novel) and that judgments about these relations may be integral to the act of reading.

18. See my *Text and Truth: Redefining Biblical Theology* (Edinburgh: T&T Clark, 1997), pp. 33-69.

pear to have been active, and in which the three "pillars" attained their reputation from their close relationship to Jesus (Gal 2:9). Yet we know next to nothing about those churches, and traces of the Jesus tradition in the Pauline letters are relatively scarce. The concept of "tradition" is needed in order to bridge the gap between the death of Jesus in around 30 C.E. and the canonical Gospels, none of which appear to predate the final quarter of the first century.[19] But we have no direct access to the early tradition; its complex dynamic is perceptible only in the evidence of literary development found within the Gospels themselves.[20] Thus, it is the Gospels that definitively articulate the early Christian reception of Jesus, giving the prior tradition (oral and written) its normative, canonical form. That does not mean that everything in the Gospels has a direct precedent in the tradition. Yet even where the evangelists innovate, the new stories or motifs derive their form and their rationale from what is already present within the tradition; they are not created out of nothing.

The Canonical Form

The canonical status of the four Gospels rests on a collective decision that took place during the mid- to late second century. In that sense, it is only around the time of Irenaeus that the tradition in its written form achieves even a relative stability and begins to fulfill its role as the normative testimony to Jesus as he was received by his first followers. The claim that Jesus' true identity is articulated in the fourfold canonical Gospel is not a neutral one but is valid only within the context of the "holy catholic church" — the social reality of which is acknowledged every time the Apostles' Creed is recited. Outside this context, other gospels can continue to flourish, and there is no historical reason to overlook them. While it is conventional to date the four canonical Gospels to the first century and the noncanonical ones to no earlier than the second, it is a mistake to assume that canonicity is tied up with historically demonstrable early datings; as a matter of fact, it is not clear that the *Gospel of Thomas* must have been written substan-

19. I assume that Mark 13:2 is *vaticinium ex eventu* (after-the-fact prophecy).

20. J. D. G. Dunn has recently argued that an "oral paradigm" should be substituted for the "literary paradigm" in the study of the Synoptics. See Dunn, *Christianity in the Making*, vol. 1, *Jesus Remembered* (Grand Rapids: Eerdmans, 2003), pp. 173-254. While Dunn may be right, lack of evidence makes it impossible to *know* whether he is right.

tially later than John or even Luke. The selection of four out of a multiplicity of gospels can be justified only on theological grounds internal to the church's faith. From this standpoint, it can be argued that it was theologically appropriate to include Luke or John in the canonical collection and to pass over *Thomas* or the *Protevangelium of James.* Although the fourfold canonical Gospel rests on the church's collective decision, that decision should not be understood as a mere historical accident or as an authoritarian ruling lacking a theological rationale.

Four, Not Three

Within the church, there are therefore four Gospels, not five (or more); and it is also important that there are four Gospels and not three. Historical Jesus research normally gives priority to the Synoptic Gospels and finds little in the Gospel of John that is usable for its purposes. It is in the Fourth Gospel that we seem to be furthest removed from empirical historical reality — although it should be emphasized that this telling of Jesus' story presupposes much the same set of historical and geographical coordinates as the others. This Gospel seems to derive from a time and place in which Jesus' actual patterns of speech have become no more than distant echoes. Instead, the Johannine Jesus speaks a distinctive language of his own, in which the central theme is his own total identification with God:

> The words that I speak to you I speak not on my own authority, but the Father who dwells in me performs his works. (John 14:10)

> I came from the Father and have come into the world; again, I am leaving the world and going to the Father. (John 16:28)

In this vertical, Godward emphasis, the evangelist discloses what is most fundamentally at stake in the story of Jesus in all its canonical retellings. In the Gospels, Jesus' story unfolds as it must on the horizontal, historical plane; and yet, if it is to have any final and ultimate significance, it must also be presented as the point of intersection between the horizontal and the vertical.[21] Jesus' life must be seen in its totality as God's act. In the life

21. This image is derived from Barth's *Römerbrief.* Commenting on "Jesus Christ our Lord" in Rom 1:4, Barth writes: "In diesem Namen begegnen und trennen sich zwei Welten,

of Jesus, it is God who is the agent no less than Jesus, and God's act is both complex, in that it incorporates all of Jesus' words and works, and simple, in that it is oriented toward a single goal: the salvation of humankind. It is the entire life of Jesus, from beginning to end, that is summed up in the statement that "God loved the world like this [οὕτως, *houtōs*] — that he gave his only Son, so that whoever believes in him might have eternal life" (John 3:16). Here the life of Jesus is set within its own proper context, originating as it does in the God whose love takes the concrete form of an act of giving, and intending as it does the incorporation of humankind within the eternal divine life. The Gospel of John differs from the Synoptics precisely because of its single-minded attempt to disclose the final theological context within which Jesus' life is set. To that end, even the *ipsissima verba* of the historical Jesus can be sacrificed.[22]

---

schneiden sich zwei Ebenen, eine bekannte und eine unbekannte. Die bekannte ist die von Gott herausgefallene und darum erlösungsbedürftige Welt des 'Fleisches,' die Welt des Menschen, der Zeit und der Dinge, unsre Welt. Diese bekannte Ebene wird geschnitten von einer andern unbekannten, von der Welt des Vaters, der Welt der ursprünglichen Schöpfung und endlichen Erlösung. Aber diese Beziehung zwischen uns und Gott, zwischen dieser Welt und der Welt Gottes will erkannt sein. Das Sehen der Schnittlinie zwischen beiden ist nicht selbstverständlich. — Der Punkt der Schnittlinie, wo sie zu sehen ist und gesehen wird, ist Jesus, Jesus von Nazareth, der 'historische' Jesus . . ." [In this name two worlds meet and go apart, two planes intersect, the one known and the other unknown. The known plane is God's creation, fallen out of its union with Him, and therefore the world of the 'flesh' needing redemption, the world of men, and of time, and of things — our world. This known plane is intersected by another plane that is unknown — the world of the Father, of the Primal Creation, and of the final Redemption. The relation between us and God, between this world and [God's] world, presses for recognition, but the line of intersection is not self-evident. The point on the line of intersection at which the relation becomes observable and observed is Jesus, Jesus of Nazareth, the historical Jesus.] Barth, *Der Römerbrief* (Munich: Chr. Kaiser, 1922), p. 5; ET, *The Epistle to the Romans*, trans. E. C. Hoskyns (London: Oxford University Press, 1933), p. 29. Incidentally, T. S. Eliot seems to derive the phrase "The point of intersection of the timeless / With time" ("The Dry Salvages," V, ll. 18-19) from Hoskyns's English rendering of Barth's imagery here: " . . . the point at which the hidden line, intersecting time and eternity . . . becomes visible" (p. 29).

22. See the still-insightful discussion in E. C. Hoskyns, *The Fourth Gospel*, vol. 1, ed. F. N. Davey (London: Faber & Faber, 1940), pp. 65-92. The evangelist "insist[s] that the tradition . . . has a meaning peering out of it at every point, a meaning which is 'beyond history,' and which alone makes sense of history. To disclose this underlying meaning of the tradition he wrote his gospel. The freedom with which he did so is nothing less than staggering to us who have been brought up within the strait fetters of the 'Historical Method,' who have almost completely lost the sense for the Problem of Theology, which is to set forth the

The Spirit of Truth

As we have seen, the theologically significant Jesus is the Jesus whose reception by his first followers is definitively articulated in the fourfold Gospel narrative. Yet Jesus is ultimately significant for us only if we believe this canonical testimony to be true, and we must therefore consider how the testimony itself enables us to reflect on the question of its own truthfulness. It does not encourage us to identify its theological truth-content simply with its empirical historical veracity. At point after point, the Gospel narratives cannot be satisfactorily harmonized, and this is a result of each evangelist's decision to retell the story of Jesus in his own way, without being constrained by his predecessors. A degree of noncorrespondence to empirical reality is, as it were, built into the fourfold testimony from the outset — for the very good reason that the story it tells is not concerned with a purely empirical reality but with God and God's saving action in the world. In Johannine language, the demonstration of its truth lies not in our own power but in the power of the "Spirit of truth," the divine revelatory dynamic immanent within the Christ event and its aftermath. That is simply to say that the promise of the Spirit is not marginal to the story that the Gospels tell. The promise does not only relate to the story of the church — as though the Spirit were the protagonist in the story of the church just as Jesus is the protagonist of the Gospels, as though Jesus and the Spirit were independent agents. Rather, the coming of the Spirit of truth is — from a Johannine perspective — the precondition for grasping and being grasped by the truth incarnated in the Gospel story. The story intends its own recognition as a true story, as the truth itself. The revelatory dynamic that occasioned the first tellings and retellings of this story continues to secure a hearing for it. We do not find out the truth, from our own resources; rather, the truth finds us.

* * *

The "quest" continues to make a necessary and important contribution to the critical study of the Gospels. It is an antidote to the docetism for which

---

nonhistorical truth that underlies all history. . . . We continually demand that an evangelist should narrate nothing but observable history, which means that we are demanding of him that he should not be an evangelist" (p. 90).

Jesus exists only in textual form; it makes the process of reception visible as such. And yet it suffers from a tendency to identify the products of its own interpretative paradigm with reality itself: the real Jesus is simply and solely the historical Jesus, and all else is just pious fantasy. As a result, it tends toward a kind of de facto atheism. Even from a historical point of view, however, it is not at all easy to detach Jesus from his first followers. Their reception of him is also his impact on them. The concrete traits of the historical Jesus belong *within* an account of the "historic, biblical Christ" and should not be allowed to take on an independent life of their own. The distinction is inevitable, but it exists only in order to be transcended. The Gospels assume that we are to speak not of Jesus alone but of Jesus in relation to God and of God in relation to Jesus; and there is no good reason not to take that assumption seriously.

The Testimony of the Biblical Witnesses

The Embodiment of God's Will: Jesus in Matthew

Dale C. Allison Jr.

Titles

How does one explicate Jesus' identity in Matthew?[1] It is perhaps natural to look initially at the titles given to Jesus in Matthew's story, for they would seem to be an easy way of saying much with little effort. The title "Messiah" places Jesus within a sacred history and makes him its culmination. "Lord" sets him above all others and calls forth obedience. "Son of Man" directs informed readers to Daniel 7 and assigns Jesus a central role in the eschatological drama.

Yet approaching Jesus' identity through titles has its drawbacks. For one thing, these titles, which come from Judaism, tend to be multivalent. They do not have constant content in Jewish literature, so their traditional connotations are imprecise. They are likewise elastic in Matthew, their exact significance not always manifest. "Son (of God)," for example, seems in some places in Matthew first to refer to Jesus' special, indeed unique relationship with God the Father: so 11:25-27. In other places it recalls Israel's status as God's "son." This is how it functions in chapter 2, where "out of Egypt have I called my son" no longer concerns Israel exiting Egypt but Jesus returning to Palestine. In still other places "Son" is connected with the messianic promise to David: so 16:13-20, where the prophecy that the

1. Portions of this essay are drawn from material previously published in Dale C. Allison Jr., *The New Moses: A Matthean Typology* (Minneapolis: Fortress, 1993) and *Studies in Matthew: Interpretation Past and Present* (Grand Rapids: Baker Academic/Baker Publishing Group, 2005). Permission granted.

builder of the temple will be God's "son" lies behind Peter's confession, as well as 26:57-68, the trial before the Sanhedrin. And in 27:43 it recalls nothing so much as the suffering righteous one of Wisdom 2.

Another problem with titles is that all of the proposed equations, including Jesus = the Messiah, Jesus = the Son of Man, and Jesus = the Son of God, are one-sided; that is, they are not really equations. Jesus redefines and enlarges and so transforms the titles more than he conforms to them. The Gospel of Matthew is not a discourse on titles but a sort of biography: it is about a person whose story is the context and content for all the appellations he draws to himself. This is one reason there are so many titles; no one label can capture Jesus' identity. Indeed, the number and variety of titles exalt Jesus, communicate his transcendent character, and imply the failure of speech to capture its elusive object. It is a general rule in ancient texts: the more titles, the more honor, and the more mystery. Greek literature often uses "many-named" (πολυώνυμος, *poluōnumos*) of the gods. The hymn in *Apocalypse of Abraham* 17 lists over three dozen names and attributes for God. A Samaritan source, *Memar Marqah* 5.4, refers to the "twenty names" of Moses.[2] And so it is in Matthew: there are so many titles because each one is in itself inadequate.[3]

A third problem with focusing upon titles is that we thereby miss much that is christologically significant. For example, between the infancy narrative and the passion narrative, Jesus works many miracles. These cannot be marginal events for the evangelist, who emphasizes that he offers us only a sample (4:23-25; 9:35–10:1, 8; etc.). No one title, however, is consistently associated with miracles. In one miracle story Jesus is "the Son of God" (14:33), in another "the Son of Man" (12:8), in another "the Son of David" (9:27), in another "Lord" (8:6). There is no consistent correlation between the doing of miracles and any particular title. So concentration on titles is an inadequate entry into this aspect of Jesus' identity.

In sum, titles in and of themselves do not give us Jesus. Matthew's Christology is rather "in the whole story," and because Matthew "portrays Jesus by means of a story no one category — teacher, healer, Wisdom in-

2. Isho'dad of Merv knows a tradition that Jesus has fully fifty-two names; see his *Commentary on Matthew* at Matt 1:23 (HSem 6:24, trans. M. D. Gibson, 5:14).

3. This is one reason why we should refrain from ranking titles in the order of their importance, or seeking the most important one, something modern Matthean scholars have sometimes attempted. I note, however, that Gregory of Nyssa, in *On Perfection*, does precisely that with the christological titles in Paul.

carnate, triumphant Son of man, not even Kyrios or Son of God — is adequate to contain that Jesus reverenced by the Church, the Jesus on whom Matthew reflects in his book."[4] And no title, it should be emphasized, refers to either the crucifixion or the resurrection.

Parallels

One advantage most of the titles do have is that they separate Jesus from everyone else. There can be only one "Son of Man" and only one "Lord," and Jesus is clearly "the Son of God" in a way that separates him from other "sons of God." Yet Jesus' uniqueness does not, for Matthew, mean that he cannot be usefully compared with others. Just as Plutarch in his biographies sets famous Greeks beside famous Romans, and just as Gregory of Nyssa likens his sister Macrina to the pagan sage Socrates and the Christian saint Thecla, so Matthew illuminates Jesus by likening him to other heroes.

Jesus and Moses

The Gospel displays a striking Moses typology.[5] It is especially strong in the infancy narrative and in the Sermon on the Mount, where Jesus sets his word over against things Moses said (5:21-48). Indeed, the Gospel begins by replaying the plot of the exodus:

- Israel's deliverer is born (1:18-25; cf. Exod 2:1-2).
- A wicked king sits upon the throne (2:1-15; cf. Exod 1:8-14).
- That king slaughters Jewish infants (2:16; cf. Exod 1:15-22).
- The hero's years after infancy go unrecounted.
- He passes through the waters (3:13-17; cf. Exod 14:21-31).
- He goes into the desert (4:1; cf. Exod 15:22ff.).
- He stays there for a period of time marked by forty units (4:2; cf. Exod 16:35).

4. David Hill, "In Quest of Matthean Christology," *Irish Biblical Studies* 8 (1986): 140.
5. In addition to what follows, see Allison, *New Moses.*

- Temptation comes in the form of hunger and idolatry (4:3-4, 8-10; cf. Exod 16:2-8; 32).
- The deliverer goes up on a mountain (5:1; cf. Exodus 19).
- We learn the commandments (5–7; cf. Exodus 20–23).

The Moses typology is also clearly present in the narrative of the transfiguration (17:1-8).[6] Jesus' face shines like the sun (17:2), as does Moses' face in Exodus 34:29-35. A bright cloud appears and a voice speaks from it (17:5; cf. Exod 24:15-18; 34:5). The onlookers — a special group of three (17:1; cf. Exod 24:1) — are afraid (17:6; cf. Exod 34:29-30). And all of this takes place on a mountain (17:1; cf. Exod 24:12, 15-18; 34:2-4) and "six days later" (17:1; cf. Exod 24:16). Moreover, Moses and Elijah, who converse with the transfigured Jesus, are the only figures in the Old Testament who speak with God on Mount Sinai/Horeb, so their presence together makes us think of that mountain. When the divine voice instructs the hearers to listen to Jesus, informed readers will infer that Jesus is the prophet like Moses foretold in Deuteronomy 18:15, 18 ("him you will listen to").

Even without introducing additional texts where Jesus is like Moses, enough has been said to indicate that we should not relegate the Moses typology to the periphery of Matthew's concerns. This typology, while never explicit, is nonetheless prominent. What is its function? No simple answer suffices. Both Moses and Jesus are many things, and they occupy several common offices. Moses is the paradigmatic prophet-king, the Messiah's model, a worker of miracles, the giver of Torah, the mediator for Israel, and a suffering servant. And Jesus is similarly a suffering servant, the mediator for Israel, the giver of Torah, a worker of miracles, the Mosaic Messiah, and the eschatological prophet-king. It would be error to isolate any one common function or title and promote it as the raison d'être for Matthew's Moses typology. The truth is more expansive than that.

One additional point about Matthew's Moses typology: too often the parallels between Jesus and Moses have been neglected in favor of focus on the differences. This may work with the Gospel of John, where the polemical edge in the comparison is undeniable, but it does not work with Matthew. In the First Gospel, Jesus' superiority to Moses is not argued. Rather,

6. Cf. David Friedrich Strauss, *The Life of Jesus Critically Examined* (Philadelphia: Fortress, 1972), pp. 544-45.

it is simply assumed. The paragraphs of 5:21-48 do, to be sure, demand more than Moses demanded, and 11:25-30 makes Jesus, not Moses, the chief mediator between God and his people. There is, however, no explicit diminishing of Moses. The parallels, which serve several functions, both literary and theological, should not be played down or deconstructed because of an anxiety to exalt Jesus over Moses. Such anxiety is not Matthew's concern, and so it makes a poor presupposition for exegesis. Our evangelist does not suffer from any Second Temple inferiority complex: it is Jesus, not Moses, who is unquestionably Lord. Matthew takes for granted, without need for argument, that just as Jesus is greater than the temple and greater than Jonah and greater than Solomon and greater than David (12:6, 41-42; 22:41-46), so too is he greater than Moses. Such is Matthew's quiet confidence, within which confidence he constructs his Moses typology. To understand him aright, then, we must follow his lead and put the emphasis where he puts it, and that is on the parallels.

Jesus and David

If Jesus resembles the lawgiver, he also resembles the greatest of Israel's kings, David. The David typology is much less prominent than the Moses typology, but there is no doubting its presence. Matthew 26:30 informs us that when the Last Supper was over, Jesus and his disciples sang "the hymn" and went out to the Mount of Olives. The geographical notice takes us back to 2 Samuel 15:30, where David, who is being plotted against by his trusted royal counselor, Ahithophel, leaves Jerusalem and goes up "the ascent of the Mount of Olives." There the king weeps and prays for deliverance (15:31), just as Jesus does in Gethsemane. The parallels between the two narratives may be set out this way:

- The subject is betrayal (26:23-25, 45-46; cf. 2 Sam 15:31).
- The one being betrayed is Israel's Davidic king.
- The place is the Mount of Olives (26:30; cf. 2 Sam 15:30).
- The hero is deeply disturbed (26:37-38; cf. 2 Sam 15:30).
- The hero prays for deliverance (26:39-44; cf. 2 Sam 15:31).
- It is night (26:20; cf. 2 Sam 17:16, 22).
- The betrayer comes to a bad end by hanging himself (27:3-5; cf. 2 Sam 17:23).

That Matthew intends the parallelism follows from the language of 27:3-10. Just as Ahithophel, the companion and friend of David (Ps 55:12-14; *m. ʿAbot* 6:3), went and hanged himself (ἀπῆλθεν . . . ἀπήγξατο, *apēlthen . . . apēnxato,* 2 Sam 17:23 LXX), so Judas, one of the twelve and Jesus' "friend" (Matt 26:50), likewise went and hanged himself (ἀπελθὼν ἀπήγξατο, *apelthōn apēnxato,* 27:5). One should further note in the Gospel accounts of the Last Supper the resonance with Psalm 41:9 — "Even my bosom friend in whom I trusted, who ate of my bread, has lifted his heel against me." Jewish tradition made the speaker of the psalm David and the friend Ahithophel (*b. Sanh.* 106b). Mark's account indeed refers the psalm to Jesus' betrayal (Mark 14:18), and the Fourth Gospel explicitly cites it in the same connection (John 13:18). Clearly, there was a tradition of likening David's betrayal and betrayer to Jesus' betrayal and betrayer.

Unlike the Moses typology, Matthew's David typology does have its correlate in a title, "the Son of David." The way that title is used, especially in the book's opening section, shows that royal connotations are to the fore. The genealogy in 1:1-17 is a royal genealogy, and "David" is its key term, occurring as it does at the beginning (1:1), in the middle (1:6), and at the end (1:17). To be the Son of David is to be Israel's king.[7]

Jesus' status as king is prominent in Matthew, and it unites much of Matthean theology. The "kingdom of God" is "his" (i.e., Jesus') kingdom (13:41). As the Son of Man who sits on his throne, he will judge and rule (19:28; 25:31, 34, 40; the last two verses call Jesus "king"). Jesus enters Jerusalem as its king (21:5) and is crucified as "King of the Jews" (27:11, 29, 37, 42). Even the Moses typology can be related to Jesus' status as king, for Jewish tradition held Moses to be a king (Philo, *Life of Moses* 1.148-49; *Mek.* on Exod 18:14).

While Jesus fulfills the Davidic covenant, at the same time he rewrites popular notions of kingship. He enters Jerusalem not on a war horse but on a donkey (21:5). Nor otherwise does he possess many of the accoutrements of royal office. In fact, the one coronation scene in Matthew is a

7. The genealogy may contain a wordplay on David's name, which in Hebrew has three consonants, the numerical value of which amounts to fourteen: d + w + d = 4 + 6 + 4 = 14. Does Matt 1:1-17 have 3 × 14 generations because David's name has three consonants whose sum is fourteen? Wordplays like this, known to the rabbis as gematria, were practiced in both Jewish and Christian circles close to Matthew's time (note Rev 13:18). In this genealogy of 3 × 14 generations, the one name with three consonants and a value of fourteen is also placed in the fourteenth spot, is mentioned three times, and is given the title "King."

mock coronation. In 27:27-31, the soldiers of the governor put a scarlet robe upon Jesus' shoulders, a crown of thorns upon his head, and a reed into his right hand; and kneeling before him, they hail him "King of the Jews."

Matthew depicts a king who does not fully exercise his sovereignty. Indeed, he seems to abdicate all of his power in the passion narrative, where he refuses to call angelic armies to his aid (26:53). This is apparent from his very posture. Before the passion narrative, and in line with his royal status throughout the Gospel, Jesus sits — that is, takes the position of authority and rest (5:1; 13:2; 15:29; 21:7; 24:3; 25:31). But after the Last Supper, he no longer sits. Instead, others sit — disciples (26:36), Peter (26:58, 69), guards (and evidently the high priest, 26:58, 62), Pilate (27:19), the soldiers at the cross (27:36). Jesus now falls to the ground (26:39), stands (27:11), and hangs from a cross (27:35). His posture during the passion reflects his temporary renunciation of authority and the lack of all comfort. The king has become the Suffering Servant of Isaiah (cf. Matt 8:17; 12:17-21).

Jesus' kingship is very strange, for it manifests itself as a sort of abdication (cf. 26:53, where he declines to call his army to his own defense). One might, however, make the theological case that his refusal to defeat his enemies with force, indeed his willingness to suffer at their hands, is a fulfillment of his own imperative to imitate God (5:48). God's own activity in the world is such that Isaiah could declare, "Truly you are a God who hides yourself" (Isa 45:15). It is certainly true that God, to all appearances, lets the freedom of the creation run riot with evil. For those who do not believe, the elusiveness or passivity of the Deity, God's apparent delight in the game of hide-and-seek, is a stumbling block, a cause for espousing deism or atheism. But maybe Matthew's Jesus encourages us to think of God's apparent passivity and silence as manifestations of an uncircumscribed love. "Love is longsuffering," or, as the King James Version has it, love "beareth all things [and] endureth all things" (1 Cor 13:7). Simone Weil once urged that "love is abdication."[8] Is this a possible reading of Jesus' kingship during his earthly ministry, especially in the passion narrative?

8. Simone Weil, *La Connaissance surnaturelle* (Paris: Gallimard, 1950), p. 267: "L'Amour consent à tout et ne commande qu'à ceux qui y consentent. L'Amour est abdication. Dieu est abdication." [Love assents to all and orders only those who assent to it. Love is abdication. God is abdication.]

Jesus and John the Baptist

There are a number of striking parallels in Matthew between Jesus and John the Baptist; they clearly belong to an editorial strategy:

John	*Jesus*
"Repent, for the kingdom of heaven is at hand" (3:2).	"Repent, for the kingdom of heaven is at hand" (4:17).
to Pharisees: "You brood of vipers" (3:7).	to Pharisees: "You brood of vipers" (12:34).
"Every tree therefore that does not bear good fruit is cut down and thrown into the fire" (3:10).	"Every tree that does not bear good fruit is cut down and thrown into the fire" (7:19).
John is rejected by "this generation" (11:16-19).	Jesus is rejected by "this generation" (11:16-19).
Herod the tetrarch is responsible for John's death.	Pilate the governor is responsible for Jesus' death.
John is seized (κρατέω, 14:3).	Jesus is seized (κρατέω, 21:46; etc.).
John is bound (δέω, 14:3).	Jesus is bound (δέω, 27:2).
Herod fears the crowds because they think John a prophet (14:5).	The chief priests and Pharisees fear the crowds because they think Jesus a prophet (21:46).
Herod is asked by another to execute John and is grieved so to do (14:6-11).	Pilate is asked by others to execute Jesus and is reluctant so to do (27:11-26).
John is buried by his disciples (14:12).	Jesus is buried by a disciple (27:57-61).

The comparison of the Baptist and Jesus was traditional; it occurs outside of Matthew (e.g., in the extensive parallels between the infancies of John and Jesus in Luke 1–2). Indeed, some sort of comparison goes back to Jesus himself, as Matthew 11:16-19 par. Luke 7:31-35 shows. But why does Matthew augment this theme? Two possibilities suggest themselves. First, John was remembered as a great prophet, as the greatest "among those born of women" (11:11), so to liken Jesus to him is perhaps to lend some of John's prophetic renown to Jesus. Second, Matthew is fond of writing up events so that they foreshadow his passion narrative, and most of the parallels just noted anticipate the Gospel's denouement. In part, then, we have here one thread in a larger literary pattern. In Matthew, the end is not confined to the ending. It rather appears throughout and thus precedes itself, so that its import cannot be missed.

Jesus and the Disciples

Matthew goes out of his way to demonstrate that the disciples around Jesus emulate their Lord in numerous particulars; his concern for showing parallels with other figures of faith thus includes both the likeness *of* Jesus to those who preceded him and the likeness *to* Jesus of those who follow him. Chapter 10 alone offers the following parallels:

The Disciples	*Jesus*
They are to heal every disease and every infirmity (10:1).	Jesus heals every disease and every infirmity (4:23).
They are to preach that "the kingdom of heaven is at hand" (10:7).	Jesus preaches that "the kingdom of heaven is at hand" (4:17).
They are to raise the dead (10:8).	Jesus raises the dead (9:18-26; 11:5).
They are to heal lepers (10:8).	Jesus heals lepers (11:5).
They are to cast out demons (10:8).	Jesus casts out demons (9:32-33).
They are to go not to the Samaritans but to the lost sheep of Israel (10:5-6).	Jesus has been sent only to the lost sheep of Israel (15:24).
They will be handed over to sanhedrins (10:17).	Jesus is handed over to the Sanhedrin (26:57-68).
They will be dragged before governors (10:18).	Jesus is taken before the governor (27:1-26).
They will be called Beelzebul (10:25).	Jesus is called Beelzebul (10:25; cf. 9:34).

What do these correlations imply? If the disciples are to imitate Jesus, the thought that others should follow their lead and do likewise lies very near to hand. One can accordingly take the phrase in 28:20, "all that I have commanded you," to be all-encompassing: the reference is not just to the Sermon on the Mount or to Jesus' speech in general but to his life in its totality. His person is a command; that is, the virtues he speaks and embodies must be mirrored by his followers. If Jesus demands the perfect imitation of God (5:48), he himself is the narrative's outstanding instance of such imitation, "the pioneer and perfecter of our faith" (Heb 12:2). Matthew implies the imperative that Ignatius delivers: "Be imitators of Jesus Christ, as he was of his Father" (*Epistle to the Philadelphians* 7.2). Matthew would also have agreed with Origen:

> Christ is set forth as an example to all believers. As he ever chose the good, even before he knew the evil at all, and loved righteousness and hated iniquity, . . . so, too, should each one of us, after a fall or an error, purify himself from stains by the example set before him, and taking a leader for the journey proceed along the steep path of virtue, so that by this means we may as far as is possible become, through our imitation of him, partakers of the divine nature, as it is written, "Whoever says that he believes in Christ should also walk even as he walked." (*On First Principles* 4.4.4)[9]

Word and Deed

The parallels between Jesus and his disciples in Matthew imply that Jesus is a moral model. The same conclusion follows from the multitude of obvious connections between Jesus' words and his deeds. If Jesus indirectly exhorts others to be meek ("Blessed are the meek," 5:5), he himself is such ("I am meek and lowly of heart," 11:29; cf. 21:5). If he enjoins mercy ("Blessed are the merciful," 5:7), he himself is merciful ("Have mercy upon us, Son of David," 9:27; cf. 15:22; 20:30). If he congratulates those oppressed for God's cause ("Blessed are those persecuted for righteousness' sake," 5:10), he himself suffers and dies innocently (Pilate asks, "What evil has he done?" 27:23). Origen perceived this long ago: "Jesus confirms all of the beatitudes

9. Origen, *On First Principles*, trans. G. W. Butterworth (Gloucester, Mass.: Peter Smith, 1973), p. 319, alt.

that he speaks in the Gospel, and he justifies his own teaching through his own example" (*Homilies on Luke* 38.1).

What we find in the Beatitudes runs throughout the Gospel. Jesus demands faithfulness to the law of Moses ("Think not that I have come to abolish the law or the prophets . . . ," 5:17-20) and faithfully keeps that law during his ministry (cf. 8:4: "Show yourself to the priest, and offer the gift that Moses commanded"). He recommends self-denial in the face of evil ("If anyone strikes you on the right cheek, turn to him the other also," 5:39) and does not resist the evils done to him ("They spat in his face and struck him, and some slapped him," 26:67; cf. 27:30). He calls for private prayer ("When you pray, go into your room and shut the door and pray to your Father who is in secret," 6:6) and subsequently withdraws to a mountain to pray alone ("He went up into the hills by himself to pray," 14:23). Jesus, moreover, advises his followers to use certain words in prayer ("Thy kingdom come, thy will be done," 6:10), and he uses those words in Gethsemane ("If this cannot pass unless I drink it, thy will be done," 26:42). He rejects the service of mammon ("Do not store up treasure upon the earth," 6:19), and he lives without concern for money ("The Son of Man has nowhere to lay his head," 8:20). He commands believers to carry crosses ("If anyone would come after me, let him deny himself, and take up his cross, and follow me," 16:24), and he does so himself (Pilate "delivered him to be crucified," 27:26). One could go on and on in this vein, citing instances of Jesus acting in accord with his speech.

In all of this Matthew is following Hellenistic tradition, which so stresses the need for teachers to live what they preach. Socrates is of course here the great model: his speech is as his life. But the motif is transferred to others. Philo for his part gives the palm to Moses (*Life of Moses* 1.29). Matthew gives it to Jesus, who exhibits the antithesis of hypocrisy, namely, congruity between word and deed. He preaches what he does and lives his own words, in order the better to recommend those words. He is his own halakah.

As animate law, Jesus is the fulfillment of God's will, Torah incarnate. This implies that his behavior is programmatic and exemplary. The Son of God first does what he asks others to do, and his character is legislation. He is, to quote Irenaeus, a consistent "example of piety, righteousness, and submission" (*Against Heresies* 2.22.4). If Aristotle regards the "good man" as the "canon" in ethics (*Nicomachean Ethics* 3.4), Matthew considers Jesus the "canon" of Christian morality. Jesus lives as he speaks and speaks as he lives. Matthew implies what Gregory of Nyssa says, that "the marks of the true

Christian are all those we know in connection with Christ. Those that we have room for we imitate, and those which our nature does not approximate by imitation, we reverence and worship" (*On Perfection*, PG 46:256C).[10]

The Coincidence of Opposites

The identity of Matthew's Jesus embraces paradoxical oppositions. When Jesus is conceived, his well-being is put in jeopardy when Joseph resolves to divorce Mary (1:18-25). Then, when he is born, the wicked king Herod wants to kill him (2:3-18). Later on, the Savior has nowhere to lay his head (8:20), and people mock him as a glutton and drunkard (11:19). Some say he is in league with Beelzebul and his demons (12:24). Respected leaders dispute his teachings and denigrate his behavior (9:2-8; 12:1-14), and his message falls upon many deaf ears (11:20-24; 13:1-17, 54-58). His forerunner, John the Baptist, is arrested, imprisoned, and beheaded (14:3-12). Eventually, one of his own companions betrays him to his enemies (26:14-16, 47-56). The other companions, in the hour of his greatest need, flee — all except one, who then denies even knowing him (26:56, 69-75). Jesus is the victim of false witnesses and unfair legal proceedings (26:57-68). Further, the crowds, once full of cheers, now demand his crucifixion and mock him (27:22-23, 39-40), while pagan soldiers, after slapping and whipping him, nail him to their most shameful and horrible instrument of torture (27:27-31, 35). He utters a cry of despair and dies in darkness (27:45-50). The first has become last.

But there is also the other side. This tormented human being who fails to bring Israel to repentance is the very same person who, as an infant, is delivered by God from his enemies (2:1-23). Later, at his baptism and subsequently his transfiguration, the Divinity is not hidden but speaks to him directly: "This is my Son, the Beloved, with whom I am well pleased" (3:17; cf. 17:5). This individual is, moreover, victorious over the devil, and demons obey his commands (4:1-11, 24; 8:28-34; 12:25-29). Angels wait upon him (4:11), and miracles proliferate. The blind see; the lame walk; celebration abounds (9:14-17; 11:1-6). All things have been handed over to the Son by the Father, for which he gives thanks (11:25-27). Jesus goes up on a mountain and there talks with Moses and Elijah; and — as though in an-

10. On the passages where word and deed do not seem to be in harmony, see Allison, *Studies in Matthew*, pp. 237-49.

ticipation of the end, when the saints will shine like the sun (Dan 12:2-3) — he is transformed: his face shines (17:1-8). When he afterward enters Jerusalem, crowds sing his praises (21:1-11). So too do children in the temple (21:15). And if he suffers torture, it is not long before he triumphantly returns to his bereft friends, having broken the bonds of death and entered into a new, heavenly existence. As if that were not enough, he receives "all authority in heaven and on earth" (28:18). The last has become first and can now comfort the distraught: "I am with you always, to the end of the age" (28:20). This is the happiest ending anyone could imagine.

Jesus' status as the coincidence of opposites is nicely illustrated by putting Matthew's transfiguration and crucifixion accounts side by side. The two narratives are twins of a sort. The disciples at the transfiguration are terrified (17:6), as are the centurion and those with him when they see the miraculous signs attendant upon the crucifixion (27:54). Only in these two places does Matthew say that people were "exceedingly afraid" (the Greek is exactly the same: ἐφοβήθησαν σφόδρα, *ephobēthēsan sphodra*). The link is small, but it prods one to observe that also common to the transfiguration and the crucifixion are the confession of Jesus as God's "Son" (17:5; 27:54) and the presence of three named onlookers (17:1, three male disciples: Peter, James, and John; 27:55-56, three female disciples: Mary Magdalene, Mary the mother of James and Joseph, and the mother of the sons of Zebedee). Moreover, these shared features exist in the midst of dramatic contrasts:

The Transfiguration	*The Crucifixion*
Jesus taking others (17:1)	Jesus taken by others (27:27)
Elevation on mountain (17:1)	Elevation on cross (27:35)
Private epiphany (17:1)	Public spectacle (27:39)
Light (17:2)	Darkness (27:45)
Garments illumined (17:2)	Garments stripped off (27:28, 35)
Jesus glorified (17:2ff.)	Jesus shamed (27:27ff.)
Elijah appearing (17:3)	Elijah not appearing (27:45-50)
Two saints beside Jesus (17:3)	Two criminals beside Jesus (27:38)
God confessing Jesus (17:5)	God abandoning Jesus (27:46)
Reverent prostration (17:6)	Mocking prostration (27:29)

Between Matthew 17:1-8 and 27:27-56 there is a curious confluence of similar motifs and contrasting images. We have here pictorial antithetical parallelism, something like a diptych in which the two plates have similar outlines but different colors. If one scene were sketched on a transparency and placed over the other, many of its lines would disappear.

Matthew's Jesus fascinates and inspires in part because his words and story give paradigmatic expression to the extreme polarities of human existence. He speaks about and suffers what human beings fear most — rejection, alienation from family and friends, misunderstanding, loneliness, doubt, torturous pain. And he speaks about and enjoys what human beings hope for most — happiness, wisdom, nearness to God, victory over death. The man of sorrows, acquainted with grief, with nowhere to lay his head, the man reviled as blasphemer, whose life ends in torture, darkness, and an agonizing question (27:46), is also the one who knows God's parental goodness, invites all to celebrate the presence of the divine utopia, and attains eternal life. The helpless man tortured on a cross is the resurrected Lord who has all authority in heaven and on earth.

Emmanuel

In Matthew 1:23, Jesus fulfills the oracle of Isaiah 7:14 and so is "Emmanuel." Matthew clarifies by adding words from Isaiah 8:8, 10: "with us is God." The gloss highlights Jesus' significance as the unique one in whom God's active presence, favor, blessing, and aid manifest themselves. This fulfills the promise that God will be especially "with" the saints in messianic times (Isa 43:5; Ezek 34:30; *Jub.* 1:17; Rev 21:3; etc.). While Matthew 1:23 does not seem to posit a preexistent being — the Son, who donned flesh — it does, in a more general sense, indicate that Jesus is the embodiment of the divine purpose and activity.

A related text appears in 18:20, which promises that where two or three are gathered in his name, Jesus is in their midst. This, as often noted, recalls a saying in the Mishnah: "But if two sit together and words of the Law [are spoken] between them, the Divine Presence [שׁכינה, *shekhinah*] rests between them . . ." (*m. 'Abot* 3:2; cf. 3:6; *Mek.* on Exod 20:24). Matthew 18:20 may indeed be a Christian reformulation of a traditional saying, in which case Jesus has been substituted for the Shekinah and so conceptualized as God's immanence.

Jesus is also the divine presence at the Gospel's conclusion, 28:16-20. Here he ends with the striking words, "I am with you always, even unto the end of the age." The speaker is like the ark of the covenant, where God dwells (Num 10:35-36), or like the Angel of the Lord, who fully represents God (Genesis 18–19), or like the Son of Man enthroned at God's right hand, whose rule is "everlasting" (Dan 7:13-14). Matthew would probably have been sympathetic with the ancient Christians who identified Jesus with God's "glory" (כבוד, *kavod* = δόξα, *doxa;* see, e.g., John 1:14 and Heb 1:3). The presence of the Deity is the presence of Jesus, and vice versa. It is fitting that Matthew's Gospel ends without Jesus ascending: the risen Lord remains with his people.

Matthew, however, does not confine Jesus' presence to the *ecclesia.* This is apparent from 25:31-46. If, as seems most likely, "the least of these my brothers" are the needy in general, so that doing good to them is doing good to Jesus himself,[11] then Jesus is "with" the suffering and the unfortunate just as he is with those who gather in his name.[12]

"Knowing" Jesus

The biographical nature of Matthew means that one comes to know Jesus first of all by reading the Gospel: the main character encounters us as we encounter the text. If the Gospel contains his words, his deeds, his story, then to know it is to begin to know him. Matthew further implies that we need to read other books too, those comprised in the Old Testament canon, because those books foreshadow, prophesy, and in so many other ways prepare for Jesus. Jesus without Moses and the prophets is not Matthew's Jesus.

But there is more to knowing Jesus than reading about him. For one thing, there is the church. Matthew twice speaks of the *ecclesia* (16:18; 18:17), of the community that knows Jesus' resurrected presence (18:20; 28:20). Although the First Gospel remains frustratingly sparse in what it tells us about this community, the church's presence is everywhere im-

11. See Arland J. Hultgren, *The Parables of Jesus: A Commentary* (Grand Rapids: Eerdmans, 2000), pp. 309-30.

12. Cf. Sarah Coakley, "The Identity of the Risen Jesus: Finding Jesus Christ in the Poor," in this volume.

plicit, and it is obvious that when followers come together for reading, prayer, baptism, and commemorating the Last Supper, Jesus is present with them. So he is known in and through the community that calls upon his name.

That, however, is not the end of the matter. Jesus again and again asks his opponents, "Have you not read?" — and of course they have, and that a thousand times (12:3, 5; 19:4; 21:16, 42; 22:31). Reading, then, is not enough. Nor is being in Jesus' presence enough, for throughout his ministry Jesus is in the midst of people who fail to perceive his real identity. What, then, is their perceptual problem? What do they lack?

The Sermon on the Mount is relentless in insisting that believers do what Jesus enjoins them to do, and that the consequences of not paying heed are catastrophic (7:24-27). One can even know much about Jesus and his wonder-working name and yet not be known by him (7:21-23). This is why reading without works is dead; so too belonging to a religious community. Epistemology and ethics are, for Matthew, inextricable. Without right conduct and purity of heart (5:8, 18-20), Jesus remains a stranger. Truly knowing him requires a certain sort of character and a certain sort of behavior. Indeed, this is so much the case that, at least in one Matthean passage, knowing is completely eclipsed by doing. In 25:31-46, those who enter into the glory of the Father fail to recognize the Savior's presence in the faces of the suffering; they learn the truth only at the eschatological judgment. So they are in Jesus' presence and carry out his will and yet, like Abraham entertaining angels unawares, know not what they do. Here ecclesiastical membership and book knowledge recede. When those at the right hand take care of the sick and clothe the needy and visit the prisoners, Jesus comes to them as one unknown, and only later do they find out who he is.[13] Clearly, to know Jesus truly is to know that what matters above all is doing God's will.

13. Does Matt 25:31-46 imply what we find in *t. Sanh.* 13.2, that "there must be righteous people among the heathen who have a share in the world to come" (cf. *Sifra* on Lev 18:5)? Cf. *Apocalypse of Sedrach* 14:5 ("There are nations that have no law, yet they fulfil thy law; they are not baptized but my divine Spirit enters them and they are converted to my baptism, and I receive them with my righteous ones into the bosom of Abraham"); Justin Martyr, *First Apology* 46.

Identity and Ambiguity in Markan Christology

Joel Marcus

The One and the Many

The identity of Jesus is the central theme in Mark's Gospel, as the evangelist makes clear from 1:1 on. In the very first verse, Mark announces that his subject is "the beginning of the good news of Jesus Christ"[1] — a designation perhaps not only for the first section of the Gospel (the prologue, which extends to 1:13 or 1:15) but also for the story as a whole. The situation may be analogous to that in the first book of the Old Testament, whose Hebrew title, בראשית *(ber'eshit),* "in the beginning," and Greek title, Γένεσις, *Genesis,* apply both to the first section (1:1–2:3 or 2:4) and to the whole work; it is a "book of beginnings." This understanding coheres with the possibility that the Gospel was intended to end at 16:8, with the empty tomb: "the *beginning* of the good news" is over on Easter morning, but "the good news of Jesus Christ" continues through the church that carries on his work through the Spirit he imparts (cf. 1:8).

The genitive Ἰησοῦ Χριστοῦ *(Iēsou Christou),* however, may be construed not only objectively ("the good news *about* Jesus") but also subjectively ("the good news that Jesus himself proclaims"): the Gospel is a message addressed to the Markan community by the risen Lord, speaking through the evangelist.[2] Already in the first verse, then, we see a hint of the

1. "Son of God" is probably not part of the original text; see Joel Marcus, *Mark 1–8: A New Translation with Introduction and Commentary,* AB 27 (New York: Doubleday, 2000), p. 141.

2. Cf. again 1:8, which implies Jesus' continued presence within the community. See

merger of Jesus' identity with that of faithful disciples who take up their crosses and follow him.

This overlap between Jesus and the disciples is presented in a variety of ways in the remainder of the Gospel. For example, both of the most frequent Markan titles for Jesus, "Son of Man" and "Son of God," have collective nuances in the Old Testament and/or intertestamental Judaism, as do the Shepherd of Zechariah 9–14, the Righteous Sufferer of the Psalms, and the Suffering Servant of Isaiah 52–53, all of which form significant background to the Markan passion narrative.[3] Moreover, various Markan passages, such as the call of the Twelve "to be with him" (3:14a), their commissioning to exercise the power Jesus bestows upon them (3:14b-15; 6:7-13), and the stories of miraculous feeding (6:30-45; 8:1-10), highlight the disciples' presence and active participation in Jesus' ministry.[4] As Jane Schaberg has pointed out, it is consonant with this participatory emphasis that each of the Markan passion predictions is followed by teaching on the subject of discipleship (8:31-38; 9:31-37; 10:32-45), as though the destiny of the Son of Man extends beyond himself to incorporate those who follow him.[5] Further, in the explanation of the parable of the sower, the Markan Jesus leaves the sower uninterpreted while allegorizing the parable's other main elements, the seed and the soils. The reason for this surprising interpretative reticence may be that the sower is meant to be understood as God, Jesus, and the Christian evangelist all rolled into one.[6]

Mark emphasizes, therefore, the important role played by disciples who are incorporated into Jesus' ministry, who thereby "enter into the

---

Marcus, *Mark 1–8*, pp. 146-47; Eugene Boring, "Mark 1:1-15 and the Beginning of the Gospel," *Semeia* 52 (1990): 71 n. 16.

3. See Joel Marcus, *The Way of the Lord: Christological Exegesis of the Old Testament in the Gospel of Mark* (Louisville/Edinburgh: Westminster John Knox/T&T Clark, 1992), ch. 8. See also Joel Marcus, "Son of Man as Son of Adam," *Revue biblique* 110 (2003): 38-61, 370-86, for the idea (already attested in the church Fathers) that "Son of Man" in the Gospels means "Son of Adam"; if this is right, then there is an organic connection between Jesus and the other children of Adam.

4. See Suzanne Henderson, *Christology and Discipleship in the Gospel of Mark*, SNTSMS 135 (Cambridge: Cambridge University Press, 2006).

5. Jane Schaberg, "Daniel 7,12 and the New Testament Passion-Resurrection Predictions," *New Testament Studies* 31 (1985): 208-22.

6. See Joel Marcus, "Blanks and Gaps in the Markan Parable of the Sower," *Biblical Interpretation* 5 (1997): 247-62.

royal power of God" (9:1, 47; 10:15, 23-25).[7] Though exegetes have laid proper stress on the negative features of the Markan disciples, this emphasis needs to be balanced with the recognition that their destiny as "fishers of people" rests not on their worthiness but upon Jesus' call (1:16-20), that in spite of everything they remain Jesus' chosen companions up until the end of the story, and that even their abandonment of Jesus there cannot annul his promise that after his resurrection they will be reunited with him in Galilee (14:27-28; 16:7).[8] The link between the identity of Jesus and that of his followers cannot be easily snapped — which is good news for the Markan community, and for later Christians as well.

After the first verse, Mark continues to highlight the issue of Jesus' identity through various rhetorical means. Among these, rhetorical questions beginning with τί (*ti*, "What . . . ?") or τίς (*tis*, "Who . . . ?") play a prominent role. For example, in the Gospel's first miracle story, the programmatic exorcism in the Capernaum synagogue, the demons call Jesus "the holy one of God" and imply his complete distinction from the demonic realm by shouting, "*What* do we have to do with you, Jesus the Nazarene? Have you come to destroy us?" (1:24). At the conclusion of this exorcism story, the human crowd in the synagogue echoes the demons' amazement at Jesus' power by exclaiming, "*What* is this? A new teaching with authority! He even gives orders to the unclean spirits, and they obey him!" (1:27). The emphasis in this programmatic story is therefore on the power that is manifesting itself through Jesus, on *what* he is doing; but this emphasis is inseparable from, and an early pointer toward, the question of *who* he is, as the conclusion of the later miracle story in 4:35-41 bears out. Here Jesus' disciples, having seen him demonstrate a godlike power over the storm, ask a rhetorical question that significantly alters the choral ending of the Capernaum exorcism: "*Who* then is this? — for even the wind and sea obey him!" Indeed, choral questions about Jesus' identity punctuate the entire first half of the Gospel (2:7; 5:7; 6:2; 8:4), thus piquing the reader's interest and preparing for the crucial inquiries in 8:27 and 8:29: "Who [τίνα, *tina*] do people say that I am? . . . But who [τίνα] do *you* say that I am?" Thereafter, the iterations of the who/what question subside, to

7. On the meaning of "enter[ing] into the βασιλεία τοῦ θεοῦ [*basileia tou theou*]," see Joel Marcus, "Entering into the Kingly Power of God," *Journal of Biblical Literature* 107 (1988): 663-75.

8. See Ernest Best, "The Role of the Disciples in Mark," *New Testament Studies* 23 (1977): 377-401.

be taken up in an altered form in the Gospel's second half by hostile authorities, who usually employ a different vocabulary (see 11:28; 14:61; 15:2).[9]

Son of David?

Another means by which Jesus' identity is revealed is a sort of boomerang effect from attempts at suppression. Someone "lets the cat out of the bag" and reveals an important aspect of Jesus' identity; others — sometimes including Jesus himself — tell that person to be silent. The rhetorical effect of such attempts at silencing, however, is not to squelch the estimate of Jesus that has been voiced but to highlight it.[10] In 1:44-45 and 7:36, for example, Jesus forbids publicity about his healings, but these commands are disobeyed and his fame becomes even more widespread. As H. J. Ebeling has shown,[11] these failed attempts reveal that Jesus' stature is so great that it cannot be hidden; paradoxically, then, the silencings serve the purpose of revelation (cf. 4:22).

In a similar way, blind Bartimaeus, upon hearing that Jesus is passing by, begins to shout, "Son of David! Jesus! Have mercy on me!" and is rebuked by the crowd (10:46-52). Some commentators, such as Werner Kelber, claim that "Son of David" is in Mark always a mistaken, inadequate estimate of Jesus, as is shown here by the fact that the person who voices it is *blind.* But probably Mark's point is the opposite: the spiritual vision of this blind man is keener than that of the bystanders who physically see.[12] Indeed, the reader is invited to adopt an attitude *opposite* to that of the squelching crowd and to admire the tenacity of the blind man who does not allow their rebuke to intimidate him but cries out all the more vehe-

9. Cf. Peter Müller, *"Wer ist dieser?" Jesus im Markusevangelium; Markus als Erzähler, Verkündiger und Lehrer,* BThSt 27 (Neukirchen-Vluyn: Neukirchener, 1995), p. 9.

10. Cf. Christopher M. Tuckett, ed., *The Messianic Secret,* IRT 1 (Philadelphia: Fortress, 1983), pp. 13-15.

11. Hans J. Ebeling, *Das Messiasgeheimnis und die Botschaft der Marcus-Evangelium,* BZNW 19 (Berlin: Töpelmann, 1939).

12. Cf. Morna Hooker, *The Gospel according to Saint Mark,* BNTC (Peabody, Mass.: Hendrickson, 1991), p. 253. Kelber points to Bartimaeus's use of *rabbouni* for Jesus in 10:51 as an indication of his inadequate Christology (cf. Peter's use of *rabbi* in 9:5), ignoring that Jesus praises Bartimaeus for his faith in the next verse. See Werner H. Kelber, *The Kingdom in Mark: A New Place and a New Time* (Philadelphia: Fortress, 1974), p. 95.

mently, "Son of David! Have mercy on me!" The triumphal entry story supports this interpretation, since there Mark evinces a positive attitude toward the Davidic expectation: the crowd hails Jesus, apparently rightly, as the one who restores "the coming dominion of our father David" (11:10). Similarly, in the case of Jesus' injunction to secrecy after Peter's confession of him as Messiah in 8:29, publicity is forbidden not because the estimate is mistaken but precisely because it is the truth, a point borne out by the positive uses of Χριστός *(Christos)* for Jesus from 1:1 on.

Kelber, however, is not completely wrong; Mark seems to have some ambivalence about Davidic messianism. I would not go as far as Theodore Weeden and Norman Perrin, who suggest that for Mark the title "Son of David"/"Messiah," like "Son of God," is always in need of correction by "Son of Man."[13] But the Markan text does at least once display reserve about the Davidic expectation, for in 12:35-37 Jesus himself raises the question of how the scribes can say that the Messiah is David's "son."

The more logical question is how they could *deny* it, since the Old Testament (e.g., Isa 11:1-5; Jer 23:5-6; 33:15; Ezek 34:23-24; 37:24; Zech 3:8; 6:12) and early Jewish traditions (see, e.g., *Psalms of Solomon* 17 and 4QFlorilegium) are nearly unanimous in linking the title of "anointed one" (= Messiah) with a coming king from the line of David. The Eighteen Benedictions speak of the Messiah as the "shoot" of David, employing terminology drawn from Isaiah 11, and the commonest term for the Messiah in rabbinic literature is "the Son of David." Nor does the New Testament seem to disagree; it contains numerous witnesses to Jesus' Davidic descent (Matt 1:6; Luke 3:31; Rom 1:3-4; 2 Tim 2:8; Rev 3:7; 5:5; 22:16), and in some passages this descent is even used as the presupposition upon which other arguments are constructed (e.g., Acts 2:30-31; 13:22-23).[14]

13. Theodore J. Weeden, "The Heresy That Necessitated Mark's Gospel" (1968), in *The Interpretation of Mark,* ed. William Telford, SNTI (Philadelphia: Fortress, 1995), pp. 89-104; Norman Perrin, "The Christology of Mark: A Study in Methodology" (1971, 1974), in *The Interpretation of Mark,* ed. William Telford, IRT 7 (Philadelphia: Fortress, 1985), pp. 95-108. The *locus classicus* for this view is Mark 14:61-62, in which the high priest asks Jesus whether he is the Messiah-Son-of-the-Blessed = Messiah-Son-of-God (on the form of apposition here, see Joel Marcus, "Mark 14:61: 'Are You the Messiah-Son-of-God?'" *Novum Testamentum* 31 [1989]: 125-41).

14. See John P. Meier, "From Elijah-like Prophet to Royal Davidic Messiah," in *Jesus: A Colloquium in the Holy Land,* ed. Doris Donnelly (New York: Continuum, 2001), passim.

But the tradition is not *entirely* univocal; Jesus *does* seem at first to be denying Davidic messiahship in Mark 12:35-37. The line of thought in the passage is clear: (a) No father calls his own son κύριος (*kyrios,* "master" or "lord"), but (b) that is the way in which David, in Psalm 110:1, addresses the Messiah; therefore, (c) David cannot be the Messiah's father, and the Messiah cannot rightly be termed his son.

Many exegetes, to be sure, reject this conclusion, asserting that the Markan Jesus *cannot* be questioning the Davidic sonship of the Messiah in 12:35-37, because elsewhere this tradition is so dominant.[15] Such exegetes generally interpret this passage in a way that takes its cues from Romans 1:2-4: Christ is *both* the Son of David *and* the Son of God.[16] In line with this harmonistic interpretation, the fourth-century anti-Gnostic writer Adamantius asserts that πῶς (*pōs,* "how") in Mark 12:35 implies questioning rather than denial of Davidic sonship, citing the LXX of Deuteronomy 32:30; Isaiah 1:21; 14:12 as parallel uses of the adverb.[17] Modern interpreters who adopt the harmonistic construal generally argue from history-of-religions parallels rather than from grammar, taking our passage as a rabbinic-style reconciliation of contradictory scriptural expectations (the Davidic descent of the Messiah on the one hand, his exaltation to heaven on the other).

In either case, such expedients are not entirely satisfactory. Our passage cites only one scripture (Ps 110:1), not two, as in the rabbinic parallels cited by the modern exegetes; moreover, its foil is a scribal opinion, and such opinions are as a rule negatively evaluated in Mark (see 2:6-8; 3:22-27; 7:5-13;

15. My argument here repeats that in my forthcoming Anchor Bible volume on Mark 8–16, in the note on "and how is he his son" in Mark 12:37.

16. See, for example, Evald Lövestam, "Die Davidssohnfrage," *Svensk exegetisk årsbok* 27 (1962): 72-82; David Daube, *The New Testament and Rabbinic Judaism* (1956; reprint, New York: Arno, 1973), pp. 158-69; Donald H. Juel, *Messianic Exegesis: Christological Interpretation of the Old Testament in Early Christianity* (Philadelphia: Fortress, 1988), pp. 142-44. This way of dealing with the passage is very old; see, for example, Tertullian, *Against Marcion* 5.60; Novatian, *On the Trinity* 11; Bede on Mark 12:37. The one glaring exception is the exegesis in *Barnabas* 12:10-11, which explicitly denies the Davidic sonship of the Messiah: "Since they are about to say that the Christ is the son of David, David himself speaks a prophecy in reverential awe, understanding the error of the sinners, 'The Lord said to my Lord, "Sit at my right side until I make your enemies a footstool for your feet."' . . . See how David calls him Lord; he does not call him son" (trans. Bart D. Ehrman, *The Apostolic Fathers,* vol. 2, LCL 25 [Cambridge: Cambridge University Press, 2003], p. 61).

17. Adamantius, *Concerning True Faith in God* (PG 11.1849-52).

9:11-13; 11:27-33; 15:31-32).[18] Certainly, as Adamantius claims, πῶς in 12:35, as well as πόθεν (*pothen,* "whence") in 12:37, can have a variety of meanings, depending on context.[19] But the Old Testament passages Adamantius cites in favor of the interrogative interpretation are not apposite (πῶς introduces exclamations rather than questions), and the immediate context in our passage, as we have seen, suggests that Jesus is aiming at refutation rather than reconciliation. This would be especially true in the hierarchical Greco-Roman world, in which "lord" and "son" were near antonyms; the father was, as it were, the lord of the son (cf. the household codes in Eph 5:21–6:9; Col 3:18–4:1). On the presumption that Mark 12:35-37 is a historical tradition and that in it Jesus is indirectly referring to himself, our passage provides prima facie evidence that he felt some reservation about the title "Son of David," either because he was not himself a Davidide (cf. John 7:42) or because of some of the connotations of that title.[20]

It is not enough, however, to say that Mark preserves a historical memory of Jesus challenging the notion of the Davidic sonship of the Messiah yet wants to affirm the post-Easter tendency to see Jesus as the Son of David. How and why does Mark put these two contradictory impulses together? Probably along the lines suggested by Romans 1:2-4: Jesus is *not (just)* the Son of David *but (also)* the Son of God.[21] The harmonistic solution that we earlier rejected as an interpretation of our passage in its im-

18. See Rudolf Bultmann, *History of the Synoptic Tradition,* 2nd ed. (New York: Harper & Row, 1968), p. 407; Marinus de Jonge, "Jesus, Son of David and Son of God," in *Intertextuality in Biblical Writings: Essays in Honour of Bas van Iersel,* ed. Sipke Draisma (Kampen: Kok, 1989), p. 96 n. 11; Marcus, *Way of the Lord,* p. 152.

19. Cf. de Jonge, "Jesus, Son of David," p. 99.

20. See Christoph Burger, *Jesus als Davidssohn: Eine traditionsgeschichtliche Untersuchung,* FRLANT 98 (Göttingen: Vandenhoeck & Ruprecht, 1970), pp. 52-59.

21. On the implication of divine sonship in 12:35-37, cf. my forthcoming Anchor Bible volume on Mark 8–16, where I point out that when the Markan Jesus uses Ps 110:1 to establish David's inferiority to the Messiah, he quotes more of the psalm than he needs to for that purpose, citing the picture of "the Lord" telling "my lord" to sit on his right until he has subdued his enemies (12:36bc). A seated position on the right hand of a deity implies co-regency with him, as is confirmed not only by Jewish texts (see *b. Sanh.* 38b and cf. Dan 7:9-14) but also by ancient iconography (see Otto Keel, *The Symbolism of the Biblical World: Ancient Near Eastern Iconography and the Book of Psalms* [New York: Seabury, 1978], pp. 253-68; Martin Hengel, *Studies in the Gospel of Mark* [Philadelphia: Fortress, 1985], pp. 175-79). The imagery of the quoted portion of the psalm, then, implies that "my lord" stands in a relation of near equality with God, an implication consonant with the continuation of Psalm 110 in the LXX, which speaks of divine begetting (Ps 110:3 [109:3 LXX]; cf. Marcus, *Way,* p. 141).

mediate context, then, is probably the right exegesis of it *in its Markan context*. But it is also true that our passage, even in that context, subordinates Davidic messianism to divine sonship, and this subordination may have to do as much with the Markan situation as with the influence of the historical Jesus.

In the Markan situation, the Davidic hope seems to be associated not only with Jesus but also with "false messiahs" (13:22; cf. 13:6). I have argued elsewhere that the latter are probably to be identified with figures such as Menachem son of Judas the Galilean and Simon bar Giora, leaders in the Jewish revolt against the Romans.[22] Mark and his community may have suffered at the hands of such messianic figures, perhaps partly because of the community's acceptance of Gentiles, and for this reason, among others, Mark's response to the Davidic image is complex. On the one hand, it is important for him to affirm that the true "Son of David" appeared many years before Menachem and Simon, manifesting his kingship to the enthusiastic acclaim of Jerusalem crowds and the accompaniment of miracles. Jesus was the authentic fulfillment of the Davidic hope, a holy warrior sent by God to free his people from an alien rule and liberate the temple; Menachem and Simon were but pale imitations (cf. John 5:43). On the other hand, Mark also sees a destructive potentiality in Davidic messianism. Where that phenomenon is defined dominantly by the nationalistic fervor of the Davidic image, those who have felt the sting of the zealotry such messianism can provoke and feed upon will naturally be inclined to deny the ultimacy of that image and to ask with the Markan Jesus how it can be claimed that the Messiah is David's son.[23]

The All-Knowing Seer and the Cry of Dereliction

Mark's ambiguity about Davidic messiahship, then, may grow partly out of the Markan community's tense relation to other messianic movements. But another aspect of Markan Christology has a deeper, more theologically significant ambiguity. This is the tension between the picture of Jesus as an all-knowing seer, which dominates the first thirteen chapters, and the pic-

22. Joel Marcus, "The Jewish War and the *Sitz im Leben* of Mark," *Journal of Biblical Literature* 111 (1992): 441-62.

23. See Marcus, *Way of the Lord*, pp. 148-49.

ture of him as an agonized, doubting sufferer, which emerges in chapters 14–15. Especially noteworthy is the contrast between 8:31; 9:31; 10:33-34, in which Jesus prophesies his imminent suffering and death (as well as his resurrection); and 14:34-39, in which he quails at the prospect of his forthcoming execution and prays to be delivered from it. Moreover, in 15:34, his last cry is not (as in Luke and John) a word of triumph but an outburst of despair at his apparent abandonment by God.

The contrast between the sections of Mark, to be sure, is not absolute. It is not just the end of the Gospel that sometimes portrays a Jesus whose knowledge is limited. In 5:30-32, for example, Jesus does not know who has touched him, and in 13:32 he confesses that no one but the Father knows the hour of the parousia, not even the Son. We have already mentioned the instances in which news of Jesus' healings spreads contrary to his own intention. Conversely, even in the passion narrative Jesus sometimes has moments of clarity, foresight, and prophetic defiance of opponents, as we shall see below. Nevertheless, just as his miracles predominate in the first half of the Gospel whereas suffering predominates at the end, so as a general rule there is a contrast between the self-confident and clairvoyant seer at the beginning and the agonized, doubting sufferer at the end.

This ambiguity probably reflects the tradition-history of Mark's Gospel: it is likely that Jesus' distress in Gethsemane and his cry of dereliction are historical memories (who would have invented them?[24]), whereas the passion predictions, at least in their present form, are products of the early church. The reasoning of Reimarus and Strauss is still cogent: if Jesus had so clearly and repeatedly predicted his death and resurrection to his disciples, they would not have been taken so off-guard when those events occurred.[25] To be sure, the "after three days" formulation does not exactly comport with later Christian belief (Jesus was thought to have been raised on the third day, not after three days) and may suggest use of an underly-

24. Cf. Celsus's attack on Jesus on the basis of the Gethsemane tradition: How can one who is divine "mourn and lament and pray to escape the fear of death, expressing himself thus, 'O Father, if it be possible, let this cup pass from me'?" (Origen, *Against Celsus* 2.24, trans. Raymond E. Brown, *The Death of the Messiah: From Gethsemane to the Grave*, vol. 1, ABRL [New York: Doubleday, 1994], p. 218).

25. Hermann Samuel Reimarus, *Fragments* (1779; reprint, Chico, Calif.: Scholars Press, 1985), pp. 130-32; David Friedrich Strauss, *The Life of Jesus Critically Examined* (1840; reprint, Philadelphia: Fortress, 1972), pp. 568-69.

ing pre-Easter tradition;[26] but if so, that tradition has been heavily if inconsistently edited to make it accord better with the actual course of events.

Nevertheless, even if Gethsemane and the cry of dereliction are closer to history than the passion predictions, we still have to account for the Markan ambiguity that results from their juxtaposition. It would be nearly impossible for Mark and his readers to ignore the contrast between the clairvoyant Jesus and the despairing one, and they would need to come up with some way of putting them together in their own minds. But how?

One way of doing so would be through the idea of *kenosis,* the sort of deliberate descent into the abyss of human experience that is spoken of in Philippians 2:6-8. In other words, the distance between the calm assurance of the passion predictions on the one hand and the agonized uncertainty of Gethsemane and the cry of dereliction on the other could be the ultimate result of a decision by Jesus to submit himself to the divine will that he drink the cup of human suffering to the full and thereby give his life as "a ransom for many" (cf. 10:45; 14:36). According to this interpretation, Mark's Christology is close to that of the Epistle to the Hebrews, especially if we read χωρὶς θεοῦ (*chōris theou,* "without God") rather than χάριτι θεοῦ (*chariti theou,* "by the grace of God") in Hebrews 2:9: "But we see Jesus, who for a little while was made lower than the angels, crowned with glory and honor because of the suffering of death, so that *without God* he might taste death for all."[27] Jesus' becoming "without God," that is, his removal from the divine presence, is a necessary part of his salvific participation in "the suffering of death" on behalf of humanity. Similar ideas recur elsewhere in the epistle; Hebrews 10:5-10, for example, links Jesus' incarnation and self-sacrifice with his desire to do God's will, and Hebrews 5:7-10 combines an exaltation motif similar to that of Philippians 2:9-11 with Jesus' tearful prayer to be saved from death, which is reminiscent of the Gethsemane tradition.

In the Markan case, to be sure, the descent into uncertainty is bumpy, unlike the smooth downward course of the kenosis envisaged in Philippians 2:6-8 (first to the slavelike condition of human existence in general,

26. See Joachim Jeremias, *New Testament Theology,* pt. 1, *The Proclamation of Jesus* (London: SCM, 1971), p. 285.

27. On the preferability of reading χωρὶς θεοῦ, see Bart D. Ehrman, *The Orthodox Corruption of Scripture: The Effect of Early Christological Controversies on the Text of the New Testament* (Oxford: Oxford University Press, 1993), pp. 146-50.

then to the further pain and humiliation of death on a cross). After the three Markan passion predictions, for example, Jesus' acknowledgment that the Son does not know the hour of the parousia (13:32) might be interpreted as the beginning of his descent into unknowing. But then several passages at the beginning of chapter 14 (14:8, 13-16, 17-21, 24-25, 27-31) strongly emphasize Jesus' knowledge of, and apparent equanimity about, future events, including his imminent suffering and death. This burst of certainty is then followed by a dark night of the soul in Gethsemane (14:32-40), at the conclusion of which Jesus seems to be prepared to be delivered to his enemies (14:41-42) and to fulfill the scriptures that speak of his death (14:49). In the next scene, he fearlessly prophesies that even his opponents will soon recognize his commensurateness with God (14:62). This confident prophecy, however, is followed by another and steeper descent into silence (15:5), passivity,[28] and the profound despair of the cry of dereliction (15:34). We may imagine these last few chapters, then, as more like a roller-coaster ride than a parachute jump — with the last and most sickening drop reserved for the end. This fluctuation in Jesus' mood and degree of certainty is not necessarily a sign that Mark's material has escaped his control. The Markan passion narrative is a real *drama*, and its hero is not a static, one-dimensional figure who always acts in a consistent and predictable manner but a full-bodied character who fluctuates, like other grand dramatic figures, between extremes of courage and fear, certainty and doubt — and thus can become an object of identification for the audience.

It is also possible to read more of an interior struggle into the Jesus of the earlier part of the Gospel and thus to reduce, though not to eliminate, the contrast with the end. This strategy is suggested by Boris Pasternak's poem "Hamlet," in which the speaker is simultaneously an actor portraying Hamlet, Hamlet himself, and Christ:

28. From 14:43 on Jesus is acted upon rather than acting, until he utters his last words in 15:34. The only partial exception is his refusal to drink in 15:23, which is a reaction rather than an action. This stress on the passivity of the Markan Jesus in the passion narrative contrasts with Calvin's position on Christ's kenosis, as described by David Steinmetz in his essay for this volume (pp. 281-82): Christ hid his divine power but did not surrender it; he chose to be a victim but was not victimized; throughout his passion he retained the power to terminate it. But if so, was he really tested in all ways as we are (Heb 4:15)? Is not victimization a part of the human condition that Christ assumed? Cf. Hans Frei, *The Identity of Jesus Christ: The Hermeneutical Bases of Dogmatic Theology* (Philadelphia: Fortress, 1975), pp. 112-15.

The buzz subsides. I have come on stage.
Leaning in an open door
I try to detect from the echo
What the future has in store.

A thousand opera-glasses level
The dark, point-blank, at me.
Abba, Father, if it be possible
Let this cup pass from me.

I love your preordained design
And am ready to play this role.
But the play being acted is not mine.
For this once let me go.

But the order of the acts is planned,
The end of the road already revealed.
Alone among the Pharisees I stand.
Life is not a stroll across a field.[29]

Here Christ becomes an actor asked to play a role in a drama he did not write but to which he is strongly attached by his love for its "preordained design" (cf. Mark 14:36, "not what I want, but what you want"). The Hamlet/Christ figure, then, is not just resigned to his fate; he actually *loves* the play, loves the design, as Shakespeare's Hamlet comes to do by the beginning of Act V, where he sees that "there's a divinity that shapes our ends/ Rough-hew them how we will" (5.2.10-11).

This way of reading Shakespeare through Pasternak suggests a different understanding of the passion predictions in Mark. They are not the bloodless utterances of a superhuman, stick-figure Jesus but intimations of a hard-won *reconciliation* to adverse destiny, which will emerge full blown at the conclusion of the struggle in Gethsemane. Like Pasternak's Hamlet, the Markan Jesus sees the big picture, feels the drama and beauty of a weighty story racing inexorably to its immensely significant conclu-

29. Boris Pasternak, "Hamlet," trans. Peter France and Jon Stallworthy, as cited in John Gross, ed., *After Shakespeare: An Anthology* (Oxford: Oxford University Press, 2002), pp. 79-80. From *Selected Poems: Boris Pasternak,* trans. Jon Stallworthy and Peter France (London: Allen Lane, 1983), p. 125. Copyright © Peter France, 1983. Forward copyright © VAAP, 1983. Reproduced by permission of Penguin Books Ltd.

sion. Yet because he, like Pasternak's Hamlet, is not playing a make-believe role but actually being asked to suffer torture and death, he can at one and the same time declare that he is ready to play his part and ask to be released from it. The worst thing would be ejection from the play, the loss of the sense of participation in the grand design; but this does not lessen the pain and dread of the solitary figure who stands at the center of the darkening stage, surrounded by the stares of hostile or indifferent spectators, facing his end alone.

Perhaps, in other words, more passion should be read into the Markan passion predictions; they should be seen as a real wrestling with his destiny by the Markan Jesus. That might help explain why the third prediction is so much more detailed than the first two: the Markan Jesus is gradually coming to grips with the full horror of what is about to happen to him. The Gethsemane scene, then, could be interpreted as the culmination of a process of reconciliation to fate that had already begun in the passion predictions, a process whereby Jesus, "although he was a son, learned obedience through what he suffered" (Heb 5:8).

But is the Markan Jesus still feeling obedient and submissive to his fate by the time he reaches his last hour? The cry of dereliction (15:34) seems to be a regression from the hard-won resignation of Gethsemane (14:41-42). Indeed, the problem may be even more radical than at first appears, since moments before he dies Jesus cries out "with a loud voice" (φωνῇ μεγάλῃ, *phōnē megalē*, 15:34; cf. ἀφεὶς φωνὴν μεγάλην, *apheis phōnēn megalēn* in 15:37). Previously in the narrative only demoniacs have cried out "with a loud voice" (1:26; 5:7). The implication may be that Jesus has entered so fully into the human condition of estrangement from God that he has actually experienced the most radical form of that estrangement, demonic possession.[30] This interpretation would cohere with the death scene's portrait of cosmic darkness (15:33; cf. Amos 8:9); the horror pressing down on Jesus is not just a meteorological quirk but the demonic power of the old age ruled by Satan. In this context Jesus' question, "Why have you abandoned me?" is parallel to the demoniacs' cry, "What do we have to do with you?" (1:24; 5:7): both express a radical sense of separation from the power and goodness of God.[31]

30. See Frederick Danker, "The Demonic Secret in Mark: A Reexamination of the Cry of Dereliction (15:34)," *Zeitschrift für die neutestamentliche Wissenschaft* 61 (1970): 48-69.

31. Among modern theologians, von Balthasar has emphasized most profoundly the radical implications of the cry of dereliction; see, for example, Hans Urs von Balthasar, *Does*

If Jesus' death is demonic, then the death scene represents an ironic, kenotic reversal of the situation in the Beelzebul controversy (3:22-30), in which Jesus is presented as "the Stronger One," whose exorcisms prove him mightier than Satan. Now it is Satan who has suddenly, albeit temporarily, gained the upper hand, and Jesus' demonic cries might almost be taken as confirming the scribes' earlier charge: "He has Beelzebul . . ." (3:22). This is not completely surprising, since there is often an ambiguity about exorcists, whose power over the demons may be seen by hostile critics as an indication that they are on the demons' side. The exorcist, therefore, inhabits a dangerously liminal space because of his commerce with the demons, and this commerce may either lead to his own possession or testify that he is already possessed.[32] The Markan Jesus' demonic possession on the cross, if that is what it is, may thus be the terrible result of his grappling with the powers of darkness — a grappling that he undertakes for the benefit of demon-possessed humanity. The "Son of the Most High God," as the Gerasene demoniac calls him (5:7), takes his place among the possessed in order that humanity may be definitively delivered from its demons. Mark, then, may understand Jesus' earlier exorcisms in the Gospels as proleptic of Jesus' own exorcism at the cross, just as he understands the healings in which Jesus raises (ἐγείρειν, *egeirein*) people from sickness (1:31; 2:9, 11-12; 3:3; 9:27; cf. 10:49) or death (5:41) as proleptic of Jesus' own "being raised" by God (14:28; 16:6).

But there is also a hope hidden in Jesus' cry of dereliction and his wordless shout *in extremis.* If these are demonic cries, it is also true that the demons shriek "with a loud voice" *as they are being exorcised.* The death scene, then, is not just a landscape of desolation and despair; it is also a scene of hope, though this hope originates in God rather than in Jesus. The screams torn from Jesus' lips are desperate, eleventh-hour acts of resistance by a power that is in process of being vanquished. The crucifixion scene thus represents the climax of old-age darkness but also the dawning of new-age light; the temple curtain, which hitherto has shielded the glory

---

Jesus Know Us — Do We Know Him? (San Francisco: Ignatius, 1983), p. 36. John Yocum criticizes von Balthasar for this, but his own exegesis of the Markan/Matthean cry of dereliction is unconvincing; see Yocum, "A Cry of Dereliction? Reconsidering a Recent Theological Commonplace," *International Journal of Systematic Theology* 7 (2005): 72-80.

32. See Joel Marcus, "The Beelzebul Controversy and the Eschatologies of Jesus," in *Authenticating the Activities of Jesus,* ed. Bruce Chilton and Craig A. Evans (Leiden: Brill, 1999), p. 263.

of God from profane view, is now suddenly torn in two (15:38), and the unchained Shekinah begins to radiate out into the universe. And as the first effect of that effulgence, a human being finally perceives Jesus' full stature: "Truly this man was the Son of God!" (15:39).

The death of Jesus, then, may be seen as the culmination of the Gospel's last and greatest exorcism (and 9:26 suggests that death is a possible result of exorcism). When the Gerasene was exorcised, the townspeople who heard about the wonder came out and saw him "sitting, clothed, and sane" (5:15) — restored, that is, from frenetic activity, nakedness, and insanity to the eschatological wholeness, the *shalom,* that is God's will for humankind. Similarly, perhaps, the "exorcism" that Jesus undergoes in his death restores him, and humanity with him, both to the human condition and to divine sonship; the centurion, seeing that he thus dies, declares, "Truly this man was the Son of God!" Throughout the Gospel up to this point, *anthrōpos* and *theos,* human and God, have frequently been opposites (1:23-24; 5:2, 7; 7:7-8; 10:27; 11:30; 12:14), and the former closely linked with Satan; Peter was preoccupied with "the things of human beings" rather than "the things of God" and was therefore under Satan's control (8:33). Now, however, these ostensible opposites are fused: "this *man* . . . Son of *God.*"[33] The opposition has been overcome and humanity restored; as once in the beginning, so now at the end of the ages, *anthrōpos* has triumphed over its enemy and has been accorded divine dignity — through the Son of Adam, the Son of Man, who is also the Son of God.[34] *Ipsi gloria in saecula* — to him be glory forever.

33. See Philip G. Davis, "Mark's Christological Paradox," *Journal for the Study of the New Testament* 35 (1989): 3-18.

34. On the godlikeness of Adam in the Old Testament and Jewish and Christian traditions, see Marcus, "Son of Man," p. 371 n. 2.

Learning and Relearning the Identity of Jesus from Luke-Acts

Beverly Roberts Gaventa

The hyphen in the title of this essay already signals the distinctiveness of the evangelist Luke. Only this evangelist extends his Gospel with a narrative of events that take place well after the resurrection and ascension of Jesus, prompting the scholarly convention of referring to the Gospel and the book of Acts as a single unit.[1] Yet Luke's distinctiveness emerges not only when he takes up his second volume but from the opening lines of the Gospel, where he provides a formal prologue announcing his aims. Luke intends that his reader Theophilus should learn here something reliable, something trustworthy, about the events that have unfolded (Luke 1:4).

Great effort has been expended on the task of identifying both Luke and Theophilus and locating their historical situation. Yet the circumstances that give rise to Luke-Acts are far from clear. Scholars generally agree that Luke wrote sometime in the 80s or 90s of the first century C.E. and that he wrote not for Theophilus alone but for other Christian readers.

1. The precise relationship between these two volumes is subject to scholarly dispute. Are they two parts of a single work or two separate works? Did Luke conceive of both volumes from the outset, or is Acts something of an afterthought? That the two share the same author is almost unanimously affirmed, however, and their common authorship is what is significant for this essay. On the dispute, see Mikeal C. Parsons and Richard I. Pervo, *Rethinking the Unity of Luke and Acts* (Minneapolis: Fortress, 1993); C. Kavin Rowe, "History, Hermeneutics, and the Unity of Luke-Acts," *Journal for the Study of the New Testament* 28 (2005): 131-57, with responses by Luke Timothy Johnson ("Literary Criticism of Luke-Acts: Is Reception-History Pertinent?" pp. 159-62) and Markus Bockmuehl ("Why Not Let Acts Be Acts? In Conversation with C. Kavin Rowe," pp. 163-66). The position of the present chapter most closely resembles that taken by Luke Timothy Johnson.

Luke is intimately familiar with the Septuagint (the ancient Greek translation of the Old Testament), which means either that he is himself a Jew or that he has extensively studied Scripture (perhaps as a "God-fearer" or proselyte).

Numerous features of Luke-Acts reflect the conventions of historical writing in the Greco-Roman world, including the preface (Luke 1:1-4),[2] the synchronous identification of events (e.g., Luke 2:1; 3:1), and the extensive use of speeches (e.g., Acts 2:14-36; 26:1b-23). For that reason, many readers examine it solely for its usefulness in historical reconstruction, unintentionally reducing Luke's intended "reliability" to questions of historical accuracy. This essay will set aside those historical questions in favor of attention to the narrative itself, asking how readers who are peering over the shoulder of Theophilus might learn the identity of Jesus from the way Luke tells his story.[3]

Learning Jesus' Identity

When Peter stands to speak at Pentecost, driven by the outpouring of the Holy Spirit, he begins the public proclamation of Jesus' identity by his followers. Luke's Gospel is replete with statements regarding Jesus' identity, to be sure. The infancy narrative finds Gabriel announcing that Mary's child "will be called Son of the Most High" and will "rule over the house of Jacob forever" (Luke 1:32-33). To the amazed shepherds, the angelic host describes him as "a Savior, Christ the Lord" (2:11). Simeon, taking Isaiah's words for his own, depicts Jesus as "a light for revelation to the Gentiles and for glory to your people Israel" (2:32). At Jesus' baptism, a heavenly voice declares him to be "my Son, the Beloved" (3:22). The opponents of God's plan also know the identity of Jesus: the devil acknowledges, "If you

2. Although see the important study of Loveday Alexander, *The Preface to Luke's Gospel: Literary Convention and Social Context in Luke 1.1-4 and Acts 1.1*, SNTSMS 78 (Cambridge: Cambridge University Press, 1993), which argues that Luke 1:1-4 is better understood as employing the style of scientific and technical manuals.

3. Narrative-critical approaches to biblical texts are now widely employed. For an important example attending to Luke-Acts in particular, see Robert C. Tannehill, *The Narrative Unity of Luke-Acts: A Literary Interpretation*, 2 vols. (Minneapolis: Fortress, 1986, 1990). See also Beverly R. Gaventa, *Acts of the Apostles*, ANTC (Nashville: Abingdon, 2003), which undertakes a narrative-critical reading that is particularly attuned to Lukan theology.

are the Son of God" (4:3), and demonic spirits greet him as "the Holy One of God" (4:34).

As the story of Jesus' ministry unfolds, these declarations are joined by discussions. Jesus' announcement of forgiveness to the paralytic prompts the scribes and Pharisees in attendance to ask, "Who is this speaking blasphemy? Who is powerful enough to forgive sin except God alone?" (5:21), setting off a conversation about the authority of the Son of Man. From his imprisonment, John the Baptist sends two emissaries to inquire of Jesus whether he is "the one who is to come" (7:19). Jesus himself asks the disciples what the crowds are saying about his identity, prompting Peter's confession (9:18-20). In the account of Jesus' trial, Pilate attempts to engage Jesus in conversation with the question, "Are you the king of the Jews?" (23:3). The Emmaus road story offers the most elegant instance of these discussions, as the risen Jesus, understood by Cleopas and his companion to be a "stranger in Jerusalem," converses with these disciples about the crucifixion of the one they had thought was to be Israel's redeemer (24:13-27).

With the Pentecost speech in Acts 2, however, the relatively private discussion about Jesus' identity comes into the open as a public proclamation by those designated as Jesus' witnesses (Acts 1:8; Luke 24:48). To be sure, the story of Pentecost is important for Luke's larger narrative in several respects. It identifies the outpouring of the Spirit as the fulfillment of Joel's prophecy. It interprets the whole of Jesus' life, death, and resurrection as the result of the plan of God. It introduces the call for repentance and baptism that culminates in the emergence of a community characterized by worship and instruction and fellowship. Although these significant Lukan concerns come together here in dramatic fashion, central to the speech is its announcement of Jesus' identity, an announcement that carries with it the implicit charge that Jesus' contemporaries were mistaken in their own conclusions about him.

This charge enters the speech with the appearance of Jesus' name in Acts 2:22b. Jesus is first described in a lengthy clause as someone whose standing with God had been made plain; he was "a man attested by God among you with powerful acts and wonders and signs which God did through him among you, as you yourselves know." With 2:23, however, the speech continues reference to Jesus ("this one"), now with a series of phrases that culminates in the finite verb "you killed." Rendered somewhat literally, the verse reads:

> This one, handed over by the appointed plan and foreknowledge of God, through the hand of lawless men you killed by nailing him to a tree.

Immediately following the assertion that "you killed" Jesus comes a second assertion, that "God raised him up by loosing the pains of death" (2:24). Here the speech introduces the contrast between the action of human beings in crucifying Jesus (which Luke nevertheless understands as part of God's plan)[4] and the action of God in raising Jesus from the dead. The verses that follow expand on this announcement of the resurrection, insisting that death was not able to maintain its grasp on Jesus, drawing on Psalm 16:8-11 and thereby preparing for the contrast between David and Jesus, and finally returning to the dramatic outpouring of the Holy Spirit. The speech ends, however, with a reiteration of the clear contrast between God's action and that of the residents of Jerusalem:

> Therefore let the entire house of Israel know with certainty that God made him both Lord and Messiah, this Jesus whom you [emphatic ὑμεῖς, *hymeis*] crucified. (2:36)[5]

Among the several things Peter's speech claims about Jesus of Nazareth, then, is that despite the fact that his deeds revealed him, residents of Jerusalem rejected that identification when they put him to death. This implied clash in understanding the identity of Jesus returns in the second major speech of Peter, and here it becomes more pronounced. The amazement that follows the healing of a man in the temple precinct in Acts 3 prompts Peter to explain how this miracle has taken place. As Peter opens the speech, he introduces Jesus with a series of contrasts between Jesus' identity and the rejection of that identity by human beings. First, Peter declares that "the God of our fathers glorified his servant [or child; παῖς,

4. The understanding that the gospel and its witnesses are governed by divine necessity (δεῖ, *dei*) or the divine plan (βουλὴ τοῦ θεοῦ, *boulē tou theou*) dominates much of Luke-Acts (e.g., Luke 2:49; 9:22; 21:9; Acts 1:16; 2:23; 4:28; 17:3; 20:27). See especially John T. Squires, *The Plan of God in Luke-Acts*, SNTSMS 76 (Cambridge: Cambridge University Press, 1993); Charles H. Cosgrove, "The Divine ΔΕΙ in Luke-Acts: Investigations into the Lukan Understanding of God's Providence," *Novum Testamentum* 26 (1984): 168-90.

5. This statement might easily be misunderstood; what "all Israel" must know concerns the identity of Jesus. The "you" who crucified Jesus refers to some residents of Jerusalem, not to all Jews or even to all residents of Jerusalem.

pais] Jesus whom you [emphatic ὑμεῖς] handed over and rejected before Pilate . . ." (3:13). Then Peter repeats: "you [emphatic ὑμεῖς] rejected the holy and righteous one and sought to have a murderer given to you" (3:14). He concludes with the astonishing charge that "you killed the author of life" (3:15).

Peter goes on to describe this as an act of ignorance and again affirms that the crucifixion and resurrection fulfill ancient prophecy (3:17-18), but that concession — however solemn — does not erase the relentless contrast between the human identification of Jesus as worthy of death and the divine identification of Jesus as God's child, as the Holy and Righteous One, even as the author of life itself. The same contrast returns, although less dramatically, in later speeches. Before the religious authorities in Acts 5, Peter and the apostles together announce that "the God of our fathers raised Jesus whom you [emphatic ὑμεῖς] killed" (5:30). When Peter proclaims the gospel before Cornelius and his household, he again underscores the actions of the Jerusalem residents "who put him to death by hanging him on a tree" (10:39).

The contrast is made again in Paul's sermon at Pisidian Antioch (13:16-41), but here an explanation is offered. As Paul recounts events before an audience of Diaspora Jews and Gentiles, he explains that the residents of Jerusalem and their leaders "did not recognize this one or the sayings of the prophets that are read each sabbath" (13:27). Although the inhabitants of Jerusalem heard Scripture read every week, and although Jesus was divinely attested, they still did not recognize him.

"Identity Changing" in the Lukan Story

That Jesus' identity is not rightly apprehended by human beings on their own should come as no surprise to the careful reader of Luke's work, since Luke-Acts includes several episodes of what might be termed "identity changing." One of the literary features of the work, and a feature that plays an important role theologically, is the tendency for characters to come into a story with one identity but leave the story bearing a strikingly different identity because of the intervention of Jesus. A simple example of this feature of Luke's narration appears in the story of the healing in Luke 8:43-48, the woman who touches Jesus' clothing. At the outset of the story, the woman is presented solely in terms of her predicament; she has been exhausted by her blood loss and by the search for healing. At the end of the story, Jesus addresses her as "Daughter," granting both her health and a sign of familial relationship.

A more elaborate example appears in the healing of the "bent over" woman in Luke 13. The story opens with the typical notation that Jesus was teaching in a synagogue on the Sabbath, when another character appears:

> Behold! A woman who had a disabling spirit for eighteen years, and she was bent over, and she was not able to straighten up at all. (13:11)

This wooden rendering of the woman's introduction shows the repetitiveness of the Greek. Beginning with the phrase "disabling spirit," the narrator depicts the outcome of her condition (she is bent over) and then states it again — with emphasis. The result is that the woman is presented entirely in terms of her handicapping condition.[6] Jesus initially addresses her simply as "Woman," but following her healing and the exchange with the synagogue official, he offers another identification for her: "daughter of Abraham" (13:16). Jesus then describes her previous condition as the result of Satan's bondage and declares that it was necessary (ἔδει, *edei*) that she be released on the Sabbath. Having come on the scene completely swallowed up by this physical limitation, she exits bearing the honorable name of her father, Abraham (see esp. 1:55, 73; 3:8).

Since healing narratives typically emphasize the severity of the affliction, the changes of identity in these stories are not especially startling. The story of Zacchaeus offers a different kind of example, a narrative of restoration rather than healing (19:1-10). Luke provides a comparatively full description of Zacchaeus. He is initially described as a "chief tax collector," a designation that is ambiguous in Luke's Gospel; tax collectors are among those who go to John the Baptist for baptism (3:12; 7:29) and who listen to Jesus' teaching (15:1; see also 18:10). That positive response nevertheless plays on the stereotype of the corruption of the tax collector (i.e., Luke notes that "even" the tax collectors came to Jesus). Zacchaeus is also said to be rich, which in Luke's story routinely signals a negative assessment (6:24; 12:16-21; 16:19-31; 18:23-25). Zacchaeus's energetic attempt to

6. In disability studies, this pattern of focusing on the person's condition to the exclusion of any other characteristic is criticized, as it would be in contemporary literature or experience. That criticism misses a crucial point of the story, however, which is precisely to bestow on the woman another identity, one that is released and restored.

see Jesus can be understood positively, but his being "short" (19:3) probably cannot.[7] These details produce an ambiguity in Zacchaeus's identification, but Zacchaeus's neighbors have no difficulty coming to their own conclusion about him, as they complain that Jesus is going to the house of "a sinful man" (19:7).

Zacchaeus's statement in 19:8 has given rise to conflicting interpretations. Conventionally, it has been read as indicating Zacchaeus's repentance: he vows that he will from this point on undertake acts of generosity and restitution. Recently, drawing attention to the present tense of the verbs, some students of Luke have argued that Zacchaeus is reporting on his customary practice: he has always treated people well.[8] However that question is resolved, the crucial declaration regarding Zacchaeus does not come from his own mouth but from that of Jesus, who announces that "today salvation has come to this house" (19:9).[9] Jesus then declares that this man too is "a son of Abraham." Whether Zacchaeus has repented or merely disclosed his usual practice, he is declared restored by Jesus: like the "bent over" woman, he also is a child of Abraham.

Luke's second volume offers a splendid example of identity changing in the first account of the conversion of Saul. Presented to readers at the death of Stephen solely in terms of his activity as a persecutor of the church (Acts 7:58–8:3), Saul returns to the narrative in Acts 9 actively seeking adherents of "the Way" and thereby fulfilling Stephen's words about the murder of Israel's prophets (7:51-53). Luke narrates Saul's encounter with the risen Jesus and then turns to the commission of Ananias (9:10-16). Instructed by the Lord in a vision to go to Saul so that Saul might be healed of his blindness, Ananias objects, reminding the Lord of Saul's history as a persecutor: "Lord, I have heard from many people about this man, what sorts of evil he did to your saints in Jerusalem. Here he has authority from the chief priests to bind everyone who calls on your name." Instead of en-

7. The Greek word ἡλικία *(hēlikia)*, translated "stature" in the NRSV, can refer to age instead, but it seems unlikely that Zacchaeus is to be thought of as young, given that he is also identified as the "chief" tax collector. On the negative perceptions attached to short people, especially short males, see Mikeal C. Parsons, "'Short in Stature': Luke's Physical Description of Zacchaeus," *New Testament Studies* 47 (2001): 50-57.

8. See especially the work of Alan C. Mitchell, "Zacchaeus Revisited: Luke 19,8 as a Defense," *Biblica* 71 (1990): 153-76. Notice also that Jesus does not declare the man to be forgiven.

9. This declaration parallels that of v. 5: "Today I must be at your house." In Luke's view, Jesus himself *is* salvation (Luke 2:30).

gaging in discussion or debate about Ananias's perspective, the Lord responds to this old identification with a new one: "Go, for he is my chosen instrument. . . ."

This exchange between Ananias and the Lord grants Saul a new identity, but it also reveals a dynamic that runs throughout these stories. What readers see in this incident is that it is not Ananias's prerogative to "identify" Saul, to decide whether he merits healing. Among the several implications of the story of the "bent over" woman is that Jesus has the authority to declare her a "daughter of Abraham." Similarly, Jesus demonstrates the salvation of Zacchaeus by labeling him as "Abraham's son" instead of "sinful man." Readers are able to learn who these people truly are only as Jesus names them. To be sure, Jesus' identity is far more complex than that of any of these characters; it cannot be learned in something as straightforward as a new name that replaces an old one (as "daughter of Abraham" replaces "bent over woman"). Nevertheless, like the identities of these others, Jesus' true identity is learned only as he reveals it.

Relearning Jesus' Identity

The example par excellence of this feature of Luke's story, and the example around whom these other identity changes take place, is that of Jesus himself. As the narrator introduces other characters, only to have them reidentified by Jesus, the narrator also introduces Jesus to readers and hearers in ways that are later amplified or corrected or redirected. By following the developing story, readers are being taught about the identity of Jesus. Major features of Jesus' identification that are later altered by the story include Jesus' kingship, his role as a prophet, his death by crucifixion, and his departure from the scene following the ascension.

Jesus as King

Prominent in Gabriel's annunciation to Mary is the identification of the child she is to bear as the king of Israel:

> The Lord God will give him the throne of his father David, and he will rule over the house of Jacob forever, and his kingdom will be without end. (Luke 1:32b-33)

Consistent with the remainder of Luke's narrative of the birth and infancy of Jesus, this statement draws heavily on Israel's own Scripture (see esp. 2 Sam 7:12-13, 16; Isa 9:7). Zechariah's reference to the "house of his servant David" (Luke 1:69) and Anna's joyous speech to those who await "Jerusalem's redemption" (2:38) underscore this identification of Jesus with the hope of Israel's restoration. Much later, Jesus' arrival in Jerusalem bears the marks of a royal entry, as he is welcomed by multitudes with the praise due a king (19:29-40).

The ascription of kingship to Jesus continues in Acts, when at Pentecost Peter interprets him as the fulfillment of God's promise to send to Israel one of David's descendants as king (Acts 2:30). In addition, the charge that Christians are declaring Jesus as "another king," threatening the power of Rome itself, figures in the riot in Thessalonica (17:7). Yet Jesus does not, at least not within the pages of Luke-Acts, occupy a throne. That fact is cruelly underscored during the passion narrative, when the Roman soldiers mock his kingship and the inscription over his cross reads, "This is the King of the Jews" (Luke 23:38; and see 23:3).

Luke's story, then, both insists that Jesus is king and acknowledges that he does not become king, at least not in the usual sense of that word. By means of this apparent contradiction, Luke importantly reframes the category, teaching his readers and hearers what it means to understand Jesus as king. In response to a question from some Pharisees, Jesus says that "the kingdom of God does not come with observation" so that people can send out notice of its arrival, because "the kingdom of God is among you" (17:20-21).[10] Two related concerns emerge here, one of which is that the arrival of God's kingdom is not subject to human prediction or control (see esp. Acts 1:6-7). The second concern is that the kingdom is already underway in the ministry of Jesus himself (see also, e.g., Luke 10:9, 11; 11:20).

This reframing of Jesus' kingship and his kingdom is susceptible of serious misunderstanding if the kingdom is understood as "merely spiritual," in the sense that it does not involve "real" authority comparable to that of the political authority of the Roman Empire. Indeed, Jesus' kingship radically undermines the authority of every empire.[11] His kingship in

10. As the note in the NRSV indicates, it is possible to translate, "The kingdom of God is within you," suggesting an inward experience, but such an exclusively private, spiritualized reading is hard to reconcile with the bulk of the Lukan story; so also Joel B. Green, *The Gospel of Luke,* NICNT (Grand Rapids: Eerdmans, 1997), p. 630 n. 54.

11. On this point, see Beverly R. Gaventa, "'Turning the World Upside Down': A Reflec-

Luke-Acts is not an escape from the world of flesh and blood; instead, it is larger than that world, encompassing it but not limited to it. In other words, the rule Luke ascribes to Jesus is cosmic in its grasp. Hints of this cosmic dimension come at least as early as the temptation narrative, where the devil enters the scene as a rival claimant to authority over all the world's kingdoms (Luke 4:5-6). Later, Jesus greets the report of his disciples that the demons yield to them with the word that he "watched Satan fall" (10:17-18), and he explicitly interprets his own authority over the demons as the sign that God's kingdom has arrived (11:20). Stories in Acts continue this pattern, as the struggle with Satan and his representatives persists into the church's life (Acts 5:3; 13:10; 19:13-20).

In addition to presenting Jesus as battling with the cosmic power of Satan (note Luke 22:3, 31), Luke shows Jesus' ascent to a throne far higher than that of Israel's past and far more powerful than that of Rome. Jesus claims that "the Son of Man will sit at the right hand of God's power" (22:69). Peter declares on Pentecost that Jesus has been not only raised from the dead but "exalted to God's right hand" (Acts 2:29-36), and Stephen sees the Son of Man standing at God's right hand (7:55-56). For the Gentile Cornelius, Peter concludes that Jesus is "Lord of all" (10:36). Jesus is king, then, in a sense that lies beyond human comprehension.

Jesus as Prophet

Alongside this cosmic kingship, Luke unmistakably places Jesus of Nazareth within the tradition of Israel's prophets. As with his kingship, this aspect of Jesus' identification is announced even before he is born, when Mary praises God for the anticipated arrival of Jesus, employing language of Scripture that has strongly prophetic overtones (see esp. Luke 1:51-53). When the infant Jesus is presented in the Jerusalem temple, Simeon draws on the wording of Isaiah (Luke 2:30-32; see Isa 42:6; 46:13; 49:6, 9; 52:10); equally important, Simeon's second oracle prophetically warns that Jesus brings judgment as well as salvation (Luke 2:34-35). The elaborate interweaving of the stories of the birth and infancy of John the

---

tion on the Acts of the Apostles," in *Shaking Heaven and Earth: Essays in Honor of Walter Brueggemann and Charles B. Cousar,* ed. Christine Roy Yoder et al. (Louisville: Westminster John Knox, 2005), pp. 105-16.

Baptist with those of Jesus further associates Jesus with the prophetic tradition.

With Jesus' sermon in Nazareth in Luke 4, the prophetic motif comes to the foreground. Unlike Mark or Matthew, Luke reports that Jesus reads from Isaiah, and he includes the passage, a passage that typifies the prophetic concern for the poor and marginalized (4:17-19; see Isa 61:1-2). In the ensuing conflict, Jesus identifies himself as a prophet (4:24) and invokes the practices of Elijah and Elisha as precedent (4:25-27). Appearing at the outset of Jesus' ministry, this scene identifies him as one who stands in the tradition of the prophets. That connection is reinforced in the healing stories. As Elisha had healed the Gentile Naaman, so Jesus heals the slave of a centurion (7:1-10; 2 Kings 5:1-14). The restoration of a widow's son recalls the healing of the son of the widow at Zarephath (7:11-17; 1 Kings 17:17-24). When messengers from John the Baptist ask Jesus about his identity, he replies in terms of his fulfillment of prophecy (7:18-23) and later interprets his impending death as the death of a prophet (13:33). Beyond these narrative details, the manifest concern of Luke for widows and the poor, and the related judgment on the powerful and the rich, clearly associates Jesus with Israel's prophets and their calls for justice.

This association carries over into Acts as well. In an early sermon, Peter openly identifies Jesus as the prophet-like-Moses, whose voice the people must hear or face the judgment of God (Acts 3:22-26). Stephen's speech also places Jesus in the company of the prophets, connecting the death of the prophets with that of Jesus himself (7:51-53). The rejection of the prophets continues in the rejection of Jesus' own witnesses that forms an important thematic thread in Acts.

While Luke carefully identifies Jesus as a prophet, he is also insistent that Jesus is more than a prophet. That point may be inferred from the discussion above about the cosmic kingship of Jesus, but it comes to expression in the narrative in other ways as well. At least as early as Luke 7:24-35, which praises John the Baptist as "a prophet" and "more than a prophet," Jesus himself contrasts the impending kingdom of God with even the greatness of the prophet John. In the same vein, Peter knows that the crowds have identified Jesus as John the Baptist or Elijah, but Peter himself acknowledges Jesus as God's own Messiah (9:18-20). More telling, the transfiguration places Jesus in the company of Moses and Elijah, yet the heavenly voice announces, "This is my Son, my chosen one" (9:35).

Jesus is, for Luke, the prophet-who-is-more-than-a-prophet. Consistent with that emerging identity, this prophet's concern encompasses Israel and more than Israel. The understanding of God's salvation as incorporating both Israel and the Gentiles is itself a prophetic motif, as Simeon makes clear in Luke 2:32 by means of Isaiah 49:6. Jesus taunts the residents of Nazareth with the recollection that Elijah and Elisha came to the aid of outsiders rather than Israelites (Luke 4:25-28). What extends Jesus' prophecy and that of his witnesses, however, is that, while their prophecy addresses Israel and anticipates Israel's role in the salvation of the Gentiles, it also addresses Gentiles directly. Gentiles are included most often as they appear with Jews among the worshipers in the synagogue (as in Acts 13:16, 26; 18:4), yet even those who are not associated with the synagogue find themselves addressed by Jesus' witnesses, as in the case of the Philippian jailer (16:25-34). In the Areopagus sermon, Paul begins with a gentle reproach of idolatry, but he concludes with a call to repentance and a warning about divine judgment (17:22-31). Jesus the prophet-like-Moses never stops being for and about Israel,[12] but this prophet is also for and about all of humankind. That universal reach does not emerge without struggle, of course. The highly developed account of the conversion of Cornelius (or, better, the conversion of Peter and the church) in Acts 10:1–11:18 emphasizes the divine decision on behalf of the Gentiles as well as the church's resistance.

Jesus as Crucified

Unlike the identifications of Jesus as king and as prophet, the identification of Jesus as crucified is not subtly reconfigured or reinterpreted; it is instead powerfully overthrown by God's vindication of Jesus in the resurrection. What Luke's readers learn about the crucifixion has to do with this vindication but also with the crucifixion as divine necessity. Luke locates the crucifixion as part of God's own plan, a plan that includes Jesus' suffering and death and resurrection, a plan anticipated in Scripture. In addition, the re-

12. This statement touches on one of the most contentious points in Lukan scholarship, namely, the stance Luke takes toward the temple, Jewish traditions, and the people of Israel. See Gaventa, *Acts*, pp. 44-48. For a collection of essays representing major viewpoints, see Joseph B. Tyson, ed., *Luke-Acts and the Jewish People: Eight Critical Perspectives* (Minneapolis: Augsburg, 1988).

current motif in Acts of the rejection of Jesus' witnesses reinforces this understanding. Just as the crucifixion does not mark Jesus as defeated, rejection of the witnesses does not identify the gospel as defeated.

The Gospel of Luke is distinctive for its admission that at least some of Jesus' followers concluded that his death meant the end of their hopes. The report of the women is dismissed as mere chatter (24:1-12). More to the point, Cleopas and his companion frankly admit to the unrecognized Jesus that they had hoped Jesus would prove to be Israel's redeemer (24:21). That their hope is now exhausted seems evident from their report that three days have passed and, while some women have reported Jesus' resurrection, the rest of Jesus' followers have seen nothing. The irony of their confession of hopelessness in the very presence of the resurrected, living Jesus reveals that their own rational capacities are bankrupt. It is only with the breaking of the bread that they, together with the remainder of the community, are able to see who Jesus truly is (24:28-35).[13]

When the moment of recognition does come at table, it not only restores their hope but connects that hope with God's long-standing plan. As Jesus himself interprets the matter directly: "Weren't these things necessary — that the Messiah should suffer and enter into his glory?" (24:26). The early sermons of Acts underscore this point: Jesus' death is not defeat, because that death has been overturned by God as an essential part of God's plan for human redemption. Although Luke offers little explanation of why Jesus' death is necessary or what it accomplishes, he nevertheless insists that God's plan includes this death.

If Jesus' death is not defeat but the confirmation of God's plan, the same is true of the rejection of Jesus' witnesses in Acts. The early attempts to silence the preaching of Peter might suggest that defeat is impending, but Luke reports instead on the growing number of the baptized (Acts 5:13-14). Stephen's martyrdom, which introduces a citywide persecution and prompts believers to flee the city, fulfills the divine plan by forcing preaching outside Jerusalem and into Samaria (8:1b-3). The repeated stories of the rejection of Paul's witness only serve to send the gospel to the next city (e.g., 13:51; 14:20; 17:10). The long concluding narrative of Paul's trials and captivity does not silence him, since he persists in preaching even to Festus and Agrippa and Bernice (26:1-32). The book of Acts culmi-

13. For reflections on the contemporary relevance of this association between the Eucharist and recognition of Jesus, see Sarah Coakley's essay in the present volume.

nates by contrasting Paul's apparent defeat (his house arrest in Rome) with his ongoing preaching and teaching of the gospel (28:30-31).

This long journey of rejection that prompts further proclamation fulfills Jesus' words in Luke 21:12-19 about the response that will meet the testimony of Jesus' disciples. The witnesses are handed over repeatedly, but they amaze their hearers with the words they persist in speaking (Acts 4:13-14; 26:24-29). In Luke's story, neither Jesus' crucifixion nor the resistance to his witnesses can be regarded as a defeat, since both take place as part of God's plan.

Jesus as Departed

The evangelist Luke is unique in his treatment of Jesus' departure, providing accounts of Jesus' ascension both at the end of the Third Gospel and at the beginning of Acts. In addition, the account in Acts 1 repeatedly emphasizes Jesus' departure. Luke specifies that it occurs while the apostles are looking on, that Jesus is taken from their eyes, that they stare into heaven. The two heavenly messengers promise that Jesus' return will resemble his departure, with no comment about Jesus' location or activity in the meanwhile (1:8-11).

This departure is reinforced in Peter's speech in Acts 3, when Peter refers to "the Messiah appointed beforehand, Jesus, whom it is necessary [δεῖ] for heaven to receive until the times of the restoration of all things" (3:20-21). The statement appears to secure the point made by the ascension account: Jesus has been removed from the human scene and resides in heaven until the parousia. And many readers, especially scholarly readers, have concluded that the Spirit or the church's own activity "replaces" Jesus in Acts.[14] Indeed, many readers of Acts think of it as the story of what the church does on its own, after Jesus has departed. Yet this aspect of Jesus' identity too is more complex than first appears.

Jesus' departure does not mean that he is disconnected from or uninvolved with the story that follows. On multiple occasions, Luke communi-

14. Hans Conzelmann's view, which distinguished between the period of Jesus and that of the church, dominated a scholarly generation. See Conzelmann, *The Theology of St. Luke*, trans. Geoffrey Buswell (New York: Harper, 1960), especially his discussion of the ascension, pp. 202-6.

cates that Jesus is shaping, directing, and sustaining the witness. Furthermore, Jesus' various actions in the story provide a framework for understanding the witness of the apostles as Jesus' work rather than their own. That is, the apostles do not so much substitute for an absent Jesus as they exemplify his present, ongoing activity. Indeed, the terminology of "absence" and "presence" is somewhat misleading. When Luke says that Jesus is at God's right hand, he surely does not mean (as some commentators do) that Jesus cannot also be present among human beings.

To begin with, Peter announces that it is Jesus who pours out the Spirit at Pentecost (2:33). This point is easily overlooked. Jesus himself earlier anticipates the baptism of the Spirit and the fulfillment of the Father's promise (1:4-5), but at Pentecost Peter identifies Jesus as the one who is pouring out the Holy Spirit. The witness of Stephen culminates in his vision of Jesus standing at God's right hand, an action often interpreted as Jesus' preparation to receive Stephen (7:56). In Acts 9, Jesus not only appears to Saul; he also speaks to Ananias with a set of instructions, so that he directs the events that follow from both sides.

Immediately after the story of Saul's conversion in chapter 9, the healing of Aeneas contains another pertinent comment. Instead of calling on the name of Jesus or declaring that it is faith in Jesus' name that heals, as occurs earlier (3:12, 16; 4:7-12), on this occasion Peter asserts to Aeneas, "Jesus Christ heals you" (9:34). This variation may be particularly important because this is one of the last healings the narrative associates with Peter.[15] This direct comment may then serve to interpret the earlier healings: any attempt to understand those healings as manifestations of Peter's own personal power is ruled out by words from his own mouth.

Later in the narrative, in the address to the Ephesian elders, Paul asserts that he received his ministry (διακονία, *diakonia*) from "the Lord Jesus" (20:24), yet another indication of Jesus' ongoing role. In the first defense speech in chapter 22, Paul repeats the story of his encounter with Jesus on the road to Damascus, adding that in the Jerusalem temple Jesus directed him to flee the city. Shortly after that scene and just prior to the removal of Paul from Jerusalem to Caesarea, the Lord speaks to Paul a

15. The healing of Aeneas is paired with that of Dorcas, which follows immediately in 9:36-43. This pattern of closely associating an event that features a male character with a similar event that features a female character occurs at several points in Luke-Acts (e.g., Zechariah and Mary in Luke 1:5-23 and 26-38; Simeon and Anna in Luke 2:25-35 and 36-38; Ananias and Sapphira in Acts 5:1-6 and 7-11).

word of encouragement and prophecy. As Paul has been a witness in Jerusalem, he must also bear witness in Rome (23:11).

To this point only those texts have been included that either refer explicitly to Jesus or refer to the Lord in a way that makes clear that the speaker is Jesus. As is well known, however, κύριος (*Kyrios*, "Lord") in Acts often refers to Jesus. For example, in 22:19-20 Paul addresses the Lord and refers to "your [i.e., the Lord's] witness Stephen," which seems to make it clear that κύριος here is the Lord Jesus, since Stephen is martyred for his witness to Jesus. A number of other passages might also be introduced into the discussion. For example, "the Lord" sends an angel to release Peter from Herod's custody (12:11, 17); at Pisidian Antioch Paul and Barnabas claim that the Lord commanded preaching to Gentiles (13:47); in Iconium the narrator reports that the Lord provides signs and wonders (14:3); in Philippi the Lord opens the heart of Lydia (16:14); and in Corinth the Lord reassures Paul and directs him to speak (18:9-10). The single reference to the Spirit of Jesus, which directs Paul and his companions away from Bithynia (in 16:7), may also be an instance of the activity of Jesus. At the very least, the ambiguity of these passages means that they *may* refer to Jesus; they cannot be firmly excluded from a discussion of the Lukan characterization of Jesus.

The most important (and probably the most overlooked) assertion about Jesus' activity in Acts comes at the high point of Paul's final defense speech in Caesarea (Acts 26). Having recounted his own overtaking by Jesus on the Damascus road as well as his own faithfulness to Israel's hope, Paul sums up his preaching. He has declared only what Moses himself declared: "that the Messiah would suffer, that as the first of those resurrected from the dead he would proclaim light both to the people and to the Gentiles" (26:23). The risen Messiah is the one who preaches light. The speech is crucial for its place in the narrative of Paul's captivity, but it is more than a summation of Acts 21–26. It points back to the words of Simeon at the beginning of Luke's Gospel: Jesus' birth means light for the Gentiles and glory for Israel (Luke 2:32). The preacher of light is not Paul but Jesus himself.

These activities suggest that the imperfect tense of Acts 1:1 is to be taken at face value. It says what it means — that Luke's first volume had to do with the *beginning* of Jesus' activity and teaching — not that he finished his actions and instruction or that he handed those tasks over to others. Jesus' ascension does not mean his absence; it simply means that his presence is no longer constrained by place and time.

Conclusion

This consideration of Jesus' identity is far from complete, having touched on some important features and slighted many others. It is tempting to cast a glance at John 21:25 and plead that should this essay canvass all the ways in which Luke identifies Jesus, an entire library shelf would not be able to contain it. The goal here has not been to catalogue every feature of Jesus' identity in Luke-Acts but to show some ways in which Jesus' identity is declared and then amplified, corrected, redirected. Readers' initial understandings are no more reliable than Peter's initial declaration that Jesus is "the Messiah of God" (Luke 9:20), an understanding that proves unable to comprehend the transfiguration (9:28-36) or to confess association with Jesus following his arrest (22:54-62).

The process of learning and relearning Jesus' identity in Luke-Acts (and the accompanying process of learning the new identities of several Lukan characters) seems particularly appropriate, given Luke's emphasis on the giving and withholding of sight and on the association of the gospel, indeed of Jesus himself, with light. Luke understands that perception, genuine sight, comes to human beings only as a result of God's gift, as is evident especially in the Emmaus road story.

Luke's two volumes then present contemporary audiences with a significant challenge about how it is that we understand who Jesus is. For many contemporary readers of the Bible, steeped in modernist assumptions about the world and its ways, understanding Jesus' identity is a matter of asking after logical or historical proof or demonstration. To affirm with Peter that Jesus is God's Messiah would require that Jesus or his representatives submit a convincing body of evidence as proofs of Jesus' accomplishments, his powers, his relationship to God. Others may read the Gospels with apparent receptivity, selecting those features of Jesus' identity that are congenial and leaving aside those that are perceived as outmoded or unwelcome. The prophetic language of Luke-Acts will be welcome in some quarters as a means of challenging contemporary practice, but the notion of Jesus' cosmic kingship will be bewildering. Still another option is chilling: the prophetic motif may be neglected in favor of a Christianity that wants to identify Jesus' kingship with contemporary political power. As different as these strategies are from one another, they share the assumption that arriving at the identity of Jesus is a matter of human intellect and volition.

Luke is radically disturbing — or at least Luke should be radically disturbing — to such sensibilities. Repeatedly, Luke demonstrates that human beings do not on their own arrive at a right understanding of Jesus' identity. Instead, they learn it through Scripture, the reading and interpretation of which play a significant role in the church's witness (see esp. Acts 13:15; 15:16-17; 17:2). They learn through instruction within the community, both from the apostles and from others (Acts 2:42; 18:24-26; 28:31). That is to say, humans are instructed about the identity of Jesus by God, by the risen Jesus, and by the Spirit. As Jesus himself rejoices, God has hidden insight from those who presume to be wise and understanding and has revealed it to the children (Luke 10:21-22).

Word of God, Messiah of Israel, Savior of the World: Learning the Identity of Jesus from the Gospel of John

Marianne Meye Thompson

The Gospel of John presents a peculiar challenge to modern interpreters who simultaneously confess Jesus as Lord and engage in historical study of the Gospels and Jesus. Paradoxically, John is the Gospel deemed least reliable in providing useful data for the quest of the "historical Jesus" but most penetrating in providing the fundamental categories for Christian confession of who Jesus ultimately was and is — Word of God made flesh, Son of the Father, resurrection and life. While these designations and metaphors may be pivotal for Johannine and, finally, Christian witness to the identity of Jesus, they play little if any role in the contemporary efforts to reconstruct the historical Jesus. Contemporary reconstructions of Jesus seek to recover his aims, his words, and his deeds, sometimes summarized in terms of "what he actually said" or "what he actually did" — the so-called indisputable facts about Jesus.[1] But what Jesus "actually said" and "actually did" are categories in which John has not achieved high marks.[2]

1. Note the number of titles that play on some variation of this theme: Robert W. Funk, Roy W. Hoover, and the Jesus Seminar, *The Five Gospels: What Did Jesus Really Say? The Search for the Authentic Words of Jesus* (1993; reprint, San Francisco: HarperSanFrancisco, 1997); N. T. Wright, *Who Was Jesus?* (Grand Rapids: Eerdmans, 1992); F. Scott Spencer, *What Did Jesus Do? Gospel Profiles of Jesus' Personal Conduct* (Edinburgh: T&T Clark, 2003). There are of course exceptions; one such, notable for its pointed title, is Leander Keck's *Who Is Jesus? History in Perfect Tense* (Columbia: University of South Carolina Press, 2000; Minneapolis: Fortress, 2001).

2. Assessments of the so-called historical reliability of John range across a broad spectrum. For presentations at opposite ends of the spectrum, see Craig Blomberg, *The Historical Reliability of John's Gospel* (Downers Grove, Ill.: InterVarsity, 2001); Maurice Casey, *Is John's Gospel True?* (New York/London: Routledge, 1996).

For many interpreters of John, it appears that the past of Jesus has been swallowed up by the present of the evangelist, or the experience and theology of the "Johannine community." John was interested in the reality and presence of Jesus for Christians of his day; in writing about the past, he rewrote it so as virtually to collapse past into present. As a result, the "historical Jesus" is scarcely visible in or recoverable through John.

Such a way of posing the problem assumes that we know what we mean by "history" and "historical." But the meaning of these terms is not transparent. On the one hand, "history" does not simply mean "the past," the sum total of all events and situations that have ever occurred. Rather, "history" refers to those events that have become part of the historical record because they made an impact and thus were remembered. In this sense, "history" refers to events in their significance within their context and in light of their subsequent influence. All history then comes to us because of the impact, negative or positive, of a person or event on individuals, cultures, institutions, and societies, and all history is in some way mediated to us through human experience and memory. On the other hand, the term "historical" refers to those things that are factual rather than fictional, to things that "really happened" in the past. But sometimes "historical" is contrasted not only to that which is fiction but to the "significance" attached to those past events. It is this sense of the term "historical" that dominates discussions of Jesus; the "historical Jesus" often designates the "past" of Jesus apart from any attribution of significance to that past. But it is precisely this sense of the term that serves inadequately to disclose the identity of Jesus, whether we are speaking of his pre- and postexistence with God, his ongoing significance for the church — or even the identity of the so-called historical Jesus.

There is no denying that Jesus as a historical figure of the past matters in the Gospel of John, and that he matters in specific and concrete ways. Two ways of construing this assertion may be ruled out. First, it is not enough to say that for John it is the sheer fact of Jesus' historical existence that matters and that John has subsequently made of Jesus what he wanted or needed to make of him. John is bound by traditions received about Jesus, and at every turn these seep through the pages of the Gospel. The Gospel traditions may be malleable, but they are not infinitely so. But, second, to say that the historical figure of Jesus matters in the Gospel of John does not mean that the identity of Jesus can be ascertained entirely through historical reconstructions of the Gospel's "undisputed facts" about him. Even if one could verify every detail of the Fourth Gospel as authentic, one would not have thereby grasped the identity of Jesus in the Fourth Gospel — the "what" that makes Jesus who he is.[3]

Word, Messiah, Savior: A Sketch of the Identity of Jesus in John

Who, then, is Jesus? This way of putting the question already suggests the way in which the answer will need to be framed: Jesus is not simply a figure of the past but one who is alive. In part, John's aim in writing his Gospel is to show that "[w]hat Jesus *is* to the faith of the true Christian believer, He *was* in the flesh."[4] Jesus was, is, and will be life for the world. Indeed, if the statement that Jesus is alive is true — and if it is not, then the Gospel bears false witness to Jesus — it will indicate that Jesus' identity cannot be limited to what can be known about him from the past, and this is what John does in fact indicate in direct and indirect ways throughout the Gospel. Jesus' past is remembered in the very narrative of the Gospel, but there is also the promise of his continued presence with his people (14:18, 23; 15:4-7), as well as that of his future coming (21:23). In brief, Jesus' identity is truly recognized only if we see him in his past, his present, and his future.

By Jesus' past we refer to the "historical" or "earthly" Jesus, the past that is partially documented in historical accounts of various sorts. But the opening sentences of the Gospel of John identify its central figure as "the Word" and, with allusion to Genesis 1:1, locate its account of this Word in relationship to God the Creator and the origins of the cosmos. Because the Word that was "in the beginning" was the agent of God's creation of all that is, the identity of that Word cannot be understood apart from relationship either to God or to the created order. Moreover, what can be said about God's relationship to the world can also be said about that of the Word: the world is answerable to its Creator (see John 1:10-11). Indeed, the Word is called God (1:1; cf. 20:28). In this sense, the identity of Jesus in John is thoroughly theological, inasmuch as it must be delineated in relationship to the God who created the world, the God whose identity is attested through the

3. For this definition of identity, see Markus Bockmuehl's discussion in "God's Life as a Jew," in the present volume.

4. E. C. Hoskyns, *The Fourth Gospel*, ed. F. N. Davey (London: Faber & Faber, 1956), p. 35.

Scriptures as the God of Israel. It follows, then, that genuine knowledge of Jesus, perhaps even genuine historical knowledge of Jesus, depends upon theological insight. To know Jesus as he "really was" in the past will require not that we strip away the theological aspects of his identity but that we bring them to bear on our understanding and articulation of who he was and is. His identity is not reducible to his past historical context.

The theological dimension of Jesus' identity shapes the way in which John portrays Jesus in every role and deed: it is as the Word of God, as the One who was the agent of creation, that the incarnate Jesus carries out his prophetic, messianic, and salvific vocation. Throughout the Gospel there are hints and reminders that in the words of Jesus it is the Word incarnate who speaks: as the unique Son, he alone makes God known (1:18); as the embodiment on earth of Jacob's ladder, he opens the heavenly realms of glory (1:51); he offers the divine gift of life in the face of death that pervades the cosmos (5:24); he has come "from above" and will return to his previous state of glory (8:22-23).

But while confession of the preexistent Word of God introduces the Gospel (1:1, 14, 18), it is the Word made flesh who heals, teaches, debates, hungers, thirsts, bleeds, and dies. The narrative indeed establishes that Jesus was a human being and that Christian faith cannot be docetic, but it does even more: it anchors the account of Jesus in an identifiable time and specific places.[5] The designations that dominate John's Gospel locate Jesus within the story of Israel in the context of the Roman Empire of the first century. Jesus enters the public scene in connection with the baptismal ministry of a Jewish prophet named John, calls Galilean fishermen to be his disciples, interprets the Torah, teaches in synagogues and in the temple, discusses and disputes with Pharisees, frequently journeys to Jerusalem, and dies by crucifixion at the hands of Roman imperial power. Jesus shares the beliefs of his fellow Jews, including the acknowledgment of one living God, the heritage received from the patriarchs, the validity of Torah and the role of Moses in giving it, the sanctity of the temple, the resurrection from the dead, and the promised ingathering of God's scattered children under the Messiah, symbolized in anticipatory fashion by the selection of

5. In my experience of teaching courses on Jesus and the Gospels, it is not the "humanity" of Jesus that causes problems for students but rather Jesus as a particular historical figure. They are not troubled that Jesus got tired, hungry, thirsty, and angry, or that he agonized in Gethsemane; but they are deeply troubled that he might have spoken words such as those recorded in Matt 15:26: "It is not fair to take the children's food and throw it to the dogs."

twelve disciples.[6] In John, Jesus alludes to the halakic regulations that allow for circumcision on the Sabbath (7:22; *m. Šabb.* 18:3–19:4); is aware of the custom of using stone jars for the waters of purification (2:6; *m. Kelim* 10:1); knows the Palestinian manna traditions of the Jewish haggadah (6:35-51) and the significance of the last day of the Feast of Tabernacles and the water poured in front of the altar (7:37; *m. Sukkah* 4:1, 8, 9). The designations used for Jesus reflect the categories that come from the Scriptures and the world of first-century Judaism: he is called prophet, Messiah, Son of Man, and King of Israel and of the Jews. His speech is replete with metaphors from Scripture, such as the vine, the shepherd, bread, and light; he interprets scriptural texts (e.g., John 6:32, 45; 10:34-36); he alludes to narratives of Israel's past, such as the sojourn in the wilderness. His public deeds and teaching take place near Passover, on the Sabbath, at Tabernacles, and at Hanukkah. These dimensions of Jesus' life are central, not incidental, to his mission as portrayed in John.

Jesus' mission is directed to "his own" (1:11), and he dies in order to save "the nation" and to "gather together the children of God who are scattered abroad" (11:48-52). The purpose of John's baptism is to make Jesus known to Israel (1:31), and he is subsequently acknowledged as the Messiah, the "King of Israel" (1:49), by "an Israelite in whom there is no deceit" (1:47) and by the crowds upon his entry into Jerusalem (12:13). Speaking with a Samaritan woman, Jesus identifies himself as belonging to "the Jews" (4:22), and non-Jews in the Gospel speak or think of Jesus as a Jew (4:9; 18:35). Virtually the entire Roman trial scene in John turns on the question whether Jesus is king of the Jews, and on this charge Pilate has him crucified (18:33, 39; 19:3, 12, 14, 19, 21). It is in the light of such data that one must read the frequent and puzzling references to "the Jews" in John — puzzling, inasmuch as the term "the Jews" often separates those so designated from others who are also clearly Jewish, including John the Baptist (1:19; 3:25) and Jesus himself (5:16, 18).[7] While in John the term does seem to distance Jesus and his followers from "the Jews," Jesus does not reject "his own," nor does he stand over against "Judaism" as a religious system.

6. For the hope of the ingathering of God's people or of the twelve tribes, see Isa 11:12; 43:5-6; 54:7-8; 56:8; Jer 23:1-5; Ezek 34:5-16; 37:20-28; see also Sir 36:11 RSV [13-16 NRSV]; 48:10; Bar 4:37; 5:5; 2 Macc 1:27; 2:17-18; *Jub.* 1:15; *Pss. Sol.* 11:2; 17:28-31.

7. For a survey and discussion of the evidence regarding "the Jews" in John, as well as additional bibliography, one may consult Raymond E. Brown, *Introduction to the Gospel of John,* ed. Francis J. Moloney (New York: Doubleday, 2003), pp. 157-88.

Although there is evidence of friction between two groups of Jews, namely, those who follow Jesus and those who do not, the conflict between them has yet to become the rift found in such early Christian documents as the epistles of Ignatius, Barnabas, or Diognetus.[8] In John, the identity of Jesus is bound up at every level with the people of Israel and their destiny, so much so that he gives his life for them.

Specifically, Jesus is the Messiah of Israel. This is the confession of the evangelist (1:17; 20:31) and of Jesus' disciples (1:41, 45, 49; 11:27), but it is also the subject of dispute and inquiry (7:26-42; 10:24). As Messiah, "the Son of God, the King of Israel," Jesus raises up a temple for God (cf. 2:19-22; 10:17-18). But it is precisely not the kind of temple that Solomon, the son of David, or his descendants would build. Similarly, he is acclaimed by the crowds as king of Israel upon his entry into Jerusalem, but his kingship will bring about his own death, not the death of his enemies. Jesus is not a king by any recognizable criteria, whether Jewish or pagan assumptions about what a king should be and do. The confession of Jesus as Messiah cannot simply be read off the surface of his life and deeds, for his messianic vocation is undertaken not in terms of the exercise of power against his enemies but as service (13:1-11) and self-giving (10:1-18; 12:23-26), and through his death on the cross. But in order to recognize this One as God's Messiah — to see, enter, and understand the kingdom that is genuinely God's kingdom (3:3, 5; 18:36) — the work of the Spirit of God is required. Recognition of Jesus as the Messiah is not the product of human logic or reason, or even of accepting his claim to be the Messiah, but of the revelation of God (6:44-45; see also Matt 11:25-27; 16:17; Luke 10:21-22). Hence, what ultimately matters for the confession of Jesus as Messiah is God's acknowledgment of him, God's witness to him (John 5:36-37; 6:27).[9]

Jesus, the Messiah of Israel, is also the "Savior of the world" (4:42). The Gospel is peppered with promises that the death and resurrection of Jesus

8. "It is outlandish to proclaim Jesus Christ and practice Judaism" (Ignatius, *To the Magnesians* 10.3); "Do not become like some people . . . , saying that the covenant is both theirs and ours. For it is ours" (*Barnabas* 4:6-7); "Christians are right to abstain from the vulgar silliness, deceit, and meddling ways of the Jews, along with their arrogance" (*Diognetus* 4.6). Translations from Bart D. Ehrman, *The Apostolic Fathers,* 2 vols., LCL 24-25 (Cambridge, Mass.: Harvard University Press, 2003), 1:251; 2:23, 139.

9. See here the helpful and insightful essay of Walter Moberly, "The Christ of the Old and New Testaments," in *The Cambridge Companion to Jesus,* ed. Markus Bockmuehl (Cambridge: Cambridge University Press, 2001), pp. 184-99.

will bring about the ingathering not only of Jesus' own people but also of all people (3:15; 10:16; 12:32, 47; see also 7:35). As the Living One, Jesus sends the Holy Spirit, the Spirit of life, from the Father (14:26; 15:26). Jesus breathes the life-giving Spirit of God into humankind as God breathed the Spirit into Adam, and as God will breathe life into the desiccated bones of the people of Israel (20:22; Gen 2:7; Ezek 37:9). Jesus' risen existence and the sending of the Spirit to bear witness to him make it possible for him to be present and known beyond the boundaries of Judea and Galilee.

There is also a brief allusion at the end of the Gospel to Jesus' expected return (John 21:22-23), and the few descriptions of the future and of what will be emphasize the twin themes of eternal life and presence — the presence of the Father, and the Son, with the people of God. The Gospel of John thus comprises in itself the whole biblical story from creation (1:1-3) to the second coming of Christ (21:22-23), implicitly identifying Jesus of Nazareth as the One who was, is, and is to come: what can be predicated of the eternal God can also be predicated of him. Word of God, Messiah of Israel, and Savior of the world: this is who he was and is and will be.

In John's witness to Jesus, these aspects of Jesus' identity are related in such a way that each determines and shapes the other. It is as the Word made flesh that Jesus is the Messiah: Israel's deliverance is an act of Israel's God, and "Messiah" is defined and redefined in terms of the embodied presence of God's own Word, who speaks words of life to his people. As the Word, the agent of creation, the Messiah of Israel delivers his people from the ultimate forces that threaten their very existence, namely, the powers of death, by subjecting himself to the powers of the Roman authorities who execute him as they would other would-be rebels. Again, it is as the Messiah of Israel that Jesus is the Savior of the world, and as the Savior of the world that he is the Messiah of Israel; and thus to gather together Israel, as a shepherd gathers his flock (10:16), is to gather together *all* God's scattered children (11:52). As Messiah of Israel, the Word incarnate accomplishes deliverance not only for his own but for the world, which was "made through him" (1:3). The mission of the Word in the world includes the people of Israel and intends their deliverance, but it also extends to the whole world, because the God of Israel is the Lord of the universe, and the incarnate Word the agent of its creation.

To be sure, it has not been easy to hold these aspects of Jesus' identity together, whether in scholarly assessment or popular piety. Ernst Käsemann once famously characterized John's picture of Jesus as "God walking on the face of the earth."[10] Here, contended Käsemann, is a portrait of the Word, of the Savior, of God — but not of one who genuinely belongs to this world, this flesh, or to Israel. It is surprising how apt many seem to find this characterization, but it is perhaps not surprising that John has contributed to acceptance of it.[11] John's descriptions of Jesus as the One who comes from above, who is one with the Father, have made it difficult not to see John's Jesus as hovering somewhat above the realities of this world and life. Interestingly, the pagan critics of early Christianity seemed to grasp the point that it is precisely in claiming this crucified human being as Son of God that the heart and offense of Christianity lies, for whereas "Son of God" and "crucified man" ought to be two different figures, Christians in fact alleged that they were one and the same. Origen reports Celsus's accusation that "[Christians say that] although we proclaim the Son of God to be Logos we do not bring forward as evidence a pure and holy Logos, but a man who was arrested most disgracefully and crucified."[12] Or, as another critic later sneered, "The deities are not inimical to you, because you worship the omnipotent God; but because you both allege that one born as men are, and put to death on the cross, which is a disgraceful punishment even for worthless men, was God, and because you believe that He still lives, and because you worship Him in daily supplications."[13] This is the "what" of the "who" to which John bears witness: the Son of God is the man who was most disgracefully crucified.

"We Saw His Glory": Sight, Insight, and Witness to Jesus

But if this Crucified One is the Son of God, how does one come to know that? For some, the answer is simple: Jesus is who he says he is. (That is, in

10. In Ernst Käsemann, *The Testament of Jesus: A Study of the Gospel of John in the Light of Chapter 17*, trans. Gerhard Krodel (Philadelphia: Fortress, 1968).

11. In fact, it has been my experience that, presented with Käsemann's description, students sometimes find it odd that one should find it objectionable. Is Jesus not, after all, "God on earth"? Did he not come to "replace" the Jewish people with a universal Christian people? And did he not offer a "spiritual" kingdom over against the worldly hopes of the Jews for an earthly, political kingdom?

12. Origen, *Against Celsus* 2.31, trans. Henry Chadwick (Cambridge: Cambridge University Press, 1965), p. 93.

13. Arnobius, *Against the Heathen* 1.36, trans. H. Bryce and H. Campbell, *ANF* 6:422, quoting his "opponent."

the terms of the well-known apologetic "trilemma," there are only three logical alternatives: Jesus was a liar, a lunatic, or who he says he is — Lord.)[14] Strikingly, although in the Fourth Gospel Jesus makes many bold claims for himself, his identity is disclosed largely through the testimony borne to him by others, and it matters greatly who says what about Jesus and that these witnesses be trustworthy. Those who bear witness to Jesus do so as the result of encounter with him. John the Baptist asserts that he has "seen and borne witness" that Jesus is the Son of God (1:34); the Samaritans announce that having heard Jesus they have come to know that he is the Savior of the world (4:42); his disciples state that he has "the words of life" (6:68); Thomas confesses the risen Jesus as "My Lord and my God!" (20:28). What is striking about all these confessions is that while they emerge from encounter with Jesus, from having seen, heard, and touched him, the substance of the confessions themselves — Son of God, Savior of the world, Lord and God — is not simply a sum reached by adding up all the right numbers. But neither is there an ugly broad ditch fixed between the historical figure and the One who is confessed in these terms. It is *in* what Jesus said and did, as well as *in* what happened to him — particularly his crucifixion and resurrection — that one may uncover what it means that he is Messiah of Israel and Savior of the world.

John's insistence that witness to Jesus emerges from encounter with Jesus creates a problem for those who have never encountered the earthly Jesus, since the same sort of encounter is no longer possible. The role of the Gospel itself is to serve as a witness to Jesus, so that those who did not or cannot encounter the earthly Jesus may know him to be life-giving and confess him as Messiah and Son of God — Lord and God (20:30-31). Those who come to this confession do so because they receive the witness of the Gospel, a "given communal embodiment of memory and witness."[15] But the Gospel does not serve as a substitute for Jesus in the present. It bears witness to the risen and living Jesus by recounting the past in light of the

14. The argument is attributed to C. S. Lewis, who famously wrote: "A man who was merely a man and said the sort of things Jesus said would not be a great moral teacher. He would either be a lunatic — on a level with the man who says he is a poached egg — or else he would be the Devil of Hell. You must make your choice. Either this man was, and is, the son of God: or else a madman or something worse." Lewis, *Mere Christianity* (1943; reprint, New York: Macmillan, 1981), p. 45.

15. Bockmuehl, "God's Life as a Jew," p. 68; see also the discussion in Francis Watson, "*Veritas Christi,*" both in the present volume.

present understanding that he is indeed living. The Gospel therefore offers its readers a link to the history of the past, as well as testimony to the One who gives life. While not identical, these are, for John, inseparable. The accountability of later interpreters to the testimony of "eyewitnesses to the word of life" is illustrated well in Irenaeus's second-century letter to Florinus, in which he asserts that as an eyewitness of the apostles, Polycarp would have recoiled in horror at Florinus's Gnostic account of their teaching. According to Irenaeus, Polycarp used to recount what he had heard the apostles say about the Lord, about his miracles and his teaching, and to do so "in complete harmony with Scripture."[16] The twofold reference to "his miracles and his teaching" and "harmony with the Scripture" demonstrates the concern both to recount the events of Jesus' life and to do so in ways that were consonant with the apostolic testimony. Likewise, the Gospel of John recounts the events of Jesus' life so as to invite people to accept the apostolic testimony of the Gospel and, like the Samaritans, to come to their own confession of faith. The Gospel directs the believer to know the Risen One whose story is told in, but cannot be reduced to, the narrative of the Gospel.

More specifically, the Gospel stakes its claim to credibility on one who was an eyewitness and who had a particular personal memory of Jesus, namely, the beloved disciple (19:35; 21:24-25). The various meanings of "seeing" in the Gospel point to the importance and character of eyewitness testimony, including that of the "disciple whom Jesus loved." On the one hand, "seeing" refers to the simple act of physical sight; on the other, it refers to perception, or spiritual insight. Statements such as "I have seen and borne witness that he is the Son of God" and "we have come to know that [he is] the Savior of the world" show that the insight that grasps who Jesus is cannot be gained entirely by what the eyes can see, but that neither can such insight dispense with what the eyes can see. A statement such as "we saw his glory" (1:14) refers to both levels: the disciples saw in Jesus and his deeds both something concrete and something beyond what is physically discernible. Insight cannot be divorced from sight — still, insight does not naturally or inevitably arise from sight (e.g., 9:39). Indeed, at times insight, which might also be understood as perception through the illumination of God's Spirit, is radically counterintuitive. This is nowhere more evident

16. Cited in Eusebius, *Ecclesiastical History* 5.20.6, trans. G. A. Williamson (New York: Dorset, 1965), p. 228.

than in Jesus' death on the cross. What it means in its historical context and what it means in the testimony of the beloved disciple and others contrast quite considerably. Sight sees the shameful death of a would-be king; the insight granted by the Spirit perceives God's glorification of the rightful King of Israel or, perhaps better, both together. Which of these shall we label "historical"?

The Gospel thus claims that a particular way of telling the story of Jesus' life and ministry has the authority of the eyewitnesses. John clearly recognizes that there are other ways to tell the story that he recounts; indeed, the Gospel is shot through with the divisions that arise over differing assessments of Jesus (1:10-13; 6:66; 7:26-42; 9:34). But not all assessments are in harmony with the eyewitnesses, and therefore not all testimony discloses the identity of Jesus. Still, even eyewitness testimony does not ensure that one will grasp the identity of Jesus. The Gospel indicates that the remembrances of the disciples were prompted by the Spirit, and that Jesus' actions and deeds were to be interpreted through the witness of Israel's Scripture, and only after his resurrection. The kind of historical account that bears witness to Jesus does not simply recount his past, but it cannot do without it.

"Afterward You Will Understand": Resurrection, Spirit, and Scripture

The Gospel of John — indeed, all the documents of the New Testament — are written from a post-resurrection perspective, and this perspective has shaped the way in which Jesus is understood. John writes the past from the perspective of the present, specifically, with the conviction that Jesus has been raised from the dead and is now "ever with the Father" (1:18). As the One who now lives with the Father, Jesus was, is, and will be the giver of life (1:1-4; 14:6; 15:1-9); indeed, his return to the Father signals that he is the Living One, the agent of creation (1:1-3), who raises the dead to life "on the last day" (5:28-29; 6:54, 57; 11:25-26). The resurrection thus functions both theologically and hermeneutically. It is the lens through which Jesus' identity as the One through whom God gives life to the world comes into focus. A prime example here is John's presentation of the signs of Jesus as life-giving and the claims of Jesus to be resurrection and life. What he claims for himself in the Gospel of John is what the resurrection confirms him to be, namely, the One who acts with the power of God to give life to the world. Jesus' "I am" statements echo the repeated assertions of the Lord God in the book of Isaiah, where God declares his unique power particularly with respect to his sole creation of the world and his continued sovereignty over it (cf., e.g., Isa 45:18; 51:12-13). Jesus' identity as God's life-giving agent takes concrete form in his giving of food to the hungry, sight to the blind, and life to the dying and the dead, and will ultimately be confirmed in the resurrection at the last day.

Put differently, to understand the identity of Jesus, one needs to understand the identity of God, "the living Father" (6:57), a reality that may be most clearly discerned in the sheer number of the Gospel's references to Jesus as Son and God as Father. The relationship of Father and Son is an interdependent relationship: Jesus is the Son because of his relationship to God the Father, and God is the Father because of his relationship to the Son. There are, to be sure, other well-known designations for Jesus in the Gospel, but each of these also indicates that Jesus is who and what he is in relationship to God. It is God's own Word that is embodied in Jesus (1:1, 14). In Jesus, God's glory dwells (1:14), even as the prophets spoke of a new "encampment" of God with his people (Exod 25:8-9; Joel 3:17; Zech 2:10). Jesus is the Son of Man who is the locus of the revelation of God's glory, particularly in his death on the cross (John 1:51; 3:14-15; 12:23). He is the One who bears the ineffable name of God (17:6, 11, 12, 26). And as the Word, who "was in the beginning with God" (1:2) and who exercises the divine powers of judgment and life, the Word is in fact called "God" (1:1; 20:28).

As already stated, John explicitly notes that the significance of some events he has narrated could not be understood until later, after Jesus was raised from the dead (e.g., 2:22; 13:7) and the Spirit of truth had been given (14:17; 15:26). Without the illumination of the Spirit, the events of Jesus' life remain opaque. So also, without the witness of Israel's Scriptures, the very identity of Jesus remains opaque. These Scriptures speak of Jesus' coming (1:45; 5:37, 46); they contain the narratives of Israel's past, such as the wandering in the wilderness, and the promises of the ingathering of God's people and God's presence with his people that make sense of Jesus' mission (Exod 25:8; 29:45; Lev 26:11; 1 Kings 6:13; Ezek 37:26-28; Zech 2:11). These Scriptures provide the texture and specific imagery used for Jesus (shepherd, king, judge, bread, light). The Gospel also claims that certain texts are actually about this Jesus (Isa 6:1-6, alluded to in John 12:41; Psalm

69, cited in John 2:17; 15:25; 19:28-29). In short, the Scriptures of Israel provide the categories and the framework for understanding the identity of Jesus as the messianic agent of God's decisive act of salvation for his people and for the world.

Conclusion

From the Gospel of John we learn that Jesus cannot be reduced to a figure of the past of human history. Indeed, he is alive. Therefore, any attempt to understand Jesus that limits him to the past and assumes that "historical" study can on its own produce adequate knowledge of him leads inevitably to a stunted grasp of who he is. The framework of the Gospel suggests as much. John's Gospel spans the biblical story from creation (1:1) to the promised return of Christ (21:22-23), and Jesus' identity must be plotted along those coordinates. Through him, God created the world; through his words and deeds, God gives life to the world; and through him, God will give life from the dead "on the last day." This cosmic and eschatological framework indicates that to restrict Jesus' identity to what can be ascertained through historical study of the past of the man, Jesus of Nazareth, is to strip away the very interpretative framework necessary to answer the question asked by inquirers in the Gospel: Who are you? (8:25).

To be sure, the Gospel explicitly and implicitly assigns a central role to eyewitness testimony to Jesus, the embodiment of the Word of God. As the embodied Word, Jesus "lived among us" (1:14), assumed our humanity, our creatureliness. The eyewitnesses speak not only of humanity in the abstract; they bear witness to a man who lived in a specific historical time and place, who held particular religious beliefs and followed particular practices and customs, and whose world was shaped by particular political and social institutions. Consequently, a failure to understand this world, the world of first-century Judaism of Galilee and Judea, and the concrete ways in which Jesus is lodged firmly within it, will entail a failure to understand Jesus. While the cosmic and eschatological framework remains essential to understanding Jesus, it does not eradicate his human and historical identity as a first-century Jew whose mission was dedicated to his people Israel.

Yet even the testimony of the eyewitnesses does not guarantee "insight" into who Jesus is. Insight requires the testimony of the eyewitnesses, but it also requires the illumination of the Spirit and of Scripture. The Gospel presents Jesus as One whose identity must be grasped in theological terms, that is, in terms of his relationship to God. Jesus is who he is — Word of God, Messiah of Israel, Savior of the world — as Son of the living Father. To strip away those aspects of his identity that set him in relationship to God, and to conceive of his identity as somehow ascertainable apart from God, is to strip away that which is indispensable to knowing who he is. The theological aspects of Jesus' identity are not a layer that can be peeled back to reveal the "real" Jesus underneath. Indeed, to frame Jesus' identity in theological terms and with reference to God is to disclose his true identity.

The Story of God's Son: The Identity of Jesus in the Letters of Paul

Richard B. Hays

In the midst of a battle against the "superapostles" who were corrupting the faith of the fledgling church he had planted in Corinth, Paul blurts out this fearful complaint:

> But I am afraid that as the serpent deceived Eve by its cunning, your thoughts will be led astray from a sincere and pure devotion to Christ. For if someone comes and proclaims *another Jesus than the one we proclaimed,* or if you receive a different spirit from the one you received, or a different gospel from the one you accepted, you submit to it readily enough. (2 Cor 11:3-4)[1]

Another Jesus?[2] Of course, Paul does not mean some other person altogether — say, Jesus Barabbas rather than Jesus of Nazareth. If the preaching of the superapostles involved a case of mistaken identity, their mistake lay not in identifying the wrong individual but in misidentifying Jesus. These other preachers were presenting an *account of Jesus* that Paul regarded as distorted. This in turn suggests that *Paul's own preaching must have included his own very specific account of the identity of Jesus, his own particular way of telling the Jesus story.* What, then, was the character of Paul's Jesus?

From one point of view, Paul offers remarkably little information

1. Scripture quotations not otherwise identified are from the NRSV.

2. It is a point of more than passing interest that Paul describes the battle in these terms, rather than saying, for example, "If someone comes and proclaims another doctrine of justification than the one we proclaimed. . . ."

about Jesus.[3] If we had only Paul's letters as a source for knowledge about the man Jesus, here is what we would know:

> Jesus was born of a woman, "under the law," that is, as a Jew (Gal 4:4). He was a descendant of Israel's great king, David (Rom 1:3). He had brothers, one of whom was named Jakobos ("James," Gal 1:19; 1 Cor 9:5). He forbade divorce (1 Cor 7:10-11), and he commanded that preachers of his message should receive financial support for their preaching (1 Cor 9:14). He instructed his followers to celebrate a communal meal in his memory (1 Cor 11:23-25). The wording of this tradition ("This cup is the new covenant in my blood") suggests that Jesus understood his impending death as a decisive event that would inaugurate a new chapter in the story of Israel's relation to God. Further, it suggests that he expected to meet a violent end, and he was right: he was crucified (1 Cor 2:2; Gal 3:1; Phil 2:8). Although crucifixion was a Roman punishment, some of Jesus' own Jewish countrymen opposed him and played a role in his violent death (1 Thess 2:14-15). He was buried; then, on the third day, he arose from the dead and appeared to many of his followers (1 Cor 15:3-8).[4]

In short, although the points of contact between Paul and the Gospels are significant, we get limited information from Paul about "the Jesus of history." He does not tell us that Jesus proclaimed the kingdom of God or that he taught in parables or that he performed healings and miracles or that he clashed with the Pharisees over interpretation of the law. (The last of these points is a remarkable silence in light of Paul's own troubled deliberations about the Torah.) Still less do we gain from Paul any sense of Jesus' individual personal characteristics: was he solemn or fun-loving, reclusive or extroverted? And what did he look like? Paul's silence on such matters is not surprising, since he was not a follower of Jesus during Jesus' earthly life; indeed, there is no reason to think that Paul ever met Jesus.[5]

3. For surveys of the critical investigation of this problem, see Victor Paul Furnish, *Jesus according to Paul* (Cambridge: Cambridge University Press, 1993); David Wenham, *Paul: Follower of Jesus or Founder of Christianity?* (Grand Rapids: Eerdmans, 1995).

4. Occasionally, it is suggested that in a few other passages Paul may allude to specific sayings of Jesus (e.g., Rom 8:15-16; 12:17; 13:8; Gal 4:6; 5:14; 1 Thess 4:15-17), but Paul himself gives no indication that these passages are based on the authority of Jesus' teaching. The "word of the Lord" in 1 Thess 4:15 probably refers to a word of Christian prophecy.

5. A statement in 2 Cor 5:16 has sometimes been understood to mean that Paul was per-

We might conclude from this brief survey of the matter that the Pauline Epistles have little to contribute to an exploration of the identity of Jesus.

Such a conclusion, however, would clash with one other salient fact: on virtually every page of his letters, Paul talks about Jesus. This fact has sometimes been obscured by the way that modernist biblical scholarship has organized information, separating out bits of "historical" data that correlate with the Gospels (as in the above sketch) from Paul's "Christology," with only the former regarded as significant for the Jesus quest. To be sure, the fragments of biographical information summarized above show that Paul's Jesus was a human historical figure of the first century C.E., but the identity of Jesus, as Paul describes it, is a much wider reality. Jesus Christ, according to Paul, is the preexistent Son of God through whom all things exist; he freely took human form and surrendered himself to suffering and death for the sake of reconciling the world to God; by virtue of his resurrection he is exalted as Lord over the world, which he transforms and sustains with his life-giving power; and he will come again to judge the world and to bring about the final redemption of all things. To speak rightly of the identity of Jesus in Paul's letters, we must take this wider, cosmic frame of reference into account.

Thus, the distinction between "the Jesus of history" and "the Christ of faith" is misleading when applied to Paul's writings. For Paul, Jesus Christ is a single person whose identity is disclosed in a seamless narrative running from creation to the cross to the resurrection to the eschaton. The historical details of his earthly life, such as his death by crucifixion, are no more and no less a part of his identity than are his role in creation and his present lordship in the community of those who call upon his name.

The aim of the present essay, then, is to trace this narrative identity through the letters of Paul,[6] following its plotline as limned in the "Christ

---

sonally acquainted with Jesus of Nazareth: "Even though we once knew Christ from a human point of view [κατὰ σάρκα, *kata sarka;* lit., according to the flesh], we know him no longer in that way." Paul's contrast, however, is not between knowledge of the human Jesus and of the divine Christ; rather, it is between the old, fleshly *way* of knowing and the new, epistemological perspective given through God's apocalyptic act of new creation. See J. Louis Martyn, "Epistemology at the Turn of the Ages," in *Theological Issues in the Letters of Paul* (Nashville: Abingdon, 1997), pp. 89-110.

6. For the purposes of this inquiry, I have surveyed not only the seven letters whose authorship is generally uncontested but also Colossians and 2 Thessalonians. The arguments against Pauline authorship of these letters are not in my judgment persuasive. I have not in-

hymn" of Philippians 2:5-11: preexistent glory, cruciform abasement, transformative exaltation, eschatological consummation. Wholly apart from the question of correspondence to the historical data given in the Gospels, what is the story of Jesus Christ told in the letters of Paul?[7]

Preexistent Glory

Jesus the Agent of Creation

Several passages in Paul's letters refer to Jesus' role in the creation of the world. The anchor point for this element of Jesus' identity is 1 Corinthians 8:6, perhaps a very early confessional formula: "For us there is one God, the Father, from whom are all things and for whom we exist, and one Lord, Jesus Christ, through whom are all things and through whom we exist." This formula is an adaptation of Israel's Shema (Deut 6:4-5), which proclaims the oneness of God as the heart of Israel's faith. By applying this language to Jesus Christ, Paul is describing him not as a second character alongside God but as (mysteriously) one with God, who brought the world into existence.[8]

As the active agent in creation, Jesus is also the bearer of divine glory, as, for example, in 2 Corinthians 4:6: "For it is the God who said, 'Let light shine out of darkness' [Gen 1:1-3], who has shone in our hearts to give the light of the knowledge of the glory of God in the face of Jesus Christ." Jesus manifests the divine glory because, in his preexistent state, "he was in the form of God" (Phil 2:6). These elements of preexistent glory and creative power are given their fullest development in Colossians 1:15-17, again perhaps part of an early confession or hymn:

---

cluded Ephesians and the Pastoral Epistles, whose authorship seems to me to be more seriously in doubt.

7. Similar approaches have been taken by Leander E. Keck, "'Jesus' in Romans," *Journal of Biblical Literature* 108 (1989): 443-60; Stephen E. Fowl, *The Story of Christ in the Ethics of Paul: An Analysis of the Function of the Hymnic Material in the Pauline Corpus,* JSNTSup 36 (Sheffield: JSOT Press, 1990); Douglas A. Campbell, "The Story of Jesus in Romans and Galatians," in *Narrative Dynamics in Paul,* ed. Bruce W. Longenecker (Louisville: Westminster John Knox, 2002), pp. 97-124.

8. N. T. Wright, *The Climax of the Covenant: Christ and the Law in Pauline Theology* (Edinburgh: T&T Clark, 1991), pp. 120-36.

> He is the image of the invisible God, the firstborn of all creation; for in him all things in heaven and on earth were created, things visible and invisible, whether thrones or dominions or rulers or powers — all things have been created through him and for him. He himself is before all things, and in him all things hold together.

These passages are strongly reminiscent of several earlier texts that speak of the role of divine Wisdom in creation (e.g., Prov 8:22-31; Wis 9:1-2, 9-10); this linkage suggests that Paul is ascribing to Jesus Christ attributes that earlier Jewish texts had associated with God's eternal creative wisdom.[9]

Closely linked to this aspect of Jesus' identity are Paul's startling declarations that Christ was the rock from which Israel drank in the wilderness (1 Cor 10:4; cf. Wis 11:4) and that the unfaithfulness of Israel's wilderness generation put Christ to the test (1 Cor 10:9).[10] Jesus Christ, who was before all things, was present in sustaining the people of Israel during the exodus, and their rebellion was therefore also in some sense against him.[11] For Paul, then, Jesus' identity is not limited to the lifespan of his activity as a Galilean prophet in Paul's own generation.

Jesus the Son of God

Paul often refers to Jesus as God's Son. The title has royal connotations, as in Psalm 2:7, and this nuance is emphasized by Romans 1:3-4 (". . . his Son, who was descended from David according to the flesh and was declared to be Son of God with power according to the spirit of holiness by resurrection from the dead, Jesus Christ our Lord"). Jesus is David's heir, who is to reign not only over Israel but also over the Gentiles (1:5), as Paul proclaims in the climactic peroration of Romans: "The root of Jesse shall come, the one who rises to rule the Gentiles; in him the Gentiles shall hope" (Rom

9. Note also the connection between Rom 10:6-7 and Bar 3:29-30.

10. The text-critical problem in 1 Cor 10:9 is difficult, but on balance Χριστόν (*Christon*, "Christ") seems to be the better reading than κύριον (*kyrion*, "the Lord"). In view of Paul's characteristic use of κύριος to refer to Jesus Christ, the textual difference may not in any case be theologically significant.

11. Nowhere else does Paul so explicitly connect God's saving and revealing activity in Israel's past to the figure of Jesus, but this one passage may be the tip of a substantial christological iceberg.

15:12). Indeed, the title Χριστός (*Christos,* "Christ"), often thought to have become for Paul merely a proper name, has by no means lost its messianic connotations, as hinted by several passages where he uses it with the definite article: "Welcome one another, therefore, just as ὁ Χριστός [lit., the Christ] has welcomed you" (Rom 15:7; cf. Rom 9:5; 15:3; 2 Cor 1:5; 2:14; Phil 1:15, 17; 3:7; Col 2:6; 3:1, 4).[12] Wherever in Paul's letters we read the name "Christ," the suggestion that he is the royal Son, Israel's expected King, is not far in the background.

More often, however, Paul's designation of Jesus as God's Son has another set of associations more prominently in view. The "sending" formulas in Galatians 4:4-5 and Romans 8:3-4 portray Jesus as preexistent Son dispatched by the Father on an errand of rescue for a world held in bondage: "But when the fullness of time had come, God sent his Son, born of a woman, born under the law, in order to redeem those who were under the law, so that we might receive adoption as children" (Gal 4:4-5).[13] These formulas envision an apocalyptic scripting of human history and speak of God's Son as a preexistent agent commissioned to enter human existence for a redemptive mission.[14]

Further, that mission requires the Son's death: "He who did not spare his own Son, but gave him up for us all, will he not also give us all things with him?" (Rom 8:32 RSV). Here the Father-Son language suggests both the *love and intimacy* within the mysterious divine reality and, at the same time, the truth that the identity of the Son is distinctively expressed in the costly *sacrificial act of his death.* (We should hear in this an echo of Abraham's offering up of Isaac: ". . . you have not withheld your son, your only son" [Gen 22:16]. The Akedah prefigures Jesus' death, as well as the blessing that his death offers to Abraham's seed.) Thus, the sacrifice of the Son is, from one point of view, the costly act of God the Father. Paul can also

12. As a glance at the concordance will show, there are dozens of instances in which Paul uses some form of the definite article with Χριστός, but it is difficult to know how many should be taken as indicators of its titular force. The ones I have cited here are among those that would merit careful study.

13. James D. G. Dunn has questioned whether Paul thought of Christ as preexistent, but his treatment of these texts in his *Theology of Paul the Apostle* (Grand Rapids: Eerdmans, 1998), pp. 277-79, is more measured than in his earlier *Christology in the Making: A New Testament Inquiry into the Origins of the Doctrine of the Incarnation,* 2nd ed. (London: SCM, 1989).

14. Cf. John 3:16-17; 1 John 4:9-10, 14.

speak of it, however, as the Son's own act of loving self-offering: ". . . the Son of God, who loved me and gave himself for me" (Gal 2:20). Consequently, the sending and death of the Son enact a mysterious fusion of agency between Father and Son. This is expressed most tellingly in the extraordinary claims of Romans 5: "But *God* proves his love for us in that while we still were sinners *Christ* died for us. . . . [W]hile we were enemies, we were reconciled to *God* through the death of *his Son*" (Rom 5:8, 10).

In such passages, the identity of Jesus is bound up inextricably with the loving, sacrificial, saving activity of God. That is why Paul can assert that "in [Christ] the whole fullness of deity dwells bodily" (Col 2:9), with the result that "in Christ God was reconciling the world to himself" (2 Cor 5:19). The reference to Jesus as "Son of God" affirms his divine origin and identity, precisely as expressed in his sacrificial death.

Jesus Prefigured in Scripture

Although Paul, in contrast to Matthew, offers few explicit proofs showing that Jesus is the fulfillment of prophecy, he does at many points suggest that Scripture prefigures the identity of Jesus. Curiously, Paul's most explicit statement of this claim has been obscured by most modern English translations. Paul begins his letter to Rome with the following words: "Paul, a slave of Jesus Christ, called to be an apostle set apart for the gospel of God, which was pre-promised through the prophets *in holy writings concerning his Son,* who came from the seed of David according to the flesh . . ." (Rom 1:1-3, my translation).[15] Here is an explicit claim that the writings of the Old Testament prophets spoke of God's Son, a claim reinforced at several places later in the letter, such as the statement that Israel was entrusted with "the oracles of God" (3:2);[16] the assertion that "the righteousness of God" is "attested by the law and the prophets" (3:21); and

15. The NRSV reads the phrase περὶ τοῦ υἱοῦ αὐτοῦ *(peri tou huiou autou)* as a modifier of εὐαγγέλιον θεοῦ *(euangelion theou),* producing the translation "the gospel of God, which he promised beforehand through his prophets in the holy scriptures, *the gospel* concerning his Son. . . ." This is a possible interpretation, but it is hardly the most natural reading of the Greek word order.

16. On "the oracles of God" as Paul's way of referring to Israel's Scripture in its role of mysteriously prefiguring Christ and the gospel, see Richard B. Hays, *The Conversion of the Imagination* (Grand Rapids: Eerdmans, 2005), pp. 98-99.

Paul's christological interpretations of Isaiah's stone of stumbling (9:33), Deuteronomy's word that is "near" the people (10:6-11), and Isaiah's Deliverer who "will banish ungodliness from Jacob" (11:26). Indeed, these passages illuminate the meaning of Paul's declaration in Romans 10:4 that Christ is τέλος νόμου *(telos nomou):* he is the goal toward which the law points.[17] Most of all, Paul's belief that the Old Testament prefigures Jesus is shown in the climactic chapter 15 of Romans, in Paul's christological reading of the Psalms (15:3, 9) and the prophecy of Isaiah about "the root of Jesse" (15:12).

Thus, for Paul, the identity of Jesus Christ is grounded in the ancient story of God's elect people Israel. His death and resurrection took place "in accordance with the scriptures," as the confessional formula of 1 Corinthians 15:3-5 insists. This hermeneutical conviction has enormous implications for opening up new insights into the identity of Jesus: Paul believes that the reader for whom the veil is removed in Christ will see in Israel's Scripture "the glory of the Lord" and will be transformed into the image of Christ that appears there (2 Cor 3:12-18).[18]

Cruciform Abasement

Jesus the Self-Giving Servant

Paul appeals repeatedly to the *pattern* of Jesus' self-giving or self-emptying for the sake of others. This theme of Jesus' exemplary self-sacrifice plays a central role in Paul's pastoral admonitions (e.g., Rom 15:1-3, 7-9; 1 Cor 11:1 [cf. 8:11]; 2 Cor 8:9; 12:9-10; Gal 2:20; 6:2; Phil 2:5-11; 3:7-17; 1 Thess 1:6).[19] The most extended of these passages is Philippians 2:5-11, where Christ is said to have emptied himself and become a slave, culminating in his death on the cross. For Paul, Christ's pattern of self-sacrificial emptying, or

17. See Richard B. Hays, *Echoes of Scripture in the Letters of Paul* (New Haven: Yale University Press, 1989), pp. 75-77.

18. Hays, *Echoes of Scripture*, pp. 122-53.

19. On the expression ὁ νόμος τοῦ Χριστοῦ (*ho nomos tou Christou*, "the law of Christ," Gal 6:2) as a designation for the pattern of Christ's burden-bearing for others, see Richard B. Hays, "Christology and Ethics in Galatians: The Law of Christ," *Catholic Biblical Quarterly* 49 (1987): 268-90; David G. Horrell, *Solidarity and Difference: A Contemporary Reading of Paul's Ethics* (London: T&T Clark, 2005), pp. 222-31.

kenosis, is a model that his followers are called to emulate: "Let each of you look not to your own interests, but to the interests of others. Let the same mind be in you that [*is*] in Christ Jesus" (Phil 2:4-5).[20] The humility (ταπεινοφροσύνῃ, *tapeinophrosynē,* 2:3) that is to characterize the community of the church reflects the character of Christ's own action: he humbled himself (ἐταπείνωσεν ἑαυτόν, *etapeinōsen heauton,* 2:8). This call to humility must have surprised Paul's first readers, for ancient popular philosophy was no more fond of lowliness and abasement than is political rhetoric in our own day. But Paul insists that the character of Jesus was shown forth in the cross and that his cruciform identity therefore provides a distinctive model to which the community must be conformed. Precisely in this way, in the midst of "a crooked and perverse generation," they will "shine like stars in the world" (Phil 2:15).

It is against this background that we should interpret a series of character qualities attributed to Christ that also set the moral tone for the Pauline churches: "the compassion of Jesus Christ" (Phil 1:8), "the love of Christ" (2 Cor 5:14; cf. Rom 8:35), "the meekness and gentleness of Christ" (2 Cor 10:1), "the steadfastness [ὑπομονή, *hypomonē*] of Christ" (2 Thess 3:5). Insofar as the community embodies these attributes, it faithfully *mirrors* the identity of Jesus to an otherwise uncomprehending world. It must always be remembered that for Paul it is Jesus' *death* in which these attributes are definitively disclosed (i.e., not in his attitude toward little children or his interpersonal sensitivity in discussion with his critics).[21]

Jesus the Paradigm of Faithfulness

In speaking of Jesus' death, we must also give careful attention to *πίστις* Ἰησοῦ Χριστοῦ *(pistis Iēsou Christou):* "the faith [or faithfulness] of Jesus Christ." Some variant of this formula appears seven times in Paul's letters (Rom 3:22, 26; Gal 2:16 [2x], 20; 3:22; Phil 3:9; see also Eph 3:12). While of-

20. On the "ethical" interpretation of the passage, and on supplying the present tense of the verb "to be" in v. 5, see Markus Bockmuehl, *The Epistle to the Philippians,* BNTC (London: A&C Black, 1997), pp. 121-25.

21. We have already noted a very few passages in which Paul refers to Jesus as an authoritative teacher (1 Cor 7:10-11; 9:14), or as the initiator of traditions that are to be kept by his followers (1 Cor 11:23-26). Though these passages may seem to us exceedingly sparse, they are present in Paul and should be noted as part of his total account of Jesus' identity.

ten translated as "faith *in* Jesus Christ," this Pauline expression refers not in the first instance to our act of "believing in" Christ but rather to Jesus Christ's gracious, self-sacrificial death on a cross. This death is simultaneously an act of human faithfulness, obedience to God "all the way to death" (Phil 2:8, my translation) — the obedience that Adam had failed to offer — and an act of divine faithfulness to the promises made to Israel. Christ's people participate in this "faith of Jesus Christ" in much the same way that they participate in the compassion or meekness of Christ: by being drawn into participation in him, they are conformed to the shape of his life. The faithfulness of Jesus is closely connected to his obedience (Rom 5:19). Yet because πίστις Χριστοῦ functions in a special way as a synecdoche for the saving event of the cross,[22] it points with particular emphasis to the climactic event in the life of "the Son of God who loved me and gave himself for me" (Gal 2:20). The faithfulness of Jesus Christ in his death on the cross is the central *defining* act for his identity; it marks him as the singular, irreplaceable individual in whom God's will for the salvation of a faithless world is made effectual.[23]

Thus, for Paul, there is no right knowledge of the identity of Jesus apart from the cross. That is why he tells the Corinthians he decided to know nothing among them except "Jesus Christ, and him crucified" (1 Cor 2:2). Paul's struggles with rival preachers often turned precisely on this issue: the superapostles in Corinth were preaching a powerful, glorious, rhetorically polished Jesus rather than a crucified Lord; the rival missionaries in Galatia sought to avoid persecution and to remove "the offense of the cross" by preaching circumcision (Gal 5:11; 6:12); and in Philippians, Paul derides his adversaries as "enemies of the cross of Christ" (Phil 3:18). Whether by precept or by example, these other early Christians were proclaiming "another Jesus" because they were not allowing the crucifixion to stand at the heart of their account of his identity. Paul, on the other hand, returns again and again to the cross as the touchstone of his interpretation of Jesus' identity (see, e.g., 1 Cor 1:23-24, 30; 2 Cor 13:4; Gal 3:1; 6:14; Phil 2:8; Col 1:20).[24]

22. Campbell, "Story of Jesus," p. 121.

23. See Richard B. Hays, *The Faith of Jesus Christ: The Narrative Substructure of Galatians 3:1–4:11*, 2nd ed. (Grand Rapids: Eerdmans, 2002), pp. xxi-lii.

24. In this respect, Paul's message presents a stark alternative to accounts that offer us a Jesus conjured out of Q and the *Gospel of Thomas*, a Jesus who is a wisdom teacher and spinner of aphorisms, a Jesus without a cross.

Jesus the Agent of Redemption

Jesus' death not only exemplifies radical obedience but also brings about the redemption of the world. Paul declares that Jesus died "for our sake," but how are we to understand the logic of this claim? Paul's letters employ a kaleidoscopic diversity of metaphors to hint at the meaning of Jesus' death for the "weak," the "ungodly," and the "sinners" (Rom 5:6-8) — that is, for "all" (2 Cor 5:14-15).

One cluster of metaphors focuses on sacrificial and substitutionary images: God put Jesus forward as a propitiation (ἱλαστήριον, *hilasterion,* Rom 3:25), or as a sin offering (περὶ ἁμαρτίας, *peri hamartias,* Rom 8:3). Closely connected to this field of images are Paul's assertions that Jesus became a curse for us (Gal 3:13), or that for our sake God "made him to be sin who knew no sin" (2 Cor 5:21). All these passages pose notorious exegetical challenges, but the common thread seems to be that Jesus' death is the death of a sacrificial victim who absorbs into himself the consequences of human sin, so that his blood has an atoning effect. Wherever we find Paul writing that God "handed him over" (Rom 4:25; 8:32; 1 Cor 11:23)[25] or that he died "for our sins" (e.g., Rom 4:25; 1 Cor 15:3; Gal 1:4; cf. Col 2:13-14; 1 Thess 5:10), we are within this metaphorical field.

The metaphor of Jesus as the paschal lamb, which appears only in 1 Corinthians 5:7, is not to be conflated with the notion of Jesus' death as atonement for sin. It adds another dimension of meaning by interpreting Jesus' death through "new exodus" imagery: it suggests both that God's work of liberating us from bondage has begun in Christ's death and that God's people must therefore, as in the Passover, "clean out the old leaven," which symbolizes the old life of impurity.

25. In 1 Cor 11:23, the phrase sometimes translated "on the night when he was betrayed" reads literally "on the night when he was handed over [παρεδίδετο, *paredideto*]." In light of the clear parallels in Rom 4:25 and 8:32, where the same verb appears, we should understand the traditional formula in 1 Cor 11:23 to refer not to Judas's act of betrayal but to God's "handing over" of Jesus to death. Beverly Roberts Gaventa has argued persuasively that this "handing over" language, beyond its sacrificial connotations, refers to God's surrender of his own Son to "anti-god powers" in order paradoxically to defeat those powers and redeem humanity; see Gaventa, "God Handed Them Over: Reading Romans 1:18-32 Apocalyptically," *Australian Biblical Review* 53 (2005): 42-53, esp. pp. 52-53. On this reading, Rom 4:25 and 8:32, along with 1 Cor 11:23, should be understood in the context of God's cosmic apocalyptic triumph over the powers. (See also my comments on "Jesus the Triumphant Rescuer," below.)

In other passages, Paul uses the metaphor of reconciliation. This language is drawn not from the imagery of the sacrificial cult but from the discourse of political negotiation.[26] Somehow, through Jesus' death, the alienation that previously separated warring parties has been overcome, and barriers have been broken down, not only between God and humanity (Rom 5:10-11; 2 Cor 5:18-20), but also between human beings who were previously at odds with one another (Rom 15:7-9).[27] Wherever we find Paul referring to "peace with God through our Lord Jesus Christ" (Rom 5:1) or the peacemaking function of the cross (Col 1:20), we see another facet of Jesus' identity, as the one who reconciles enemies through surrendering his own life.

Thus, through a variety of different metaphors, Paul portrays Jesus' death as the pivotal event in the salvation of the world. Jesus is the one who was given up (or gave himself up, as in Gal 1:4; 2:20) to bring about this mysterious redemptive outcome.

Transformative Exaltation

Jesus the Agent — and First Fruits — of New Creation

Paul's proclamation of Christ crucified, however, is not the end of the story. As 1 Corinthians 15 declares, after his death and burial "he was raised on the third day in accordance with the scriptures," and he appeared to a chain of witnesses, culminating in Paul himself. This astounding turn in the story vindicates Jesus as "Son of God with power" (Rom 1:4). In this way, it discloses a new dimension of his identity: "For he was crucified in weakness, but lives by the power of God" (2 Cor 13:4). The resurrection, effected by God the Father (Gal 1:1; 1 Thess 1:10), reconfirms Jesus' relation to the Father, for he is now exalted to the right hand of God, where he intercedes for us (Rom 8:34).

The resurrection of Jesus also spills over into saving effects for the world. He was "raised for our justification" (Rom 4:25), and his resurrec-

26. Cilliers Breytenbach, *Versöhnung: Eine Studie zur paulinischen Soteriologie,* WMANT 60 (Neukirchen: Neukirchener Verlag, 1989).

27. This theme is given an especially rich ecclesiological development by the author of Ephesians (Eph 2:11-22).

tion is both the source and attestation of his life-giving power: "If the Spirit of him who raised Jesus from the dead dwells in you, he who raised Christ from the dead will give life to your mortal bodies also through his Spirit that dwells in you" (Rom 8:11; cf. 6:4-11). This effusion of life is not merely a secondary effect of the resurrection of Jesus; it is integral to his identity, for while "'the first man, Adam, became a living being' [Gen 2:7], the last Adam became a life-giving spirit" (1 Cor 15:45). Consequently, his identity cannot be understood apart from the company of those who are destined to share his resurrection (1 Thess 4:13-18): he is the "first fruits of those who have fallen asleep" (1 Cor 15:20-23), the "firstborn from the dead" (Col 1:18). To know who he is is to know him as the "firstborn within a large family," who will ultimately share in his glory (Rom 8:29-30).

For Paul, Jesus is the antitype of Adam: "For as all die in Adam, so all will be made alive in Christ" (1 Cor 15:22). He is (to borrow a term from Hebrews) the ἀρχηγός *(archēgos)* of a new humanity, the initiator and representative figure of a whole new creation brought into being through his obedient death and resurrection from the grave.

Jesus the Triumphant Rescuer

By virtue of his resurrection, Jesus is frequently portrayed by Paul as *Christus Victor,* as one who has come to "snatch us out of the grasp of the present evil age."[28] The metaphor of liberation sounds again and again through Paul's letters. Christ has set us free (Gal 5:1); we are no longer captive under the law (Gal 4:3-5; Col 2:14), no longer enslaved to the powers of sin and death (Rom 6:18; 7:25; 8:2), no longer separated from God by the principalities and powers (Rom 8:31-39). Even though the completion of this rescue operation remains in the eschatological future (1 Thess 1:10; Rom 8:18-25; 11:25-27), the resurrection has assured Jesus' ultimate triumph, so that Paul can already exclaim, "Thanks be to God, who gives us the victory through our Lord Jesus Christ" (1 Cor 15:57).

28. This is J. Louis Martyn's colorful translation of Gal 1:4. Martyn, *Galatians,* AB 33A (New York: Doubleday, 1997), p. 81.

Jesus the Benefactor

With extraordinary frequency, Paul represents Jesus as the source of peace and blessing. This theme appears not only in Paul's characteristic salutations and benedictions, where we find various versions of the χάρις (*charis*, "grace") formula (Rom 1:7; 16:20; 1 Cor 1:3; 16:23; 2 Cor 1:2; 13:13; Phlm 25; etc.), but also scattered profusely throughout the letters, in endless variation but always identifying Jesus as the giver of wonderful gifts and consolations. He is the source of the "free gift of righteousness" (Rom 5:15-17; 6:23) or "harvest of righteousness" (Phil 1:11), of "eternal life" (Rom 5:21), of "the blessing of Christ" (Rom 15:29), of "the peace of Christ" (Col 3:15; 2 Thess 3:16; cf. Rom 5:1), of the "yes" to all God's promises (2 Cor 1:19-20), of "redemption" (Rom 3:24-26), of "the grace of God" (1 Cor 1:4), of "encouragement" (Phil 2:1), of "eternal comfort and good hope" (2 Thess 2:16), and on and on. In short, Jesus is represented as the *benefactor and sustainer* of the community of faith, an inexhaustible fountain of grace.

Jesus the Kyrios

Jesus can be such a benefactor only because he is exalted to the right hand of God and now reigns "until he has put all his enemies under his feet" (1 Cor 15:25). As the Risen One, Jesus is now *Lord;* accordingly, κύριος (*kyrios*, "Lord") is one of Paul's favorite titles for Jesus. The title signifies his sovereign authority. To confess him as "Lord" is at the heart of Christian practice (Rom 10:9; 1 Cor 12:3), and to make such a confession is a performative, self-involving act of submission to him. Consistent with this image of submission, Paul describes himself as the slave of Christ (Rom 1:1; Gal 1:10); he can also apply the metaphor (if it *is* a metaphor) to his fellow apostolic workers (Phil 1:1; Col 4:12) and to all who are called into Christ's service (1 Cor 7:22). That is why, Paul argues, Christians should not pass judgment on one another: they are all slaves of Christ and therefore accountable to no one other than their one true Master (Rom 14:4; cf. 14:7-12; Col 3:22–4:1). As the Master, Jesus sends his slave Paul on whatever errands he chooses and works through him to spread the gospel (Rom 1:5; 15:18-19; 1 Cor 3:5; 4:1; Gal 1:16; 1 Thess 3:11). Yet it is precisely as Christ's slave that Paul also receives the authorization that empowers his apostolic work (e.g., 1 Cor 4:1-5; 2 Cor 10:7-8; Gal 1:10-12).[29] Only for that reason can he make the extraordinarily bold claim that his mission is to "take every thought captive to obey Christ" (2 Cor 10:5).

The portrayal of Jesus as *kyrios* carries with it one further set of sweeping implications about Jesus' identity, for *kyrios* is the word characteristically used by the Septuagint (the ancient Greek translation of the Old Testament) to render the Tetragrammaton, the unutterable name of God. Paul can thus quote Old Testament passages that in their original context refer to the God of Israel and interpret them as references to the Lord Jesus Christ. The most striking instance of this is Philippians 2:9-11, which declares that God highly exalted the crucified Jesus so that

> at the name of Jesus every knee should bend . . .
> and every tongue should confess
> that Jesus Christ is *kyrios*,
> to the glory of God the Father. (2:10-11)

The text echoes Isaiah 45:22-23, a relentlessly monotheistic text:

> Turn to me and be saved,
> all the ends of the earth!
> For I am God, and there is no other.
> By myself I have sworn,
> from my mouth has gone forth in righteousness
> a word that shall not return:
> "To me every knee shall bow,
> every tongue shall swear."

Thus, according to Philippians 2:9-11, the obedient submission that was to be rendered to God alone is now to be directed to Jesus Christ. Similarly, Paul appropriates Joel 2:32 — "Then everyone who calls on the name of the Lord shall be saved" — as a word that pertains to those who call on *Jesus* as Lord (Rom 10:9, 12-13).[30] Paul's identification of Jesus as Lord thus converges with his "Son of God" language to underscore the mysterious

29. On this theme, see Dale B. Martin, *Slavery as Salvation: The Metaphor of Slavery in Pauline Christianity* (New Haven: Yale University Press, 1990).

30. See C. Kavin Rowe, "Romans 10:13: What Is the Name of the Lord?" *Horizons in Biblical Theology* 22 (2000): 135-73.

oneness of Jesus with God. Only for that reason can he be the one in whom faith/trust is rightly to be placed (Gal 2:16; Phil 1:29; Col 2:5; Phlm 5).

Jesus Embodied in the Church

We come now to what may be the most startling aspect of Paul's portrayal of the identity of Jesus: Paul and his communities know Jesus Christ not only as Lord — not only as the Master who holds sovereign authority over the church — but also as personally united with his people in such a way that they become his "body." He is actually present in and through them. After the resurrection, Jesus' identity is not confined to a single localized physical body; he embraces and receives into himself all those whom he calls. Consequently, he manifests his identity to the world through this complex corporate reality.[31]

The well-known "body of Christ" text in 1 Corinthians 12 makes this point forcefully: "For just as the body is one and has many members, and all the members of the body, though many, are one body, so it is with Christ" (12:12). As Paul develops the analogy, he does *not* say that the *church* has many members, like a physical human body.[32] Rather, he says that *Christ* has many members, which, like the members of the human body, have diverse functions. Thus, the term "Christ" in 1 Corinthians 12:12-27 refers to this multimembered corporate entity. The seriousness with which Paul takes this claim is illustrated by his use of the same image earlier in the same letter, in his vehement argument against the Corinthians' practice of going to prostitutes: "Do you not know that your bodies are members of Christ? Should I therefore take the members of Christ and make them members of a prostitute? Never!" (6:15).

The more closely we study Paul's letters, the more we are forced to recognize that this is for him not merely a figure of speech. The church really *is* the body of Christ, because Christ lives in us: "I have been crucified with Christ; and it is no longer I who live, but it is Christ who lives in me" (Gal 2:19b-20a).[33] The line of distinction between Christ and his people has be-

31. Later Christian theology referred to this corporate aspect of Christ's identity as the *totus Christus,* the "whole Christ" (Augustine, *On Christian Doctrine* 3.31.44).

32. Many students are surprised to discover that the term ἐκκλησία (*ekklēsia*, "church") appears in the passage only at 12:28.

33. Paul's "I" here is not merely autobiographical but also exemplary; he presents his

come blurred if not erased altogether. "My" personal identity has been taken up into Christ.

Here, if anywhere (someone might protest), surely we must make a distinction between the historical man Jesus and the risen "supernatural" Christ. After all, Paul never calls the church "the body of Jesus." A careful examination of the evidence, however, shows that such a distinction does not consistently stand. The key text is 2 Corinthians 4:10-11: "[We are] always carrying in the body the death of Jesus, so that the life of Jesus may also be made visible in our bodies. For while we live, we are always being given up to death for Jesus' sake, so that the life of Jesus may be made visible in our mortal flesh." What Paul says of himself applies more generally to the identity and vocation of the church: our lives and our bodies become the locus of the manifestation of *Jesus'* life. Here, as elsewhere, "Jesus" and "Christ" are names that Paul can use interchangeably to refer to the same person.

If that is so, then our investigation of the identity of Jesus must take into account the numerous passages in which Paul describes the participation of the church in Christ's sufferings, in the power of his resurrection, and in the resultant transformation of human social experience within the body of Christ.[34] Our understanding of the identity of Jesus Christ will somehow have to include his present embodiment in the community of those called by his name, a community that lives in suffering and weakness but also displays, in a distinctive way, the hope of freedom from sin and abolition of divisive distinctions of nationality, social rank, and gender.

We must hasten to say that claims about the church as the theater of the identity of Jesus always remain subject to the eschatological reservation: we see through a glass darkly. Paul describes himself as being in the agony of childbirth "until Christ is formed in you," that is, in the Galatian churches (Gal 4:19). This suggests that we do not yet see Christ's identity rightly displayed in the church. On the one hand, Paul can write that "all of us, with unveiled faces, seeing the glory of the Lord [Jesus] as though re-

---

experience of dying to his old life and living in union with Christ as a model or pattern that he expects all Christians to share. See Beverly Roberts Gaventa, "Galatians 1 and 2: Autobiography as Paradigm," *Novum Testamentum* 28 (1986): 309-26.

34. See especially Rom 6:3-11; 8:17, 29-30; 2 Cor 12:7b-10; Gal 3:27-29; 6:14; Phil 3:7-11; and Col 1:24 — the last of these the extraordinary text in which Paul declares that through his own sufferings he is "completing what is lacking in Christ's afflictions for the sake of his body, that is, the church" (Col 1:24).

flected in a mirror, are being transformed into the same image from one degree of glory into another" (2 Cor 3:18). Here is the eschatological vision, already shining forth in the community (see also Col 1:27). On the other hand, Paul never forgets that "we hope for what we do not see" (Rom 8:25), and that the identity of Jesus Christ will be fully manifest in the church only when he comes as the Savior from heaven, who "will transform the body of our lowliness [ταπεινώσεως, *tapeinōseōs;* cf. Phil 2:8] that it may be conformed to the body of his glory, by the power that also enables him to make all things subject to himself" (Phil 3:20-21 NRSV alt.).

Eschatological Consummation

Jesus the Agent of Final Judgment and Salvation

Paul's account of Jesus contains a prominent eschatological element. The same Jesus Christ who was the preexistent creator, who was crucified and rose from the dead, will also come at the end of the age to judge the world and to complete his saving work. The image of Jesus as judge, though it is highlighted in the creeds and in the church's iconographic traditions, strikes late modern sensibilities as offensive, and it has fallen into neglect in our time. In Paul, however, we find repeated references to Jesus as the agent of eschatological judgment: "For all of us must appear before the judgment seat of Christ, so that each may receive recompense for what has been done in the body, whether good or evil" (2 Cor 5:10; see also Rom 2:16; 14:4; 1 Cor 4:5; Phil 1:10; 2:16; 1 Thess 5:23).

Alongside such images, however, we find Paul more often proclaiming that the purpose of Christ's future coming is to bring to completion the salvation of his people. Paul portrays Jesus not only as judge but also as advocate who intercedes for us in the final judgment (Rom 8:33-34). His intercession will succeed against all cosmic accusers and adversaries, for nothing can separate us from "the love of God in Christ Jesus our Lord" (Rom 8:35-39). He will come as the eschatological "Deliverer" (Rom 11:26), and he will *rescue* us from "the wrath that is coming" (1 Thess 1:10). He will gather his people to be with him forever (1 Thess 4:16-17; 2 Thess 2:1) and complete the good work that he has begun among them (Phil 1:6) by banishing ungodliness, taking away their sins, and sanctifying them entirely (Rom 11:26-27; 1 Cor 1:7-8; 1 Thess 5:23). At Christ's future coming his people will be fully conformed to him and share his glory (Rom 8:29-30; Phil 3:20-21; Col 3:4).

"That God May Be All in All"

Paul's story about the identity of Jesus contains one last surprising twist. At that eschatological day, when every knee bows and every tongue confesses that Jesus Christ is Lord, when his triumph over all things, including the power of death, is complete and all things are put under his feet in subjection — then, at that moment, he will hand over the kingdom to God the Father. "The Son himself will also be subjected to the one who put all things in subjection under him, so that God may be all in all" (1 Cor 15:24-28). Thus, the grand conclusion of the plot shows that the identity of Jesus Christ is still consistent. In the day of eschatological consummation, he is still the same obedient, self-emptying Son on whose act of radical self-giving the salvation of the world depends. If the story had any other ending, he would indeed be "another Jesus."

Jesus' Identity and Ours

Paul's Jesus Christ is the protagonist of an epic story that moves from creation to the climactic events of cross and resurrection to the final judgment and salvation of the world. Thus, Paul's account of Jesus has the unity of a personal identity unfolded across time. Jesus the weak, suffering servant is not a contradiction or a paradox alongside Jesus the triumphant, conquering Lord. The identity of Paul's Jesus is encapsulated precisely in the narrative line and cannot be abstracted from it.

Someone might ask what value there is in seeking a synthetic account of Jesus as a character in Paul's letters. Is it purely a literary parlor game? Will this project merely retrace a mythological plot that corresponds neither to the historical reality of the life of Jesus nor to the theological needs of our own time? My answer to this is twofold.

First, if critical history is our interest, there is great value in asking how Jesus looked through Paul's eyes, since Paul is our earliest extant witness. The usual procedure of taking the Gospels (written twenty to forty years later) as the primary frame of reference and asking how Paul matches up is historically anachronistic. The first step is to clarify what *Paul* tells us about the identity of Jesus; only then, as a second step, can we compare Paul's Jesus to information from other sources. One striking result of this procedure is to show that the account of Jesus as Lord and Redeemer of the world is not — as is sometimes asserted — a late doctrinal invention of the church in the second or third century; rather, it belongs to the very earliest layers of tradition to which we have access.

Second, reckoning with Paul's account of the identity of Jesus requires us to expand the frame within which we decide what is "real." If "reality" is rightly described by Paul's declaration that "one has died for all, therefore all have died," then his next moves follow compellingly: we no longer know κατὰ σάρκα *(kata sarka)*, according to the flesh; the old has passed away. We are living in the realm of new creation (2 Cor 5:14-17). Our very concept of personal identity undergoes a mind-stretching transformation, including our own personal identities: we are transformed by the story of Jesus Christ, and we find ourselves living *within* that story rather than at a critical distance from it. If Paul's story of Jesus Christ is true, then we too have been crucified with Christ and will be raised with him. In the story of Jesus Christ we find our own.

"Time Would Fail Me to Tell . . .": The Identity of Jesus Christ in Hebrews

A. KATHERINE GRIEB

Thou within the veil hast entered, robed in flesh,
our great High Priest:
Thou on earth both Priest and Victim in the eucharistic feast.[1]

The Epistle to the Hebrews has more intense christological reflection per square inch than any other extant early Christian writing. "Time would fail me to tell"[2] of even a fraction of the identity of Jesus Christ in this beautiful sermonic text. Yet even a limited overview offers an important perspective for understanding the person and work of Jesus Christ. Thus, in a necessarily terse treatment, I will summarize the author's christological argument, look briefly at the notion of "identity" in a literary text, then go on to explore three distinctive features of the construction of the "identity" of Jesus Christ in Hebrews. I will conclude with a reflection on Hebrews' usefulness for discerning how Scripture speaks to us today.

The Christological Argument of Hebrews

The most cursory review of Hebrews' argument attests to its rich christological depth. Within the first four verses of the opening paragraph,

1. From the hymn "Alleluia! Sing to Jesus," words by William Chatterton Dix (1837-1898). *The Hymnal 1982* of the Episcopal Church, USA, ##460, 461.

2. Hebrews 11:32. Scripture quotations not otherwise identified are from the NRSV.

the author[3] contrasts the one (Son) and the many (prophets); the various ways God spoke in the past and the way God has spoken "in these last days," through the Son; the exalted, enthroned Son and the angels. Hebrews identifies the Son in terms that describe his roles and actions: appointed heir of all things, the One through whom God created the world; the radiance of God's glory, the exact likeness of God's very being; the One who sustains all things by his powerful word; the One who has made purification for sins; the One who has taken his seat at the right hand of the Majesty; and the One who has become superior to angels and has inherited the name more excellent than theirs.

In the subsequent catena of biblical texts, the Son is called "the firstborn" (1:6) and addressed as "God" (1:8) and "Lord" (1:10). Though "for a little while . . . made lower than the angels," now he is "crowned with glory and honor because of the suffering of death" (2:9). He is the pioneer, or initiator (ἀρχηγός, *archēgos*), of salvation, "bringing many children to glory," whom God perfected through suffering (2:10). He has destroyed the devil, who has the power of death, and rescued those enslaved by the fear of death (2:14-15). As "a merciful and faithful high priest," he has atoned for the people's sins. Tested through suffering himself, he can help those presently being tested (2:17-18). He is "the apostle[4] and high priest of our confession" (3:1). In midrashic "sidebars" to the argument, the Son is compared favorably to God's servant Moses (3:2-6), while "Jesus" is playfully fused with Joshua (4:8).[5]

Sent from God ("apostle," 3:1), the Son is suggestively identified with God's living and active word (also the penetrating purity of God's wisdom[6]), which, like a two-edged sword, examines and judges the heart, and before whose eyes all are naked (4:12-13).[7] The theme of Son of God as

3. I shall refer to both the text and its unknown author as "Hebrews" unless there is reason to differentiate between them.

4. Uniquely in the New Testament.

5. The names "Joshua" and "Jesus" are the same in Greek.

6. See Wis 7:23-24. God's effective word is described in, e.g., Isa 55:10-11.

7. Origen's reference to those "who have truly borne the Word of God, living and active, sharper than any two-edged sword," suggests martyrdom as *imitatio Christi* in *An Exhortation to Martyrdom* 15 (trans. Rowan A. Greer, *Origen: An Exhortation to Martyrdom, Prayer, and Selected Works* [New York: Paulist, 1979], p. 52). The event of the Crucified, Risen One becomes the cause of the martyr's death, while word of him, in the Scriptures and in exhortations like Origen's, becomes the means of discerning a call to it.

high priest is explored at length in 4:14–5:10. The passage's conclusion (5:7-9), bracketed by two still-unexplained references to priesthood after the order of Melchizedek, refers to "the days of his flesh,"[8] in which the Son "learned obedience through what he suffered," which is then glossed, or explained — importantly — as "having been made perfect." Through this process of perfection through suffering, he has become "the source of eternal salvation."[9] After being warned about the perils of falling away, the hearers are encouraged to hope with "a hope that enters the inner shrine behind the curtain, where Jesus, a forerunner[10] on our behalf, has entered" (6:19-20, anticipating chapters 8–10). Jesus is then once more described as "high priest . . . according to the order of Melchizedek" (6:20), which is finally explained in chapter 7.

The Melchizedek typology demonstrates the superiority of the priesthood of Jesus Christ to that of the Levitical priesthood. Jesus is the guarantor of "a better covenant" (7:22). Here is the fullest account of Christ as "a high priest, holy, blameless, undefiled, separated from sinners, and exalted above the heavens" (7:26). The identities of Son and high priest are now completely fused: Jesus is both "a Son who has been made perfect[11] forever" (7:28) and a high priest "seated at the right hand[12] of the throne of the Majesty in the heavens" (8:1). This fusion enables the next step in the argument, which describes Jesus Christ as "a minister in the sanctuary and the true tent," the heavenly One (8:2-5). Jesus is the "*mediator* of a better covenant" enacted through better promises (8:6). "New covenant" language (Jer 31:31-34) contrasts Israel's broken covenant with this one, by which God will be merciful toward their iniquities and remember their sins no more.

Hebrews describes the architecture, furnishings, and liturgy of the earthly tabernacle's sanctuary with particular attention to the rite of atonement for Yom Kippur at the mercy seat. The ancient wilderness tabernacle rite is "a symbol of the present time" (9:9) and the current Levitical priesthood, which treats only externals, not purification of the conscience

8. The associated words "prayers and supplications, with loud cries and tears" may allude to Gethsemane traditions.

9. An instance of *hapax legomenon* (a word or phrase that appears only once) in the New Testament; see Isa 45:17.

10. Also unique to Hebrews in the New Testament.

11. The word translated "made perfect" is also used in the LXX for the consecration of a high priest.

12. Where the Son has previously been located, as early as 1:3.

(9:9). By contrast, Christ, "high priest of the good things to come"[13] in the more perfect (heavenly) tabernacle, entered once for all into the holy of holies, obtaining "eternal redemption" by means of his own blood through the "eternal Spirit"[14] (9:11-14). He mediates a new covenant by which those called may receive the promised eternal inheritance, because his death inaugurates the testament[15] that frees them from transgressions of the first covenant (9:15-17; cf. Jer 31:34; Heb 8:12). The wilderness tabernacle reminds the hearers that the first covenant was also inaugurated by blood (9:18-20; cf. Exod 24:8), for "without the shedding of blood there is no forgiveness of sins" (9:22). The singular effective atoning act of Christ in the heavenly sanctuary (9:24) is contrasted with the earthly repetition of the Yom Kippur rite by Levitical priests. Since Christ has effectively atoned for sin, his second appearance will not deal with sin but will save those eagerly waiting for him (9:28).

The futility of multiple sacrifices of bulls and goats, which can never take away sins (10:4), is further contrasted with the singular obedient self-offering of Christ, described at the point of his incarnation. As he enters the world, Christ speaks the words of Psalm 40:6-8 ("Sacrifices and offerings you have not desired . . ."), then adds, "See, . . . I have come to do your will," the will by which "we have been sanctified through the offering of the body of Jesus Christ once for all" (10:5-10). The Levitical priests who "stand" daily offering sacrifices are contrasted with the completed work of Christ, who "sat down" at the right hand of God to wait for his enemies to be made a footstool (10:11-13; Ps 110:1). Jeremiah 31:33-34 is quoted once more to reiterate that Christ's completed saving work is available to believers.

A second appeal to follow Jesus "by the new and living way that he opened for us" through the veil of his flesh (cf. 6:19-20) is combined with further strong warnings against the dangers of apostasy (10:19-31). The community's earlier courage during persecution is recalled, and they are assured that "the one who is coming" will not delay. God's Righteous One is not to shrink back but to have faith (πίστις, *pistis,* 10:32-39; cf. Hab 2:3-4). In chapter 11, the word πίστις ("faith," or perhaps better, "faithfulness") serves as the catchword link to the catalogue of Israel's faithful ancestors in the style of

13. Reading the textual variant at 9:11.

14. Another *hapax legomenon* in the New Testament.

15. The same word is used for "testament" (or "will") and "covenant," allowing this wordplay.

Sirach 44–50 and Wisdom 10:1–11:14. Repetition of "by faith[fulness]" links Abraham (who trusted God's ability to create Isaac and to raise him from the dead) and Moses (who gladly suffered "abuse . . . for the Christ," unafraid of Pharaoh, because he saw the One who is invisible). Many brave martyrs "of whom the world was not worthy" died unrewarded because God's plan required "that they would not, apart from us, be made perfect."

If Sirach chooses the high priest Simon ben Onias, gloriously vested in full liturgical splendor, as the climax of his series of faithful Israelites, Hebrews reaches the rhetorical *telos* of its argument with the paradox of the crucified high priest. This second reference to Jesus as initiator (ἀρχηγός) and now also perfecter of the faithfulness of the sermon's hearers (12:2) leads to the extended metaphor of athletic discipline needed for running the race that Jesus ran (enduring the cross, disregarding its shame, taking his seat at God's right hand) and grounds an appeal to imagine whatever painful trials the hearers are enduring as the temporary discipline of their loving Father, meant for their good. Another powerful warning against abdication of the privileges of sonship follows. They are not to refuse "the one who is speaking," "the one who warns from heaven," for God is a consuming fire (12:25-29).

In the final chapter, biblical promises of God's faithfulness accompany directives for an ethical life. Because "Jesus Christ is the same yesterday and today and forever" (13:8), they are not to be carried away by strange doctrines or love of money but to engage in community-building practices and to identify with those who are poor, imprisoned, and facing torture. The claim "we have an altar from which those who officiate in the tabernacle have no right to eat" (13:10) refers to Jesus' saving death on the cross, now redescribed in liturgical language. Since the sacrificial animals were burned "outside the camp" (cf. Lev 16:27) and Jesus also suffered "outside the city gate," the community is also to go "outside the camp" to bear abuse as he did (13:11-13). Finally, the sermon's hearers are blessed with the prayer that "the God of peace, who brought back from the dead our Lord Jesus, the great shepherd of the sheep," will enable them to do his will "through Jesus Christ, to whom be the glory forever and ever" (13:20-21).

In summary, then, Jesus Christ is "both a sacrifice for sin and . . . an example of godly life":[16] One whose preexistence and exaltation are assumed; whose crucifixion (a shameful criminal death wrought by Gentile

16. Proper 15, *The Book of Common Prayer* of the Episcopal Church, USA (1979), p. 180.

soldiers) is reinterpreted as the liturgical blood sacrifice to end all sacrifices, offered in the heavenly sanctuary in the roles of both victim and priest; the pattern of whose death is intended as encouragement for his own, who are to follow him through the veil of the heavenly sanctuary with their own lives.

"Identity" within a Literary Text

Whenever we attempt to discern the identity of Jesus Christ in Hebrews or in any other literary text, several possible interrelated construals of the term "identity" assert themselves: *sameness,* or continuity through time; *distinctiveness,* or identifiability; and *singularity,* or particularity disclosed through characteristic words or actions.[17]

"Identity" as *sameness* suggests that things are identical if and only if they have all their essential properties in common. In terms of personal identity, sameness and oneness are related, as in the doctrine of the simplicity of God. To say that God is One is to say that there is no admixture of elements within God nor any constraint external to God that could prevent God's consistency and faithfulness. To the extent that God's being is known in God's action, the identity of God, construed as sameness, is seen in history. Quoting Rowan Williams, "If there is one God, the acts of that God should, *prima facie,* be consistent." Thus, "the canon of Hebrew Scripture can itself be read both as an effort to articulate the deepening sense of the oneness of God's act . . . and as the perception of that oneness in and through the *overcoming* of the dramatic ruptures in Israel's history."[18] Hebrews employs this concept of identity as sameness in 13:8 — "Jesus Christ is the same yesterday and today and forever" — and in its many uses of the word "eternal," several of which are unique to Hebrews.

"Identity" as *distinctiveness,* in the sense of identifiability, involves a continuum, or spectrum, of knowledge about a person: from mere "identification" provided by bureaucratic forms, to "identifying features" that enable a person to be spotted in a crowd, to "identifying behavioral characteristics"

17. For a fuller treatment of "identity" as it relates to philosophy and theology, see Sarah Coakley, "The Identity of the Risen Jesus: Finding Jesus Christ in the Poor," in this volume.

18. Rowan Williams, *On Christian Theology* (Oxford: Blackwell, 2000), p. 21. Robert Jenson in particular has called our attention to this facet of identity.

such that people can exchange stories and recognize that they are talking about the same person. Deeper knowledge of someone in this sense involves disclosure, whether voluntary or involuntary, of an interiority that can be known, at least in part. There is mystery at the heart of another. In the case of God, involuntary disclosure seems impossible: God's gracious self-revelation invites deeper communion, yet at least in this life, our knowledge of God's mysterious self is always only partial. Hebrews assumes this concept of identity when it speaks of God's continuing self-disclosure, first in the prophets and then, in these last days, in the Son who radiates God's glory and imprints his being (1:1-3). Hebrews also insists that to be encountered by the Word/Wisdom of God is ourselves to be known and uncovered involuntarily in radical heart surgery. The judgment of God in Christ pierces and penetrates the depths of the human persona (4:12-13), and we are forced to recognize ourselves as "creatures" transparent before our Creator.

"Identity" as *singularity*, what makes someone a particular person and no one else, concerns, as Hans Frei puts it, "the specific uniqueness of a person, what really counts about him."[19] What Frei calls the "unsubstitutable particularity" of Jesus Christ is rendered narratively by describing his characteristic words and actions. Although God's being is known in his acts (so Barth), Jesus' identity is also rendered in the passion narrative, when Jesus is no longer acting but is instead acted upon. In literature, as in life, identity is tied to character, characteristic words and actions typically rendered through narrative. The series of events we call "plot" shapes character, and characters acting "in character" advance the plot. Hebrews uses this understanding of identity when it insists that "although he was a Son, he learned obedience through what he suffered" (5:8) and when it holds up the characteristic pattern of going "outside the camp" as an example for believers to imitate (13:13).

Distinctive Features of the Identity of Jesus Christ in Hebrews

A fuller treatment of the identity of Jesus Christ in Hebrews would locate its distinctive Christology within the canonical context of the rest of the New Testament, comparing its soteriology with that of other early Chris-

19. Hans W. Frei, *The Identity of Jesus Christ: The Hermeneutical Bases of Dogmatic Theology* (Philadelphia: Fortress, 1975), p. 37.

tian voices. If New Testament Christologies divide roughly into two types (two-stage and three-stage schemas), depending on whether preexistence is assumed, Hebrews clearly joins Paul[20] and John's Gospel[21] as instances of the second type. Yet three features of Hebrews distinguish it from other soteriologies of the New Testament: (1) the rendering of the identity of Jesus Christ through the medium of an intra-trinitarian conversation quoting Scripture; (2) the fusion of "platonic" spatial realism and "apocalyptic" temporal realism as a frame for the discussion; and (3) the rare (before Chalcedon) dialectic of preexistent and exalted divinity together with full participation in and solidarity with humanity under death's reign. Close attention to these aspects of Hebrews is our present task.

Intra-trinitarian Conversation Quoting Scripture

Uniquely in Hebrews, Jesus Christ's identity as human Savior is spoken by the triune God using the language of Israel's Scriptures. Christ's saving work is described in an ongoing intra-trinitarian conversation about the sermon's addressees, who are privileged to overhear God's gracious words concerning them.

The Epistle to the Hebrews surpasses all the other New Testament books in its use of Israel's Scriptures.[22] Four sorts of references may be distinguished: direct quotations (e.g., 1:5); indirect quotations, allusions, or echoes (e.g., Ps 110:1 at 1:3 and throughout); interpreted summaries of biblical events in the record of God's revelation (e.g., 1:1; chapter 11); and biblical titles, names, or topics upon which Hebrews elaborates (e.g., Son of God, Melchizedek, angels). The author's working canon privileges the Pentateuch and the Psalms (Ps 110:4 alone is mentioned some ten times). Jeremiah (e.g., at 8:8-12; 10:16-17) and Isaiah (e.g., at 2:13; 9:2-8) also receive special weight. The argument consists largely of sustained exegesis of four blocks of biblical texts through which it moves: Psalm 8, Psalm 95, Psalm 110, and Jeremiah 31.[23]

20. The possibly hymnic fragment in Rom 1:3-4 notwithstanding; see Phil 2:5-11.

21. Especially the prologue (1:1-18) and 17:5.

22. See Simon Kistemaker, *The Psalm Citations in the Epistle to the Hebrews* (Amsterdam: van Soest, 1961), p. 13.

23. George B. Caird, "The Exegetical Method of the Epistle to the Hebrews," *Canadian Journal of Theology* 5 (1959): 44-51.

Hebrews' interest in the Scriptures is unremittingly christological. The Bible is searched for what it says about Jesus, the Son through whom God has spoken in these last days (1:2). Definitions and titles matter less to the author than the narrated action and passion of Jesus Christ: "*That* Jesus Christ *has come* he knows apart from the Old Testament (2:3-4). But *who* exactly the One is who has come and *what* he means and is before God and for [humanity] — this he learns and explains from the history of Israel as it speaks out of the Old Testament."[24]

The identity of Jesus Christ as revealed in Scripture and its implications for those who belong to him[25] are not trivial, the author insists: it could be literally a matter of life and death. The sermon's hearers are in serious danger, both physically and spiritually.[26] Scriptural interpretation is not a leisurely exploration of hypothetical possibilities but a practical "word of exhortation" (13:22) to a congregation that is experiencing actual temptations to fall away in the face of concrete pressures better known to the author/preacher and the congregation than to us. A context of present active persecution need not be assumed, but the author recalls the community's past trials and seems to expect more.

Second Temple writers often introduce biblical quotations with formulas ("it is written," "according to the scripture") or with references to a specific book or prophet, but Hebrews depicts God *speaking* through Scripture, using expressions such as "he says," usually in the present tense and the active voice. Whether the quotation's author is identified (as in 9:19-20; 12:21) or his identity is either irrelevant or too obvious to mention (as in 2:6), God's living and active Word (4:12) speaks "today, if you hear his voice" (3:7).

Strikingly in Hebrews, as we listen to Scripture we hear (a) what God says to the Son (1:5-13; 5:5-6), to a person like Abraham (11:18), and to us (13:5);[27] (b) what the Son says to God (2:12-13; 10:7), interceding for the con-

24. Markus Barth, "The Old Testament in Hebrews: An Essay in Biblical Hermeneutics," in *Current Issues in New Testament Interpretation,* ed. William Klassen and Graydon F. Snyder (New York: Harper, 1962), p. 57.

25. See Markus Bockmuehl, "The Church in Hebrews," in *A Vision for the Church: Studies in Early Christian Ecclesiology in Honour of J. P. M. Sweet,* ed. Markus Bockmuehl and Michael B. Thompson (Edinburgh: T&T Clark, 1997), pp. 133-51.

26. At least in view are the clear and present dangers of unbelief, apostasy, fatigue, heresy, persecution, amnesia, dullness, and death.

27. We also infer that God speaks to and about angels (1:5, 7).

gregation (7:25) and promising to proclaim God's name there (2:12-13); and (c) what the Spirit says to the congregation (3:7-11; 10:15-17).[28] To listen to Scripture as part of the congregation (ideal hearers) of Hebrews, then, is to overhear a dialogue between the Father and the Son that both concerns us (5:1) and takes place in our midst (2:12). This intimate soteriological conversation (God's speech to God about our salvation) is not hidden from us but disclosed through biblical texts. What happens in the Godhead is revealed to us in Scripture. Although it is always only something of God's mystery that is disclosed, God's spoken words and God's works are God's own testimonies. God is self-disclosing, testifying (a word used repeatedly in Hebrews for God's revelation in Scripture) in ways we are urged to hear.

"Platonic" Spatial Realism and "Apocalyptic" Temporal Realism

The identity of Jesus Christ in Hebrews is framed by the unusual combination of "platonic" spatial realism and "apocalyptic" temporal realism.[29] By platonic spatial realism I mean Hebrews' assumption that the wilderness tabernacle was made after the pattern God showed to Moses: "See that you make everything according to the pattern (τύπος, *typos*) that was shown you on the mountain" (8:5, recalling Exod 25:40). Like the Aaronic priests during the wilderness era, their spiritual successors in the Levitical priesthood perhaps contemporary with the author of Hebrews[30] worship in a sanctuary that is only "a sketch and shadow of the heavenly one" (8:5).

This temporary sanctuary "made with hands" is, in Hebrews and in other contemporary Jewish writings, contrasted with another sanctuary "not made with hands" (9:11, 24; cf. Mark 14:58; Acts 7:48).[31] Early Chris-

28. The Father and Son do not address the Spirit, nor does the Spirit address them, but the Spirit speaks to us of God.

29. The word "platonic" is set in self-distancing quotes because, as Leander Keck quips, "ideas don't have addresses," and because Jewish writers of the Second Temple period were all Hellenized after the conquests and occupation strategies of Alexander the Great. "Apocalyptic" is in quotes to acknowledge the current debate about the complexities of its use, a subject beyond the scope of this paper.

30. For the way time works in the sermon, which is debated, see the second half of this section.

31. For related ideas, see 1 Cor 3:16; 6:19; 1 Pet 2:4-6.

tian use of this contrast may trade on the oracle of Nathan in 2 Samuel 7:12-14, used in *testimonia* with Psalms 2, 89, and 132. In Mark's Gospel, the false witnesses seem to expect the replacement of Herod's newly renovated temple with something even greater there in Jerusalem. John's Gospel also knows this *Tempelwort* tradition, because the "mistake" is explained in terms of the temple of Jesus' own body, to be destroyed and raised again in three days (John 2:13-22). Qumran's Temple Scroll envisions the construction of an alternative temple, apparently as theological critique of the false priesthood in Jerusalem. Since the construction plans are fantastic, by definition impossible for human hands, the ideal temple may have existed only in the mind of God.[32]

In Hebrews, the tabernacle[33] not made with hands is the real one, eternally present in the heavens. It was necessary for Christ to enter into that holy of holies as our great high priest and there to offer himself as perfect sacrifice in order to secure our redemption (9:11-24). Jesus' crucifixion has thus been redescribed liturgically in cosmic proportions as the world-altering reality that has inaugurated human salvation.

Hebrews' platonic spatial realism is combined with an apocalyptic temporal realism in which God's time has graciously invaded human time in the person and work of Jesus Christ. Time is notoriously difficult in Hebrews, in spite of an abundance of apparently clear temporal markers in the text.[34] The first verses mark the contrast between "long ago" (πάλαι, *palai,* lit., [days] of old) and "these last days," when God has spoken to us by a Son. The day of judgment looms ahead and is drawing near (10:25); "the one who is coming will come and will not delay" (10:37); Jesus will appear a second time (9:28) to bring salvation to those who are eagerly waiting for him. As long as it is still called "today," the door into God's gracious rest remains open (3:13-19), and here the temporal confusion begins: is the

32. "Only" in this context is an exclusive, non-derogatory term: existing in the mind of God is ultimate reality.

33. Hebrews nowhere references the Jerusalem temple explicitly. Whether the wilderness tabernacle/tent (which later evolved into Solomon's temple after David brought the ark of the covenant to Jerusalem) has anything at all to do with the second temple and whether the Herodian temple is still standing at the time of Hebrews' writing are matters of considerable debate.

34. A helpful older article is C. K. Barrett's "The Eschatology of the Epistle to the Hebrews," in *The Background of the New Testament and Its Eschatology,* ed. W. D. Davies and David Daube (Cambridge: Cambridge University Press, 1956), pp. 363-93.

"today" of the wilderness generation recalled from Numbers 13–14 the same as the "today" of Psalm 95, which redescribes what is entered from "the land" to "rest," and also the "today" of the hearers in 4:9, to whom a sabbath rest remains?

Moreover, how are these apparently clearly delineated temporal markers to be reconciled with Hebrews' repeated references to things "eternal": "eternal salvation" (5:9), "eternal redemption" (9:12), "eternal Spirit" (9:14), "eternal covenant" (13:20)? Other puzzling temporal claims abound: though long dead, Abel still speaks (11:4); Moses suffered abuse for the Christ (11:26); resembling the Son of God, Melchizedek remains a priest forever (7:3). The most complicated temporality concerns the tabernacle and its rites of atonement. In 9:8, the Holy Spirit indicates that the way into the sanctuary has not yet been disclosed while the first tabernacle still stands, and "this is a symbol of the present time," in which ineffective sacrifices are still offered (9:9-10).

Wilderness tabernacle typology frames the language of redemption: "without the shedding of blood there is no forgiveness of sins" (9:22), which is why our great high priest had to offer himself as pure sacrifice in the heavenly sanctuary once for all (9:24, 28).[35] The wilderness tabernacle had not stood since the time of the first temple. So "the present time" must be the "today" of the author/preacher and congregation, and the actions of the ancient tabernacle serve (by analogy) to critique the present-day temple priests, who are still offering sacrifices both annually and daily (10:1-4, 11).[36]

Whatever temporality is assumed, human time pales in comparison to God's time, just as the human tabernacle is but a sketch and shadow of the heavenly one. The apocalyptic temporal realism of Hebrews requires that the heavenly reality of redemption in Christ Jesus once for all "dislocate" all other times, making them types of God's eternity.

35. Unless his appearing in God's presence refers to his session at the right hand (Psalms 8 and 110). Christ's death and session tend to be conflated.

36. If Hebrews was written after 70 C.E., another reading may be required, and the time of "today" may need to be located back in the wilderness.

Preexistent and Exalted Divinity in Radical Solidarity with Humanity

The identity of Jesus Christ in Hebrews effectively combines three-stage preexistence/exaltation Christology with fully experienced humanity and radical solidarity with those subject to suffering and death. No other New Testament text so clearly puts the full deity and entire humanity of Jesus Christ side by side in what we might call pre-Chalcedonian paradox. The Johannine Jesus embodies the fullness of deity, and the line between deity and humanity is clearly expressed: "You are from below, I am from above; you are of this world, I am not of this world" (John 8:23).

The contrast with Hebrews at this point could not be clearer: it was necessary (ὤφειλεν, *ōpheilen*) for the Son to be made like his brothers and sisters in every respect[37] so that he might become a merciful and faithful high priest (2:17). Jesus had to be tested in every way as humans are so that he might sympathize with our weaknesses (4:15). He had to partake of our mortality so that through death he might free those enslaved by the fear of death (2:14-15).[38] Therefore, the prayer to be delivered from the hour of death that the Johannine Jesus spurns (John 12:27) must be embraced by the Son of God in Hebrews (5:7-10) in order for him to be qualified for the office of high priest. It is a required part of his formation. Neither side of what will become the Chalcedonian formula is compromised in Hebrews; the full deity of Jesus Christ is not eclipsed by his entire humanity. Rather, the Son's assumption of "flesh and blood" (2:14) is essential to his work both on earth and in the heavenly sanctuary. Thus, preexistence/exaltation Christology is combined in Hebrews with radical human solidarity and empathy hard-won through participatory suffering and death as "flesh and blood."

The identity of Jesus Christ in Hebrews extends beyond Christology to anthropology. What is the human creature that God should remember it? What originally was the psalmist's question to God about humanity is here spoken back to humanity as God's own word (2:6-8a). Just as Scripture in Hebrews discloses something of the inner life of God, it also shows us what it is to be truly human. We see Israel's unfaithfulness (3:13-19) and faithful-

37. This is glossed to exclude sin in 4:15.

38. See Patrick Gray, "Brotherly Love and the High Priest Christology of Hebrews," *Journal of Biblical Literature* 122 (2003): 335-51.

ness (11:1-40); Moses' fearful confession before God, "I tremble with fear" (12:21), and our bold confession, like Moses' boldness before the king (11:27), "The Lord is my helper . . . I will not be afraid" (13:6). Exegesis for Hebrews includes not only the Word of God to humanity but also the words of humanity to God. Both words of trembling and words of trusting are honored as part of the great conversation where the voice of the living God names the question in the human heart by means of Scripture, reveals God's purpose in Jesus Christ to address that yet unasked question, and speaks Scripture as a word of exhortation in response to God's prior Word. The human situation has been fully understood and comprehended in God's ongoing purpose; therefore, the human task is to trust and obey.

Conclusion: God Has Spoken to Us by a Son

Philosophical theologians have pondered the question of how God speaks, and especially how God speaks through biblical texts. Predictably, the issue is most acute for those who wish to found biblical and theological ethics on some version of divine command theory. Nicholas Wolterstorff has argued for the retrieval of a hermeneutical practice that reads the Christian Bible to discern what God is saying thereby.[39] His hermeneutic assumes that Scripture is intrinsically a medium of divine discourse, an assumption widespread within Christianity for at least the first 1500 years. Whatever the merits of his argument, Wolterstorff's premise should lead exegetical theologians directly to Hebrews. There, more than anywhere else in Scripture, we find theological reflection about the implications of God's speech through biblical texts and God's speech by a Son.

A similar hermeneutical retrieval is needed in the area of Christian social ethics. Hebrews' "word of exhortation" (13:22) binds Christology to ethics throughout its argument, and its final chapter treats material that is self-evidently relevant to the formation and nurture of Christian community: hospitality to strangers; solidarity with the suffering; the sanctity of marriage; proper attitudes toward money and possessions; support of leaders. The use of *imitatio Christi* as a warrant for social ethics is pervasive within the New Testament. What is distinctive about Hebrews is its use

39. Nicholas Wolterstorff, *Divine Discourse: Philosophical Reflections on the Claim That God Speaks* (Cambridge: Cambridge University Press, 1995).

as a warrant for solidarity with those who are politically at risk and suffering hardship.[40] The identity of Jesus Christ in Hebrews calls us to follow him, our Shepherd and perfect sacrifice, "outside the camp."

* * *

"Time would fail me to tell . . ." of the identity of Jesus Christ in Hebrews so as to do justice to the rich complexity of this early Christian sermon. Hebrews is an exquisitely beautiful and multifaceted argument for the person and work of the Son of God as the high priest of Israel who offered himself once and for all time "a full, perfect, and sufficient sacrifice, oblation, and satisfaction, for the sins of the whole world."[41] Here deity and humanity in their fullness meet in Jesus Christ, God's Word, God's Wisdom, and God's Witness for those "outside the camp." "Today," when we hear his voice, may we not harden our hearts.

40. See my "'Outside the Camp': *Imitatio Christi* and Social Ethics in Hebrews 13," forthcoming.

41. From the Great Thanksgiving, *Book of Common Prayer,* p. 334.

Moses and Jonah in Gethsemane: Representation and Impassibility in Their Old Testament Inflections

Gary A. Anderson

Basic to the identity of Jesus in the thinking of the early church were his representative nature and his impassibility. God did not just resurrect a man on Easter Sunday; rather, in that act he committed himself to raising all those who are joined in faith to him. Robert Jenson puts the matter in a characteristically laconic fashion: while Jesus rests in the grave, the Father faces a dilemma. He can either "have his Son and us with him into the bargain, or he can abolish us and have no Son, for there is no Son but the one who said, 'Father, forgive them.'"[1] Certainly, one of the reasons the early church labored so hard to make sure that Jesus was fully man was so that this representative aspect would be efficacious. What has not been assumed cannot be healed.

The other feature basic to Christ's identity was his impassibility. Christ became one with us through his suffering on the cross. But suffering is of course a dangerous element to introduce into the Godhead, because suffering is something that happens *to* a person, and as a result, it can *change* a person. When Jesus prays in Gethsemane that his cup of suffering be removed, an element of reservation is introduced. Is Jesus a free agent in this story?[2] Most readers are going to answer, vigorously, Yes! But if Jesus really doubted, that is, if he experienced the sort of vacillation that is common to the human condition, is it possible that the larger project of human salvation was truly at risk? Had the man Jesus not come down on the right side

1. Robert W. Jenson, *Systematic Theology,* vol. 1, *The Triune God* (New York: Oxford University Press, 1997), p. 191.

2. On this problem, see the discussion of Robert Jenson in the present volume.

of the matter, was all lost? Christian theology has never wanted to assert this. And so the Christian tradition has coined an impossible phrase to account for this conundrum: Christ suffered *impassibly*. The doctrine of divine impassibility in Christian dress has meant that God's intimate involvement with the human condition did not set at risk his providential purpose of redeeming the created order. David Hart has put the matter well: "For God to pour himself out . . . as the man Jesus is not a venture outside of the trinitarian life of indestructible love, but in fact quite the reverse: it is the act by which creation is seized up into the sheer invincible pertinacity of that love, which reaches down to gather us into its triune motion."[3]

The question I would like to pose in this essay is whether these two notions that appear so quintessentially christological — representation and impassibility — have an analogy in the Old Testament.

Moses and the Nature of Representation

Certainly, one of the most dramatic moments of intercession in the Old Testament is the moment when Moses speaks to God just after Israel has venerated the golden calf (Exod 32:1-6). No sooner has Israel been given a set of commands that solemnize her election as God's very own people than she violates one of the most important of them. God, in understandable indignation, turns to address his prophet Moses:

> Hurry down, for your people, whom you brought out of the land of Egypt, have acted basely. They have been quick to turn aside from the way that I enjoined upon them. They have made themselves a molten calf and bowed low to it and sacrificed to it, saying: "This is your god, O Israel, who brought you out of the land of Egypt!" (Exod 32:7-8)[4]

It is worth noting that already in this first address to Moses, God sets up a peculiar triangular relationship: he takes Moses into his confidence to dis-

3. David Bentley Hart, "No Shadow of Turning: On Divine Impassibility," *Pro Ecclesia* 11 (2002): 202. One should also compare the judicious and informative treatment of the problem by Ellen Davis in her essay "Vulnerability, the Condition of Covenant," in *The Art of Reading Scripture*, ed. Ellen F. Davis and Richard B. Hays (Grand Rapids: Eerdmans, 2003), pp. 290-93.

4. Scripture quotations not otherwise identified are from the NJPS.

cuss the matter of Israel's sin, but in so doing he indicates from the very inception the state of alienation between himself and Israel. Israel, God declares, is not my people but *your* people; it is *you, Moses* (!), who brought them up out of Egypt. This peculiar turn in diction creates the necessary space between God and Israel that will allow God to deal with this people in a less than salutary fashion.

Having shown his hand, God gets right to the point:

> I see that this is a stiffnecked people. Now, let Me be, that My anger may blaze forth against them and that I may destroy them, and make of you a great nation. (32:9-10)

Israel's disobedient nature is inarguable; it is established on the grounds of the quickness with which she has overturned the mandates of the recently minted Sinaitic covenant.[5]

What is most striking here is the textual echo of the story of Noah.[6] For way back in Genesis, not long after the creation of the world itself, God became fed up with the lawlessness and violence that had run rampant on the face of the earth and took aim to destroy the world. Only Noah was found sufficiently worthy to survive this cataclysm; and he was told to build an ark so that he, his immediate family, and a representative sample of the animal kingdom might survive the chaotic waters.

Yet there is a significant difference between these two stories. Noah, though a survivor of the flood, achieved this status in a more or less passive manner. Yes, of course, he built the ark, and loaded the animals onto it, but he took no stance for or against what God proposed to do. Not to put too fine a point on it, he simply went along for the ride. Whereas Noah was simply "remembered" by God (Gen 8:1), Moses stridently demands that God remember his prior commitments:

> "*Remember* Your servants, Abraham, Isaac, and Israel, how You swore to them by Your Self and said to them: I will make your offspring as numerous as the stars of heaven, and I will give to your offspring this

5. Elsewhere I have called this the Bible's doctrine of "immediate sin," which is not really different from what the Christian West would call "original sin." See Gary Anderson, "Biblical Origins and the Problem of the Fall," *Pro Ecclesia* 10 (2001): 17-30.

6. On this point, see the excellent discussion of R. W. L. Moberly, *At the Mountain of God: Story and Theology in Exodus 32–34*, JSOTSup 22 (Sheffield: JSOT Press, 1983), p. 92.

> whole land of which I spoke, to possess forever." And the LORD renounced the punishment He had planned to bring upon His people. (Exod 32:13-14)

Moses, for his part, stands in a much different relationship to the impending cataclysm. Unlike Noah, Moses is taken into God's confidence and consulted about what is going to transpire. For if God simply wished to announce a judgment, he could say: "I see that this is a stiffnecked people and so I will let My anger blaze forth against them and will destroy them, and make of you a great nation." Such a statement would draw an almost exact analogy to the story of the flood. And so we could justly wonder whether Marcion was not correct about the irascible nature of Israel's jealous [g]od.[7] But note what God in fact says: "I see that this is a stiffnecked people. *Now, let Me be,* that My anger may blaze forth against them and that I may destroy them, and make of you a great nation."

In acting this way, God sets a condition on his rage and requests Moses' permission before he proceeds. A rabbinic midrash captures the tenor of this request just about perfectly:

> God said to Moses after the incident of the Golden Calf, "Let me at them, and my anger will rest on them and I will get rid of them." Is Moses holding back God's hand, so that God must say "Let go of me"? What is this like? A king became angry at his son, placed him in a small room, and was about to hit him. At the same time the king cried out from the room for someone to stop him. The prince's teacher was standing outside, and said to himself, "The king and his son are in the room. Why does the king say 'stop me'? It must be that the king wants me to go into the room and effect a reconciliation between him and his son. That's why the king is crying, 'Stop me.'" In a similar way, God said to Moses, "Let Me at them." Moses said, "Because God wants me to defend Israel, He says, 'Let Me at them.'" And Moses immediately interceded for them.[8]

7. Marcion, an influential second-century heretic, taught that there was a radical dichotomy between the Old and New Testaments. Indeed, for him, the jealous [g]od of the Old Testament was inferior to the God of Jesus.

8. *Exodus Rabbah* 42:9 as cited in Yochanan Muffs, "Who Will Stand in the Breach? A Study of Prophetic Intercession," in *Love and Joy: Law, Language, and Religion in Ancient Israel* (New York: Jewish Theological Seminary, 1992), p. 34.

It is not solely that God requests Moses' help in this matter; he also signals the manner by which Moses can be most effective. God tells Moses that should he leave God alone, God will make of him a *"great nation."* But this way of putting the matter clearly calls to mind the earlier promise God made to the very father of the nation he wishes to destroy (Gen 12:2). By framing his request this way, God sets up the most formidable argument that can be used against him. God cannot destroy Israel, because of the *promise* to which he is eternally bound.

Moses begins his argument, however, from a slightly different direction. First, he denies categorically any degree of ownership over this people. Though God has "flattered" Moses by naming him as the one who brought Israel out of Egypt (Exod 32:7), Moses will have none of this. "Let not *Your* anger, O LORD, blaze forth against *Your* people, whom *You* delivered from the land of Egypt with great power and with a mighty hand" (32:11). Having laid the responsibility for the exodus on God's shoulders, Moses considers the tremendous investment God himself has made in this very venture. He reminds God that one of the most central concerns in leading Israel out of Egypt with all sorts of supernatural deeds ("with great power and with a mighty hand") was to make it publicly clear to one and all just who was the true sovereign Lord. Pharaoh had his own doubts about the matter right from the start and so refused to release Israel. "Who is the LORD that I should heed Him?" he jeeringly asked Moses in reply to his request (5:2). As a result of such insolence, God let Pharaoh persist in his stubborn refusals so that "I may gain glory through Pharaoh and all his host; the Egyptians shall know that I am the LORD" (14:4). And now, Moses reminds God, if you destroy her in the wilderness, your *glorious reputation* that you worked so hard to win will come to naught. "Let not the Egyptians say," Moses urges, "'It was with evil intent that He delivered them, only to kill them off in the mountains and annihilate them from the face of the earth'" (32:12).

But Moses does not let the case rest here. He rejoins the opening that God has provided him. He recounts the nature in which God bound himself to a specific people when he first promised to make *them* "a great nation" (32:10; cf. Gen 12:2): "Remember Your servants, Abraham, Isaac, and Israel, how You swore to *them* by Your Self and said to *them:* I will make *your* [plural] offspring as numerous as the stars of heaven, and I will give to *your* [plural] offspring this whole land of which I spoke, to possess forever" (32:13). Having been reminded of his obligations, the Lord "renounced the punishment He had planned to bring upon His people."

A key feature of this entire narrative is the strongly *representational* role that Moses plays. As Yochanan Muffs has argued so brilliantly, Moses is not simply an exemplary human being standing before God. *He, in fact, represents part of God to God.*[9] He assumes a part of the divine personality such that one cannot properly pick out the full characterization or identity of God by attending only to what the subject identified as "God" in the story says. Indeed, to follow the literal sense in this fashion is to fall quickly into heresy. For good reason, Marcion latched onto this text and questioned whether any sober-minded reader could abide such a capricious God; and more recently, Harold Bloom has vigorously nodded in agreement with this second-century figure.[10]

But Muffs sidesteps this difficulty by arguing that who God is in this story is a combination of what both God and Moses say. "God allows the prophet to represent in his prayer His own attribute of mercy," Muffs declares, "the very element that enables a calming of God's [angry and vindictive] feelings."[11] Because the prophet is a necessary, nonnegotiable element in the rendering of the identity of God, the midrash can go so far as to say that God wept when Moses was ready to hand over his soul to death: "God said, Who will stand against Me on the day of wrath? (cf. Ps 94:16). This means, Who shall protect Israel in the hour of My anger? And who will stand up in the great eschatological war for My children? And who will speak up for them when they sin against Me?"[12] Moses is a *necessary* actor in the narrative that depicts God's character. The identity of God would be different without him.

Yet Moses' psychic connection with God is not the only representational aspect on the table. Moses is also strongly tied to the people Israel. Indeed, as the dialogue between Moses and God continues and the immediate threat of destruction is set aside, a new issue surfaces: whether God will renew his close ties to Israel and accompany her personally to the promised land. Again, God tries to sever Moses from the people Israel. But when Moses sees the great favor he has won in God's eyes, he is not in any way content. For Moses, favor becomes a valuable commodity only when it is deployed to Israel's benefit. "Now, if I have truly gained Your favor," Mo-

9. Muffs, "Who Will Stand in the Breach?" pp. 33-34.

10. Harold Bloom, *The Book of J* (New York: Grove Weidenfeld, 1990).

11. Muffs, "Who Will Stand in the Breach?" p. 33.

12. See *Midrash Tanhuma* to the *parasha* (weekly Torah portion) *Va-ethanan* (Deut 3:23–7:11), as cited in Muffs, "Who Will Stand in the Breach?" p. 33.

ses answers, "pray let me know Your ways, that I may know You and continue in Your favor. Consider, too, that this nation is Your people." And God replies: "I will go in the lead and will [deliver you to safety]" (Exod 33:13-14). Clearly, God is interested only in Moses, as he ignores the second half of Moses' request ("Consider, too . . ."). And so Moses must step back into the breach to confront his benefactor: "Unless you go in the lead, do not make *us* leave this place. For how shall it be known that *Your people* have gained Your favor unless You go with *us*, so that *we* may be distinguished, *Your people and I*, from every people on the face of the earth?" (33:15-16). At this point the Lord acquiesces. Israel is fully back in his good graces, and God agrees to accompany Israel personally to the promised land.

Only one portion of Moses' request has not been addressed. Moses has prayed that God will make known to him his ways. In order to do this, God has Moses ascend Mt. Sinai a second time to receive a second set of the stone tablets. And on top of that mountain, the Lord passes by Moses and proclaims:

> The LORD! the LORD! a God compassionate and gracious, slow to anger, abounding in kindness and faithfulness, extending kindness to the thousandth generation, forgiving iniquity, transgression, and sin; yet He does not remit all punishment, but visits the iniquity of parents upon children and children's children, upon the third and fourth generations. (34:6-7)

These attributes of God — which become known as the "thirteen attributes" in Jewish tradition — are often reused in the Bible by various intercessors to remind God of his compassionate nature and to persuade him to show mercy on his people.[13]

This remarkable revelation of God's overwhelmingly compassionate nature will be an important tool for Moses' subsequent intercession on behalf of Israel. For in the book of Numbers, when Israel is given the opportunity to enter the land of Canaan to lay claim to what her God has promised, she will think twice and refuse to enter. As a result of Israel's

13. On these attributes, see Muffs, "Who Will Stand in the Breach?" pp. 20-24. For a sample of how they are used elsewhere in the Old Testament, consult Pss 86:15; 103:8; 145:8; Joel 2:13; Neh 9:17. See also the discussion of Uriel Simon, *The JPS Bible Commentary: Jonah* (Philadelphia: Jewish Publication Society, 1999), pp. 35, 37.

disobedience, God will react in a manner very similar to his response to the golden calf. The accompanying table lays out the parallel texts:

Exodus 32	*Numbers 14*
9The LORD further said to Moses, "I see that this is a stiffnecked people. 10Now let Me be, that My anger may blaze forth against them and that I may destroy them, and make of you a great nation."	11And the LORD said to Moses, "How long will this people spurn Me, and how long will they have no faith in Me despite all the signs that I have performed in their midst? 12I will strike them with pestilence and disown them, and I will make of you a nation far more numerous than they!"
11But Moses implored the LORD his God, saying, "Let not Your anger, O LORD, blaze forth against Your people, whom You delivered from the land of Egypt with great power and with a mighty hand. 12Let not the Egyptians say, 'It was with evil intent . . .'	13But Moses said to the LORD, "When the Egyptians, from whose midst You brought up this people in Your might, hear the news, 14they will tell it to the inhabitants of that land. . . .
13Remember Your servants, Abraham, Isaac, and Israel, how You swore to them by Your Self and said to them: I will make your offspring as numerous as the stars of heaven, and I will give to your offspring this whole land of which I spoke, to possess forever."	17Therefore, I pray, let my Lord's forbearance be great, as You have declared, saying,
	18*'The LORD! slow to anger and abounding in kindness; forgiving iniquity and transgression; yet not remitting all punishment, but visiting the iniquity of fathers upon children, upon the third and fourth generations.'* 19*Pardon, I pray, the iniquity of this people according to Your great kindness, as You have forgiven this people ever since Egypt."*

14And the LORD renounced the punishment He had planned to bring upon His people.

20And the LORD said, "I pardon, as you have asked."

The key difference between these two prayers is the introduction of the thirteen attributes into the body of the petition. What Moses desires to know in Exodus 33:13 ("Now, if I have truly gained Your favor, pray let me know Your ways . . .") turns out to be much more than a moment's curiosity. The knowledge he receives establishes the very basis of subsequent appeals for clemency. God has provided Moses with the legal grounds on which he can pursue his claims against God.

Clearly, one part of the christological analogy is in place. Moses, like Jesus of Nazareth, has been called to represent his people before God. Indeed, the representation is so strong that the delineation of our characters in the simple plotlines of Exodus 32:7-14 and Numbers 14:11-20 turns out to be quite complex. Because Moses, as Muffs puts the matter, assumes the role of one side of the divine personality, it is not clear that the dialogue is between a human prophet and a God who is totally other. Rather, God has involved Moses in this prayer in such a profound manner that the character we can pick out as "God" is somehow the combination of what our human and divine subjects say.

If we were to paraphrase Jenson, we could say that the God of Israel faces a dilemma: he can either have his prophet and Israel with him into the bargain, or he can abolish Israel and have no Moses, for there is no Moses but the one who said, "For how shall it be known that Your people have gained Your favor unless You go with us, so that we may be distinguished, *Your people and I,* from every people on the face of the earth?" (Exod 33:16).[14]

This is a powerful story, but also a potentially disturbing one. If we

14. Tertullian (155-230 C.E.), in his work *Against Marcion,* had already seen the christological analogy at work here and found in this text a potent witness to the christological mystery: "Pitiable are ye . . . since you know not Christ, prefigured in the person of Moses, as the one who prayed to the Father, and offered His own life for the salvation of the people. It is enough, however, that the nation was at that instant really given to Moses. That which he, as a servant, was able to ask of the Lord [an allusion to Moses' response to God: 'Thou shalt not do this; or else destroy me along with them'], the Lord required of Himself. For this purpose did He say to His servant, 'Let me alone, that I may consume them,' in order that by his entreaty, and by offering himself, he might hinder (the threatened judgment), and that you might by such an instance learn how much privilege is vouchsafed with God to a faithful man and a prophet" (*Against Marcion* 2.26, trans. Peter Holmes, *ANF* 3:318, alt.).

concede that God's identity is revealed by the interaction of prophet and Lord, we still leave open the question of what would happen should the prophet prove unfit for the job. Does all of Israel's sacred history stand in the balance? Is Moses' own psychic strength, which allows him to stand in the breach before God, that trustworthy? The midrash, as we saw, gives voice to these very fears when it depicts God as crying when Moses hands his soul over to death: "Who will protect Israel from Me now that Moses is gone?" God laments. This is a gripping yet troubling account. Is God so much a part of the natural order that he becomes totally dependent on fallible human intermediaries? Even the most reverent reader of the Bible hesitates here. In order to shed further light on the problem, let us turn to the figure of Jonah.

Jonah and the Nature of Impassibility

The book of Jonah is structured around two themes: getting Jonah to Nineveh so that he can deliver his message, and teaching this reluctant prophet why his task is necessary. Let's begin with the first. Jonah's mission to the Ninevites opens with the Lord's command in 1:1 and resumes again in 3:1 with a reiteration of the same. It is useful to see just how similar the opening lines of these respective chapters are.

Jonah 1

1The word of the LORD came to Jonah
son of Amittai: 2"Go at once to
Nineveh, that great city, and proclaim
judgment upon it; for their wickedness has come before Me." 3Jonah,
however, started out to flee to
Tarshish from the LORD's service.

Jonah 3

1The word of the LORD came to Jonah
a second time: 2"Go at once to
Nineveh, that great city, and proclaim
to it what I tell you." 3Jonah went at
once to Nineveh in accordance with
the LORD's command.

One might assume that the intervening narrative about Jonah's experience on board the ship has taught him that the Lord's call is impossible to flee, and so now, in chapter 3, he is voluntarily acting in compliance with it. This, however, does not seem to be the case. First, although Jonah has learned that he cannot flee from his prophetic task, instead of confessing the error of his ways and telling the sailors to drop him off at the next harbor (a distinct but unmentioned possibility), he informs them that they must cast him overboard in order to have respite from the storm. Jonah, by this action, anticipates his more brazen attitude of chapter 4: it is better to die than to comply with a command that one finds morally repugnant. But God will not let the matter rest at that. It seems he is bound and determined that Jonah reach Nineveh. For this reason, a fish is appointed to swallow Jonah and disgorge him upon dry land.

But just as Jonah refused to pray while in the hold of the ship even after being discovered by the ship's captain (1:6), so he is silent upon entering the fish. Only after three days — a common idiom in the Bible for denoting the passage of a period of time that is long but not overly so[15] — does he finally pray. This scene reminds one of the famous remark ascribed to Mark Twain, recounting his travel by ship to Europe. "After one day I was so sick I was afraid I was going to die," he quipped; "a few days later I was afraid I wasn't going to die!" Jonah's prayer of contrition is forced from his mouth by an aggressive God hell-bent on getting him to Nineveh.

While in Nineveh, Jonah makes a perfunctory trip through the city proclaiming that in a mere forty days the city will be no more. Just as Jonah has feared, his cry of judgment falls on receptive ears, and all the inhabitants of the city, from the king to the lowly oxen, undergo acts of self-mortification amid the hope that God will relent from his decree and show mercy.

Indeed, this is precisely what happens. Jonah, for his part, is greatly distressed and has harsh words for God:

> O LORD! Isn't this just what I said when I was still in my own country? That is why I fled beforehand to Tarshish. For I know that You are a compassionate and gracious God, slow to anger, abounding in kindness, renouncing punishment. (4:2)

Jonah's displeasure is shocking. As readers, we are ignorant at the beginning of the tale as to what motivates Jonah's flight from God (1:1-3). Is it the difficulty of the job (large city, many sinners?), the fact that the city is some distance from his home, fear about his prophetic reputation, or maybe the fact that the people are not Israelites?[16] To the reader, any of

15. See Simon, *Jonah*, p. 19.

16. This last reason is a favorite explanation among many modern Christian readers. It simply does not work in the context of the book.

these is possible, but Jonah's answer briskly brushes them all aside. This prophet is in agony because he knows that God is "compassionate and gracious, slow to anger, abounding in kindness, renouncing punishment" (4:2). In short, the very formula bequeathed to Moses as a means of forestalling a harsh decree turns from being beneficent to the world to just the opposite! What was to become the primary means of averting the wrath of God becomes the source of Jonah's moral outrage.

Jonah, the reader learns, is a rigorous moralist. He believes that the world's affairs should be conducted according to the exacting standards of the law and that any divergence to the right or the left is worthy of quick and sure punishment.[17] In spite of, or perhaps better, *because of* being forced to deliver a quite different message, Jonah will not give up on his sense of dissatisfaction that borders on outrage. Rather than returning home — *west,* toward Israel — Jonah declares his desire to die and obstinately heads *east.* There he builds a booth in which to sit and watch what will become of the city. Evidently, he hopes that God's initial leniency will be shown to have been hopelessly optimistic, if not downright foolish, and the destruction of the wicked city will shortly take place.

What is striking here is that we see what happens when our appointed Mosaic prophet does not rise to the accepted standard of his office. It is not the case that all bets are off and God's rage will now burst forth unchecked. In fact, God had the system rigged from the beginning. He was going to get Jonah to Nineveh no matter what.

And here is the answer to the theological problem raised by the story of Moses' prayer of intercession. There we worried about the manner in which God seemed to tie his identity to the role of a certain human agent. If that agent proved fallible, would God's wrath get the better of him? In the story of Jonah, we see the bottom line: if we have to choose between a narrative that will preserve human free choice but compromise God's mercy and a narrative that will compromise human choice in order to effect God's mercy, the direction God will take is clear. And this, I would argue, is precisely what the theological tradition has tried to affirm through the doctrine of impassibility. It is not that God is indifferent to his creation in the way in which the

17. See the discussion of St. Thomas Aquinas on justice and mercy in the *Summa Theologica* I.21.3. It is not unjust for God to show mercy on the guilty; it is like someone paying a creditor 600 denarii when only 200 are owed. It is not an unjust action; it is an excessive one. And just as the sinner will "owe" a punishment of some sort for his crimes, so God is free to take less payment (measured in terms of punishment) than is due.

Greek philosophical world would have construed it. God is intimately bound to his creation, but that boundedness cannot and will not compromise his providential ends. John Webster has put the matter well:

> Precisely because God's will is sovereign, it can freely and without loss or impairment take the prayers of creatures into its service, and allow itself to hear in the creature an echo of itself. God is not constituted by these others; his will is not battered into submission; rather, through them God demonstrates the kind of liberty which is proper to Himself, a liberty which is not threatened by but exercised in Moses' prayer, Jonah's refusal, and the Son's anguish in the Garden.[18]

But the story does not end here. For the genius of the book of Jonah is the way it underscores the theme of prophetic participation in the life of God. God could leave Jonah in his funk and, like a mother or father faced with a toddler's tantrum, simply hope that with the passage of time things will change. Or maybe he could give up on Jonah altogether. Why not? Isn't it God's prerogative to do such? Yet just as God *provided* a fish to make Jonah do his bidding, God now *provides* a plant to grow up over Jonah's head and offer some shade: "The Lord God *provided* a ricinus plant, which grew up over Jonah, to provide shade for his head and save him from his distress [רָעָה, *raʿah*]. Jonah was very happy about the plant" (4:6, my translation).

This plant, which arises to shade Jonah's head, seems to be as well a token of God's care and concern for Jonah. For the masculine suffix ("*his* distress") unequivocally informs us that the distress in question is that of Jonah's own person, not what the sun might produce. Moreover, a rich set of ironies is set in place. Just as we could say that penance and contrition saved the Ninevites from the consequences of their wickedness (רָעָה, 1:2; 3:8, 10), so this plant has been sent to "save" (לְהַצִּיל, *lehatsil*) Jonah from his distress (רָעָה).[19] Jonah perceives that this token of "salvation" is God's act of trying to make amends after all is said and done. Jonah apparently understands the plant as something sent to placate his anger, a token that he is not completely in the wrong.

18. John Webster provided these comments as a response to a version of this paper at the Society of Biblical Literature conference in Philadelphia, November 2005.

19. Even better, one could say that just as the acts of self-mortification taken on by the Ninevites demonstrated their dependence on God, so the sun sent to smite Jonah demonstrates his own dependence on God — as great as that of the Ninevites he despises.

But this is not God's design. The distress from which he wishes to deliver Jonah is his own strict moral calculus about how the world should be administered. Evidently, God has determined that no rational argument is going to win the day with Jonah. If anything has been learned up to now, it is the strength of Jonah's resolve. God will have to use other means to show Jonah that he is not as self-sufficient as he has thought. And it is for this pedagogical purpose that the plant has been sent in the first place. No sooner has it been given than it is taken away. This provides God the opportunity to allow Jonah to indict himself.

Let's compare Jonah's attitude toward Nineveh with his attitude toward the plant. When Jonah sees that Nineveh has been sustained by God's mercy, he assumes the attitude we saw earlier on the ship — he wishes to die: "Please, LORD, take my life, for I would rather die than live" (4:3). A world bereft of justice, he believes, is not worth inhabiting. God, in evident perplexity, asks: "Are you that deeply grieved?" (4:4), which we might gloss: "Are your moral scruples that rigorous that turning a benign eye on this city really does you in?" To this query, Jonah does not give answer. As at the beginning of the book, he departs in silence, evidently hoping that the city will soon return to its wayward ways so that he can enjoy a moment of *Schadenfreude* at God's expense. Justice is no trifling matter to this earnest prophet.

God intervenes by providing Jonah with a plant that offers him some shade, an act that appears to be a gesture of reconciliation. But as soon as Jonah begins to take solace in it, God sends "a sultry east wind" to destroy the plant so that the sun can beat down on him. Jonah is forlorn and mutters to himself, "I would rather die than live" (4:8). Now God has Jonah in a corner. He poses his question again: "Are you so deeply grieved," to which he adds a brief clarification, *"about the plant?"* (4:9). For the first time in the story, this model of self-control loses his cool. Jonah breaks his silence, lashing out at God in defiant anger: "Yes [I am very angry, indeed about that plant!], so deeply that I want to die." In this fashion, Uriel Simon writes, "Jonah unwittingly passes sentence on [himself by] the disproportion of his reaction: the fact is that he was not nearly as troubled by the salvation of Nineveh as he is by the death of the plant. He confesses that the broad assault on divine justice did not provoke him nearly as much as the personal attack on his own well-being."[20]

20. Simon, *Jonah*, p. 44.

Given the ridiculous position that Jonah has now put himself in, God can close the book with a sharp counterquestion, the answer to which we never hear Jonah give: "And should not I care about Nineveh, that great city, in which there are more than a hundred and twenty thousand persons who do not yet know their right hand from their left, and many beasts as well!" (4:11). According to Jewish tradition, Jonah answers God by reciting the closing lines of the prophet Micah:

> Who is a God like You,
> Forgiving iniquity
> And remitting transgression;
> Who has not maintained His wrath forever
> Against the remnant of His own people,
> Because He loves graciousness! . . . (Mic 7:18)

Whatever Jonah's response, the reader sees the untenable position he has put himself in. God is not content simply to use this reluctant prophet to forgive Nineveh; he wishes also to educate him. For ideally, the prophet is supposed to represent both God to the people (in order to proclaim justice) and the people to God (in order to plead for mercy).

Conclusion

It is God's fundamental desire that any prophet who would speak to and for Israel would participate in God's manner of conducting the affairs of the world.[21] Sometimes, as in the case of Moses, this means being sufficiently knowledgeable about God's *character* (the thirteen attributes) and *promises* that he can remind God of them in time of need.[22] The biblical

21. So Hans Urs von Balthasar: "The whole dialogue between God and man passes through Moses in such a way that he must not only continuously represent God's standpoint over against the people, but can equally continuously set out before God the standpoint of the people, where this is at all defensible. . . . [YHWH], who has bound himself to Israel, is quite simply no longer free. . . . The mediator must defend what is divine against God: God's commitment and obligation against God's freedom, God's will to bestow grace against his punitive righteousness, ultimately God's 'weakness' against his strength." Balthasar, *The Glory of the Lord*, vol. 6, *Theology: The Old Covenant*, trans. Brian McNeil and Erasmo Leiva-Merikakis (San Francisco: Ignatius, 1991), p. 191.

22. Karl Barth writes, in regard to Moses' prayer: "Is not this to flee from God to God,

narrative is constructed such that this is a *real* act of bargaining.[23] Absent Moses and his bravery, Israel will cease to exist.

But the story fails as soon as we reduce it to some theory of divine accommodation. For attributing to God the expression of wrath is not the same as attributing to God such bodily appendages as hands or feet. *The expression of divine wrath or grief is necessary in order to bring the importance of human participation into highest relief.* The point is worth repeating: when Moses and God go head to head in Exodus 32–34, the identity of God is not represented solely by what the character marked "God" says in the dialogue. The identity is fleshed out by the combination of the two voices. Through the prophets, God has invited Israel into his own person, and unlike Noah, they have a material effect on how the world's affairs are conducted. In the midrash, God rues the day Moses departs from this world. As Muffs has so clearly shown, God has not only left himself open to intimidation; he has *required* it. Yet God has not been so cavalier as to hand over his providential designs to a wayward and often fickle humanity lock, stock, and barrel. His providential plan will not be deterred.

In the book of Jonah, we see what happens if the prophetic counterpart refuses to play his part. Given a choice between human participation and God's intentions to forgive and heal, the latter must always win. But even in this case, it is not sufficient simply to "win." A forgiven Nineveh is

---

to appeal from God to God?" Barth, *Church Dogmatics* 4/1, trans. G. W. Bromiley (Edinburgh: T&T Clark, 1956), p. 426. Or consider Barth on the person of Moses himself: "[Moses] was the man who heard and mediated the Word of God, advising and leading and, in fact, ruling the people, not in his own power, but in that of the Word of God which he heard and mediated. And we know, too, that he was the man who prayed for Israel in his solitariness with God, in a sense forcing himself upon God, keeping Him to His promises and earlier work as the covenant Lord of Israel, and being approved and heard by God. He was the man who anticipated in his relationship to Israel the mission ordained for it in its relationship with the nations as the meaning and scope of the covenant which God had concluded with it. He steadfastly represented the people before God even at the risk of his own person and his own relationship with [YHWH]. . . . The mystery of the grace of God is the mystery of this man, and of the connexion between him and that One. The elevation of Israel stands or falls with his election. . . . To look to God meant to Israel to look to this man, to hear God to hear the word of this man, to obey God to follow his direction, to trust God to trust his insight" (pp. 429-30).

23. St. Thomas, who believes in the predestination of the saved and the damned alike, nevertheless declares with full confidence that the prayers of the elect contribute to another's predestined state. See his discussion in the *Summa Theologica* I.23.8.

not the same as an educated prophet. The book does not end with the success of the prophetic mission (Jonah 3:10). Rather, the whole book turns on the drama of chapter 4 and whether Jonah can learn what his role in this affair should have been, with the hope that he will play it more faithfully should the occasion arise again.

In brief, representation and impassibility in their Old Testament inflections take seriously God's intimate emotional involvement with humankind. Yet however passionate the divine/human encounters may appear, they never call into question the benevolent ends toward which God is driving the story. God is love, and as such he desires to involve humankind in the administration of the world to which he is so devoted. Moreover, as the close of the book of Jonah shows so clearly, it is not enough for God to impose obedience. God wants his prophets to offer their service willingly. God allows himself to be dependent upon the prayers of Israel's great intercessors, but in so doing he does not set his providential plans at risk. For it is precisely God's sovereignty that makes our freedom possible.

Perhaps this is the answer the Old Testament would provide to the conundrum of Gethsemane. The man Jesus makes a free decision, but there is no way to imagine that the Son would do anything but obey the Father and drink that cup. The advantage of the Old Testament is that we need not explore this thorny problem in the context of a single moral agent. The Old Testament can split the problem (precisely because the idea of "incarnation" is present in a less concentrated form)[24] across two narratives and so ask and answer a question that cannot be put to the person of Jesus. Placing Moses and Jonah in Gethsemane, we can see that God, through the agent appointed to represent God before humanity and humanity before God, does suffer — but he does so impassibly.

24. On the notion that God incarnates himself within the people Israel, see Michael Wyschogrod, "Incarnation," *Pro Ecclesia* 2 (1993): 208-15, esp. pp. 212-13.

Isaiah and Jesus: How Might the Old Testament Inform Contemporary Christology?

R. W. L. Moberly

Christian attempts to understand Jesus have long drawn on Israel's Scriptures in general, and the book of Isaiah in particular, as a prime resource. In this they have followed the lead of the New Testament. This essay suggests one way in which Christians might continue to do so today.[1]

Setting Out the Problem

The classic construal of Isaiah as a "Fifth Gospel" strongly articulates the Christian significance of this book. Jerome influentially said in the prologue to his Latin translation of Isaiah (a prologue that was included in the Vulgate): ". . . he should be called an evangelist rather than a prophet because he describes all the mysteries of Christ and the Church so clearly that you would think he is composing a history of what has already happened rather than prophesying about what is to come."[2] Yet despite Jerome, and

1. For different and fuller proposals by Christian scholars who have studied Isaiah extensively, see H. G. M. Williamson, *Variations on a Theme: King, Messiah, and Servant in the Book of Isaiah* (Carlisle: Paternoster, 1998); Christopher R. Seitz, "Of Mortal Appearance: Earthly Jesus and Isaiah as a Type of Christian Scripture," in *Figured Out: Typology and Providence in Christian Scripture* (Louisville: Westminster John Knox, 2001), pp. 103-16. For an overview and appraisal of Christian approaches to Isaiah, see Brevard S. Childs, *The Struggle to Understand Isaiah as Christian Scripture* (Grand Rapids: Eerdmans, 2004).

2. *Biblia Sacra iuxta Vulgatam versionem*, vol. 2, 3rd ed. (Stuttgart: Deutsche Bibelgesellschaft, 1983), p. 1096. Despite the generalizing nature of Jerome's contention, it may well be that Isaiah 53 is the primary envisaged passage. In the 1820s, Herbert Marsh, a

even before the advent of modern critical historical awareness, which has tended to dismiss the "Fifth Gospel" construal out of hand, it was not always obvious exactly how Isaiah functioned as such a Gospel — at least, if one bothered to read more than a few famous texts in relative isolation from their literary context.

One luminous moment came in the late fourth century when Ambrose, bishop of Milan, directed the new convert Augustine, who was preparing to be baptized, to read Isaiah.[3] Ambrose apparently did not specify precisely why Augustine should read Isaiah or what he would find there, but Augustine presumed that it was because of the book's heralding of the gospel and the call of the Gentiles. Augustine obediently began Isaiah at the beginning — and failed to understand what he was reading. Since he supposed the rest of the book would be comparable, he laid it aside. Although this was with the intention of resuming his reading later, when better fitted for it, he never in fact did so. It was the Psalms, not Isaiah, where Augustine encountered Christ in the Old Testament, and it was the Psalms that he expounded at length and in depth. Ambrose's expectation that Isaiah could be picked up and read by an intelligent catechumen (who in fact possessed one of the finest minds in the history of the church) in such a way that Christ would be encountered there came to grief on the simple fact that this is not an obvious or straightforward reading of the text — even for someone predisposed, indeed positively expectant, to find Christ there, and for whom metaphorical and figural readings, of one kind or other, were taken for granted.

The advent of a better-developed historical knowledge than was generally available to the ancients enables us to see clearly why Augustine should have found his task so difficult. On any reckoning, the early chapters of Isaiah are not an easy read. The organizing principle and purpose of the text are far from self-evident, and its referent is likewise sometimes unclear.[4] But the text's general concern seems to be the problematic conduct

---

senior British biblical scholar, could still depict Isaiah 53 in the Jerome-like language that has characterized many Christian interpreters down the ages: "[W]e have a plain and literal description of our Saviour's sufferings, death, and burial: indeed no less plain and literal, than any historical narrative could be, which was written after the events themselves had taken place." Marsh, *Lectures on the Criticism and Interpretation of the Bible* (London: Rivington, 1842), p. 431.

3. The story is recounted in Augustine's *Confessions* 9.5.

4. For example, the vividly sketched context for Isaiah's meeting with Ahaz, and Isaiah's

and disposition of the people of Jerusalem, and also its king, and the bearing of this upon the fate of the city in times of enemy aggression — fairly clearly, that of the Assyrian empire.[5] This is juxtaposed, however, with language about divine initiative and transformative power, together with images of a glorious Jerusalem in an unspecified future. In terms of an ancient prophetic concern for YHWH's dealings with Jerusalem and its people, it is possible to make some sense of the text, though it remains unstraightforward; but to introduce reference to Jesus Christ seems simply extraneous and obfuscating ("He's not there, so don't waste time and go into contortions trying to find him there").

When you add to this historical awareness the contemporary ideological anxiety that to read Israel's Scriptures in Christian categories can be seen as in some sense a hostile takeover bid (hostile because generally resisted by a majority of Jews),[6] then one may wonder whether the conception of Isaiah as in any sense a "Gospel" may not best be quietly laid aside and left in the history books where it belongs.

Things are not so simple, however, if one wants to take seriously the Christian conviction that Jesus in a fundamental way "fulfills" Israel's Scriptures (a conviction disputed indeed by Jews from the outset but upon whose validity the New Testament is premised, in full recognition of extensive Jewish refusal). For although this conviction all too commonly reduces

challenge to Ahaz genuinely to believe in YHWH in time of trouble (7:1-9), leads into a famous though contextually somewhat puzzling sign of the child Immanuel (7:10-17), which in turn leads into a series of visions "on that day" (7:18-25) and a series of divine messages to the text's narrating voice, presumably Isaiah (8:1, 5, 11). The initial setting fades from view, leaving a lack of any clear setting, and the train of thought is in places difficult to follow.

5. Assyria is specifically named in 7:17, 18, 20; 8:4, 7; 10:5, 12, 24, and other subsequent passages.

6. Among leading Christian Old Testament interpreters, both Rolf Rendtorff and Walter Brueggemann, in different ways, have emphasized the need for rethinking Christian theological approaches to the Old Testament in the light of a proper understanding of, and respect for, Judaism; see Rendtorff's "Toward a Common Jewish-Christian Reading of the Hebrew Bible," in *Canon and Theology: Overtures to an Old Testament Theology,* trans. Margaret Kohl, OBT (Minneapolis: Fortress, 1993; ET from German of 1991), pp. 31-45; and Brueggemann, *Theology of the Old Testament: Testimony, Dispute, Advocacy* (Minneapolis: Fortress, 1997), pp. 80-83, 87-89, 107-12. Childs has taken issue with both in his "Does the Old Testament Witness to Jesus Christ?" in *Evangelium, Schriftauslegung, Kirche: FS Peter Stuhlmacher,* ed. Jostein Ådna et al. (Göttingen: Vandenhoeck & Ruprecht, 1997), pp. 57-64; and in his *Struggle,* pp. 292-96.

to arguments over proof texts, it is at heart a conviction that the vision of God, the world, and the people of God in Israel's Scriptures is taken to its fullest limit and best realizes its rich potential in the person and work of Jesus. If Jesus constitutes the best, and in important senses definitive, understanding both of the nature and purposes of God and of the nature and purpose of human life, then he should enable our better and truer understanding of our world and all that is in it — which includes that scriptural matrix that was from the outset so crucial for articulating his identity.

To be sure, the Christian conviction that Jesus is definitive is properly a conviction about the ultimacy of Jesus and not about the ultimacy of our formulations (however much one seeks to hold together the reality of Jesus and the witness of the church), for we will all stand before him as our judge. The truth of Jesus is a mystery in the proper sense — not a puzzle to be solved, but an all-encompassing reality that appears ever greater the more we enter into it; and the less we enter in, the more likely we are to misunderstand and misrepresent. The history of the church, not least in relation to the Jewish people, patently shows the recurrent failure of Christians to see what they should see and to be what they should be. So acknowledgment of sin and error, and corresponding repentance, must be integral to Christian thought and life. With regard to Christian handling of Israel's Scriptures, all forced and tendentious readings, or manipulative uses, must be acknowledged and renounced. Yet if the Christian conviction about Jesus is right, then one sign should surely be its heuristic fruitfulness.

Contextualizing Isaiah within Christian Scripture

The conviction that Jesus "fulfills" Israel's Scriptures has been embodied, among other ways, in the formation of the Christian canon, in which Israel's Scriptures are now juxtaposed with, and read alongside, the apostolic witness to Jesus. The formation of the Christian canon continues and extends a principle already at work in the formation of Israel's Scriptures — that the writings included have an enduring significance beyond that of their originating context. These texts have been considered so to articulate that which is true of God, Israel, and the world that they have been preserved so as to have a normative force for subsequent generations who seek to stand in meaningful continuity with that Israel that descends from Abraham, was brought out of Egypt, and entered into covenant with YHWH at Sinai.

This process embodies at least two assumptions. First, writings that are enduringly significant must be open to being read in ways, and be found to have meanings, not necessarily envisaged by either author or original audience. When the originating context recedes, and when the text is combined with other texts from different times and contexts, and when it is read in a wide variety of life situations, then the text can become meaningful in fresh and unpredictable ways. To be sure, a disciplined awareness of the text's likely original sense can be a valuable critical control in its responsible reuse, especially for handling anxieties about indisciplined or misguided uses.[7] Nonetheless, the point of a good springboard is not an endless bouncing upon it but rather a graceful entry into the swimming pool.

Second, if writings are to be significant for enabling successive generations to stand in faithful continuity with their foundations, then there must be an implicit "rule of faith" in their reading and appropriation. If the point is to enable a community to sustain a certain kind of identity and way of thinking and living in the world, then that community must have some overall sense of the kind of meaning that is to be found in its writings — their drift, their tenor — to enable them to perform this function. This, of course, gives rise to constant debate about material whose prima facie tenor seems at odds with what the community has come to regard as appropriate. Nonetheless, such debate should be a sign of life for all communities with strong textual foundations.[8]

This means that when the book of Isaiah is read as part of Christian Scripture, it is being contextualized in a way that creates certain expectations — not least that the material will properly be found meaningful in ways that overlap with, but are distinct from, both an ancient historical reading within the context of ancient Israel and a Jewish reading that presupposes its own particular recontextualization of the scriptural text

7. The history of Jewish and Christian biblical interpretation is full of such debates, for example, in the medieval Jewish reinstatement of the *peshat* (plain meaning) in relation to *derash* (applied meaning), or in the Protestant Reformers' reinstatement of literal sense in relation to allegory.

8. An interesting analogy to Jewish and Christian engagement with the Bible is afforded by the continuing American engagement with its eighteenth-century constitution, whose wording is constantly extended in ways beyond those envisaged in its originating context, in interaction with the patterns of life of the American people; see Jaroslav Pelikan, *Interpreting the Bible and the Constitution* (New Haven: Yale University Press, 2004).

within Judaism. How might this work? There are, I think, necessarily both metaphysical-cum-theological assumptions (to do with God's providential purposes and the belief that Israel's God is definitively revealed in Jesus) and textual-cum-literary assumptions (to do with various kinds of metaphorical and figural modes of reading) that jointly operate and play upon each other. To be sure, such a Christian hermeneutic may be complex. For example, a traditional Jewish objection to seeing Jesus as the "fulfillment" of those passages that speak of a Davidic king bringing justice and peace (Isa 7:14; 8:23–9:6 [9:1-7 Eng.]; 11:1-9) is simple: "If Jesus is the Redeemer, why is the world so unredeemed?" Christian reading of these passages in relation to Jesus is inseparable from the fundamental reconstrual of messiahship and salvation that runs through the Gospels and the rest of the New Testament, and so is hardly straightforward.[9] But rather than remaining at the level of principle, it may be helpful to consider specific practice.

God and Humanity in the Book of Isaiah: Exaltation and Abasement

How, then, might Isaiah contribute toward a contemporary restatement of the identity of Jesus?[10] My approach will not be in terms of perhaps the most obvious, and time-honored — either to start with Isaiah and trace a historical trajectory to the New Testament and beyond, or to start with the New Testament's explicit citation of Isaiah, or to start with those passages in Isaiah that are familiar to many Christians from liturgical use. Rather, I will offer a reflection on resonances between Isaiah and the New Testament when both are read as canonical Scripture in the context of Christian faith.

9. A valuable discussion of this issue, in relation to Martin Buber's formulation of the classic Jewish objection, is Paul Meyer, "The This-Worldliness of the New Testament," in *The Word in This World: Essays in New Testament Exegesis and Theology* (Louisville: Westminster John Knox, 2004), pp. 5-18.

10. Throughout this essay I work with the biblical text in its received form, seeking to read it with total imaginative seriousness, without prejudice to the standard debates about composition and redaction, tradition-history and historicity. I take it for granted that awareness of these debates will at the least nuance how one expresses matters and influence what one infers, or does not infer, from the text.

I start with some of the words of Mary's Song, the Magnificat:

He has shown strength with his arm,
he has scattered the proud in the thoughts of their hearts;
He has brought down the mighty from their thrones,
and has exalted the lowly;
The hungry he has filled with good things,
while the rich he has sent away empty. (Luke 1:51-53)

A truth about God has become evident through its impinging upon the everyday world, in this case in God's choice of the peasant girl Mary to be the mother of a child who is to be the sovereign Lord over God's people. To be sure, the perception of this reality is not straightforward and requires discernment — the unsympathetic and the literalist might insist that unless and until Caesar and his minions (ancient or modern) are removed from their current positions of power, the language means little; and since the emperor Augustus was still well ensconced in Rome, and King Herod in Judea, and Roman imperium experienced no notable blips around the time of Jesus' birth, then our text could be a pious but vacuous expression of fantasy — at best an opiate for the marginal and miserable. Yet to take seriously Mary's Song means to rethink the nature of human greatness and significance in the light of God and to recognize that what counts may be found in places that are far removed from the centers of political power, whose own significance is thereby fundamentally reenvisioned.

Mary's Song can be used heuristically to direct our attention to an important and recurrent yet widely underrated theme in Isaiah:[11] exaltation and abasement.[12] Isaiah focuses throughout on the city of Jerusalem, capi-

11. For example, J. Clinton McCann Jr., "The Book of Isaiah — Theses and Hypotheses," *Biblical Theology Bulletin* 33 (2003): 88-94, surveys recent scholarly trends and offers fresh proposals for biblical-theological reflection on Isaiah but makes no mention of this material. I am unaware of any recent discussion of Isaiah that focuses upon this theme.

12. The resonance of the Magnificat with Hannah's Song in 1 Samuel 2, and with some of Israel's psalms more generally, is a reminder that this theme within Isaiah is well represented in other parts of the Old Testament also (traditio-historically, of course, linkages between Isaiah and the Psalms are natural in Jerusalem-oriented literary collections). Deuteronomy 8, with its contrast between a divine humbling that teaches the nature of human life (vv. 2-3) and a human self-exaltation that leads to a forgetful narrowing of human sensibility (vv. 14-18), would also be germane to the discussion. Notable too is Prov 6:16-19, where the first of the things that YHWH hates is "high [i.e., haughty] eyes."

tal of the kingdom of Judah, and on its inhabitants. Within the geopolitical world of the eastern Mediterranean in the Iron Age, Jerusalem was a small and seemingly insignificant entity when set alongside the historic civilizations of Egypt and Mesopotamia. Of course, within the perspective of Israel's canonical writers, Jerusalem has a significance quite other than that which would be apparent in military or economic terms, a significance dependent upon God. For Jerusalem is a place that YHWH has chosen, where Solomon's temple on Mt. Zion mediates YHWH's presence, and where YHWH's chosen house of David rules, all of which is presupposed by Isaiah. Thus, within Isaiah's particular world, Jerusalem indeed represents importance and greatness. But how is all this construed?

After an introductory, apparently summarizing portrayal of Isaiah's message in chapter 1, the theme of exaltation and abasement becomes central in chapter 2. An initial vision of Mt. Zion in "future days" sees it as the highest of the mountains and raised up above the hills (2:2), where the imagery intrinsically suggests majesty and desirability, such that nations will be drawn to it as a place of God's truth and justice (2:3-4);[13] this vision should encourage faithfulness in the present on the part of the "house of Jacob" (2:5).

The opening vision stands in stark contrast to the remainder of the chapter, where faithfulness seems absent. As the text continues, the imagery turns to what the land of Israel is full of — enormous wealth and military resources (2:7), those things that are generally taken to constitute human greatness. But they are accompanied by religious practices and personnel[14] that characterize nations other than Israel (2:6),[15] and by religious practices that are simply idolatrous (2:8), for they accord divine honor to their own handiwork. In the prophet's vision, the consequence is clear: the abasement

13. The fact that, geographically, Zion is a modest hill, smaller than most in the hill country of Israel, is of course an integral presupposition of the prophetic vision.

14. The text of Isa 2:6 is problematic. I follow many commentators in providing an appropriate object to the verb מָלְאוּ (*mal'u*, "are full of") either by emending the difficult מִקֶּדֶם (*miqqedem*, "from the east") to מִקְסָם (*miqsam*, "divination") or by supposing that the latter has dropped out through haplography (unintentional omission of the visually similar word).

15. This, of course, reflects the prophet's judgment as to what should characterize Israel in distinction from other nations, a judgment that has been "received" through the processes of canon formation. It is not incompatible with historical likelihood that Isaiah's perspective was not a majority perspective in his own context, that is, that for many Israelites, diviners may have been commonplace and uncontroversial (which seems a natural implication of 3:2).

of humanity,[16] which is reduced to terror before YHWH (2:9-10). An inversion is explicit in 2:11 — human attempts at exaltation are brought low, while by contrast, YHWH, indeed YHWH alone, is exalted.[17]

This vision of divine exaltation and human abasement is followed by another, couched in terms of YHWH's "day," a day that is emphatically "against" (ten times in 2:12-16) "all that is exalted and high, and . . . all that is raised up" (2:12). This is then spelled out in terms of things that are intrinsically high (trees, mountains, towers) or otherwise grand (ships) — clearly, metaphorical depictions of human pride and self-aggrandizement — all of which will encounter the same inversion (2:17). Next is another picture of human terror before YHWH, and the recognition of the futility of the costly objects of adoration (2:18-21). This picture leads to a final appeal, comparable to the appeal in 2:5 that follows the vision in 2:2-4, to "cease from mortals" (2:22), that is, to cease trusting in human attempts at exaltation rather than trusting in YHWH. Implicitly, the chapter's opening vision of an exalted temple on Zion, the locus for God's teaching of justice and of peace, points to the "better way" that those addressed in 2:6-22 should heed. But as the text stands, we are faced with the juxtaposition of two starkly different visions of possible futures.

The vision of "YHWH's day" does not specify whether it is conceivable for humans to attain exaltation. Indeed, would the language of "YHWH alone exalted" necessarily exclude humans from exaltation? In the next passage in which the language of exaltation and abasement is explicitly used, this issue is addressed:

> Humanity is bowed down, people are brought low,
>   and the eyes of the high are brought low.
> But YHWH of hosts is high in justice,
>   and the holy God shows himself holy in righteousness. (5:15-16)

At first sight, this seems simply to repeat the language of chapter 2. Yet when read in its own context of chapter 5, which opens with the song of

16. The language of the chapter seems deliberately to generalize what has begun specifically with "the house of Jacob," even though YHWH's dealings with Israel, focused upon Jerusalem, still constitute the frame of reference.

17. There is interesting variation in the terminology for abasement and exaltation; e.g., YHWH's exaltation is depicted with verbs other than those used for attempted human exaltation, presumably as a tacit differentiation of the genuine from the spurious.

the vineyard where YHWH seeks justice and righteousness in his people, the language acquires fuller meaning.[18] Thus, despite the rhetorical contrast between God and humanity, the concern of the language is not to exclude but rather to implicate and change the human: Israel is to embody those moral qualities that characterize YHWH himself — to practice justice and righteousness, because this is how YHWH himself acts. The point, then, of the contrast within the passage is *instructive,* to explain the true sense of "being high." True human exaltation is shown to be founded in the kind of moral practice that is characteristic of God, over against widely held but mistaken alternative construals, such as the possession of much property (5:8) or the indulging of pleasure (5:11-12), which have disastrous consequences. In the attainment of such true human exaltation, God is exalted and his holiness displayed.

Alongside these passages, we should note also Isaiah 33, which contains oracles of deliverance from a "destroyer" who "is to be destroyed" (33:1). Here it is said of YHWH that he is exalted and dwells on high and that "he fills Zion with justice and righteousness" (33:5), and YHWH says for himself, "Now I will arise, now I will be high, now I will be raised up" (33:10). The consequence of YHWH's arising is that those in Zion who are sinful and godless are terrified at the prospect of the fire of the divine presence (33:14), while, on the contrary, those who live in justice and integrity — displaying YHWH's qualities — will come to dwell "on the heights" (33:15-16a).

In brief, these passages depict an understanding of exaltation as a characteristic of the one God, which may also become a characteristic of humans who embrace the way of YHWH through living with integrity (practicing "justice and righteousness"). But those humans who try to exalt themselves on their own terms thereby encounter the opposition of YHWH and will, sooner or later, be abased by him. Given the explicit repetition of this theme, and the structurally weighty position of chapter 2 within the book as a whole, I suggest that one may properly, if with restraint, use this theme heuristically for an overall construal of Isaiah. Strikingly, the language and/or conceptuality recur with reference to those three figures within Isaiah that have most consistently been read (predictively, metaphorically, figurally) in relation to Jesus — king, prophet, servant.

18. Here I draw on my "Whose Justice? Which Righteousness? The Interpretation of Isaiah V 16," *Vetus Testamentum* 51 (2001): 55-68, esp. pp. 63, 67.

Isaiah's encounter with the specious King Ahaz (7:1ff.) leads into various passages that speak of a Davidic king who will show the appropriate royal qualities that have, by clear implication, been lacking in Ahaz himself.[19] One of the most famous (9:1-6 [2-7 Eng.]) speaks of a child/son who is characterized by divinely resonant epithets,[20] one who will establish the Davidic throne "with justice and with righteousness." Although the language of exaltation and abasement is not used, our heuristic key indicates that this royal figure is appropriately understood as sharing in YHWH's exaltation because of his practice of YHWH's qualities.

With this Davidic king one can contrast the fall from heaven of the "Day Star, Son of Dawn," an archetypal figure whose resonances extend far beyond his contextual embodiment as the king of Babylon (14:1-23). This figure is marked by wanting a position in the heavens and a throne on high (14:13), with an explicit desire to be like deity, like Elyon ("the Most High," 14:14b). Yet the figure is brought down (where the passive probably implies the action of God) to the lowest depths imaginable, those of Sheol and the Pit (14:15), and denied even the conventional glory of a royal tomb (14:18-19). The reason for this is his lack of justice and righteousness; that is, he is brought down because of his destructive and murderous actions (14:20a).

When Isaiah has a vision of YHWH in royal majesty, in which YHWH sits on a throne that is "high and raised up" (6:1), this vision is clearly connected with that of chapter 2. Thus, we might reasonably read Isaiah's confession of sin in this vision as appropriate self-abasement, and the purging of his lips and his undertaking of his commission as a degree of exaltation; the prophet in his responsiveness to the vision demonstrates true conformity to the will of YHWH.

Later in the book, in what appears also to be a vision of some kind, it is said of the servant of YHWH that "he will be high and raised up and very exalted" (52:13). The terms that have earlier been used of YHWH and his throne are now used of a human figure, the servant of YHWH, as an interpretative preface to the account of his suffering and humiliation (52:13–53:12). On this most famous passage within Isaiah, I would make just three comments. First, no matter how much one tries to "think historically" of a

19. Ahaz's speciousness is exemplified by his use of pious language that Isaiah perceives to be merely evasive of genuine engagement with God (7:10-13).

20. "Wonderful Counsellor" (פֶּלֶא יוֹעֵץ, *pele' yo'ets*) resonates strongly with YHWH's being wonderful in counsel (הִפְלִיא עֵצָה, *hipli' 'etsah*, 28:29); "Mighty God" (אֵל גִּבּוֹר, *'el gibbor*) is likewise used of YHWH (10:21).

figure in the world of captive Judah as the primary referent of the prophetic vision — be it Duhm's "leprous rabbi" or, more likely, the prophet himself taking on Israel's role as servant[21] — the resonance of the language with the New Testament's portrayal of the suffering, death, and resurrection of Jesus is inescapable for the Christian imagination; whether or not Jesus thought of himself in these terms, the important consideration is that Christians should (heuristically) think of Jesus in these terms. Second, although the servant does not as such perform the "justice and righteousness" that is expected of Israel and its rulers, in his own particular way he is clearly fully obedient to YHWH's demanding will, and it is because of this that the section ends, as it began, with affirmations of the servant's eventual position, which will benefit "many" (53:10-12). Third, it is because of the servant's astonishing faithfulness in humiliation that he is seen to be raised to that position of exaltation that characterizes God himself — and those who embrace God's ways.[22]

Isaiah and Christology

If we return to the Gospels, the resonance of Isaiah's portrayal of exaltation and abasement with many of the sayings of Jesus is readily apparent. Most obviously, perhaps, "all who exalt themselves will be humbled, but all who humble themselves will be exalted" (Luke 14:11; 18:14; Matt 23:12), which each time rounds off a depiction of self-dispossession. Jesus uses Isaiah's depiction of the Day Star, Son of Dawn, with reference to the town of Capernaum, where people knew Jesus well and had seen his acts of power but would not repent: "And you, Capernaum, would you be exalted to heaven? You will descend to Hades" (Matt 11:23); the imagery appropriate to a king can be applied to human pride more generally.

Indeed, the idea of inverting usual priorities of exaltation and superiority lies at the very heart of Jesus' teaching, not least with regard to his own mission and practice. So, for example, the passion predictions and their se-

21. See Seitz, "Of Mortal Appearance," p. 114; Brevard S. Childs, *Isaiah*, OTL (Louisville: Westminster John Knox, 2001), p. 412.

22. The exaltation of the servant is also reminiscent of the exaltation of Zion in 2:1-4 in the astonishing effect it has on "nations" (גּוֹיִם, *goyim*, 52:15; 2:2), implying perhaps (in conjunction also with 42:1-4) that the exalted servant embodies or enables that drawing to the ways of God that is the destiny of Zion.

quels in Mark. When Peter attempts to correct Jesus' depiction of his role as Messiah in terms of suffering and dying, Jesus responds with, "Those who want to save their life will lose it, while those who lose their life for my sake, and for the sake of the gospel, will save it" (Mark 8:35). When the disciples argue about their position in some kind of pecking order, Jesus responds with, "Whoever wants to be first must be last of all and servant of all" (9:35). When James and John request top places in Jesus' kingdom and the others get annoyed with them (because they got in first?), Jesus responds with, "Whoever wants to be great among you must be your servant, and whoever wants to be first among you must be slave of all" and goes on to point out that this corresponds to his own priorities, which are "not to be served but to serve and to give his life a ransom for many" (10:43-45).

At the structural level of the New Testament's total portrayal of Jesus there are strong resonances also. Most clear perhaps among the evangelists is John's portrayal of the cross: the place of apparent weakness, shame, and death when Jesus is lifted up on the cross is the place of exaltation and glorification, where humans are drawn to the truth of their being (John 3:14-15; 12:23-33). Paul's portrayal depicts Jesus' self-emptying as the form of human life whereby Jesus construed his equality with God (Phil 2:5-8); the consequent exaltation of Jesus to the highest position imaginable (2:9-11) concludes with a citation of Isaiah's vision of general human acknowledgment of the definitive reality of the one God (Isa 45:23) as realized in and through what Jesus has done (Phil 2:10-11). Paul's further personal testimony to his own revaluation of what previously he had valued the most, his relinquishment of all so as to know Christ and the power of his resurrection (3:2-11), can be seen as modeling a Christian appropriation of Christ's pattern of abasement and exaltation.

Such explicit citations and the conceptual resonances between the book of Isaiah and the New Testament portrayal of Jesus are so readily apparent that I will move directly to the role all of this might play in articulating the identity of Jesus in a contemporary context.

First, a proposal for how we might think christianly in the light of Scripture as a whole. How should Isaiah's vision of "YHWH's day" be understood?[23] The vision is of a kind of ultimate reality, by which ill-founded

23. Here I draw on my "Christ in All the Scriptures? The Challenge of Reading the Old Testament as Christian Scripture," *Journal of Theological Interpretation* 1 (2007): 79-100, esp. pp. 98-100.

human aspirations to greatness and grandeur are found wanting and are overturned — when God appears and confronts human pretension with divine truth. This also implies an urgent transformation of current ways of living in the light of what will ultimately be seen to be of lasting value. Even in the context of the book of Isaiah on its own terms, the nature of the vision is such that it is not possible to pin it down or restrict its reference to any particular moment or event (for like so much within Isaiah, unlike Jeremiah or Ezekiel, there is a notable lack of historical specificity). However much one may see an event such as the fall of Jerusalem in 587 as an instantiation of the vision, that 587 fall is neither final nor definitive. From a Christian perspective, however, the coming of Jesus, and supremely, his death and resurrection, is precisely that event within history that is final — not in the sense that history does not continue, but in the sense that God has definitively revealed and enacted his judgment on the world. This judgment is such that, at any subsequent point in this world or beyond, that which is revealed in the life, death, and resurrection of Jesus remains the ultimate yardstick by which all human aspiration and endeavor are measured by God and either affirmed or found wanting. It is not that human self-aggrandizement cannot now continue, but the nature of, and the reason for, its ultimate futility has been definitively disclosed. It thus becomes appropriate to see the self-revelation of God in Jesus as the supreme realization of Isaiah's vision of "YHWH's day." It is not that this is what Isaiah intended but that this is what his words can be seen to entail when they are read as part of Christian Scripture.

Second, a proposal for formulating Christology in relation to Jewish-Christian dialogue. On the one hand, we must continue to say (in line with much historical-critical work) that the "godlike" language and predicates used of the Davidic king or the servant of YHWH do not imply the "divinity" of the figure in the kind of way that Christians have often supposed, for humans can be depicted with terms used of God when they display qualities of God. This should enable greater Christian openness to recognizing that of which Isaiah speaks in Jewish, and indeed other, contexts — whenever and wherever humans faithfully embody God's priorities, whether or not Christ is acknowledged.

On the other hand, this is not to imply that Christians should abandon belief in the divinity and finality of Christ. To the contrary, our proposal to construe Isaiah's "day of YHWH" in the light of Christ is one way of approaching John's understanding of Jesus as the human face of God, such that

Isaiah "saw his glory and spoke about him" (John 12:41). If Jesus is the definitive embodiment and realization of the God whose purpose is to overturn misguided human self-seeking and to replace it by self-giving integrity as the pattern of human fulfillment in the image of God, then Christians have the stronger reason to take Isaiah's vision with utmost seriousness.

To be sure, the content of Christian proclamation, the saving lordship of Christ, cannot be separated from a mode of proclamation that enters into the reality of that lordship by itself embodying the pattern of abasement and exaltation, of death and resurrection, as Paul makes so clear in Philippians 2–3. If the divine exaltation of Christ is promoted by methods that utilize unregenerate patterns of human power and exaltation, then its nature and meaning are thereby intrinsically distorted (as critics of Christendom have not been slow to point out).

Third, some reflections on what can be involved in making theological and christological proposals in the light of Scripture. Isaiah's depiction of God is strongly moral and relational. God's exaltation and holiness are not only explicitly construed in morally demanding terms of justice and righteousness, and in opposition to that which does not display these qualities, but what is said of God is said only and always in relation to its bearing upon humanity. There is no biblical account of God that does not also implicate Israel and the church. Thus, a theology or Christology that is informed by these texts should likewise resist accounts of God or of Jesus that do not directly bear upon human self-understanding and moral practice.

Further, Isaiah moves the believer to be suspicious of any close alignment between human glory/power and the presence of God. For it is all too likely that what humans admire, esteem, and strive for will be potentially idolatrous, that is, the symbolic embodiment of activity and qualities that are not rooted in the genuine pursuit of God's justice, righteousness, and holiness. To be sure, an alignment between what seems naturally desirable and what is of God is not precluded, at least on a wider Old Testament canvas, and not least with regard to the Old Testament portrayal of David.[24] But despite this caveat, the thrust of Isaiah is certainly to suggest a

24. This seems to be one of the points of the story of Samuel's anointing of David. After Samuel has had to be reminded that God does not look on the outward appearance but on the heart (1 Sam 16:6-7), thus establishing the independence of God's choice from conventional human attractiveness, it is then possible to recognize that God's choice may indeed be outwardly attractive (16:12). Similarly, those who have been weaned off the self-aggrandizing attractions of political power are those who may then best be entrusted with it.

hermeneutic of suspicion toward common understandings of human grandeur; the servant of YHWH is no David, for he is entirely without the kind of attractiveness that would naturally or instinctively draw human beings to himself (Isa 53:2). So too we should remember that Jesus' earthly ministry met far more apathy, bafflement, and hostility than it met warmth, understanding, and acceptance, and it ended in abandonment and an agonizing execution. The recurrent Christian desire to commend faith in Christ by pointing to attractive and successful people who profess the faith (athletes, singers, actors, etc.) is entirely understandable — yet it risks promoting an enlightened self-interest in which grace is cheapened and the whole counsel of God diminished.

Moreover, it follows that there must necessarily be "paradoxical" and "nonconformist" dimensions in understanding Christ — the exaltation of the humble and the humbling of the exalted. In this general context, many of the emphases of liberation theology, and some feminist theology, as well as ideological suspicion, with their critiques of rather too comfortable "establishment" perspectives on theology and life, need continuing and renewed attention. The suspicion that too much theology and Christology is self-interested and complacent can hardly be met without an engagement with the implications of the biblical text that is genuinely searching and unsettling.

Conclusion

If an orthodox creedal confession of Christ is to continue to be meaningful and recognized as true in the churches, it must be seen to do at least two things. On the one hand, it must preserve the mystery of God, eschewing both the rationalist confidence that supposes the mystery of God to be reduced through a knowledge of Christ and the agnostic doubt that supposes meaningful knowledge of God to be impossible. On the other hand, it must enhance the mystery of life, enabling a way of seeing the world, and of life in it, that is more clear-eyed, more truthful, more compassionate, more faithful.

This essay has sought, in a preliminary way, to suggest how these concerns might perhaps be realized through a reading of Old and New Testaments together as Scripture. For it is as we learn to draw on the full resources of Scripture for knowing God in Christ that we become better able to discern the work of God in the world more generally; and we become better able to avoid the self-deceptions and idolatries that so regularly afflict us, better able to be channels for the furthering of God's good purposes for his world.

The Testimony of the Church

The Word and His Flesh: Human Weakness and the Identity of Jesus in Patristic Christology

Brian E. Daley, SJ

"But you — who do you say that I am?" (Mark 8:29). Jesus' blunt question to the disciples, it is often said, remains one of the driving questions of Christian faith: the question, for all those who desire to follow him, of how we understand his identity. For the church of the first several centuries, this question was, to a large degree, raised and focused by the scandal of his human weakness: his suffering and death, of course, but also his human growth and his human needs, as witnessed by the New Testament, as well as the limits his finite human nature imposed on his actions and knowledge. If he is truly the Messiah of Israel and the eschatological giver of God's Holy Spirit, as early Christians were generally ready to confess, what sense can one make of his human ordinariness and obscurity, his human vulnerability and mortality? And if those limiting qualities are taken to be essential to the narrative of how he has actually become humanity's Savior and Lord — if his death, as Jesus himself suggests on the road to Emmaus (Luke 24:26), is in fact the divinely ordained prelude to his resurrection and entry into messianic glory — how must one conceive of *him* as the subject of that narrative?

The classical understanding of Christian orthodoxy, formed in the early church over seven or eight centuries of preaching and controversy and expressed in a growing stream of biblical commentary, theological argument, creedal confessions, and conciliar formulas, was and continues to be that Jesus is himself the Son of God: the eternal Word "by whom all things were made," who in time has become a human among humans, in order to transform and liberate the humanity he has made his own, even to offer humanity a share in the life of God. Classical Christian orthodoxy confesses that the Jesus who revealed God's will and God's love in works and words of power is "one and the same" as the Jesus who slept in the boat, who wept for Lazarus, and who suffered on the cross: God the Son, humanly "personalizing" the transcendent fullness of the divine Mystery in the body and mind, the relationships and limitations, of his own fully human life. The Second Council of Constantinople (553) expresses this central, irreducible paradox of Christian orthodoxy in the clear, if confrontational, terms of a canonical ultimatum:

> If anyone says that the Word of God who performed miracles was someone other than the Christ who suffered, or says that God the Word was *with* the Christ "born of a woman" (Gal 4:4) or was *in* him as one in another, but does not confess that our Lord Jesus Christ, the Word of God made flesh and made human, is *one and the same,* and that both the miracles and the sufferings which he voluntarily endured in the flesh belong to the same one, let that person be anathema.[1]

What I would like to suggest in this essay is that this classical understanding of the single, paradoxical identity of Jesus developed precisely as part of an ongoing struggle in the early church to grasp and express the saving meaning of his real human limitations and human sufferings, assuming that they are proper to a subject who is not simply and exclusively a human being. Taking these limitations seriously — limitations that include his human passivities, his ability to experience grief and to suffer and die — was always a challenge for early believers, because such passivities seemed to conflict both with his role as God's herald and Savior and with the paradigmatic character of his human behavior. Yet the alternative was to disregard the contents of the Gospel narrative, and to depreciate his humanity in a serious way.

Through the process of protracted, often sharply polemical reflection on the implications of this paradox, early Christian theologians developed a grammar for language about Jesus that staked out the conditions for *identifying* him in the fullness of apostolic faith — for saying, as far as human and Christian speech can say, just who and what Jesus is, how the reality of God is involved through him in the history of the world, and what

1. Second Council of Constantinople, canon 3, trans. J. Neuner and J. Dupuis, *The Christian Faith in the Doctrinal Documents of the Catholic Church* (New York: Alba House, 1982), p. 159, alt.; emphasis mine.

God has done for us in him. Only in knowing his identity, patristic Christology suggests — only in being able to name Jesus for who and what he is — do we begin to understand our own human identity and our ultimate vocation.

Clearly, it is impossible here to offer a full summary of the growing sense of both the complexity and the simplicity of the identity of Jesus in the writings of those Fathers considered to represent the mainstream of early Christian orthodoxy. What I would like to do is to offer four "snapshots," four brief and impressionistic characterizations, of the ways four Greek theologians from the second to the seventh century — Irenaeus, Athanasius, Cyril of Alexandria, and Maximus the Confessor — invite us to conceive of the identity of Jesus. My hope is that this will provide us with a sense of developing consistency within the early classical tradition of Christology, one that builds on the New Testament witness yet moves well beyond it philosophically and theologically, and that it will provoke us to deeper reflection for ourselves.

Irenaeus of Lyons

Writing from the frontier region of Gaul around the year 185, Irenaeus tried, in his massive work *Against Heresies (Adversus haereses),* to confront the recurrent "Gnostic" tendency in religious thought, which had already made its presence felt in the small circle of Christian believers, and which continues, in various ways, to have its appeal: the tendency to deconstruct the continuity and credibility of the public world, including the institutions and religious traditions we live in; to look on matter and the body, as well the responsibilities we bear toward the material and bodily world, as part of an illusory realm, the creation of a lesser god, the fruit of a superhuman conspiracy or a cosmic mistake; to see human freedom, the redemption of the human spirit from illusion and enslavement to history, as possible only through a radically revisionist narrative of our origins, which calls us to disregard the accepted realities of daily life and find our meaning within ourselves, in the secret "enlightenment" communicated to an elect few. For Christian Gnostics of the second century, such as the Valentinians, the source of this redeeming knowledge was thought to be the Savior Jesus: not the earthy Jewish prophet of the four Gospels but the representative of an archetypal *pleroma* of heavenly actors, whose doings long antedate the history of the material world and who engage in this present history only to rescue from it those few who can see the illusion of matter, flesh, and human institutions for what it is.

Irenaeus's concern, through all the twists and turns of his proclaimed "unmasking and refutation" of Gnostic teaching, is to argue for the unity and religious relevance of what ordinary Christians regard as the real world — the unity of God as Creator and Savior; the unity of the biblical narrative, of the created universe, of the human person, of the worldwide church and its message — and to insist that it is in *this* world, in *this* history, in *this* body, for all their limitations, that the gospel of redemption through Christ is already on the way to fulfillment. Only in such a unified framework of time and space is there an intelligible form to the story of human alienation and hope, a convincing proclamation of good news. And in this unified narrative, the identity of Jesus as both divine Word and fleshly human being is clearly the paradoxical heart of the story of salvation, the link between source and goal, promise and fulfillment.

So Irenaeus criticizes the Gnostics, in book 3 of *Against Heresies,* for being unaware

> that [God's] only-begotten Word, who is always present with the human race, united to and mingled with the work of his hands,[2] according to the Father's pleasure, and who became flesh, is himself Jesus Christ our Lord, who did also suffer for us, and rose again on our behalf.[3]

By experiencing in himself every stage and aspect of human growth, while communicating to his own body and to the human family in solidarity with him God's own incorruptible life, Irenaeus's Word made flesh becomes the unique Mediator, the only one capable of restoring friendship and *communio* between humanity and its Creator.

In explaining Jesus' work of mediation in book 4 of *Against Heresies,* Irenaeus lays special emphasis on the revelation of God's glory — of God's life-restoring presence to the human mind and senses — which only Jesus, as Word and Son in human form, can achieve. For Irenaeus, it is the revelation of God in the historical, fleshly Jesus that is the heart of redemption:

2. The Greek word here is *plasma:* that which is shaped by God's hands, thus "creation" in its most palpable sense.

3. Irenaeus, *Against Heresies* 3.16.6, ed. A. Roberts and J. Donaldson, *ANF* 1:442, alt.

> For the manifestation of the Son is the knowledge of the Father; for all things are manifested through the Word. . . . For the Lord taught us that no one is capable of knowing God, unless he be taught of God — that is, that God cannot be known without God — but that this is the express will of the Father, that God should be known. . . . For by means of the creation itself, the Word reveals God the Creator; and by means of the world, the Lord as maker of the world; and by means of the formation [of the human creature], the craftsman who formed him; and by the Son, that Father who begot the Son. . . . And through the Word himself who had been made visible and palpable, the Father was shown forth; and although all did not equally believe in him, still all did see the Father in the Son: for the Father is the invisible of the Son, but the Son is the visible of the Father.[4]

By revealing his splendor in the incarnate Word, God communicates life to mortal creatures, draws them into the vital *communio* of his own radiance.

In identifying the saving work of Christ with his presence on earth as incarnate Word, God made real flesh, Irenaeus looks even beyond Christ's revelatory role to connect his person with the continuing sacramental life of the church. So in book 5 of *Against Heresies*, he emphasizes the importance of the Eucharist, taken in this life to be our bodily nourishment, as a pledge of the fullness of the redemption that will be achieved for us in the resurrection of our own material, mortal bodies. It is only because the Word of God has actually become flesh and blood himself, he insists, that the Eucharist, the food that conveys his flesh and blood to us in liturgical signs, can be for us a promise of everlasting life. Here, as before, Irenaeus emphasizes the complex identity of Jesus, God's eternal Word who has made our limited, visible, material nature his own, as itself the key to the church's present faith in him as Savior, and to her hope that our flesh will share in the salvation he offers.

For Gnostic Christians, the passible, limited body and the whole visible, bodily order of fragile human relationships and limiting human institutions constituted the world from which Christ came to save us by secret knowledge. Irenaeus, by contrast, and with him the growing consensus of Christian tradition, proclaims the body, the church, and the world as forming together the locus of salvation, precisely because in the person of Jesus the life-giving Word has made all of these things his own.

4. *Against Heresies* 4.6.3-6 (*ANF* 1:468-69, alt.).

Athanasius of Alexandria

It is no exaggeration to say that Athanasius's whole long career as bishop and theologian was occupied with the church's fourth-century struggle to identify who and what Jesus is. Born in the closing years of the third century, Athanasius was elected bishop of Alexandria in 328, three years after the presbyter Arius had been excommunicated by the Council of Nicaea, essentially for his insistence that the Son of God is himself the first and noblest of creatures. But the issues raised by Arius and his followers were not resolved by Nicaea's creed and canons; until his death in 373, Athanasius continued to fight for a strong conception of Jesus' identity as fully divine — from the early 340s, by an increasingly explicit emphasis on the importance of the Nicene Creed's formulation that the Son is "of the same substance as the Father."

Undoubtedly, both "Arian" and "Nicene" approaches to Jesus' identity were the agenda of theological families rather than organically developed theological systems; undoubtedly, too, the way Nicaea's "substance" language was accepted, understood, and eventually extended to include the Holy Spirit's relationship to the Father grew slowly throughout the fourth century and found different expressions among different authors.[5] Still, the thinking opposed by Athanasius throughout his career had a relatively consistent pattern: the well-established tradition of Platonic and earlier Christian thought that saw God's activity in the world as communicated in steps, and that conceived of the Son and the Holy Spirit, God's mediating agents in creation, as themselves produced, even "created" by a wholly transcendent Father, as God's first steps in self-communication. As such, Son and Spirit were understood to participate in the Father's being and operations to such a preeminent extent that they might legitimately be called "divine," even "like the Father in all things"; but they were seen as less than the Father in their being, simply because the Father alone is the primordial source of all that is.

Part of the Arian argument, it seems, came from scriptural references to the limitations of knowledge professed by Jesus, the Word made flesh, in passages such as Matthew 24:36, as well as from the New Testament witness

5. On the fourth-century controversies surrounding Arius and Nicaea, see, most recently, John Behr, *The Nicene Faith* (Crestwood, N.Y.: St. Vladimir's, 2004); Lewis Ayres, *Nicaea and Its Legacy* (Oxford: Oxford University Press, 2004).

to Jesus' ability to grow and change (e.g., Luke 2:52) — both seen as features not of divine substance but of the world of "becoming."[6] Similarly, the suffering of Christ was seen as a crucial part of the limitation and vulnerability that prove the creaturely status of the Son.

Against this "Arian" view, Athanasius argued with increasing energy throughout his life for a view of the Word — and in his later works, also of the Spirit — as fully equal with the Father in being and life, fully one reality with the Father, precisely because both Word and Spirit accomplish within creation what only God, and not a creature, can do. For Athanasius, the transcendent Logos, or active Reason, of God, eternally generated by the Father within the divine Mystery itself, is commissioned to be the Father's active and ordering presence in the world. God, as God, is totally "other" than creation; nothing that belongs to the created realm (which for Athanasius means brought into being from nothing) can be called "divine" in the strict sense. So God the Word and God the Spirit, whom baptismal faith instinctively recognizes as divine because they impart to creatures a share in divine life, must be seen as *other* than creation, but not *distant* from it: not part of creation, yet so actively involved in it, so present to it for its good, that they can direct, order, and heal it from within. This presence to creation of the Word who is not a creature is realized most fully, Athanasius argues, in his incarnation.[7]

In Athanasius's decades-long campaign to refute the Arian position in all its many shades and to promote a strong sense of the Son's full status as God, even after he has made a human form, or "body," his own, the scandal of Jesus' limitations and sufferings, as well as their crucial importance to his identity as Savior, play a critical, if complex, role. This is made clear in what may be his earliest works: the pair of apologetic treatises, written probably in the early 330s, known as *Against the Pagans (Contra gentes)* and *On the Incarnation (De incarnatione)*. These essays offer an elaborate argument for the plausibility of the Christian conception of an incarnate, saving, crucified Logos by telling the story of how humanity, originally created to participate in the ordered rationality of the divine Logos, and so to

6. The most penetrating analysis of Arius's theological position and its philosophical and cultural roots remains Rowan Williams, *Arius: Heresy and Tradition* (London: Darton, Longman & Todd, 1987; rev. ed., Grand Rapids: Eerdmans, 2002).

7. For helpful synthetic presentations of Athanasius's theology, see Alvyn Pettersen, *Athanasius* (London: Geoffrey Chapman, 1995); Khaled Anatolios, *Athanasius: The Coherence of His Thought* (London: Routledge, 1998).

share in the divine quality of incorruptibility by knowing God, lost that gift by fatal choices. Humanity therefore needed to be redeemed, reshaped in God's image, endowed again with unending life, by the Word's coming to share in our world, our wounded physicality, and even our death.

After poignantly describing the effects of human sin on the descendants of Adam and Eve in the early chapters of *On the Incarnation,* depicting sin as a growing epidemic that has robbed humanity of its rationality and vitality and reduced it to being dominated by greed and violence, Athanasius points out the only remedy left to the Logos, as just and compassionate Creator: to take on human corruptibility and mortality himself and to overcome death in his own person, through his identity as incarnate Word:

> To this end [the Word] took to himself a body capable of death, that it, by partaking of the Word who is above all, might be worthy to die in the place of all, and might, because of the Word which had come to dwell in it, remain incorruptible, and that from then on corruption might be kept from all by the grace of the resurrection.[8]

In this treatise, Athanasius identifies the saving effect of the Word's incarnation in two principal ways: as his restoration of vital energy within the vulnerable human community "in putting away death from us and renewing us again"; but equally as his revelation to fallen human minds of the Word's power and presence, restoring to them the similarity to himself that makes them rational and holy.[9] Like Irenaeus, Athanasius is convinced that the Word's self-revelation in human terms itself opens up the new possibility of human participation in God's immortality.[10] Even Jesus' death on the cross — for ancient minds, the principal obstacle to belief in his divine identity — Athanasius describes as a moment of revelation: only a real death, a death inflicted by the violence of others, a death in public view, could qualify as the prelude to definitive resurrection and victory:

> He accepted on the cross, and endured, a death inflicted by others, and above all by his enemies, which they thought dreadful and ignominious and not to be faced; so that when this also was destroyed, both he him-

8. Athanasius, *On the Incarnation* 9, trans. A. Robertson, *NPNF*² 4:40-41, alt.
9. *On the Incarnation* 16 (*NPNF*² 4:45).
10. See, e.g., *On the Incarnation* 54 (*NPNF*² 4:65).

> self might be believed to be the life, and the power of death might be brought utterly to nought.[11]

Jesus' passion reveals most forcefully, for Athanasius, the cost to God of his decision to restore humanity by taking our weakness to himself, but also its effect on faith.

Athanasius returns to the troubling issue of the weakness of the incarnate Word in his *Third Oration against the Arians,* written probably in Rome toward the end of his second exile, in 345-346. In this somewhat rambling treatise, he deals in detail with the scriptural arguments advanced by the opponents of Nicaea against the notion that the Word, generated by the Father and capable of incarnation, even of suffering, could be "of the same substance" as the Father. Athanasius's refutation of Arian exegesis follows a single form: the one Mystery proclaimed in the Gospels is that indeed "the Word has become flesh," the divine Son has taken on a body such as ours, to communicate through that human body a new revelation of God and new vitality; therefore, those passages in Scripture that ascribe to the Son vulnerability or ignorance, or even a creaturely dependence on God, are to be taken as referring to his acquired humanity, his "flesh," and not to his core identity as God the Word. The Gospel narrative presents us with a Jesus whose identity is complex, paradoxical; yet that identity is itself both the key to right interpretation of Scripture, for Athanasius, and its central message of salvation.

Athanasius goes on to apply this principle to Jesus' physical and mental suffering, in Gethsemane and on the cross:

> Wherefore of necessity when he was in a passible body, weeping and toiling, these things which are proper to the flesh are ascribed to him, together with the body. . . . And as to his saying, "If it be possible, let the cup pass" (Matt 26:39), observe how, though he thus spoke, he rebuked Peter, saying "You are not thinking the things that are of God, but those that are human" (Matt 16:23). For he willed what he deprecated — and that was why he had come; but *his* was the willing (for this was why he came!), but the terror belonged to the flesh. Therefore as a human being he utters this speech also; and yet again, both were said by the same one, to show that he was God, willing this himself, but that having become human, he had a flesh that was in terror. For the sake of this flesh he

11. *On the Incarnation* 24 (*NPNF*[2] 4:49, alt.).

> combined his own will with human weakness, that by destroying this he might, in turn, make humans undaunted in face of death.[12]

Athanasius is not yet ready — as Augustine and later Maximus the Confessor would be — to acknowledge explicitly in the incarnate Word two naturally distinct wills, two fully operative (if utterly incommensurate) levels of psychological and cognitive activity. For him, the decisive, conscious agent in the life and works of Christ, even in his moments of most abject suffering, is the Word who is divine. Fear, pain, ignorance, mortality are all proper to "flesh" — *our* flesh, humanity in its fallen state, deprived of the clarity of vision and incorruptibility of life that God intended for us when he originally shaped us in the image of the Son. Yet Athanasius argues repeatedly that the Word, by making these weaknesses of "the flesh" his own, has begun to transform and heal them. So he sees in Gethsemane and Calvary the testing place of the saving identity of Jesus: Jesus experiences there, as his own, a true human terror, a sense of abandonment in the face of death, yet remains willing to carry out the eternal plan of sacrificial love, which is both his own and his Father's.[13]

Cyril of Alexandria

Athanasius's learned and strong-minded successor in the first half of the fifth century, Cyril of Alexandria, exerted perhaps the most formative influence on what have become the classic Christian language rules for speaking of the complex identity of Jesus the Savior. Taking "body" and "flesh" in the fullest sense of their biblical usage, to signify not only biological materiality but mind, feelings, and will, Cyril speaks of the human Jesus not as an "assumed man," as some of his Antiochene contemporaries would do, but as "one Christ along with his flesh, the same at once God and a human being."[14] Cyril's emphasis on the radical unity of Christ as subject of all that is predicated of him, and on the divine Word as the basis and central focus of that unity, is rich with implications for his portrait of Jesus. In his celebrated *Third Letter to Nestorius* [of Constantinople], writ-

12. Athanasius, *Oration 3 against the Arians* 56-57 (*NPNF*[2] 4:424, alt.).

13. This is emphasized also throughout *On the Incarnation;* see especially 27-32, 46-55.

14. Cyril, *Third Letter to Nestorius* 12, anathema 2, trans. Lionel R. Wickham, *Select Letters* (Oxford: Clarendon, 1983), p. 29, alt.

ten in the autumn of 430 — a manifesto on the orthodox understanding of the Savior as the basis for continuing communion in faith and sacrament between the two prelates and their churches — Cyril insists that this sense of Jesus' unity as subject is the warrant for our worship of him, "without separating and parting the human and God as though they were mutually connected [only] by unity of rank and sovereignty. . . ."[15] An awareness of this unity enables the participant in a eucharistic liturgy to recognize in the sacramental gifts "not mere flesh (God forbid!) or the flesh of a man hallowed by connection with the Word . . . , but the truly life-giving flesh belonging properly to God the Word himself."[16] It presents Christ's priestly sacrifice on the cross, identified as such typologically in the letter to the Hebrews, as the Son's offering of his own body to the Father, "for us and not for himself."[17] And it provides the real justification for Cyril's insistence, throughout his quarrel with Nestorius, on the importance to orthodoxy of Mary's traditional title, "God-bearer" *(Theotokos),* since the church believes that the eternal Word of God "united what is human to himself in his own concrete individuality *(kath' hypostasin)* and underwent fleshly birth from her womb."[18]

The dispute between Cyril and the representatives of the Antiochene exegetical and theological tradition — Nestorius, Theodoret of Cyrus, and their teachers Diodore of Tarsus and Theodore of Mopsuestia — was not primarily a dispute about the fullness of Christ's humanity, as has sometimes been suggested, a dispute in which the Antiochenes were primarily concerned with emphasizing that humanity, while the Alexandrians offered it only lip service. Rather, the main differences seem to lie in different senses of the relevance of history and time to salvation, and of the ontological and existential boundaries between God and the world. For Antiochenes such as Theodore or Theodoret, the saving and transforming encounter of humanity with God, with all the freedom from corruptibility, passion, and sin that it promises, is a gift reserved in its fullness for the eschatological future, a new "state" *(katastasis)* that at present is realized only by the risen Christ, and pointed to by Scripture and the symbols of the church's worship. The world we presently live in is separated by an unbridgeable gulf from God

15. *Third Letter to Nestorius* 4 (Wickham, p. 19, alt.).
16. *Third Letter to Nestorius* 7 (Wickham, p. 23, alt.).
17. *Third Letter to Nestorius* 9 (Wickham, p. 25).
18. *Third Letter to Nestorius* 11 (Wickham, p. 29, alt.).

and his eternity, in the Antiochene view, and the main task of theology is to keep its language about God pure from anything that might confuse these realms, or imply some limitation or circumscription of God's being. For Cyril and his followers, by contrast, the news of the incarnation of the Word is precisely that the God who is ontologically "other" than creation has now become personally present within it, has made a human creature his own embodiment, united it to his own concrete existence, or *hypostasis,* identified himself with the full individual nature of a man, so that the creative and healing energies proper to God are now accessible in time, in the person of Christ and in the church that is his body. As a result, while Theodoret lays strong emphasis, in his polemical treatises against Cyril, on the importance of keeping the Word free from any suggestion of sharing in human suffering, Cyril insists with equal force that the Christian message of salvation rests on the paradoxical but literal ascription of human suffering — acquired through incarnation — to God the Word.

Cyril's reason for insisting on this living paradox of a divine Word who suffers, not as God, but still truly suffers in his own flesh,[19] is not simply to head off the Antiochene criticism that his portrait of Christ compromises the divine attribute of impassibility. Rather, it is central to his soteriology that the Word made flesh should indeed suffer what we humans suffer, but in a way free from the elements of compulsion, self-preoccupation, and fear that normally accompany our own suffering.[20] He is fully human, yet human in a freer, more virtuous way than we can be — in a way that offers us both a model and an unattainable norm — because he is himself God the Son. As Cyril remarks in his *Scholia on the Incarnation,* "He has reserved to his [human] nature that it should be superior to all."[21]

In an interesting fragment of book 7 of his *Commentary on John* (written before the controversy with Nestorius began), Cyril makes this same point with reference to human grief, with which Jesus is said to have struggled at the death of his friend Lazarus (John 11:33-34). The Fourth Gospel

19. See J. Warren Smith, "Suffering Impassibly: Christ's Passion in Cyril of Alexandria's Soteriology," *Pro Ecclesia* 11 (2002): 463-83.

20. See Cyril, *Second Oration to the Royal Ladies* (PG 76:1393B); cf. Smith, "Suffering Impassibly," pp. 463-64.

21. Cyril, *Scholia on the Incarnation of the Only-Begotten* 37, ed. Philip E. Pusey, *Cyrilli Archiepiscopi Alexandrini Opera* 6 (1875; reprint, Brussels: Culture et Civilisation, 1965), pp. 574-75; trans. Pusey, *St. Cyril, Archbishop of Alexandria, Five Tomes against Nestorius,* etc. (Oxford: J. Parker, 1881), pp. 232-33.

tells us that Jesus "was indignant and was troubled" as he stood before Lazarus's tomb. Cyril writes:

> Since Christ was not only God by nature, but also a human being, he suffers in a human way along with everyone else. But when grief begins to be stirred up in him, and the holy flesh is inclined to shed tears, he does not allow it to suffer this in an unrestrained way, as usually happens with us. "He was indignant[22] in the Spirit" (John 11:33): that is, in the power of the Holy Spirit he rebukes his own flesh, so to speak. . . . For this is the reason the Word of God, powerful in every way, came to be in flesh — or rather, came to *be* flesh: that by the activities of his own Spirit he might strengthen the weaknesses of the flesh, and set this nature free from an earth-bound way of thinking, and might re-shape it to be concerned only with what pleases God. For surely it is an illness of human nature to be tyrannized by grief; but this, too, has been abolished first in Christ, along with our other illnesses, that it might come over from him to us.[23]

In the complex subjective identity of the Word made flesh, the inner dialogue between these two complete and wholly different realms of being leads to a new subordination of what is human to God, and to new human freedom from the tyranny of our passions — a freedom now accessible to us all through Jesus' own person.

Maximus the Confessor

The immediate solution to the bitter fifth-century dispute between Cyril of Alexandria and the Antiochene theologians over how to conceive and

22. The Greek word in John 11:33, ἐμβριμᾶται *(embrimatai),* is usually translated as indicating deep emotion: "he was deeply moved" (RSV), "he was greatly disturbed" (NRSV), "[he was in] great distress" (JB). The original meaning of the verb is "to snort" and is used for horses, but in its (fairly infrequent) application to human beings it appears to mean "to express anger," "to rebuke indignantly" (cf. Dan 11:30 LXX; Matt 9:30; Mark 1:43). Cyril clearly understands the verb to mean that Jesus "rebuked" his own flesh, in the power of the Holy Spirit, for its tendency to be undone by grief. It is in response to this inner, divine rebuke that his human nature is then said to be visibly "troubled" but ultimately healed of this weakness.

23. Cyril, Fragment on John 11:33-34 (ed. Pusey, 4:279-80).

express the identity of Jesus — although by no means a final, comprehensive solution — was the formulation of Christian faith in his person hammered out by the Council of Chalcedon in 451 and appended to the normative creeds of Nicaea and Constantinople I as a kind of hermeneutical key. Rejecting any formulation that might suggest a permanent separation or an indiscriminate confusion of the human and the divine in Jesus, insisting on the full reality of both levels of his existence as a single person, the language agreed on at Chalcedon confesses him to be

> one and the same Son, our Lord Jesus Christ: the same one perfect in divinity and perfect in humanity, truly God and truly human . . . recognized in two natures without confusion, without change, without division, without separation, with the difference between the natures in no way removed through the union; rather, the distinctive property of both natures is preserved and comes together in a single *persona* and a single concrete individual *(hypostasis)*.[24]

The language of the Chalcedonian formula was carefully woven together from a variety of earlier conciliar and theological texts, representing both sides of the debate as well as earlier stages of agreement between them.[25] Yet the formula offered a divided Eastern Christendom little respite from the bitter disputes of the 430s and 440s. For theologians sympathetic to the Antiochene tradition, for ecclesiastical politicians looking for consensus, and for most Western theologians, it seemed a welcome and even-handed compromise; but for the great majority of monks, clergy, and faithful outside the main cities of the Eastern Empire, as well as for a number of Eastern Christian intellectuals of the late fifth century, it was an equivocation, a failure to acknowledge the centrally divine identity of the Savior as the core of even his human experiences and acts. For those who rejected the Chalcedonian formula, in the fifth century and afterward, only the terminology of Cyril's later letters, centered on the formula "one nature of the Word, made flesh," captured the vital, mutually expressive unity of the human and the divine elements that determined the identity of Jesus.

24. Text in Giuseppe Alberigo et al., ed. and trans. Norman P. Tanner, *Decrees of the Ecumenical Councils,* vol. 1 (London/Washington: Sheed & Ward/Georgetown, 1990), p. 86, alt.

25. For an analysis of the text, see Aloys Grillmeier, *Christ in Christian Tradition,* vol. 1, 2nd ed. (London: Mowbray, 1975), pp. 543-54, and the literature cited there.

In the second quarter of the seventh century, the Emperor Heraclius's efforts to reunify the Eastern Empire led to new efforts on the part of his court bishops to find a way of construing the official Chalcedonian Christology that might be acceptable to dissident Christians. Patriarch Sergius of Constantinople (in office 610-638), borrowing a phrase from Pseudo-Dionysius's *Letter 4*, cautiously advanced the theory that all the human activities of Christ, mental and bodily, were manifestations of "a single theandric operation" *(mia theandrikē energeia)*, flowing forth from God's power and using his human nature as a created instrument. Sergius seems quickly to have refined this position in a somewhat more psychological direction, arguing in letters from the late 620s onward that the human experiences and actions of Jesus all express the single *will* and operation of the second person of the Trinity, even though they do so through the instrumentality of the complete human nature that God the Son has made his own. It was in response to this attempt to reread Chalcedon yet again that Maximus the Confessor was to make his name, and bear final witness with his life.

A well-educated native of Constantinople, born about 580, who had spent some years as a bureaucrat at the imperial court, Maximus became a monk about 613 and eventually moved west with other Byzantines to escape the Persian invasion of western Asia Minor, settling around 628-629 in Carthage, where he kept up a lively theological correspondence throughout the Greek-speaking world. For Maximus, Sergius's new interpretation of the Chalcedonian formula amounted to a tacit denial of its central affirmation about the identity of Jesus: the completeness of his two utterly incommensurate, fully functioning realities — that of God and that of a human being — yoked together in the unique historical particularity of a single individual. Every nature, Maximus argued, to be completely itself, must be completely operational; a nature, after all, in classical Aristotelian terminology, is a substance (i.e., a definable kind of being, a "what") considered as a principle of operation. And since willing and desiring are integral to all intellectual natures, and form part of what we mean by consciousness, to deny that Jesus possesses a full human will *(thelēma physikon)*, which by natural impulse seeks its own human welfare, is to deny the fullness of his human nature, affirmed by the tradition of faith and canonized at Chalcedon.

For Maximus, as for Athanasius three centuries earlier, the test case of Jesus' identity in the Gospels, in terms of consciousness and will, is the scene of his agony in Gethsemane. But while Athanasius construed that story in terms of a tension between the Word and his "flesh," Maximus sees at play simply an instance of what is implied more broadly by the Christology of Chalcedon: Jesus' two natures, with all their faculties and operations, remain intact and distinct, but his single hypostasis — his unique individual *way (tropos)* of being God and being human — gives a different modality to both his eternal existence as Son of God and his historical existence as son of Mary. Jesus is, as Maximus remarks in several places, "divine in a human way and human in a divine way."[26] For the human will and the other human faculties of Jesus, this divine modality, communicated by the divine hypostasis whose nature it is, brings that human nature to its own creaturely perfection. So he writes of the Gethsemane scene, in *Opusculum 7*, that Jesus' prayer for deliverance was a clear expression of his humanity's natural dynamism toward self-preservation.

> On the other hand, that it [Jesus' human will] was completely deified and in agreement with the divine will, that it was always moved and formed by it and remained in accord with it, is clear from the fact that he always carried out perfectly the decision of his Father's will, and that alone. So, as a human being, he said, "Not my will, but your will be done" (Luke 22:42). In this he offered himself to us as a model and norm for putting away our own wills to fulfill God's will perfectly, even if we should see death threatening us as a result. . . . He had, then, a human will. . . . Constantly and completely divinized by its assent to, and its union with, the Father's will, it was, to put it precisely, divine by union, not divine by nature; so it truly became, and so it should be called. But it never departed from its natural constitution by being divinized.[27]

In a number of his writings, Maximus stresses that it is precisely the unique structure of Jesus' person that contains and reveals the promised eschatological structure of human salvation.[28] In the identity of Jesus, Maximus discovers the full reality of grace, laid open to us in the divine modality of Jesus' humanity, and sees there at the same time the full realization of human nature as it was created to be. "Divinization," a hallowed term in

26. See, e.g., Maximus, *Letter 15* (PG 91:573B); *Letter 19* (PG 91:593A2-B1); *Opusculum 4* (PG 91:61BC); *Opusculum 7* (PG 91:84B-D); *Disputation with Pyrrhus* (PG 91:297D-299A).

27. *Opusculum 7* (PG 91:80D, 81D).

28. See *To Thalassius,* question 60 (CCSG 22:73.10-19).

the Greek patristic tradition for the goal of God's gracious work in redeemed humanity, is thus for him both a gift beyond the resources of human nature and the full realization of what God intended that nature to become. It has first been achieved, Maximus argues, in the person of Christ.

Concluding Reflections

In the four Greek Fathers whose treatment of Christ we have briefly surveyed, it is his human weakness — the limitation of his energy, strength, and intellect, his ability to suffer and die — that both raises the greatest challenge to the church's proclamation of his lordship and stimulates the most profound theological reflection on what it might mean to say, with the centurion at Calvary, "This person truly was Son of God" (Mark 15:39). Irenaeus's opposition to Gnostic portraits of Christ clearly rests on an affirmation of the central importance of Jesus' innerworldly materiality — a realm that for Gnostic thought was irreducibly alien to God — for the full message of salvation. Athanasius, two centuries later, sees in the suffering of Jesus the full proof that God's Word has taken on the complex, damaged human reality Athanasius calls "flesh," and has begun to transform it by making it the vehicle of revelation and renewed life. Cyril of Alexandria, along with his fifth-century contemporaries, develops a more nuanced technical vocabulary for speaking of the identity of Jesus — of what is single and what is twofold in his identity, and how they are related — and argues that in the very act of making our human weakness his own, the Son of God has begun to transform us, to give us virtue and life in place of sin and death, simply by being both God and fully human at once. Maximus the Confessor, in the seventh century, continues to reflect on the structure of Christ's person, using the vocabulary of Cyril and the Council of Chalcedon; for Maximus, Christ's will is especially the place in which human freedom begins to share in the transcendent freedom of God, and to choose, by the grace Christ communicates, the destiny for which God created humanity in the beginning.

All of these portraits of the person of Christ are way stations in a continuing process of Christian reflection on who Jesus really is and what he means for us: reflection that is rooted in the narrative of the Gospels and the apostolic witness and returns constantly to the New Testament for judgment and verification. These patristic readings of the Gospels are framed, certainly, by particular New Testament affirmations about Jesus that set the hermeneutical conditions for reading the longer narratives of his life and work: by the schema in Philippians 2:5-11 of the self-emptying and glorification of one who in the beginning is "equal to God"; by the portrait in Hebrews 4:14–5:10 of Jesus, Son of God and high priest, who "learned obedience through what he suffered"; and above all, perhaps, by the affirmation in the opening verses of the Fourth Gospel that the Word "who was in the beginning with God . . . became flesh and dwelt among us" (John 1:2, 14). Yet patristic reflection on the person of Christ clearly expresses a tradition of faith and understanding that moves into realms of discourse and conceptuality the New Testament writers could never have imagined or understood, a tradition that continues to evolve wherever Christians receive and think about the gospel. As Athanasius argues in defense of the creedal language of Nicaea, the fact that both the supporters and the opponents of Arius could use similar scriptural texts and phrases to undergird their opposed positions made it necessary for the Council to employ "strange" terms — terms taken from philosophy and science rather than Scripture — as interpretative norms for ensuring that the Scriptures themselves would be understood in the way the Christian tradition had always taken them, and the New Testament's apostolic authors had intended them.[29]

If we are to make sense, ourselves, of the classical Christian understanding of Jesus' identity that emerges in these and other early Christian writers, we must keep several cautions in mind. The two distinct "substances" or "natures" early theology sees in the person of Christ are, of course, two wholly incommensurable realities — not two parallel species of being competing for center stage. The one does not rule the other out. And the one "person" the church recognizes as "owning" these two substances or natures is not classically understood in the way modern Westerners conceive of a person, defined by being a unique, self-contained pole of consciousness and free decisions, capable of forming relationships with other, equally distinct persons. In the classical understanding of both the triune God and Jesus Christ, "persons," or hypostases, are irreducible individual subjects of predication and attribution; yet the heart of both these Mysteries, for Christian faith, is that the three related "persons" in God

29. See Athanasius, *Defense of the Nicene Definition* 5.18-24, esp. 21; cf. Origen, *On First Principles* pref. 2.

share a single consciousness and will, a single substance, and that the one "person" of the incarnate Word possesses both an infinite divine mind and will and a complete human mind and will like our own. For the post-Chalcedonian understanding of the person of Christ, the Mystery of the gospel is that God the Son — "one of the Holy Trinity" — is "selved" in the full human knowledge and freedom of the son of Mary, and expresses in Jesus' human life and actions what it is to be Son of the Father and giver of the Spirit. The one who is "God from God, light from light," in Nicene language, has lived out in a human life, in a human body and mind, with all their inherent vulnerability and promise, what eternal Sonship means, so that we too who call Jesus "Lord" might also dare to call God "Father" and to live in his Spirit as God's sons and daughters.

In a famous passage in its Pastoral Constitution on the Church in the Modern World, *Gaudium et Spes,* the Second Vatican Council makes this same link between the identity of Jesus and the identity to which all of us are called, in grace:

> In reality it is only in the Mystery of the Word made flesh that the mystery of humanity truly becomes clear. For Adam, the first human being, was a type of him who was to come, Christ the Lord. Christ, the new Adam, in the very revelation of the Mystery of the Father and of his love, fully reveals humanity to itself, and brings to light its very high calling.[30]

In the Greek Fathers we have surveyed here, that same Christian intuition is expressed with increasing clarity and wonder. In the person of Jesus — a human being who, at the moment of his most abject human weakness, is recognized as "truly Son of God" — the ancient faith of Christians finds both the pledge of God's indomitable love and the form of our human vocation. The identity of Jesus, however we parse it, is meant to be the pattern and promise of our own.

30. *Gaudium et Spes,* §22, trans. Paul Lennon, in *Vatican Council II,* ed. Austin Flannery (Northport, N.Y.: Costello, 1996), p. 185.

The Eucharist and the Identity of Jesus in the Early Reformation

David C. Steinmetz

There was no quest for the historical Jesus in the sixteenth century, because the necessary preconditions for such a quest were lacking. For Luther and Calvin, to say nothing of their Catholic and Protestant contemporaries, the historical Jesus was precisely the Jesus who was portrayed in the Gospels. Sixteenth-century theologians saw no slippage between the biblical portrait of Jesus and the historical reality that lay behind it, even though they were well aware of some difficulties in the biblical text. In the end, they regarded such difficulties as theologically trivial and capable of satisfactory resolution through renewed study.

Debates over the identity of Jesus in the early Reformation were therefore not prompted by the kind of historical-critical questions that interest biblical scholars in the present. The issue for sixteenth-century theologians was the meaning of Jesus' teaching in the Gospels and not its historical reliability. Debates over the identity of Jesus in the Reformation were prompted by other considerations. They occurred primarily in the context of debates over the nature of the Eucharist. Critics of Catholic sacramental theology found they could not talk about the presence of Jesus Christ in the Eucharist without clarifying what they believed about his identity. Who was Jesus, after all, and what could he have meant to imply about himself when, as the Gospel of Matthew reports, he broke bread and told his disciples to "take, eat, this is my body" (26:26)?

Early Protestants were fairly certain they knew what Jesus did not mean. In their view, he did not mean to suggest that bread and wine had been miraculously transformed, or "transubstantiated," into his body and blood. The word "transubstantiation" describes the medieval Catholic theory of Christ's real presence. It rests on a distinction between the substance of a thing (what it really is) and its accidents (how it appears to observers). Ever since the Fourth Lateran Council in 1215, the Catholic Church had insisted that consecrated bread and wine were transformed by the power of God into the substance of Christ's body and blood without altering their accidental qualities. Observers could detect no change in the consecrated elements or distinguish them from unconsecrated by taste, appearance, weight, or smell.

Jesus Christ and the Eucharist in Zwingli's Theology

For Huldrych Zwingli, the principal Reformer of Zurich, the theory of transubstantiation seemed fatally flawed.[1] While Zwingli conceded that Christ was in some way present when the Eucharist was celebrated, he denied that Christ was present in the bread and wine. Zwingli's eucharistic theology was heavily influenced by his reading of four biblical texts: one from Paul (Rom 1:25), two from John (4:24; 6:63), and a final one from Matthew (26:26). Romans 1:25, which complains that the Gentiles "served and worshiped creatures rather than the Creator," was to Zwingli a warning that reverence for consecrated elements might prove to be an ascription to creatures (namely, bread and wine) of an honor that belongs only to the invisible and transcendent God. In his view, the common practice of honoring the Eucharist by reserving consecrated elements for adoration was an inexcusable lapse into the primal sin of idolatry.[2]

Zwingli's distrust of the material culture of late medieval religion was reinforced in his mind by John 4:24, a text that affirmed "God is a Spirit" and should therefore be worshiped "in spirit and in truth." Incense, images, candles, holy water, stained glass windows — even music — represented for Zwingli an externalization of worship that obscured the imma-

1. For an introduction to Zwingli's eucharistic views, see Jaques Courvoisier, *Zwingli: A Reformed Theologian* (Richmond: John Knox, 1963), pp. 67-78; Gottfried W. Locher, *Zwingli's Thought: New Perspectives* (Leiden: Brill, 1981), pp. 20-23, 220-28; "The Shape of Zwingli's Theology," *Pittsburgh Perspective* 8 (June 1967): 5-26.

2. For important texts from Zwingli in English translation, see "On the Lord's Supper," in *Zwingli and Bullinger*, ed. G. W. Bromiley (Philadelphia: Westminster, 1953); *Commentary on True and False Religion*, ed. Samuel M. Jackson and Clarence N. Heller (Durham, N.C.: Labyrinth, 1981).

terial character of God and the internal nature of Christian worship. God transcends material objectification, and spiritual worship requires a radical simplification of its external forms.

Zwingli's principal objection to material things as means of grace was encapsulated in his reading of John 6:63: "the flesh" (or, as Zwingli understood it, "the material world of which flesh is a useful symbol") "counts for nothing," since it is "the Spirit" who "gives life." The soul or inner person can be touched and moved only by the direct action of the Holy Spirit. External rites, including baptism and Eucharist, are incapable of conveying grace. They belong to the world of "flesh" and are therefore spiritually incompetent. Whatever grace is given when the Eucharist is celebrated must be given directly by the Holy Spirit to the souls of the faithful rather than channeled through bread and wine. Why this distrust of sacraments as means of grace was not extended to preaching — which is, after all, itself a material act — remains an unresolved question in Zwingli's theology. Perhaps the invisibility of speech separated it for Zwingli from the world of "flesh" to which the more obviously material sacraments belonged.

The problematic text for Zwingli was the so-called words of institution in Matthew 26:26: "Take, eat, this is my body." If the consecrated elements were creatures rather than the Creator, if God was to be worshiped without material objectification, and if bread and wine belonged to the spiritually impotent world of "flesh," then what could Jesus have possibly meant by calling the bread his body? Zwingli was not impressed by the argument of Andreas Bodenstein von Carlstadt that Jesus was simply pointing to his body when he uttered these words to his disciples.[3]

Zwingli found help in a letter from a Dutch jurist, Cornelius Hoen, who claimed to have been inspired by the theology of the fifteenth-century Dutch theologian Wessel Gansfort. Hoen suggested that the verb "is" in the phrase "this is my body" should be read as "signifies." There is certainly precedent in the "I am" sayings from the Gospel of John for reading the verb "to be" in a metaphorical sense. When Jesus called himself the good shepherd, the gate of the sheepfold, or the true vine, he was not speaking literally. The verb "to be" in these cases does not mean identity but a very

3. For a brief introduction to Carlstadt, see my *Reformers in the Wings*, 2nd ed. (New York: Oxford University Press, 2001), pp. 123-30; or E. Gordon Rupp, *Patterns of Reformation* (Philadelphia: Fortress, 1969). Ronald J. Sider offers a sympathetic interpretation in *Andreas Bodenstein von Karlstadt: The Development of His Thought, 1517-1525*, SMRT 11 (Leiden: Brill, 1974).

important similarity. So too, argued Hoen, when Jesus said, "this is my body," the statement should not be taken literally. Jesus meant only that the bread and wine signified his body, not that they were identical with it. Zwingli was persuaded by Hoen's reasoning and embraced his interpretation as his own.

With these four texts in mind, Zwingli constructed a complex doctrine of the Eucharist that had past, present, and future dimensions.[4] The past dimension of Zwingli's eucharistic theology is the aspect most frequently cited, though, unfortunately, not always correctly. Zwingli understood the celebration of the Lord's Supper as a "remembrance" of the life, death, and resurrection of Jesus Christ, though Zwingli's eucharistic liturgy was not a wistful recollection of things past and gone. Memory for Zwingli was a faculty that took a datum from the past and made it a living part of the present. It did so in order to enable a person or a group to function properly in the here and now.

Children provide a good example of what Zwingli had in mind. In Zwingli's world, children learned at an early age to manage a variety of common tasks: ride a horse, lace a shoe, even fix a broken shelf. When they were middle-aged, they used such lessons from their youthful past to ride their own horses, lace their own shoes, and fix their own broken shelves. Memory brings past lessons into the present to enable human beings to function. Otherwise — to quote a German proverb — Johann may never do as an adult what little Hans failed to learn as a child.

What is true of individuals is also true of groups. Groups need to remember why they were constituted in order to achieve their goals in the present. Nothing is more pathetic than a once-vigorous political party that has forgotten its first principles. Loss of memory is the first stage in the dissolution of a human personality or the decline of a particular social group.

The church that celebrates the Eucharist is not engaging in a nostalgic escape from the present to another place or time, where the problems of the

4. The Anabaptists were clearly indebted to Zwingli, rejecting with him a bodily presence of Christ in the Eucharist and stressing the presence of his glorified body at the right hand of the Father. Some Anabaptists allowed for a spiritual presence of Christ and emphasized solidarity with him in his suffering. Faith, memory, gratitude, and suffering were the words underlined by Anabaptists. See John D. Rempel, *The Lord's Supper in Anabaptism: A Study in the Christology of Balthasar Hubmaier, Pilgram Marpeck, and Dirk Philips* (Scottsdale, Pa.: Herald, 1993).

present do not matter. The primary movement of memory for Zwingli was not from present to past but from past to present. The Holy Spirit takes a crucial datum from the church's past (in this case, the death and resurrection of Jesus Christ) and makes it as real to believers in the present as the bread and wine they share. It does so in order to prevent the dissolution of the church's identity and so enable it to achieve in the space and time in which it lives the purposes for which it was established. The Eucharist is about memory because memory is essential to proper human functioning.[5]

But the Eucharist is also about hope. It is a simple meal eaten in anticipation of the lavish banquet to be shared in heaven at the end of time. Participation in the Eucharist is a public confession that God's kingdom will come and God's commandments will be done, all evidence to the contrary notwithstanding. For Zwingli, the Eucharist underscored the church's conviction that history is never out of control but always subject to God's providence. The future, like the past, belongs to a God whose purposes are benign and whose promises are reliable.

Zwingli reserved his most complicated argument for his discussion of the relation of the Eucharist to the present. That Christ is remembered and that the kingdom of God is anticipated are certainly important themes in any eucharistic theology. But the faithful gathered around the host — especially the newly hatched Protestant faithful who a few short months before had attended Catholic mass — expected Christ the Lord to appear at his own eucharistic celebration. Was that a hope Zwingli shared, or was the price of reform in Zurich the loss of Christ from the Eucharist? Was the Eucharist for Zwingli nothing more than an inner psychological event, a mnemonic device established to remind a church, always tempted to amnesia, of the central tenets of the gospel, lest it forget who and what it is? Was Zwingli nothing more than the prophet of an absent Christ? Zwingli certainly didn't think so.

However, in order to explain how Christ was and was not present, it was essential for Zwingli to insist on a sharp distinction between the two natures of Christ. His starting point was the orthodox Christology of the ancient creeds. With the early Fathers, he confessed that in the incarnation

5. Gottfried W. Locher stressed the importance of understanding how Augustinian Zwingli's view of memory was. For Augustine, memory is a faculty that deals with past, present, and future, though Zwingli was particularly interested in the connection of memory with the present. See Locher, "Shape," p. 23.

the divine Word, the second person of the Trinity, assumed human nature. The human nature of Christ was "anhypostatic," in the sense that it did not exist prior to, or apart from, its assumption by the divine Word, and "enhypostatic," in the sense that its continued existence depended on its continued union. Moreover, it was finite. Finitude marked Christ's humanity at every stage of his life: his incarnation, death, resurrection, and ascension. At no time, in Zwingli's view, was Christ's human nature divinized, except, of course, in the limited sense that the humanity of the risen Christ was no longer subject to death.

Confessing the finitude of Christ's human nature made what Zwingli regarded as an essential soteriological point. Christ assumed human nature, not angelic, and human nature is indisputably finite. Only if Christ bore the finite nature common to all men and women (sin only excepted) could he stand in the presence of God as their high priest and intercessor. He could not be the perpetual representative of a group of which he was not a member or to which he no longer belonged. When the creed proclaimed that the risen Christ is "seated at the right hand of God, the Father Almighty," Zwingli understood this affirmation quite literally. In his view, Christ's risen humanity could be in one place at a time and in one place only. *X* marked the spot. Any blurring of the line between the divine and human natures would threaten the integrity of the saving work of Christ.

Not that Zwingli knew exactly where "the right hand of God the Father" was. What was clear was that it was remote, transcendent, inaccessible — a distant place that could not be reached by human initiative. If Christ were to be present in the eucharistic service (leaving to one side the question of the locus of his presence), he could only be present in such a way as not to threaten the claim that his humanity remained "seated at the right hand of God."

Zwingli made three suggestions to address the problem this affirmation created. The first suggestion focused on the Eucharist as a sign of a present reality. The Eucharist is not merely a remembrance of Christ's past death and resurrection or a foretaste of his future coming in glory — though it is both of those things. It is also a sign that the redeeming work of Christ as mediator and intercessor continues unabated in the present. The risen Christ is never idle, and the "right hand of God" is a place of endless activity on behalf of the redeemed. The confession that Christ's finite humanity is "seated at the right hand of God" is therefore very good news for the church and ought to be celebrated.

The second suggestion rested on the doctrine of the Trinity. Zwingli thought the role of the Holy Spirit was crucial in any sound eucharistic theology. He believed the Spirit could make Christ so present to his followers that the seemingly unbridgeable gap between the finite human being "seated at the right hand of God the Father" and the congregation gathered around the eucharistic elements could in fact be bridged. Where the Spirit of the Lord was present in the church, there too Christ was present.

Zwingli turned to the doctrine of the two natures of Christ for his third suggestion. While the human nature of Jesus Christ remained finite, even after the resurrection, his divine nature continued to be infinite. That meant that Christ could be present to the church, not only by the action of the Holy Spirit, but also by the immediate presence of his divine nature itself. Of course, Christ's divine nature never appears in disembodied form. Because it is hypostatically united to Christ's human nature, the bond uniting them can never be severed. Wherever Christ is present, he is always present in both natures.

Zwingli centered the locus of Christ's presence in the worshiping community. Worshipers were the many grains formed by the action of God into one loaf. Zwingli scholars even suggest that what took place in the Eucharist for Zwingli was a kind of "transubstantiation" of the worshiping community into the body of Christ.[6] This action took place prior to (or, at the very least, apart from) eating and drinking the consecrated bread and wine — which, as Zwingli made painfully clear on more than one occasion, could never be for him a means of grace.

Zwingli saw the Eucharist as a "visible sign of an invisible grace." In his view, the "invisible grace" normally antedated the "visible sign." Worshipers did not eat the bread or drink the wine in order to receive grace but because they already had. At its core, the Eucharist was an act of "thanksgiving." Believers shared the elements to express gratitude for what they had received and to confess their faith publicly. The material objects used in Zwingli's Eucharist belonged, in other words, to the visible response of the church to the invisible action of God. At no time were they regarded by Zwingli as channels of the grace they celebrated.

6. Courvoisier suggests that the language of "transubstantiation" is particularly appropriate; see *Zwingli,* p. 76.

Jesus Christ and the Eucharist in Luther's Theology

Luther did not reject out of hand all of the propositions about the Eucharist Zwingli defended.[7] He agreed with Zwingli that transubstantiation was an unsatisfactory explanation of the mystery of Christ's real presence, though like his Catholic opponents he located Christ's presence in the elements of bread and wine. The problem with transubstantiation from Luther's point of view was that it required the faithful to believe two miracles: (1) that Christ was really present and (2) that his presence required the reduction of bread and wine to their accidents. For Luther, one miracle sufficed. Christ was substantially present in the Eucharist, but so too were the bread and wine.[8]

Luther also agreed with Zwingli that the Eucharist was not a sacrifice. It was not something the priest offered to God for the sins of his congregation, not even when understood as a re-presentation of the unique sacrifice of Christ in unbloody form. The Eucharist was a gift God gave to the church. That is why both Luther and Zwingli preferred to regard it as a "benefit" or "testament" rather than as a sacrifice.

"Testament" was a particularly important word for early Protestants. A testament is a one-sided contract that offers bequests to a beneficiary on the death of the testator. The contract is not made with a beneficiary but on his or her behalf. When Christ the testator died, he fulfilled the condition of his one-sided contract and offered to the church the benefits of his death and resurrection. The church did not in any sense merit such gifts but received them as the undeserved bequest of the testator. The Eucharist is therefore not for Luther and Zwingli a place where sacrifices are offered but where benefits are received.

Rejection of the doctrine of transubstantiation as well as the notion that the Eucharist was a sacrifice marked negative points of agreement between the two Reformers. Positively, they agreed to regard the Eucharist as a visible Word of God, that is, as a proclamation in visible rather than audible form of Christ's death and resurrection. The Eucharist therefore offers Christ, not to God the Father, but to the worshiping congregation. The

7. For a brief treatment of Luther's eucharistic theology, see Paul Althaus, *The Theology of Martin Luther* (Philadelphia: Fortress, 1966), pp. 375-403. See also chapter 7, "Scripture and the Lord's Supper in Luther's Theology," in my *Luther in Context*, 2nd ed. (Grand Rapids: Baker, 1995, 2002), pp. 72-84.

8. The most important of Luther's polemical works against Zwingli are found in *Luther's Works* 37 (Minneapolis: Fortress, 1962).

Word of God — that is, the lively and life-giving voice of the living God — is the instrument by which God created the world and through which he will renew it. It is the fundamental sacrament of which baptism and Eucharist are visible forms.

But there the agreements end and the disagreements begin to multiply. Luther dismissed Zwingli's reading of John 6:63: "the Spirit gives life" but "the flesh counts for nothing." The "flesh" that God condemned was not the material world but the self-centered self that stands in opposition to God. Flesh in this text has to do with alienation, not materiality, and idolatry is a sin that can be committed in the complete absence of material objects. Whenever fallen human beings — whom Luther characterized as hearts turned in on themselves — trust what is not God as God (even if it is something as good as human love or as enduring as human friendship), they commit the primal sin of idolatry. No one commits idolatry by trusting the material channels for grace God has established in baptism and the Eucharist. They are trustworthy because they rest on God's promise. Not to trust the promise is not to trust God.

Luther was also not impressed by Zwingli's understanding of the phrase in the creed "seated at the right hand of God the Father." The "right hand of God" is obviously metaphorical language. In biblical language, the "right hand" is the place of honor from which a ruler reigns. Since God reigns everywhere, "the right hand of God" is not so much a place as an assertion of God's universal sovereignty. Whereas Zwingli thought of the "right hand of God" as remote, transcendent, incredibly distant, Luther thought of it as immanent. That the risen Christ is at God's right hand is another way of asserting that Christ is everywhere present in his risen humanity.

Luther's view of the risen Christ rested on a Christology markedly different from Zwingli's. While Zwingli insisted on the finitude of Christ's risen humanity, Luther was willing to concede that something unprecedented had happened in the resurrection. Although Christ continued to bear a human body, it was a body no longer subject to limitations of space and time. Indeed, the body of the risen Christ could even walk through the door of a locked room to appear suddenly in the midst of his disciples. Luther thought what had occurred in the resurrection was a transfer of attributes *(communicatio idiomatum)* in which Christ's human nature took on some of the characteristics of his divine nature — including the trait of ubiquity.[9]

9. The radical Reformer Caspar Schwenckfeld argued against Luther that Christ

The chasm Zwingli posited between the congregation of believers on earth and the finite humanity of Christ in heaven dissolved for Luther. Luther saw no need to bring Christ down from heaven. Christ was already present on earth. He was present in the bread and wine, even before they were consecrated. Luther taunted Zwingli with the claim that the ubiquity of Christ's body meant it could be found everywhere, even in a peasant's bowl of pea soup (though — as Luther warned wryly — no one could locate Christ by stirring vigorously). If the risen Christ is where the Father reigns, he is never distant from the worshiping congregation. The ascension did not mean for Luther, as it did for Zwingli, that Christ had left the world's space and time but only that the mode of his continuing presence in the world had changed. The central problem for Luther's eucharistic theology was therefore not distance from the world but inaccessible immanence within it.

Luther drew a simple distinction in German between a thing being present *(da)* and being accessible *(dir da)*. The risen Christ is present *(da)* in ordinary bread and wine. But he is accessible to the church *(dir da)* only in the Eucharist. God has attached his promise to the Eucharist. It is there and not in ordinary bread and wine that Christ is savingly present in the full reality of both natures, truly human and truly divine. Luther affirmed the physical real presence of Christ and therefore insisted on a literal reading of the verb "is" in the words of institution. The Eucharist is not a mere sign pointing to a distant reality or even an icon through which the power of a distant divine reality is present. It is the thing itself. When Jesus said "this is my body," he meant what he said.

The question whether unbelievers receive the body and blood of Christ when they participate in the Eucharist was largely moot for Luther's opponent, Zwingli. After all, in his view Christ was not present in the bread and wine at all. Believers received grace directly from God and participated in the Eucharist as an expression of their gratitude for grace already received. Believers and unbelievers alike, when taking the elements, received only bread and wine.

But Luther answered the question whether unbelievers receive the

brought his own heavenly, or "uncreaturely," body with him in the incarnation and that it was possible to engage in an internal eating of Christ's body and blood that could precede, accompany, or follow any external eating. For a brief introduction and bibliography, see my *Reformers in the Wings*, pp. 131-37.

body and blood of Christ with a resounding yes. The presence of Christ was not dependent on the faith of the communicant or the piety of the celebrant but on the reliability of God's promise. Even if an irrational creature — say, a mouse — were to eat the consecrated host, it would eat the body and blood of Christ. Nevertheless, faith was essential in order to receive the saving benefits of Christ's presence. Unbelievers received the body and blood of Christ, but they ate and drank to their own damnation. Benefits, Luther warned, were restricted to believers.

Jesus Christ and the Eucharist in Calvin's Theology

Calvin was appalled by Luther's doctrine of the ubiquity of the body of Christ.[10] A ubiquitous body was in Calvin's view no human body at all but only a "monstrous body" that had lost its proper form. While Calvin was critical of Zwingli on many points, he agreed with him that Christ's humanity was finite or it was no longer human. Christ was, as Zwingli had correctly argued, "seated" in his finite humanity "at the right hand of God," a remote and distant place. The problem for Calvin, as for Zwingli, was how to bridge this chasm.[11]

Nevertheless, Calvin agreed with Luther that the material elements of bread and wine were in fact means of grace, a point Zwingli energetically denied. When the consecrated elements were offered to a worshiping congregation, Christ was offered, even if the congregation lacked faith. Indeed, Calvin wanted to argue for a real presence of Christ in the Eucharist, though his Christology forced him to argue for what he called a "spiritual real presence," an apparent oxymoron that bemused and annoyed his Lutheran critics.

10. The best general introduction to Calvin is still François Wendel, *Calvin: Origins and Development of His Religious Thought,* trans. Philip Mairet (Grand Rapids: Baker, 1950, 1963, 1997). Especially important on his eucharistic thought is Kilian McDonnell, *John Calvin, the Church, and the Eucharist* (Princeton: Princeton University Press, 1967). See also Brian A. Gerrish, *Grace and Gratitude: The Eucharistic Theology of John Calvin* (Minneapolis: Fortress, 1993); and my *Calvin in Context* (New York: Oxford University Press, 1995).

11. In addition to Calvin's *Institutes of the Christian Religion,* ed. John T. McNeill, LCC 20-21 (Philadelphia: Westminster, 1960), one should consult Calvin's treatises against Lutheran theologians Joachim Westphal and Tilemann Hesshusen in *Selected Works of John Calvin: Tracts and Letters,* ed. Jules Bonnet and H. Beveridge, vol. 3, reprint ed. (Grand Rapids: Baker, 1983).

Calvin offered four explanations to support his view that Christ was substantially present in the Eucharist. His first explanation rested on a redefinition of the word "substance." What, asked Calvin, was the substance of Christ's body? It was certainly not its bones, sinews, and tissue. The substance of Christ's body was its power and effect for human salvation. Wherever the power and effect of Christ's body was present, the substance of Christ's body was truly present.

Calvin's second explanation depended on a characterization of faith as an ecstatic act. When believers received the Eucharist, they were in Calvin's view elevated by faith to the "right hand of God," where they gazed on the risen Christ. In this account, the chasm between heaven and earth was bridged, not by the descent of Christ, but by the ascent of the church. Calvin obviously did not have in mind a literal ascent. However, to what extent this "ascent" was an inner psychological act of the human imagination and to what extent a gift of fresh insight by the Spirit was left unclear.

Calvin adopted his third and fourth explanations from Zwingli — though he revised them sharply on one crucial point. For Zwingli, the locus of Christ's presence was the church; for Calvin, it was the Eucharist itself. Nevertheless, both argued that Christ's presence depended on the action of the Holy Spirit (Calvin's third explanation) and the hypostatic union of Christ's divine and human natures (Calvin's fourth). Indeed, the whole Christ was present in the Eucharist, even if the finite human body remained at the right hand of God.

The Lutherans christened Calvin's fourth explanation the *extracalvinisticum*, because of a passage in the *Institutes* that suggested Christ's divine nature continued to perform after the incarnation all the functions the second person of the Trinity had performed prior to it. So even while Jesus was asleep in a boat on the Sea of Galilee, his divine nature continued to function as the ordering principle of the universe, regulating wind and wave and tide. The Latin phrase Calvin used to describe the undiminished divine activity of the God-man, Jesus of Nazareth, was *etiam extra carnem*, "also outside the flesh." *Extra carnem* was another way of saying the God-man never ceased to do what God the Son had always done.

For Calvin, the humiliation of the kenosis was that Christ hid his divine power, not that he surrendered it. Indeed, Calvin found it impossible to see how Christ's death could have been a totally free act of submission if he had relinquished his boundless power. Because he retained throughout his suffering and death the power to terminate it, his passion was an absolutely free choice. In this respect, the divine nature guaranteed the undiminished integrity of the human. Christ chose to be victim; he was not victimized.

This state of affairs did not change with the ascension. Christ's divine nature continued to operate "outside the flesh," even in the Eucharist. And if Christ was present in the Eucharist, he was present in both natures. How could he not be, given the hypostatic union? Calvin asked that theologians grant only (1) that Christ's human nature was finite and (2) that his infinite divine nature was hypostatically united to it, and they had conceded the possibility of a "spiritual real presence." In short, for Calvin the "whole Christ" was present in both natures, "but not wholly," so long as the finite humanity remained seated at the right hand of God. *Totus Christus sed non totum.*

Calvin's argument seemed like nonsense to Lutherans like Joachim Westphal and Tilemann Hesshusen, who suspected that Calvin was a "crafty sacramentarian" whose "spiritual real presence" was another form of "substantial real absence." At the very least, Calvin seemed to them to have taken away with one hand what he conceded with the other. Lutheran theologians insisted on a glorification of Christ's risen humanity that overcame the finite limitations so crucial to the arguments of Zwingli and Calvin. Calvin did not accommodate them.

Calvin did agree with Luther that Christ was truly offered to the worshiping congregation in the Eucharist, even if the members of the congregation lacked faith. What he did not accept was the notion that unbelievers could receive Christ's body and blood. To explain what he had in mind, he posited the doctrine of a "double mouth." In order to receive bread and wine, one needed only a physical mouth. In order to receive Christ's body and blood, one needed the additional mouth of faith.

Faith did not make Christ present. Calvin was adamant on that point. Christ was offered to the congregation, whether it received him or not. But there was an important difference for Calvin between offering and receiving. Unbelievers were offered Christ but received only bread and wine. Believers were offered Christ and received both Christ and the consecrated elements. In his rejection of the notion that unbelievers do in fact receive Christ, Calvin broke decisively with Luther.

Conclusion

If Zwingli, Luther, and Calvin were asked to identify Jesus, they would undoubtedly have pointed to what they regarded as the historically reliable narrative of his life, death, and resurrection in the four Gospels, a narrative anticipated in the Old Testament and further explicated in the New. As they saw it, Christians were called to obey this Jesus and no other.

At the same time, explaining Jesus as he was offered to them by the Gospels was no simple task. It compelled them to use the complex language of the ancient creeds. In their view, the Bible taught — in substance if not in words — that the second person of the Trinity assumed humanity, though not a human being, in Jesus of Nazareth. This incarnate Lord bore two natures, fully human and fully divine, hypostatically united in one person. When Luther indicated at the beginning of the Smalcald Articles that he had no quarrel with the Catholic Church over the doctrine of the Trinity or the two natures of Christ, he could have been speaking for Zwingli and Calvin as well.

Their differences emerged in the context of their discussions of the Eucharist. Zwingli and Calvin argued it was essential for Christ's humanity to remain finite, even after the resurrection and ascension. Christ could not be our high priest if he no longer bore our humanity. However, they rejected as faulty reasoning the claim that the presence of Christ's finite humanity in heaven precluded its presence on earth. In the end, both defended a kind of "spiritual real presence," though Zwingli located it in the church and Calvin in the bread and wine.

Luther thought there was ample evidence in the New Testament that the risen Christ had undergone a transformation. His body was no longer subject to temporal and spatial limitations. Therefore, it could be physically present whenever the Eucharist was celebrated. The good news for Luther was that Christ was not only present but accessible. As Luther saw matters, the problem for eucharistic theology had never been a chasm between heaven and earth but the existence on earth of a presence that eluded human grasp.

The disagreements among the Protestant Reformers richly illustrate the point that debates about the nature of the Eucharist are so intertwined with debates about the identity of Jesus that it is impossible to separate them for very long. The line from the hymn, "O young and fearless Prophet of ancient Galilee, thy life is still a summons to serve humanity," evokes one kind of eucharistic theology.[12] The line from the Christmas carol, "Veiled in flesh the Godhead see, hail the incarnate Deity," evokes quite another.[13] While it is not clear that the eucharistic encounter with Jesus depends on having the theory exactly right, it is clear that ideas do matter. Martin Kähler may have been right when, faced with the limitations of human reasoning about God, he suggested that the intellectual as well as the moral life of Christians needs to be justified by faith. But his suggestion does not change the fact that eucharistic theologies have no obvious way to transcend the theories about Jesus on which they rest. Theories about Jesus inspire exactly the eucharistic theologies they deserve. It could hardly be otherwise.

12. "O Young and Fearless Prophet," words by S. Ralph Harlow, 1931. *United Methodist Hymnal* (1989), #444.

13. "Hark! the Herald Angels Sing," words by Charles Wesley, 1739; alt. George Whitefield, 1753, et al. *United Methodist Hymnal* (1989), #240.

The Identity of Jesus Christ in the Liturgy

Katherine Sonderegger

Though fully (yet not exhaustively) an earthly, historical human being, Jesus Christ is unique among his fellows for being known principally through worship.[1] This fact is often recognized implicitly — people consider the Bible a religious or churchly book — yet its radical scope and depth are rarely sounded. One theologian who did so squarely, though by no means solely, was John Calvin. In the *Institutes of the Christian Religion,* Calvin expressed the point with characteristic economy: "This, then, is the true knowledge of Christ, if we receive him as he is offered by the Father: namely, clothed with his gospel."[2]

This is a strange claim to make in the contemporary world. We are accustomed in our age to assuming that a personal life is more properly and deeply known through discovery than through manifestation. The true self lies hidden, we are inclined to say, and it is only with distance — perhaps of time, perhaps of affection — and unrestrained investigation that the true inwardness of a life is uncovered. This is so natural to us that examples seem clichéd. The biography of a former U.S. president discloses aspects of the self — secret characteristics, hidden flaws — that can be known and revealed only now. Old diaries, brought to light after a person's

1. I should say at the outset that this essay has a rather narrow scope. I have aimed to be ecumenical as far as possible in my presentation of Christ's identity in liturgy, but it is not possible to include everything relevant to the topic. Certainly, much more could be said about the complex and demanding field of liturgical theology; the private life of prayer; the perspectives of Pentecostal, low-church, and nonliturgical traditions; and the transforming force of Christian *practice!*

2. John Calvin, *Institutes of the Christian Religion* 3.2.6, trans. F. L. Battles, LCC 20:548.

death, disclose a deep passion or fear or ambition that would never have been recognized during the person's life. Or, more rarely, the emerging evidence of a person's private acts points to hidden strengths and quiet heroism that give us a deeper appreciation for the life lived than anything known in that person's public face. Underneath all that, we often say, what is she really like? Who is he, really? This pattern of seeking deeper, revolutionary truths has been applied in our modern age to Jesus of Nazareth, and we should not be surprised. In this, as in all other aspects of his earthly journey, Jesus is the Representative, the Everyman. In an age of exposure, his is the greatest secret, his life the deepest unveiling. The hunger to strip away the public face and to enter into the deeper truth of *this* life is nearly insatiable — in America, at least. And we would very much mistake this hunger did we not see in it the piety of our present age: we seek to know Jesus more truly, more fully, more properly than he can be known in the church's vestments.

Now it is just this division of the seamless life of Christ that cannot be true of him, Calvin tells us, especially of him: "For just as he has been appointed as the goal of our faith, so we cannot take the right road to him unless the gospel goes before us. And there, surely, the treasures of grace are opened to us; for if they had been closed, Christ would have benefited us little."[3] The firm, assertive tone of this passage disguises from us its setting in Reformation controversy: in this chapter Calvin aims his considerable rhetorical skill against the medieval teachings of "implicit" and "unformed" faith. These allow, Calvin charges, a Christian knowledge of Jesus that rests principally, in the former, upon the authority of the church and, in the latter, upon the bare, factual knowledge of Christ "outside us." But we need not adopt Calvin's larger, polemical purposes to accept his starting point, namely, Christ clothed in his gospel.

Here Calvin makes use of a distinction that is prescient of our situation. Christ is not directly identical with his gospel, yet he does not appear without it. As with us, the older theologians knew that Jesus of Nazareth could be described apart from personal confession of faith in him. They recognized that a third-person characterization could be drawn up of this life: he was born during the reign of Caesar Augustus; he knew the Judean prophet John the baptizer; he taught in the northern region of ancient Israel, the Galilee, at times drawing great crowds, at times, controversy; he

3. Calvin, *Institutes* 3.2.6 (LCC 20:548).

spent his last days in Jerusalem during the Passover festival; he was condemned by the high priest and Pilate and executed by common hanging on a crossbar; his women disciples kept watch at the cross; and his male disciples survived him, perhaps because they posed no threat, perhaps because, in fear and discouragement, they fled.

Such a summary of Jesus' earthly life fits what philosophers inspired by Bertrand Russell call "knowledge by description": Jesus is simply the one who fits these descriptions, the one these statements are about. They answer the question, Who is Jesus? by giving a string of third-person descriptions beginning, He is the one who. . . . For Russell, this is just what a name is: it stands surety for a long list of descriptions and allows us quickly to pick out and know the one named in this way. Readers familiar with the complex school of narrative theology will recognize the force of this definition of names. For some narrative theologians, Jesus just is this one, depicted in unforgettable and unique ways in the Gospels, who fits the descriptions unfolded there. In Hans Frei's memorable phrase, his "unsubstitutable identity" is the "mysterious coincidence of his intentional action with circumstances" depicted in this unfolding of events and human aims.[4]

Now, it would not be entirely fair to Frei, I hasten to add, to leave him associated altogether with such "knowledge by description." Indeed, the very premise of Frei's short work *The Identity of Jesus Christ* is that Jesus is the One who is "present" — manifested and available and forceful — to us who know him. Jesus is the union of identity and presence in such a way that to know who he is is to know that he lives. So strong is this joining of "about-ness" and "immediacy" that Frei can compare our knowledge of Christ to Anselm's proof for the existence of God in the *Proslogion.* Just as we might paraphrase Anselm's argument as the premise that to know the word "God" is to know that God exists — an "analytic proposition" in Kant's terms — so Frei's premise is that to know the name "Jesus" is to know that Jesus lives. His identity is as the Present One. In all of this, Frei's study of Calvin was not in vain! For such epistemological distinctions as Russell's or Frei's were unknown in the sixteenth century, but the concepts were not.

4. Hans W. Frei, *The Identity of Jesus Christ: The Hermeneutical Bases of Dogmatic Theology* (Philadelphia: Fortress, 1975), pp. 82, 94.

The Identity of Jesus as Redeemer

For Calvin, knowledge of Jesus Christ that was merely "about him" — knowledge made up of third-person descriptions — was "bare" or "cold" knowledge of a "Christ who is external to us." Not so do we know Christ truly. Calvin can speak in rather astonishing terms about the self-presence or immediacy of Christ to the believer: "Christ is not outside us but dwells within us. Not only does he cleave to us by an indivisible bond of fellowship, but with a wonderful communion, day by day, he grows more and more into one body with us, until he becomes completely one with us."[5] Here Calvin powerfully sets forth Jesus Christ's uniqueness. Drawing on Romans 8, Calvin sees the work of the Holy Spirit to be the direct engrafting of Christ into the believer such that to know him truly and fully is to know him as given to us. In the language of the *Book of Common Prayer* — and the Gospel of John — we pray that "he may dwell in us, and we in him." This is to know Christ, clothed in his gospel.

Now, there are two aspects of this proper knowledge of Christ, joined together: that Jesus is more deeply known in his image as Redeemer, and that "Redeemer" is essential to the incarnate Word, revealed in Scripture. Jesus Christ is most truly, fully, and properly the Redeemer; that is what it means to address him as Christ, the Messiah, or King, of Israel. He is anointed at his birth and at his baptism and in his ministry and at his death as the Ruler of his people, the One who is to redeem, deliver, and save the covenant house of Israel. "Everyone is searching for you," the disciples tell Jesus, and he answers, "Let us go on to the neighboring towns, so that I may proclaim the message there also; for that is what I came out to do" (Mark 1:37-38 NRSV). Again, it is tempting to see such confessions in the Gospels — "my food is to do the will of him who sent me" (John 4:34) — as the unfurling of an office or vocation that a particular life assumes. As with the whole Latin tradition, Calvin knows the language of Christ's "offices": Jesus can be seen as the perfecter and exemplar of the anointed Prophet, Priest, and King. But we misunderstand this category of "office" should we think of a self lying behind — or more, disguised or disfigured by — the public work that is given for him to do. The relation between person and work in Jesus Christ is not one of public, available, and distorting role versus hidden, deeper, and truer inner self. Rather, Jesus is the One

5. Calvin, *Institutes* 3.2.24 (LCC 20:570-71).

who is "about his Father's business." His person is realized, known, and manifested in his work: just that is what it means to be a redeemer, the Redeemer. This joining and enfolding of self and office is expressed with luminous precision in the Johannine proclamation: I am the Way, the Truth and the Life (John 14:6). The "Way" of Jesus' life, his public works of teaching, healing, exorcism, and debate; his prophetic acts; his calling and confirming of disciples; his unsparing onrush toward Jerusalem; the torture and cross and grave; the manifestation of his glory and homeland: all of these just are his Truth and Life. There is no better, deeper, or truer knowledge of Jesus than this. To know him properly is to know his proclamation, his Way of redeeming love.

It may seem, then, that the epistemic way to Jesus of Nazareth is a narrow road indeed. Is there no historical or anthropological knowledge of him apart from this "high christological" doctrine of him as Redeemer and King? Calvin's teaching of a Christ clothed in his gospel appears to *entail* that a comparison of Jesus to other "redeemer figures" is an empty task — and this, despite the fruit many glean from such work. This teaching appears to entail that investigations into first-century peasant life or Second Temple Judaism or literary and imaginative reworkings of New Testament material are all futile — despite their attractiveness and the instruction many receive from them. In short, this emphasis upon Christ as anointed Ruler of Israel threatens to make real knowledge of Jesus impossible in the absence of confession of him as the church's Lord and Savior. What the church teaches, we know and pray and confess; and the learning stops there. But how can this be? Is not any fully human life — even a life we may confess as also divine — intelligible in more than one way, especially in more than a codified, institutional, and creedal way? Can church doctrine be exhaustively and exclusively correct in just this way? On what grounds, after all, can we say that Jesus is known properly in his gospel, in his life within us as Redeemer; or only pallidly or not at all? Is this not what the medieval logicians called a perfect *petitio principii:* assuming as true what one sets out to prove?

Here I think we may find more room, more flexibility and grace, in the concept of Redeemer, the Savior of Israel, than we have feared. It *does* set its own stern demands. This Stone that is set for the falling and rising of many is just the hard contour of the very notion of Redeemer. Like the notion of Savior, or the secularized notion of beloved, Redeemer implies *relation,* a tie to others who are redeemed, saved, or loved. Moreover, redemption, like salvation or love, is parallel to (not identical with) what J. L. Austin termed a "performative utterance": the word itself brings about a state to the speaker or the listener.[6] Consider Austin's celebrated example of a promise. The very notion of a promise or vow is one that implies an act or state that involves the speaker, simply by uttering the vow. Now, to be sure, the promiser may not intend to carry out the vow — though this does not make her less of a promiser! — and a well-intentioned promiser may never make good on the vow, however honest the intent. And we can certainly call to mind many great works of literature in which love declared is ridiculed or spurned or answered too late: the speech-act of love is often refused; indeed, just this is the story of the gospel. But nothing about the notion of promise or love or redemption need involve us in this tangle of subjectivity, a very dense tangle all its own. What Austin's concept illustrates imperfectly is the odd notion of a redeemer: to be one, to be the perfect One, is to act for others, for them and for their sake, so that who this One is is what this One does, and does for us. If Jesus is in fact the anointed Messiah and King, the Redeemer of the world, he must be known as such if we are to know him as he is. And just this is confession, praise, and prayer to and in him.

Notice that such knowledge is oddly and "improperly" consistent with refusing the offer of his acting for us and for our sake. And here the roominess and grace of this name, Redeemer, emerge. I may acknowledge that Jesus is Redeemer in a third-person way: *Christians* claim that Jesus is the anointed King and Judge (but *I* reserve judgment). I may "mention" this identity but not "use" it (to borrow another philosophical distinction), so that I might say, Jesus is given the title Redeemer (but *I* do not confess or apply or use that title). And I may disbelieve the notion, or even that such a notion is appropriate for me: Jesus did not (in fact) redeem the world or did not (could not) redeem me. But oddly, wonderfully, this is just what "Redeemer" implies. The disbelief, the refusal, the distancing and alienation are the very states a redeemer meets with victorious love and self-giving. Not the healthy but the sick require a physician. Properly, a redeemer is confessed and known as such; improperly, a redeemer is indicated by repudiation and indifference toward him.

Now, such an identity — Jesus Christ is Lord and Savior — does not

6. J. L. Austin, *How to Do Things with Words*, 2nd ed. (Cambridge, Mass.: Harvard University Press, 1962, 1975), p. 6; on the notion of promising, 1-11.

entail belief in and confession of all church doctrine and all scriptural events, teachings, and depictions. That would be a confession that the church or the Bible is as such the Redeemer, known properly only in this way. Scripture and church teaching *testify* to Jesus Christ as Redeemer, and the world has heard this name through these testimonies. But Jesus himself is Redeemer; it is he who is to dwell within us with saving power. The exegetical, historical, literary, and anthropological study of these testimonies will continue, and some studies will lead some readers to doubt the accuracy or sequence or setting of the biblical accounts. It is a separate task, a pressing and complex one, to sort out the historical weight and reliability of the Gospel stories about Jesus and his circle. But whatever historical judgment we in the end may make about particulars in the New Testament, what we must say here is that the identity of Jesus as Redeemer, King, and Savior demands of us another judgment: will we know him properly as he is, clothed in his gospel? Will we confess him as he presents himself, as Redeemer? This decision, the act of faith, is not an act *opposed* to knowledge, a desperate hurtling over the skepticism, doubt, and reserve of our age, but rather a proper, deep, and true knowledge, the meeting of the Redeemer as he is by the very ones in need of this personal saving work. This meeting is what we properly call worship: the liturgy, or work of the people.

The Redeemer Known in Liturgy

From earliest times, the liturgy of the community has fallen into two halves, the service of the Word and the service of the Table (the Lord's Supper, or Holy Communion). There are variants, of course, and the wide divergence of practice expected of a broad and long-standing tradition. Indeed, whole continents have been shaken by the conflicts among Christians in the proper celebration of the Supper and the right use of Scripture in teaching, doctrine, and morals. Yet we need not have uniformity in liturgical practice or history of worship to recognize that Christians have by and large acknowledged their Redeemer through reading of Scripture, both Old Testament and New, prayers, hymns, and preaching; and remembering the Redeemer's passion, resurrection, and return in the Supper he gave to his disciples. In the service of the Word, Christians recall and honor the church's ancient testimonies to Christ's redeeming work, and they listen to these words in order to hear afresh a Word spoken to them from the living Lord. This memorial action is central, certainly, to the Holy Communion as well. The words used in the great majority of consecrating prayers to authorize this act of worship are "Do this in memory of me." Little wonder that the architect of Christianity in the West, St. Augustine, considered memory one of the central mysteries of the human intellect and a gracious trace of the triune God in whose image rational creatures were made. For our aims, however, the memorial act of worship is assumed into and serves a higher one: the knowledge and confession of the living Redeemer, the One present to his congregation. It is just this knowledge, after all, that marks out the proper acknowledgment of the Redeemer — knowing the One who has met the lost, met me, with victory, so that he is within me and within his community as the Good News of deliverance. Just how is Christ present, then, in these services as living Lord, the near Redeemer?

Service of the Word

We may begin where most Christian services do, with the service of the Word. For many Protestants, until the widespread influence of liturgical renewal, the service of the Word simply was Christian worship. It remains so for most Independent and Reformed Church worship. Here we have a structure that most resembles a monastic office or the Morning and Evening Prayer offices of the English Reformation: congregational recitation of psalms, lections from the Old and New Testaments, prayers of confession and intercession, congregational and choir music, and sermon. In each and in the whole, Christ is known and present as he is, the living Redeemer. Such presence has been thoroughly examined in the Supper, somewhat less in the sermon, and even less in the entire shape of the service of the Word; yet Christ in fact makes himself known as he is throughout all the acts of worship. Calvin gives us a slight indication of this path when he reminds us that "we cannot take the right road to him unless the gospel goes before us." More directly, we may follow the lead here of the pioneers of Vatican II liturgical theology — Edward Schillebeeckx, Henri de Lubac, Karl Rahner — who described Christ himself as the "Primal Sacrament" of the church, a Foundation that gives new significance ("trans-signification") to every act of symbol, sign, and praise. Jesus Christ is the origin and ground of all worship of him; such worship manifests him and teaches him — not simply *about* him — through his own gracious presence.

Consider the service of the Word as a whole. The shape of this service makes out of a crowd a congregation, out of the lost sheep disciples. These distinctions are central to the shape of the Gospels. Early in Jesus' ministry, he encounters the crowds, the *ochloi* in Greek. They press into doorways; they mass around a house such that a paralytic in search of healing must be lowered through the roof; they follow him in such great numbers that he must climb into a fishing skiff and put out into the lake to teach them. These crowds are the "lost sheep of the house of Israel," the "least" and "little ones," the hungry, desperate, and possessed. They are drawn to Jesus by his reputation as a healer and by his "teaching with authority," so that his fame spreads throughout the region. Now, such crowds are hardly reliable allies of Jesus! They seek signs and seek them again; they hear and hear but do not understand; they proclaim him "blessed" and curse him before Pilate. They strike the shepherd and are scattered. Such are the people and leaders who press into the doorway of the church.

The entrance rite, much abbreviated in a service of the Word, marks out all the same the movement Christians make, in season and out, to conform themselves to the crowds, to press into the doorway to see him and hear him gladly, to remember that they are the lost and hungry and that they reject the very One they seek. Thomas Cranmer's sixteenth-century prayer of general confession — a public rite of repentance for the English Church that has since spread to all churches — conforms the penitent to this crowd-like shape. The phrases, redolent of Old and New Testaments, have shaped generations of worshipers across the denominations: "we have erred and strayed from thy ways like lost sheep, we have followed too much the devices and desires of our own hearts, we have offended against thy holy laws, we have left undone those things which we ought to have done, and we have done those things which we ought not to have done." Indeed, in the entrance rite to Cranmer's eucharistic rite, the priest reads "comfortable words" — the verses of Scripture read out over the penitents — drawn from Matthew's depiction of Jesus as wise Teacher and comforter of "the babes": Come unto me all ye that labor and are heavy laden and I will refresh you (Matt 11:28). Even in the movement of the faithful to the Communion table, then, the echo of this broad shaping can be heard: the crowd is called into the Redeemer's presence.

Now, in this initial shaping during the service of the Word we may be tempted to overlook the true subject of the conformation, Jesus the Redeemer. Just as we cannot know Jesus properly and fully apart from his gospel of grace, so we cannot be gathered as the lost and rebellious without his presence as Redeemer, stepping out ahead of us, drawing us to him. To phrase this epistemically, we do not know Christ as Redeemer because we examine our own lost state or inner disposition of pride or indifference; rather, we know our state and need because we have known the Redeemer. Theologically, this is expressed in the doctrine of prevenient grace: God's act of gracious pardon and drawing near always precedes and gives rise to our seeking him. Scripturally, we might say that the crowds drew together — were formed as such — because the Good Shepherd came and gathered to him the sheep (John 6:44; 12:32). Liturgically, we may say that people are drawn from the highways and byways to come into the great banquet hall: we are the crowd that masses around the church doors to see what and who is within.

This moment of motley assembly, where we see ourselves as Christ has found us and looked upon us, passes into the deeper knowledge of the Redeemer, present to his congregation and people. Here the conforming work of Christ in his Spirit is most closely allied to his identity as King of Israel: his own are shaped into a congregation that enters the Lord's gates with praise. Christians become a "people," the *laos* in Greek, a laity conformed to the people and house of Israel. In most services of the Word, especially in the Protestant form that stands independent of the celebration of the Holy Communion, the opening verses from Scripture are typically drawn out of the Psalms. An invitatory psalm marks the entrance into congregational recitation of the Psalms in Morning and Evening Prayer; in turn, these underscore the shaping of the crowd into the congregation that goes its way "into his gates with thanksgiving, and into his courts with praise" (Ps 100:4). The reading of Scripture, from Old and New Testaments, the offering up of prayers "on behalf of ourselves and others," the lifting up of voices in congregational hymns, and the bringing in procession the oblations and alms to set before the Lord — all of these are inherited from the liturgical shaping of the house of Israel in temple and synagogue. The sermon, a setting out of the "true and lively word" received in a fresh listening to Scripture, again reaches back at least to synagogue practice and seems to stand behind Jesus' proclamation of the Jubilee in Luke 4. Conformed by Christ's own presence and name as Messiah to the congregation and household of Israel, Christians in the service of the Word know more deeply and fully the

Christ of the gospel as they recognize themselves as graciously engrafted into the worship of the Lord God of covenant Israel.

Nor is this all. The deeper and fuller knowledge of Christ, the Redeemer, is patterned into the worshiper by the final conformation of the crowd into the Messiah's own flock, shaped by his gracious presence into disciples. The relation of disciple to Master and Redeemer is, to be sure, enacted throughout the service: these positions of crowd, congregation/people, and disciples are not so much serial as they are coincident. Christians know Christ as the One who came to the lost, the covenanted, and the called, not one after the other, but rather all at once, even as in the Supper worshipers know Christ as the One welcomed, followed, and rejected, all in one meal and communion. This coincidence, however, is not directionless or without a pattern. Rather, the service of the Word progresses from crowd to disciple, or perhaps better, from outer communion to innermost, the disciples who are called friends. All elements remain within the service as a whole — the prayer of confession, for example, can be moved from the opening rite to its heart, near the pastoral prayer — yet the weight of each alters as the service moves to its end.

To be a disciple is to find oneself conformed to Jesus as the "Man of Prayer," to learn from the Teacher how to pray. Across the churches, the liturgies of Word and Table include the prayer Jesus taught his disciples, the Lord's Prayer. We are invited to join with disciples in ancient Galilee, in the church of all ages, in the worldwide communion of the church that now circles the globe, in the patterning of ourselves as the Lord's disciples, the ones who are "bold" to call God, "Our Father." There is little in liturgy that more closely enacts Calvin's maxim that Christ must indwell us and grow into us ever more deeply than the universal use of the Lord's Prayer. Here, Christians pray not to Jesus but to Jesus' Father, and just this is our deeper knowledge of and communion with Christ.

Note that we stand here before the innermost mystery of Christ's life lived for us and for our sake. There is a third-person aspect to our knowledge of Jesus within the service of the Word. Our prayers and praise do not take the form of direct address to Jesus, with rare exceptions. Our Scripture readings from the New Testament and, typologically, from the Old, offer a third-person, descriptive account of Jesus. We learn about him there. But the Scriptures are placed always within this deeper community of prayer and discipleship. They are taken up within the prayer directed to the "God and Father of our Lord Jesus Christ." This practice can give students of the service of the Word the impression that the liturgy is more "theological" than "christological," more patterned, that is, on the praise of the One God of Israel than on the Son, the Redeemer. The Supper, it appears, is designed to right that imbalance and, in just that way, to complete the liturgical action of the people of God. But the knowledge of and communion with Christ within the service of the Word are far richer than this analysis suggests.

To be a disciple is to know Christ as the mediator of prayer, the Redeemer of our life with and before God. In prayer through his name, we enter into the communion of the Father and the Son, their unity in the Spirit. We know Christ now not as object of thought or praise but rather as subject, the Way, who in his prayer to the Father gathers us up as his own, to speak through his Spirit. This is the knowledge of Christ that echoes the christological vision of Hebrews: Jesus as pioneer and perfecter of faith, the first of a large family, the intercessor at God's right hand. The corporate, representative power of Christ — his reality as Last Adam — comes to the fore here. Our human words are taken up into the divine Word, the Speaking that was before all worlds, and through which all worlds came to be. This redeeming work of sanctifying our words comes to its climax during the service of the Word in the recitation of the Lord's Prayer. Here the crowd and people of God formally and materially become the disciples of Christ. Within the Gospel of Matthew (the order is rather different in Luke), this prayer is taught the disciples and the crowds after the calling and designating of the Twelve but before the transfiguration, before the final testing by Jesus' opponents, before the triumphal entry, before rejection, cross, and grave. This is a prayer set within Jesus' Galilean ministry, within the time of crowds and healings and spreading fame. It is seedtime, not harvest. The Lord's Prayer, then, captures and enacts the frailty of discipleship, the full range of Christ's redeeming work to those he draws near.

Still ahead for Simon Peter is his repudiation of Jesus as Master, as well as his friendly counsel to Jesus to put his mind on "earthly things"; still ahead for the Twelve, their flight when the Teacher is arrested and arraigned, and their puzzled examination of one another, "which one of them it could be" who would betray him; still ahead for them all — the crowds, the people, the disciples — is the final test, the bitter cup, the rejection and cruel death; and ahead for us all, the dying and rising to new life that is the promise and hope of all creatures, the final conformation to Christ, the Redeemer of the world. The Lord's Prayer locates us all as those called to him, who cling to his words yet cannot stay awake one hour, cannot leave behind our membership in the crowds or satanic opponents, cannot remain faithful, cannot remain. It is to such that Jesus comes and teaches the prayer. Each petition confirms us as disciples who, in their need, know their Redeemer: the cry for bread; the longing for forgiveness; the nearness, daily, of the Gethsemane trial and night; the hunger for the royal kingdom and its glory. In knowing these petitions as our own, we know the relation that is most deeply and comprehensively tied to Christ, the Savior: we know him as the One who came to save sinners. In this confession, we gain knowledge of Christ objectively, to be sure, but more than this knowledge about Christ, we gain knowledge through and in him. We pray in his name and through his prayer the petitions of betrayers, redeemed by the Betrayed.

The service of the Word, then, leads us naturally to the traditional loci for encountering Christ within worship, the gospel proclaimed and the Passion Supper celebrated.

Word and Table

There are few places more controverted in theology than the mode and form of Christ's presence in sermon and Holy Communion. And though knowledge of Jesus Christ as Redeemer is perhaps even more central to the gospel proclaimed than to the eucharistic rite, the mode of presence of Jesus to the faithful in the Supper has been deeply church-dividing and remains the central ecumenical rupture into the modern age.[7] Indeed, the groundbreaking agreement between the Worldwide Lutheran Federation and Rome over the church-dividing doctrine of justification (1999) only underscores the depth and bitterness of the eucharistic debate. Even an agreement on the "chief article," as Lutherans have termed the justification doctrine, cannot bring a unified Table to the Lutheran and Roman communions. How much more to the parties that looked on with interest but from the outside in the Orthodox, Anglican, and Protestant worlds! There is unity, to be sure, in baptism, and that sacramental act, along with the private devotional prayers of the faithful, remains the clearest sign of the undivided Redeemer within the Christian world. But the rupture of communion in the

7. For further reflection on Christ's presence in the Supper, see the essay by David Steinmetz in this volume.

Supper only highlights the primacy of Word and Table as places of Christ's unique presence to the church. We might even say that the Word preached stands in the same center for Protestants that the Table does for eucharistic churches: the luminous midpoint from which Christ is known and received. We cannot hope to mediate these two centerpieces nor reconcile the eucharistic divide through a doctrinal analysis of Christ's presence and identity in liturgy such as we are carrying out here. Indeed, to do so, or to hope to do so, would be to transfer the locus of Christ's unique presence as redeeming Word from church to lecture hall and study. If Christ is most deeply known through worship, the very division in the churches over the Supper and the differing weights given to the sermon must teach us too, in these mean times, about the Redeemer of the fragmented and the lost.

More fruitful for our time of divided Christendom is the delicate relation of Word and sign *(signum* or *sacramentum)* to matter *(res)* and action in both preaching and celebrating the Lord's Supper. Here we focus not so much on sacramental doctrine, however that is understood for either Eucharist or sermon, but rather on how these liturgical acts lead the worshiper into deeper and fuller knowledge of Christ. To phrase this in more liturgical language: we inquire not so much about the mode of Christ's presence as about the illumination of the believer by the light of the One believed. This is in fact *the* test case of our original claim, that Jesus Christ stands apart from his fellows by being known more truly in worship than in any other form. In our earlier liturgical discussion of the service of the Word, we examined the shape and direction of the whole, the confirmation of the worshiper to the myriad fellowships gathered together by the Redeemer. And this is fitting, as the service of the Word is joined to the eucharistic action into a single rite, so that Word and action are joined both within the Supper and beyond, in the rite as a whole. The formal element, or sign, of this movement from crowd to disciple is now joined to the matter of preaching and Supper so that the immeasurable richness of Christ can be known materially and concretely.

For a last time, we may turn again to Calvin's maxim, that Christ is known best clothed in his gospel; or, to borrow language from Karl Barth, that the content of Christ is not given apart from its form, "the Word of God in the sign of the word of [the human]"[8] as Scripture, proclamation,

8. Karl Barth, *Church Dogmatics* 1/2, §19.2, trans. G. W. Bromiley (Edinburgh: T&T Clark, 1956), p. 500.

revelation. We can see this more readily in preaching. Here the Word proclaimed is already in its "natural" form as human word: the divine Word is the content in the "secondary form" of ordinary, creaturely words. The sermon is recognized by its particular task and force as gospel. It proclaims and is servant of Christ. Often this takes the form of a sermon on a Gospel text, so that the Jesus depicted in the New Testament lesson is the One set out as the Redeemer. But it need not be so straightforwardly christological, nor is the church well served by this habit of preaching only from Gospel texts. To "speak by way of the Son" is not always to speak directly about Jesus, the Son! Rather, the sermon is to set out God's redeeming nearness, the promise of deliverance and its manifestation throughout the history of the congregation and people of God. The preacher in words and presence brings together the indirect, third-person knowledge about Jesus, promised or recalled, with the immediate and confessional knowledge of Christ as living Redeemer.

We must state such claims, however, with care. The preacher does not "become" Christ, nor does the preacher, however fine, become the "clothing" of the gospel. Not in this way would we learn something more and deeper about Jesus, the Redeemer! There are no sinful creatures who take Christ's place in his person and work, none who represent or exemplify Christ as subject of the atonement and new life. Rather, the preacher, as with all other creatures drawn to Christ, sets out, depicts, and enacts the motion from crowd to disciple, and the need and rebellion that accompanies and identifies these states. The preacher and the sermon simply are the words that cry out for redemption; they are the testimony of one who has been drawn into the Word's light. These words, then, have not been prized out of the fallen world of natural language. Rather, they speak about Jesus with the temptations, errors, misunderstandings, and rebellions that characterize the human encounter with the Redeemer. But they deepen our direct and proper knowledge of him when they enunciate even in the third-person descriptions of Jesus the true and mystical communion of Christ with the fallen and lost. This is the setting forth of Christ's death until he come.

Just so might we see the union of Word and matter, content and form in the Passion Supper of Christ. Here the natural likeness, or homologue, of Word to fallen word is not directly present; rather, we see bread and wine, the elements of the Supper, proclaimed as Christ's body and blood. The unconsecrated element of this sign, then, is mute in itself, unlike the sermon. Its very material is the artifact of human labor and natural growth. For this reason, the Holy Communion is properly a sacrament, as preaching is at best only indirectly such. The principal sacraments, recognized by all Christian churches, baptism and the Lord's Supper, constitute this "mute" element, the natural and creaturely product of earth. (It may be this very concentration of the sacramental action on that which is of the earth, or earthy, that sets forth the principal from the secondary sacramental practices of the church.) To this natural element is added the word or sign: in baptism, the prayer over the water, which recounts the history of salvation by water; in the Supper, the words of institution and the prayer over the elements, which recount the history of salvation in the passion of the Redeemer and the calling down of the Spirit. In both, the prayer unites the sacrament with the service of the Word, conforming the celebrant and people into the disciples of the Redeemer; in both, the description of salvation as unfolding narrative is taken up in the proclamation that this hour and these lives are themselves knit up in this redeeming work. The words of institution, themselves a complex element in eucharistic controversy, reproduce in a summary, often stylized form the words Jesus spoke over the bread and wine of his last meal with his disciples. All the elements of discipleship are crystallized in these words: the frailty and need, the "super-substantial bread," the trial and sleep, and the final betrayal and fleeing away. To recite and hear these words is to be conformed directly into the ones who need in life and death the Redeemer of the lost.

But it is the final gift of this sacrament that it does not spring directly from the Last Supper, the night of betrayal and passion, but rather from the first worship of the disciples after the threshold of death had been crossed. It is a festival of the resurrection. For this reason, it is the sign of signs: it is the speaking of the mute, the living of the dead, the reconciliation of the enemy. Christians learn more deeply and truly of Jesus in the Eucharist as nowhere else because here the living Christ takes the *res* of his death and our betrayal and sets them forth as the bread of heaven, the food of angels. The very act of hallowing and buying back — redeeming — the lost is exemplified and enacted by bread of affliction becoming the body of the Redeemer, and these in turn the food of the living Lord, the flesh that is food indeed. Those who eat of this bread will live forever (John 6:51): this Johannine promise repeats the knowledge of the Redeemer, confessed by every living disciple. To know this is to know Christ, clothed in his gospel.

The Identity of the Risen Jesus: Finding Jesus Christ in the Poor

Sarah Coakley

The Problem

"Who, or why, or which, or *what,* is the Akond of SWAT?"[1] wrote Edward Lear in one of his more elusive nonsense poems. No less elusive, however, is the somewhat parallel question, Who, or why, or which, or *what,* is the "risen Jesus"? This essay will attempt to probe this misleadingly simple theological question afresh. In particular, it will propose a *systematic* solution to the task of analyzing how historical, dogmatic, and what we might call "spiritual," or "ascetic," approaches to the quest for Jesus' identity might relate and mutually inform one another. The task is a curiously complicated one, as we shall see. Not only is there still great difficulty, even after two hundred years of "historical Jesus" research, in bringing modern, historical-critical discussions about the identity of "Jesus" into clear relation to the older, dogmatic reflection on his "person"; but there is little consistent confidence within contemporary systematics about the means and possibility of a *direct* relation to the "risen Jesus" now, about what this claim might mean, and about how the probative recognition of him might occur. Indeed, we might say that this last, pressingly existential question has been all but occluded — embarrassedly repressed, even — in the era of obsession about the "historical" identity of Jesus.

Let me take a telling example of this modern trend, by way of introduction. Nearly fifty years ago, in the heyday of the second "quest for the

1. Edward Lear, "The Akond of Swat," in *The Complete Nonsense of Edward Lear,* ed. Holbrook Jackson (London: Faber & Faber, 1947), p. 257.

historical Jesus," there was a notoriously frustrating debate between Rudolf Bultmann and Ernst Käsemann on the continuity, or lack thereof, between the historical Jesus and the risen Christ.[2] After observing for a while the interesting spectacle of these titans in combat, the insightful commentator might have begun to discern that the two were apparently arguing at cross-purposes: what Bultmann meant by "the historical Jesus" (which he so strenuously denied had any continuity with the risen Christ of Paul and the Gospels) was *not* what Käsemann meant by the term "Jesus" (which he equally emphatically insisted had to be personally continuous with the risen Christ). Nor did "continuity" have the same valence for them. For Bultmann it meant full and complete identity, identity in *all* characteristics, between the prior and latter states (Jesus and the risen Christ) — and that is what he wanted to deny. For Käsemann it meant merely a contentful enduring of certain *key* characteristics between the two — and that is why he insisted on it.[3] Untangling these confusions about identity seemed to leave little room, ironically, for serious spiritual analysis of what it could mean to encounter Jesus *now*.

Three lessons appear to have emerged from this rather tortured and exhausting debate of the 1950s, yet it is questionable whether these lessons have been brought forward consciously into today's continuing fascination with the "identity of Jesus" as (purportedly) capable of delivery by New Testament scholarship. New quests for the historical Jesus have, since Bultmann, succeeded older quests, in sometimes confusing waves of fashion;[4] yet the analytic, *philosophical* distinctions that need to be drawn in order to avoid repeating some of the mistakes about the category of "identity" implicit in the Bultmann/Käsemann debate are often absent from the empirical rehearsal of the New Testament "evidences," even now.

In the first section of this essay, then, I shall rehearse these lessons, but

2. Käsemann conveniently recapitulates the various moments in this debate in "Sackgassen im Streit um den historischen Jesus"; ET, "Blind Alleys in the 'Jesus of History' Controversy," in *New Testament Questions of Today*, trans. W. J. Montague (London: SCM, 1969), pp. 23-65. Käsemann is responding to Bultmann's "Das Verhältnis der urchristlichen Christusbotschaft zum historischen Jesus" (Heidelberg: Carl Winter, 1960).

3. See Käsemann, *New Testament Questions of Today*, pp. 43-58.

4. We should note that the most recent decades of historical Jesus work have witnessed a fantastic range of hypotheses about Jesus' "real" identity — from Cynic teacher to "marginal Jew," from Gnostic partner of Mary Magdalene to conscious reformer of Jewish patriarchalism.

always with an eye to our specific theological goal of clarifying what might be at stake in using historical reconstructions — *one* means of epistemic access — to help identify the *risen* Jesus. From here, in the second section of the essay, I shall turn to the ontological pole and go on to place these distinctively modern, historiographical problems in a more robustly christological context of analysis; I shall attempt the tricky task of mapping what we have learned from the modern, *historical* debates about Jesus onto the older, *dogmatic* debates about his "person" and "natures." This somewhat risky undertaking cannot, however, be effected without generating some further important distinctions in which analytic philosophy of identity can also come to our aid. Our continuing task will be to clarify quite what meaning of "identity" we are after when we inquire about the personal identity of Jesus, and particularly of the risen Jesus. The results of these first two (admittedly somewhat arduously cerebral) sections will then open us onto the substantial proposals of the third, in which the most novel dimension of my argument will emerge. Here I shall shift back again to the epistemological pole and discuss one specific way of recognizing this identity of the risen Jesus in our contemporary lives, in the context of ministry to the poor and dispossessed. Following leads laid down in the New Testament, but particularly in the fourth-century Cappadocian fathers' theology of donation to the poor, I shall argue that the parable of the sheep and the goats in Matthew 25:31-46 presents us with the suggestion of a surprising, indeed we might say "apophatic,"[5] form of epistemic transformation required for the *full* acknowledgment of the identity of the risen Jesus. I shall close with some systematic conclusions about the relation of practices to theory in this proposed account of the meaning of the identity of the risen Jesus and of our graced access to him — the "Godhead here in hiding."[6]

The "Identity" of Jesus: The Historical Approach

Let us turn, then, to three lessons that I see to have emerged from the Bultmann/Käsemann debate of the late 1950s on the historical Jesus, and to

5. That is, one that defies normal speech and categories.

6. The words of the eucharistic hymn, trans. Gerard Manley Hopkins, are from St. Thomas Aquinas, *Adoro te devote.*

how their enunciation might help us untangle the knotty question of the risen Jesus' "identity."

First, the debate showed the disjunction between the "historical Jesus" and the "risen," or "biblical," Christ to have been a specifically nineteenth-century product, and one arguably infused from the start with a false positivism about the capabilities of historical reconstruction. For according to this disjunction, the "historical Jesus" had connoted what one could get *hold of*, verify with the scientific tools of modern research, whereas the "risen Christ," if needed at all, was decidedly elusive: he could easily become a sort of gnostic, wafting idea or — when rescued to some extent by Bultmann and his ilk — a code for an internal existential *response* by the believer.[7] Käsemann was rightly concerned about being asked to make this ostensibly false choice between Jesus and the Christ, yet his own proposals of reconstruction arguably slid back toward the perils of the first, "historical" alternative. So the question remained: how could one avoid the false disjunction from the outset? Was it not fueled precisely by a misleading historical positivism on the one hand and a pervasive and question-begging coyness about "supernaturalism" on the other? Had the possibility of a direct encounter with the *risen Jesus* been covertly erased even as the disjunction between the historical Jesus and the biblical Christ had been endlessly rehearsed?

Second, the Bultmann/Käsemann debate underscored the persistent ambiguity of the very term "historical Jesus." For Bultmann it seemingly had the primary meaning of "historians' Jesus," a product therefore of a fallible, human enterprise, and not a proper *basis* for faith; to found belief on such a reconstruction could only, as he argued in *Faith and Understanding*, be a manifestation of works righteousness.[8] For Käsemann, however, the same term at least sometimes meant the "earthly [or pre-Easter] Jesus," with which — necessarily, he argued — there had to be some substantial continuity if the "risen Christ" was not to evaporate into a docetic or ghostly visitant.[9] So here, second, the question remained: how *should* one

7. The danger of this aspect of Bultmann's Christology is illuminatingly — but sympathetically — discussed throughout James F. Kay, *Christus Praesens: A Reconsideration of Rudolf Bultmann's Christology* (Grand Rapids: Eerdmans, 1994).

8. See Bultmann, *Faith and Understanding* (London: SCM, 1969), ch. 1, for the clearest enunciation of this point.

9. See, e.g., *New Testament Questions of Today*, p. 48: the "historical Jesus" is "among the criteria of [the] validity" of the New Testament kerygma, and thus he is an "irreplaceable Je-

construe the significance of the "historical Jesus" (and in which sense) for understanding the identity of Jesus?

And then third, the debate revealed a connected muddle — or evasion — that lurked in the same nineteenth-century Jesus/Christ disjunction. The fascination of the choice between *two* (and only two) alternatives in this debate had led the "biblical Christ" and the "risen Christ" to become virtual synonyms (over against the "historical Jesus"). This caused an insidious blurring that occurred just as the false disjunction was driven home, that is, a blurring between *ontological* states of Jesus' identity (whether earthly or risen) and *epistemological* forms of response to him (whether through historical research or decisions of faith). Too often, it seemed, the first and second "questers" reduced the former to the latter category: they made the question of Jesus' identity *either* a matter of human historical reconstruction *or* of equally human responses of faith (albeit animated, purportedly, by prior divine grace). The *actual* earthly or risen Jesus threatened to disappear from view into a sort of *noumenal* no-man's-land — except, as was notoriously quipped against Bultmann, when he put in a miraculous appearance between 10 and 11 on a Sunday morning at the behest of a gifted Lutheran preacher.[10] Probably this last evasion (or reduction) was at least as much the effect of modernistic coyness over supernaturalism as was the initial disjunction between Jesus and Christ itself. But I suspect that it also arose — as I have hinted — from an unacknowledged neo-Kantian presumption that the divine per se was now epistemologically off-limits, except insofar as *we* construct it. The idea, for instance, that one might actually "see" the risen Jesus himself, today, now, in some important and transforming way that involves response to *his* proffered identity, came implicitly to be regarded as fantastic and precritical — so much so that the possibility could seemingly not even be mentioned. It is such coyness that this essay seeks to address and contest.

---

sus." In *Jesus Means Freedom* (Philadelphia: Fortress, 1969), Käsemann gives another reason why the "historical Jesus" is so crucial to him, namely, as criterion of judgment against a potentially corrupt or idolatrous view of "Jesus" presented by the church (see p. 151).

10. This quip is of course only partly fair to Bultmann's christological position. James F. Kay concludes his insightful study of Bultmann's Christology by distinguishing three strands within it, which are often not held in perfect balance by Bultmann himself: the mythical (or storied) Jesus; the pre-Easter, historical figure; and the contemporary, eschatological presence of Jesus in the Word of proclamation (see Kay, *Christus Praesens*, pp. 174-75).

But meanwhile, today, the idea still endures in some quarters that the question of the identity of Jesus can be *settled* by appeal to historical reconstruction, that is, by reference to what we have just called the "historians' Jesus." Why else, one might say, are there the continuing popular frissons of excitement occasioned by the Jesus Seminar, by Marcus Borg, or by John Dominic Crossan? The idea of *settling* the identity of a past figure in this way, after all, is not obviously stupid; it might be regarded, surely, as relatively uncontentious in historians' circles if applied to some other past figure (Socrates or Genghis Khan, for instance) on whom historical details are relatively scarce and mediated through texts and traditions with a distinct slant to them. Despite the fact that philosophers might balk and inquire much more closely what precisely the quest for identity could entail (a point to which we shall return),[11] historians are generally at ease with the task of an assiduous and critical gathering of evidence for the characterization of a past life, in this loose sense of "identity." Yet in the case of Jesus, such a historical approach is obviously *pre-theological.* By definition it shrinks what can be said of Jesus to what secular historians regard as appropriate to their task and duty and so necessarily consigns him to the past. What are the alternatives, then, if this secular reduction is to be avoided?

The rest of this essay will be devoted to sketching *one* such alternative, one in which the historians' Jesus, as we have defined it, can indeed continue to play a certain significant role (although not a primary or decisive one) in answer to the question of Jesus' human identity, and in which a certain boldness about a claimed access to the risen Jesus *himself* will be a salient feature of the discussion. But to arrive at this alternative, we first have to renounce the modern dualism (as it still bedeviled Bultmann and Käsemann) between the historical Jesus and the Christ of faith *tout court* — at least as it appears to apply *ontologically* to the identity of Jesus; and we have to probe both through and behind the disjunction. It appears, then, that we need to be dealing with *four* items for discussion and analysis rather than two: the "historians' Jesus" and the "response of faith to 'Christ'" at the epistemological level, and the "earthly Jesus" and the "risen Jesus" at the ontological level. Whereas the first two items are clearly *dis-*

11. Modern analytic philosophy distinguishes (a) discussion of the problem of "identity" as "sameness" between items with identical characteristics (the issue of the so-called "identity of indiscernibles") and (b) discussion of the problem of "personal identity" through time and change.

tinct forms of human analysis and response (though maybe not as cleanly disjunct as some would have it), the latter two items are arguably *personally* identical: they constitute descriptions of the same person at different times — an issue that we must now explore.[12]

The "Person" of Christ: The Dogmatic Approach

We have noted how tempting it is to impose the modern template of a Jesus/Christ disjunction onto the issue of the person of Jesus himself. But in this way modern, *historiographical* debates about the "person" of Jesus can become confusingly entangled with premodern, essentially *metaphysical* debates about the "person" *(hypostasis)* of Christ. In fact, there seem to be three forms of temptation toward such confusion, each equally seductive and equally misleading christologically.

The first form of temptation causes one to slide straight back to the epistemological pole. It assumes that talk about "Jesus" is a matter of establishing *fact,* while talk about "Christ" is a matter of establishing *value* and eliciting *response.* The crudest version of this misapprehension is the naive empiricist attempt to justify an ascription of divine identity to Jesus by reference to historical evidences, a ploy that has in the past much exercised evangelical and British empiricist approaches to Christology, but that I take to be a category mistake: evidences may at best *suggest* the presence of divinity, but they cannot logically compel such a conclusion. To cite a recent essay by Rowan Williams, the response of faith to Christ is *not* a matter of dispassionate factual investigation, but "everything depends, in our reading of the gospels, on whether the story displaces or decentres us, whether we read it as an address to us, a call to *dispossession.*"[13] Williams goes on to deny that fact and response can be rent apart here, as might appear to be the case: "There is no path to a secure portrait of Jesus independent of how he has been responded to. . . . Part of the 'reality' we seek is that the history of Jesus did indeed begin the process that led to the definition of faith in the Christian sense."[14] In

12. For discussion of the continuity in personal identity of the earthly and risen Jesus in the Pauline Epistles, see the essay by Richard Hays in the present volume.

13. Rowan Williams, "Looking for Jesus and Finding Christ," in *Biblical Concepts and Our World,* ed. D. Z. Phillips and Mario von der Ruhr (Basingstoke: Palgrave Macmillan, 2004), p. 150; emphasis mine.

14. Williams, "Looking for Jesus and Finding Christ," p. 151.

other words, not only is the quest for facts about Jesus strongly entangled with implicit issues of valuation, but there is also an underlying metaphysical *reality* — Jesus — with whom both historians and believers have to do; the temptation to slice him in half is to be sternly resisted. Yet that temptation may come in another two forms as well. The modernistic template may suggest, second, that *clarity* may be achieved in the area of "Jesus," whereas *mystery* necessarily attends the figure of "Christ"; or, third — and worse — that the *humanity* of the God/man is ascribed to "Jesus" and the *divinity* to "Christ." But in both cases this is to divide the natures.

Only when we have shaken off these misapprehensions like dust from our feet can we proceed to less misleading ways of framing the metaphysical question about Jesus' own identity. What we have suggested so far, then, is that this *one* "person" is the subject both of historical inquiry and of the arousal of faith; that he is no less personally mysterious and elusive in his earthly life than in his risen existence; and that (from the perspective of faith, not of "secular" historical research) we must speak of his personal, "hypostatic" identity in the incarnation as involving a *coexistence* of the human with the divine.

Once we are talking about hypostasis as the locus of Jesus' identity, we have declared a sort of dogmatic fiat (some would say by a mere sleight of hand): we have not exactly clarified the issue intrinsically, but at least we have shed certain modernistic muddles. The word "hypostasis" in fact merely serves here as a placeholder for a strong metaphysical claim: that Jesus was God's Son incarnate. It does not provide an answer to the notoriously complex philosophical problems of "personal identity" in general — indeed, it complicates them! Whereas debates about personal identity in analytic philosophy focus on whether to appeal to mental states (memory in particular) or to physical ones (bodily features) as criteria of identity through time,[15] the concept "hypostasis" does nothing to *solve* such debates in this christological context; it merely trumps them in Jesus' case by appeal to an unchanging, divine locus of identity (the Logos, the second person of the Trinity) that is inseparably conjoined to a human nature at the incarnation.

Is, then, the risen Jesus *also* human in his identity? The question is, in a

15. A fine, if now somewhat dated, collection of essays that gives the flavor of the analytic debate is Amélie Oksenberg Rorty, ed., *The Identities of Persons* (Berkeley: University of California Press, 1976).

sense, a trick one, and it has had no clearly unanimous answer from the Christian theological tradition.[16] However, if we take the Gospel appearance narratives as broadly credible, we must surely answer yes rather than no: this risen Jesus seemingly *claims* to be the same Jesus who taught and healed and suffered and died — thus meeting the mental/memory criterion for personal identity — and he is recognizable to at least some of his followers and acquaintances, has wounds and scars consistent with an experience of crucifixion, and has a voice that also evokes recognition — thus meeting the physical criterion. So the risen Jesus is the same Jesus as was known to his disciples before his arrest, trial, and death. Yet it seems that his personal identity has also undergone significant change: he is strangely unrecognizable at times to some who knew him before (an epistemic problem that we shall address shortly), he moves around in ways incompatible with normal human bodiliness, and he is perceived as densely "present" in ways and places not strictly compatible with ordinary human physical existence. Perhaps we must therefore call the risen Jesus "human" in some expanded, intensified, or transformed sense; no longer simply "*a* man," he is rather — as Luther would have put it — the "proper man," as only one who is also God can be: God "for us."

But this conclusion of course raises further complications for our identity issue. For especially as the era of physical resurrection appearances seems to draw to a close in the biblical text, we are again pushed up against the question of how *physical* criteria of identity could continue to apply in the identification of the risen Jesus. What has now become of the individual who was/is Jesus? Simply to resummon the patristic argument of metaphysical fiat at this point may not adequately satisfy us: it may strike us as too much lifted away from the known contours of individual bodily existence. Docetism again looms. Perhaps, then, we need to step back and distinguish several *different* ways in which we now see that the question of the identity of Jesus may be tackled, and also to return to the question of what part, if any, may be played in this by the modern project of historical reconstruction.

At one level of discussion, as we have now shown, the question of Je-

16. At the Reformation this question became inextricably entangled with debates in the *Abendmahlstreit* about the sort of presence Christ has at the Eucharist. Those denying a "real," that is, physical, presence would also be inclined to question the risen Jesus' present "human," bodily availability in general. For discussion of these Reformation-era controversies, see the essay by David Steinmetz in the present volume.

sus' identity is metaphysically straightforward, if deeply mysterious and unique: for those who subscribe to an orthodox Christology, Jesus simply *is* God incarnate; his identity *is* the divine hypostasis of the Word. As such, the mystery of his personhood has an apophatic dimension qualitatively different from the mystery of every human personhood; for he, alone among humans, is also God. But if it be objected that this claim merely begs the question of the relation of this metaphysical pronouncement to historical manifestation, we have to acknowledge the challenge and take some riskier and more complicated steps. First, we have to summon the bag and baggage of the philosophically contested criteria of mental and physical identity through time and inquire how those criteria could possibly apply to a God/man who has undergone death and resurrection. Let us suppose, for a moment, that this first task will not defeat us, by dint of some clever analogical reasoning. After all, contemporary philosophers such as Derek Parfit have made the ingenious claim that a personal identity over time may be more akin to a lake with its ever-changing shores than to a strictly stable entity;[17] and if ordinary persons can maintain their malleable identity no less than mutable lakes, surely it is logically possible that Jesus' divine/personal identity can also endure — in and through certain notable bodily transformations of the passion and resurrection — and retain the capacity to be recognized even *as* a resurrection body.

But things get yet tougher to handle hereafter, for it seems that the Gospels and Epistles also press on us the thought that the risen Jesus' identity is to be found (if not always easily recognized) even when *individual* resurrection appearances are not in play. Specifically, he is to be found in "the breaking of bread" (Luke 24:35), and in the faces of the poor, the destitute, the sick, and the imprisoned (Matt 25:31-46). And further, if Paul's theology of the church as the "body of Christ" (Romans 12; 1 Corinthians 12) is to be taken as more than a mere metaphorical frill, he is also to be identified, more generically, in the very mystery of the life of the church, his ecclesial body. Analytic identity theorists may at this point throw up their hands in horror: where is the identity of Jesus then *not* to be found — "Split the wood and I am there"? — and this query certainly has merit. But perhaps it is just at this juncture that we can rescue our historians' Jesus and at last give him something to do *theologically.* Simultaneously, however, we can also introduce our own distinctive proposal about the relation

17. See Derek Parfit, *Reasons and Persons* (Oxford: Clarendon, 1984).

of continuing Christian *practices* to the capacity for graced recognition of the identity of the risen Jesus. Here, at last, historiographical and dogmatic criteria of Jesus' identity finally come together, undergirded epistemically by the necessary sustaining matrix of the Christian practices of meditation, prayer, sacrament, and — as we shall now proceed to explore — acts of mercy to the poor.

Jesus Christ in the Poor: A "Spiritual Sense" Approach

In a famous essay on meaning, J. L. Austin once averred that the word "same" (like other difficult-to-define words such as "real" and "exists") is one of a group in which "the negative use wears the trousers."[18] Whatever we think of the gender ascription here, we immediately see what he means: we tend to know when something, or someone, is *not* the same as another, but it is much harder to say definitively when it, or she, *is* the same. And thus perhaps oftentimes — or so Austin indicates — it is better not to try too hard. It may be, I suggest, that such a semantic intuition will help us now discern the proper *christological* use of the historians' Jesus for the broader issue of Jesus' identity. To attempt to found, or more precisely to *justify*, faith in historical research is, or so I have argued, a category mistake of some spiritual magnitude, but that is not to say that historical research cannot play some significant, if secondary, role as "negative" testing for claims to the identity of Jesus.[19] It can "wear the trousers," to use Austin's

18. J. L. Austin, "Truth," in *Philosophical Papers* (Oxford: Clarendon, 1961), p. 88; see also *Sense and Sensibilia,* reconstructed from the manuscript notes by G. J. Warnock (Oxford: Clarendon, 1962), p. 70.

19. I want to be clear what I mean by "negative" in this context. First, I do not mean "negative" in the sense of either "hostile" or "destructive"; I mean it rather in the sense of "chastening" or "constraining." Nor do I mean that "positive" (in the sense of "sustaining" or "fulfilling" or "contentful") reflection on Jesus cannot be supplied both by meditative and prayerful study of the canonical biblical literature (a requirement for any Christian spiritual life) and, indeed, by historical-critical study of Jesus (which can often be in fruitful interplay with biblical meditation). My point is, first, that we must most carefully avoid the supposition that we can ever catch and hold Jesus, let alone justify our belief in him, by way of historical evidences; and thus, second, that the continuous need to chasten and correct our own incipient blasphemy or idolatry in this area can in one degree be importantly addressed by the use of historical evidences for that ("negative") purpose. (Indeed, historical Jesus research can be used no less significantly against a false captivity of Jesus by the church, and a

phrase. The kinds of conclusions that secular historians may gather about a past person's identity (in the loose sense, discussed above, of character qualities or distinctive personal beliefs and actions) can at least indicate when a claim about that person is palpably errant. Thus, for instance, if a self-proclaimed Christian believer avers that Jesus was not a Jew (a denial on which so much hung in the twentieth century),[20] or if she insists that Jesus tells her that being obedient to him should rightly result in worldly influence and financial success (a supposition not absent from certain forms of twenty-first-century spirituality), we may appropriately object, not only on intra-Christian biblical grounds, but also on *historical* grounds that this cannot be the same Jesus who lived and taught and walked about and was crucified in Palestine at a known period in the first century C.E.

And so here, finally, we reach the nub to which the foregoing argument has eventually led. If historical evidences can properly supply only *negative* tests on Jesus' earthly personal identity, what are to be the appropriate *positive* tests in the case of Jesus' risen identity? To extend our gender metaphor, a little provocatively: if historical evidences "wear the trousers" in the matter of the identity of Jesus, where are we to find the more alluring and enveloping *skirts* of this issue?[21]

The investigation of the identity of the risen Jesus surely shares something with the investigation of the identity of any other *living* human person, but it also has something entirely unique to it. What it shares with the investigation of living personhood, it seems to me, is the possibility of relationship: I do not only grasp but am also grasped by the living mystery of the "other" (something not possible in the same way, note, in a detective's investigation of the technical identity of a dead body or in the secular his-

---

smug presumption that he is available only to the creedally orthodox, as it can against more individual manifestations of fantasy or self-righteousness.) I shall argue shortly below, however, that this continuous task of a "negative" use of *historical* evidences must always be balanced, indeed undergirded, by a *spiritual* erasure of self-certainty, in and through the Holy Spirit, who alone discloses the identity of the risen Jesus to us.

20. On the Jewishness of Jesus, see Markus Bockmuehl, "God's Life as a Jew," in this volume.

21. One cannot help recalling here the famous remark of R. H. Lightfoot that "we trace in [the Gospels] but the *outskirts* of his ways" (*History and Interpretation in the Gospels* [London: Hodder & Stoughton, 1935], p. 225; emphasis mine). I do intend a gender allusion, in the sense that, as we shall see, a very particular, and normally undiscussed, form of epistemic receptivity is here required of us, which is spiritually transformative rather than gender-stereotypical.

torian's reconstruction of a deceased personality). But what is unique to the risen Jesus, if his hypostatic identity qua second divine person is to be properly intuited and responded to, is the necessity of my first being grasped, not just by the living mystery of the person of Jesus himself, but by that in God (what Christians call the Spirit) that so *dispossesses* me that I can truly "see" Jesus and not merely my own face at the bottom of a well. Note that with "dispossession" I am picking up a theme we earlier saw adumbrated by Rowan Williams, but I am giving it now a particular significance, in terms of the transformative, even destabilizing conditions of entry into inner-trinitarian participation. In other words, what is needed — in the richest theological sense of identifying the risen Jesus — is some prior, interruptive undoing of epistemic blockage, some mending of the blindness of the ravages of sin, in order that the person of Jesus might truly be identified. Paul memorably puts it thus, heading off a proto-Gnostic threat before he discloses his teaching on the body of Christ: "No one can say 'Jesus is Lord' *except by the Holy Spirit*" (1 Cor 12:3); and in the contemporary period, Hans Urs von Balthasar has expressed a similar sentiment, precisely in relation to the problem of our contemporary obsession with the historical reconstruction of Jesus: we need, he says, to avoid "fixing [our] eyes so narrowly on the historical aspect of Christ's revelation, as the thing of ultimate importance, that [we] neglect the Holy Spirit."[22] In other words, to "see" God (the Son) — to identify the risen Jesus — involves a profound epistemic transformation, one that may first throw me out of kilter but can ultimately knit me participatively into the life of the Trinity. And *this* is why acknowledging the identity of Jesus is different from any other such identifying of persons.

Let me now try, in what remains of my essay, to spell this suggestion out a little further. I have attempted in a recent publication ("The Resurrection and the Spiritual Senses," in my *Powers and Submissions*)[23] to explicate the possible conditions for contemporary "seeing" of the resurrected Jesus by reference to the patristic "spiritual senses" tradition. This tradition charts in some detail the proposed capacity of our gross physical senses to undergo profound transformative change, or sharpening, in the Spirit, in order to

22. Hans Urs von Balthasar, *Love Alone Is Credible,* trans. D. C. Schindler (San Francisco: Ignatius, 2004), pp. 149-50.

23. Sarah Coakley, *Powers and Submissions: Spirituality, Philosophy, and Gender* (Oxford: Blackwell, 2002), ch. 8. The essay is also now in Phillips and von der Ruhr, *Biblical Concepts and Our World,* pp. 169-89.

come ultimately into desired recognition of, and union with, the risen Jesus. The tradition is founded creatively in the work of Origen, especially in his *Commentary on the Song of Songs,* but Origen's own rendition of this type of epistemology is rendered problematic by its sharp Platonic disjunction between "inner" (spiritual) and "outer" (physical) senses and its consequent squeamishness about the final redeemability of flesh. The adjustments made to Origen's approach by the fourth-century Gregory of Nyssa, I argue in *Powers and Submissions,* present a telling and creative alternative, in which spiritual senses are developed by the grace of the Holy Spirit and through patient Christian practice over a lifetime of purgation and transformation, *starting with the raw material of the "fleshly-minded"* (as Gregory himself puts it in the introduction to his *Commentary on the Song*).[24] In other words, for Gregory, it is precisely the stuff of my flesh that is redeemed, rather than discarded, in this process toward Christic recognition and union. Yet what is also distinctive to Gregory's account is an insistence that a dethroning darkness — a blinding of normal sight and intellectual power — will necessarily attend any *close* approach to intimacy with the bridegroom, Christ; the soul must enter the destabilizing realm of the unconscious and adopt the ostensibly "feminine" posture of virgin/lover in order to reach the goal of closeness and embrace of the Logos.[25] She (for it is she) must exercise her epistemic responses in new, and subtle, ways — by dark touch and taste and smell (the supposedly lower senses of classical philosophy, now elevated to superior significance) — if Christ is to be truly encountered. Only through this lengthy process is the soul sufficiently cleansed to be able to see, and thus also to *reflect,* the beauty of the risen Jesus: "So too," says Gregory, "the soul reflects the pure image of that unsullied Beauty, when she has prepared herself properly and cast off every material stain. Then may the soul say — for she is a kind of living mirror possessing free will: When I face my Beloved with my entire surface, all the beauty of His form is reflected within me."[26]

24. See Coakley, *Powers and Submissions,* pp. 136-39, for a brief discussion and comparison of Origen and Gregory of Nyssa on this theme.

25. I discuss in detail the issue of how gender is not merely destabilized but substantively remade as relationship to Christ, according to Gregory of Nyssa, in *Powers and Submissions,* ch. 9. To read Gregory as reestablishing a "worldly" view of "femininity" would be entirely to miss his subtlety here.

26. Gregory of Nyssa, *Commentary on the Song of Songs* 15, trans. and ed. Herbert Musurillo, *From Glory to Glory* (Crestwood, N.Y.: St. Vladimir's Seminary Press, 1995), p. 282.

Why, then, do I argue that the spiritual senses give us the final epistemic key to the problem of the identity of the risen Jesus? It is partly because I see this tradition as able to explain, retroactively, certain characteristic features of the New Testament stories of the resurrection that otherwise remain obscure or quirky: the possibility of being with the risen Jesus and *not* recognizing him, for instance; having to go through a personal process of change or of particular ritual acts in order to "see" him; the context of uncertainty and disturbance and "fear" in which the resurrection is distinctively encountered; or the significance of women's testimony to the resurrection that was so quickly sidelined or superseded. But also, more systematically, I wish to highlight the significance of the spiritual senses because I take it they indicate a particular sort of knowing that is alone *appropriate* to the mystery of the identity of Jesus: a knowing by destabilized unknowing, a knowing by so-called "feminine" desire, a knowing by a gradual spiritual transformation and merging into the object of longing.

Predictably, perhaps, my initial essay on this theme produced some vehemently negative response: it is surprising, but noteworthy, how committed most contemporary theologians seemingly are to the *impossibility* of any present *physical* reidentification of the risen Jesus at all, of whatever sort. Ingolf Dalferth, scolding me for what he saw as a major category error, put it uncompromisingly thus: "*'seeing' the risen Christ* is not a case of seeing at all, but a metaphorical way of expressing the fundamental change of life brought about [in the believer in relation to the resurrection]."[27] But I beg to differ. If we cannot, by definition, respond to Jesus' identity through our bodies — our eyes, our hands, our lips, our ears — what is the cost to our Christian principle of incarnation? Who is "wearing the trousers" here? And that is why, in the closing portion of this essay, I wish — doggedly — to repeat, and extend, this earlier line of argument on the spiritual senses with a further responsive suggestion. I want to say that that supposed "*impossibility*" (as Dalferth puts it) of relating physically to the risen Jesus is really, and more truly, a profound *possibility* of a paradoxical and "apophatic" sort — one that intrinsically undercuts my natural longings to control and predict the epistemic outcome. And it seems to me that even the New Testament authors already show us — and the patristic authors on the spiritual senses ramify this approach — that the spiritual or

27. Ingolf U. Dalferth, "The Resurrection: The Grammar of 'Raised,'" in Phillips and von der Ruhr, *Biblical Concepts and Our World*, p. 202; emphasis original.

epistemic conditions for the recognition of the risen Jesus (involving crucially, as I have hinted, a radical dispossession to the Spirit) demand a cumulative tangle of *practices* — meditative, sacramental, but also moral — in order to sustain this paradoxical form of unknowing/knowing.[28]

The repetitive emptying of self, in the Spirit, toward the possibility of seeing and finding Jesus has to be formed and shaped first by deep positive meditative immersion in the narrative of the Gospels, to be sure, but no less also by the sort of *rupture* of expectation that the sacramental breaking of bread implies.[29] He is made known in "the *breaking* of bread" (Luke 24:35), but only because his *death* is proclaimed "until he comes" (1 Cor 11:26).[30] It is through this paradox of making and breaking my sense of Jesus that my true sense of Jesus, by grace, emerges. It involves a sort of "turning," and "turning" again — as the Magdalene did before she recognized the gardener for "Rabboni" (John 20:14, 16) — that I am ever engaged in as I seek the identity of the risen Jesus. By the same token, in my moral life, in my intended acts of mercy, though it is Jesus I seek to obey and emulate, it is always in the *erasure* of expectation that Jesus truly presents himself to me — in the entirely unromantic other, in the exhausting and defeating poverty of my neighbor, in the nuisance of the beggar at my gate. And that "apophatic" lesson surely sustains the insights of the parable of the sheep and the goats in Matthew 25:31-46, if anything does. The paradoxes of this parable are striking and powerful: the true recognizers of Jesus are precisely the ones who are unaware of it (25:37-39); yet presumably their moral antennae have in some sense been trained, spiritually if unconsciously, and by repetitive breakage, to respond to the identity of Jesus in

28. Marianne Sawicki develops a somewhat similar line of approach to practice and resurrection in *Seeing the Lord: Resurrection and Early Christian Practices* (Minneapolis: Fortress, 1994), and does so in a way that gives close attention to particular New Testament evidences. However, she does not systematically develop the apophatic dimension of the argument in the way I am suggesting here.

29. It strikes me that the "doing in memory" of the Eucharist might itself be seen as a sort of extension of the identity criterion of "memory" for the existence of persons through time, but here extended by means of Jesus' followers *identifying themselves* with the body of Jesus, who has to suffer passion and death.

30. I have discussed in more detail this reading of the eucharistic "breaking" as a questioning and chastening of desire in my recent Hensley Henson Lectures, Oxford 2005. A discerning reading of the Emmaus story as both "demanding and surprising," especially in a Jewish/Christian context, may be found in R. W. L. Moberly, *The Bible, Theology, and Faith: A Study of Abraham and Jesus* (Cambridge: Cambridge University Press, 2000), ch. 2.

those whom they serve. Jesus is found precisely in the incarnational *physicality* of these poor and destitute to whom they have given their acknowledgment and aid; Jesus is ignored, unrecognized, despised, by those who fail so to will and act. Such is not merely a question of ethical rectitude, let alone a worthy project of human self-improvement; it is a subtle matter of *seeing* — of identification and response. And perhaps more: for according to at least one strand in patristic exegesis of Matthew 25, what is given back to us by the poor whom we serve — Jesus himself — is far greater a gift than anything we could ever give to them.

It is Gregory of Nyssa's elder brother Basil who expresses this point with the greatest spiritual acuity and daring. Although all the Cappadocian fathers insist on the revolutionary social significance of donation to the poor[31] — the possibility thereby of upending the network of class and privilege that sustains the order of the world — it is Basil who first presses home the radical point that gifts to the poor are not really free donations at all but rather the paying back of an initial debt that God lays on us even as we are created. Since life itself is a gift, all of life is also a repayment. If we are all debtors to start with, then our response to the poor is not some good civic duty of supererogation but a *necessity* — which, however, to our great surprise, issues in yet further divine gift, the gift of being given Jesus back by the poor. As Basil puts it, "And you, whatever fruits of beneficence you do yield, you gather up for yourself; for the grace of good

31. This is a striking theme throughout the writings of the Cappadocian fathers: see, e.g., Gregory of Nyssa, *Sermones*, ed. Günter Heil, GNO 9 (Leiden: Brill, 1967), pp. 93-127; and, for Basil and Gregory of Nazianzus on the same issue, see M. F. Toal, trans., *The Sunday Sermons of the Great Fathers*, 4 vols. (Chicago: Regnery, 1955-63), 3:325-32; 4:43-64. Two of the most important homilies by Gregory of Nyssa on *philanthropia* to the poor are presented, with commentary, by Adrianus van Heck, ed., in *Gregorii Nysseni de pauperibus amandis orationes duo* (Leiden: Brill, 1964). A compendium of patristic and later interpretations of Matthew 25 can be conveniently found in Sherman W. Gray, *The Least of My Brothers: Matthew 25:31-46 — A History of Interpretation* (Atlanta: Scholars Press, 1989). However, Gray is mostly interested in whether the text calls readers to care for all the poor or only for Christians, and this leads to neglect of other themes that the patristic authors (such as the Cappadocians) also cover. I am much indebted, in this final section of my essay, to Brian E. Daley's lecture "Building a New City: The Cappadocian Fathers and the Rhetoric of Philanthropy," *Journal of Early Christian Studies* 7 (1999): 431-61; and also to the continuing work of Susan R. Holman on the theme of poverty in the patristic era: see her recent *The Hungry Are Dying: Beggars and Bishops in Roman Cappadocia* (New York: Oxford University Press, 2001).

works and their reward is returned to the giver. Have you given something to a person in need; what you have given becomes yours, and is returned to you with an increase."[32] Gregory of Nazianzus, Basil's great friend and collaborator, finishes his great sermon "On the Love of the Poor and Those Afflicted with Leprosy" with a similar sentiment, expressly summoning the paradoxes of Matthew 25:

> If therefore I have convinced you of anything, O Servants of Christ, who are my brothers and my fellow heirs, let us, while there is yet time, visit Christ in His sickness, let us have care for Christ . . . , let us give to Christ to eat, let us clothe Christ in His nakedness, let us do honour to Christ, . . . not only with precious ointments, as Mary did, not only in His tomb, as Joseph of Arimathea did . . . ; but let us honour Him because the Lord of all will have mercy. . . . Let us give Him this honour in His poor, in those who lie on the ground here before us this day, so that when we leave this world they may receive us into eternal tabernacles, in Jesus Christ our Lord.[33]

The Cappadocian view of acts of mercy, then, must finally be seen as intrinsically connected to the question of the identification of Jesus: to know Christ *is* to have served the poor, to have felt the indebtedness of the very gift of life that animates such service, yet also to have received the identity of Jesus back afresh in the process.[34]

So "Who, or why, or which, or *what,* is the risen Jesus?" As we have seen, when we ask about the conditions for the recognition of the identity of Jesus, we are asking a deep and complicated question, one in which epistemic, sacramental, and moral factors are profoundly entangled, as well as necessary speculations about the metaphysics of divinity. We have come a long way from the "quest for the historical Jesus," with its optimistic positivism about "the facts." Along the path we have suggested a "trou-

32. Basil, in Toal, *Sunday Sermons of the Great Fathers,* 3:327.

33. Gregory of Nazianzus, in Toal, *Sunday Sermons of the Great Fathers,* 4:63-64.

34. Perhaps this is most beautifully expressed in Gregory of Nyssa's explicitly christological remarks: "Do not look down on those who lie at your feet, as if you judged them worthless. Consider who they are, and you will discover their dignity: they have put on the figure (πρόσωπον) of our Savior." Van Heck, *de Pauperibus* 8.23–9.4, cited in Daley, "Building a New City," p. 451. The connection of my line of thought here to the close of Dale Allison's essay in the present volume on Jesus' identity in Matthew is perhaps worthy of comment.

ser"-like role — significant but circumscribed — that historical investigation can and indeed should play in responding to the identity of Jesus, but we have been far more interested in developing less well-worn lines of approach. Thus, we have identified some of the confusions caused by the superimposition of modern disjunctions between Jesus and the Christ on traditional christological metaphysics and have attempted to give new coinage to that metaphysics with the help of analytic reflection on philosophical criteria of personal identity. Finally, we have suggested that the full recognition of the identity of Jesus may be a unique and lifelong task, one that necessarily "skirts" — as I have put it — the borderlands of desire and unknowing; it is the product of an only gradually emerging spiritual and erotic maturity, and rooted transformatively in sacramental practice, prayer, and service to the poor. But only in the light of union, it has been suggested, will our epistemic responses be fully cleansed and engaged to receive it; only then shall we realize that we have seen Christ most fully in the "least of our sisters and brothers"; only then, indeed, shall we know, with the appropriateness of a continuing and paradoxical unknowing brokered by the Spirit, the full mystery of the identity of the risen Jesus, the mystery, in fact, of "Godhead here in hiding."

Epilogue: Who Is Jesus Christ for Us Today?

Reflections on a Pilgrimage

Beverly Roberts Gaventa and Richard B. Hays

"We wish to see Jesus."

The pilgrimage undertaken in this volume has offered many vantage points from which to seek and learn the identity of Jesus. The necessity of multiple vantage points is already suggested by the rich diversity of presentations of Jesus in the biblical texts themselves. For example, Matthew identifies Jesus as the very presence of God ("God with us," 1:23) and renders the story of Jesus in tones that are unmistakably drawn from biblical accounts of Moses and David. John reaches back to creation itself to insist that Jesus must be understood in relationship to God and the whole created order. The letters of Paul address communities of believers with the claim that they themselves participate in the death and resurrection of Jesus — that they are, through Jesus, both transformed and transforming of the world. And canonical reflection on Jesus' identity allows us to see Moses and Jonah as antecedents for Jesus' struggle in Gethsemane.

Beyond the canonical witnesses to Jesus lies the vast wealth of continuing reception of biblical reflection on Jesus. We have glimpsed the early church's endeavor to articulate Jesus' saving identity while simultaneously expressing his genuine human limitations. And we have seen how the early Reformers' varying understandings of Jesus focused on their understandings of his presence at the Eucharist.

At a number of points in our pilgrimage, we have recognized that Jesus is not only the object of our pilgrimage, the one whom we set out to see and understand; Jesus is also the one who calls us on a pilgrimage of worship and service. Our response to his call is invariably flawed, but the changed direction of our lives is nonetheless real. While it is easy and fashionable to lament the failings of Jesus' followers, it remains improbable, as Charles Marsh has observed, that anyone would ever read Nietzsche or Derrida and be inspired to open a soup kitchen.[1]

At this point in the pilgrimage, as we reach the end of this book, it might seem highly desirable to render a picture of Jesus in a pithy sentence or two. Given the media realities of our time, that strategy would have great market value. Yet the wealth of sites on our pilgrimage means that a brief statement sketching the identity of Jesus is impossible. Indeed, no "sound-bite" Jesus can ever be faithful to the evidence, because the testimony of the variety of witnesses to Jesus — past, present, and future — cannot be collapsed into a sixty-second summary.

Readers who find themselves chafing at that observation may suspect that sheer pedantry is at work here, that we are exercising a scholarly penchant for making things more complex than need be. It may be helpful, then, to consider the rich complexity of our own individual identities, each with as many aspects and nuances as we have relationships. The testimony to that identity given by a coworker would differ from that given by a spouse or by a neighbor or by a childhood friend — in fact, no two reports would be exactly the same. No sound bite, however truthful, can capture the complete identity of any individual.

Some Christians will find themselves uncomfortable with our insistence on the wealth of descriptions of Jesus, not because they suspect that it is obfuscating, but because they fear that it compromises the gospel. Yet given the diversity of biblical witnesses to Jesus, orthodoxy actually *demands* that we speak about Jesus in more than one way. To privilege one part or another is to reckon with a diminished Jesus, a Jesus whose personal identity is less fully rounded than the complex Jesus offered us by the great cloud of witnesses in the Christian tradition.

So how can we move forward with and among this great cloud of witnesses? How can we affirm the riches of the pilgrimage without devolving into chaos or sheer relativism? We can start by articulating as clearly as possible the common ground shared by the many pilgrims who, across time, have sought and borne witness to the Jesus to whom Scripture points. The varying studies in the present volume reflect the broad convergence articulated in the introduction about genuine interpretation of the

1. Charles Marsh, *The Beloved Community: How Faith Shapes Social Justice, from the Civil Rights Movement to Today* (New York: Basic, 2005), pp. 5-6.

identity of Jesus. As we look back over these studies, we may summarize once again some of the key elements of that convergence.

- Attempts to understand Jesus of Nazareth must recognize that he was a part of the Judaism of his day.
- Jesus is reliably attested and known in the Scriptures of the Old and New Testaments. The whole of the canonical witness is significant, which means that the church must always be engaged in deep and careful reading of these texts.
- The canonical witness to Jesus continues in the church's interpretative tradition. The tradition is not an artificial accretion that can be freely discarded. Rather, it is the community's time-tested unpacking of the fuller meaning of the biblical testimony. At the same time, ongoing critical reflection on the tradition's interpretation of Jesus' identity, in dialogue with Scripture under the guidance of the Holy Spirit, is itself an element of the tradition.
- Jesus is not dead; he lives in the present as the Lord of the church and of the world. He can be encountered in the community of his people, the body of Christ. He is present in life-giving power in the church's sacraments. And the church continues to meet him anew whenever it befriends the poor and those who suffer.
- Jesus is always a disturbing and destabilizing figure, not the guarantor of any established order.

The Gospel of John concludes with a twofold affirmation — an assurance that the testimony it offers is reliable, and an acknowledgment that it is, of necessity, only partial: if all the things that Jesus did were reported, "the world itself could not contain the books that would be written" (21:25 NRSV). Thus, John's telling of the story has no end. Nor does the pilgrimage of those who wish to see Jesus.

Recommended Reading

Allison, Dale C. *Jesus of Nazareth: Millenarian Prophet.* Minneapolis: Fortress, 1998. Over against some recent interpretations that deny Jesus' own apocalyptic convictions, Allison mounts a strong argument in favor of Jesus as an eschatological prophet. Schweitzer's interpretation of Jesus is here reintroduced and reinvigorated.

Barton, Stephen C., ed. *The Cambridge Companion to the Gospels.* Cambridge: Cambridge University Press, 2006. A collection of essays on the canonical Gospels, intended for the educated general reader. The book has three sections: "Approaching the gospels: context and method"; "The gospels as witnesses to Christ: content and interpretation"; and "The afterlife of the gospels: impact on church and society."

Bauckham, Richard. *God Crucified: Monotheism and Christology in the New Testament.* Grand Rapids: Eerdmans, 1999. A provocative argument that even in the earliest stages of Christian tradition, believers interpreted Jesus as sharing in the unique identity of Israel's God.

Bockmuehl, Markus. *This Jesus: Martyr, Lord, Messiah.* Edinburgh: T&T Clark, 1994. A historically sophisticated but concise and readable exploration of the identity of Jesus. Bockmuehl locates Jesus firmly within first-century Judaism while also showing the organic continuity between Jesus and the emergent faith of the early church.

———, ed. *The Cambridge Companion to Jesus.* Cambridge: Cambridge University Press, 2001. This collection treats a variety of historical and theological topics, ranging from criteria used in the "quest" to the global significance of God's victory in Jesus Christ.

Borg, Marcus J., and N. T. Wright. *The Meaning of Jesus: Two Visions.* San Francisco: HarperSanFrancisco, 1999. Two prominent authors on the Jesus of history set forth their divergent positions in a cordial debate.

Burridge, Richard A., and Graham Gould. *Jesus Now and Then.* Grand Rapids: Eerdmans, 2004. An engaging and lucid introduction to interpretations of Jesus that begins with the New Testament but also explores the formulations of the creeds and contemporary debates.

Dahl, Nils Alstrup. *Jesus the Christ: The Historical Origins of Christological Doctrine.* Edited by Donald H. Juel. Minneapolis: Fortress, 1991. This important collection of Dahl's scholarly essays focuses on the crucifixion as the anchor point for christological reflection and highlights the role of memory in the early church's preservation and transmission of traditions about Jesus.

Davis, Ellen F., and Richard B. Hays, eds. *The Art of Reading Scripture.* Grand Rapids: Eerdmans, 2003. A collection of essays by an interdisciplinary team of scholars, proposing ways to renew the church's practices of biblical interpretation. The present volume is intended as a companion to this book.

Dunn, James D. G. *Jesus Remembered.* Vol. 1 of *Christianity in the Making.* Grand Rapids: Eerdmans, 2003. A massive study that concentrates on the impact Jesus made on his first disciples during his mission and on the oral tradition process through which that impact was recalled.

Frei, Hans W. *The Identity of Jesus Christ: The Hermeneutical Bases of Dogmatic Theology.* Philadelphia: Fortress, 1975. An influential theological meditation on the way in which Jesus' identity and presence are conveyed through the medium of narrative.

Hurtado, Larry W. *Lord Jesus Christ: Devotion to Jesus in Earliest Christianity.* Grand Rapids: Eerdmans, 2003. A major study of early Christian texts, canonical and noncanonical, that contends that worship of Jesus as divine began, not with the creeds and councils, but in the earliest stages of the church's life.

Johnson, Luke Timothy. *Living Jesus: Learning the Heart of the Gospel.* San Francisco: HarperSanFrancisco, 1999. A reflective study, by a noted critic of recent "quests" for the historical Jesus, of the ways in which the living presence of the risen Jesus is encountered in the spiritual practices of the Christian life. The second half of the book sketches the distinct portraits of Jesus offered in the four Gospels.

Keck, Leander E. *Who Is Jesus? History in Perfect Tense.* Columbia: University of South Carolina Press, 2000. With a view to both historical investigation and contemporary implications, Keck explores four major issues regarding Jesus: his Jewishness, his teaching, his death on the cross, and his significance for the moral life.

Meier, John P. *A Marginal Jew: Rethinking the Historical Jesus.* 3 vols. New York: Doubleday, 1991-2001. A masterly multivolume study of the historians' Jesus that combines exhaustive research with careful argumentation and lucid presentation. A fourth volume will deal with several enigmas surrounding Jesus and with historical issues surrounding his death.

O'Collins, Gerald, SJ. *Christology: A Biblical, Historical, and Systematic Study of Jesus.* Oxford: Oxford University Press, 1995. This study integrates contemporary research on the biblical portrait of Jesus with the church's continuing tradition of receiving and reflecting on the gospel, from the church Fathers and the early Councils to the issues raised by modern theology. O'Collins presents the mainstream of Christian orthodox faith in Jesus in a thoughtful and balanced way.

Placher, William C. *Jesus the Savior: The Meaning of Jesus Christ for Christian Faith.* Louisville: Westminster John Knox, 2001. Organized around traditional topics of incarnation, ministry, the cross, and resurrection, this unconventional treatment of Jesus is deeply engaged both with the church's traditions and with contemporary life.

Powell, Mark Allan. *Jesus as a Figure in History: How Modern Historians View the Man from Galilee.* Louisville: Westminster John Knox, 1998. Following an overview of the early stages of historical research concerning Jesus and an introduction to the methods used, Powell discusses the work of the Jesus Seminar, John Dominic Crossan, Marcus J. Borg, E. P. Sanders, John P. Meier, and N. T. Wright.

Ratzinger, Joseph (Pope Benedict XVI). *Jesus of Nazareth: From the Baptism in the Jordan to the Transfiguration.* Translated by A. J. Walker. New York: Doubleday, 2007. A synthetic theological presentation of Jesus as the one human being through whom God was and is definitively present and revealed. Ratzinger's study is notable for its constructive use of Old Testament texts and patristic sources.

Sanders, E. P. *Jesus and Judaism.* Philadelphia: Fortress, 1985. A highly influential study of Jesus in relation to first-century Judaism. Sanders identifies Jesus as a prophet of Jewish restoration eschatology.

———. *The Historical Figure of Jesus.* New York: Penguin, 1993. Here Sanders draws on his earlier work to produce a full treatment of Jesus' life intended for the general reader.

Schweitzer, Albert. *The Quest of the Historical Jesus.* Translated by W. Montgomery. New York: Macmillan, 1968 (original 1906). Schweitzer's work continues to be required reading, both for his trenchant review and critique of the nineteenth-century studies of Jesus' life and for his own forceful proposals about Jesus.

Stanton, Graham. *The Gospels and Jesus,* 2nd ed. Oxford Bible Series. Oxford: Oxford University Press, 2002. Written for the general reader, this is a clear and helpful introduction to the distinctive features of the four Gospels and the problem of reading these texts as sources for historical knowledge about the identity of Jesus. The volume also contains a helpful chapter on gospels outside the New Testament canon.

Theissen, Gerd, and Annette Merz. *The Historical Jesus: A Comprehensive Guide.* Minneapolis: Fortress, 1998. This useful guide introduces the major historical issues in a format designed for instruction, including detailed study tasks and full citation of nonbiblical texts.

Vermès, Géza. *Jesus in His Jewish Context.* Minneapolis: Fortress, 2003. Vermès, professor emeritus of Jewish studies at Oxford University and an authority on the Dead Sea Scrolls, has also written five books on Jesus. This one is an informative collection of essays seeking to place Jesus within his Jewish environment.

Williams, Rowan. *Christ on Trial: How the Gospel Unsettles Our Judgment.* Grand Rapids: Eerdmans, 2000. This book comprises a series of meditations that reflect on the distinctive witness of each of the Gospel writers as to the identity of Jesus Christ. Williams shows how those accounts end up putting believers "on trial" as well and explores several meanings of judging and being judged.

Wright, N. T. *Jesus and the Victory of God.* Vol. 2 of *Christian Origins and the Question of God.* Minneapolis: Fortress, 1996. An artful (and controversial) study that interprets Jesus as a Jewish eschatological prophet who understood himself to be proclaiming and enacting the return of Yahweh to Zion and the end of Israel's exile.

Yoder, John Howard. *The Politics of Jesus,* 2nd ed. Grand Rapids: Eerdmans, 1994. A pioneering effort "to throw a cable across the chasm which usually separates the disciplines of New Testament exegesis and contemporary social ethics" (p. 3). Yoder argues for the political relevance and normative claim of Jesus' example of nonviolence. The second edition adds a series of epilogues that update the argument of the original 1972 edition.

Index of Names

Index of Scripture References